Semantic Multimedia and Ontologies

Yiannis Kompatsiaris · Paola Hobson
Editors

Semantic Multimedia and Ontologies

Theory and Applications

 Springer

Editors
Yiannis Kompatsiaris, Dipl Eng, PhD
Informatics and Telematics Institute
Thermi-Thessaloniki
Greece

Paola Hobson, BSc, PhD, MBA
Chartered Engineer
Motorola Labs
Basingstoke
UK

ISBN: 978-1-84996-722-8   e-ISBN: 978-1-84800-076-6

British Library Cataloguing in Publication Data
A catalogue record for this book is available from the British Library

Printed on acid-free paper

9 8 7 6 5 4 3 2 1

Springer Science+Business Media
springer.com

Acknowledgments

This work was partially supported by the European Commission under contracts FP6-001765 aceMedia and FP6-027685 MESH.

Contents

Contributors

Rajeev Agrawal
Kettering University, Flint, MI, USA and Wayne State University, Detroit, MI, USA
e-mail: ragrawal@kettering.edu

Yannis Avrithis
Image Video and Multimedia Laboratory, School of Electrical and Computer Engineering, National Technical University of Athens, Athens, Greece
e-mail: iavr@image.ntua.gr

Juan José Burred
Communication Systems Group, Technische Universität Berlin, Sekr. EN 1, Einsteinufer 17, 10587 Berlin, Germany
e-mail: burred@nue.tu-berlin.de

Iván Cantador
Universidad Autónoma de Madrid, Madrid, Spain
e-mail: ivan.cantador@uam.es

Pablo Castells
Universidad Autónoma de Madrid, Madrid, Spain
e-mail: pablo.castells@uam.es

Òscar Celma
Music Technology Group, Universitat Pompeu Fabra, Barcelona, Spain
e-mail: oscar.celma@iua.upf.edu

Michael Christel
School of Computer Science, Carnegie Mellon University, Pittsburgh, PA, USA
e-mail: christel@cs.cmu.edu

Stavros Christodoulakis
Laboratory of Distributed Multimedia Information Systems and Applications (TUC/MUSIC), Technical University of Crete, Chania, Crete, Greece
e-mail: stavros@ced.tuc.gr

Stamatia Dasiopoulou
Multimedia Knowledge Laboratory, Centre for Research and Technology Hellas,
Informatics and Telematics Institute, Thermi-Thessaloniki, Greece
e-mail: dasiop@iti.gr

Cathy Dolbear
Ordnance Survey Research Labs, Southampton, UK
e-mail: Catherine.Dolbear@ordnancesurvey.co.uk

Bianca Falcidieno
Istituto di Matematica Applicata e Tecnologie Informatiche, Consiglio Nazionale
delle Ricerche, Genova, Italy
e-mail: falcidieno @ge.imati.cnr.it

Miriam Fernández
Universidad Autónoma de Madrid, Madrid, Spain
e-mail: miriam.fernandez@uam.es

Farshad Fotouhi
Wayne State University, Detroit, MI, USA
e-mail: fotouhi@wayne.edu

Roberto García
Human-Computer Interaction Research Group (GRIHO), Universitat de Lleida,
Lleida, Spain
e-mail: rgarcia@diei.udl.cat

William I. Grosky
University of Michigan-Dearborn, Dearborn, MI, USA
e-mail: wgrosky@umich.edu

Martin Haller
Communication Systems Group, Technische Universität Berlin, Sekr. EN 1,
Einsteinufer 17, 10587 Berlin, Germany
e-mail: haller@nue.tu-berlin.de

Alexander Hauptmann
School of Computer Science, Carnegie Mellon University, Pittsburgh, PA, USA
e-mail: alex@cs.cmu.edu

Paola Hobson
Motorola Labs, Basingstoke, UK

Jane Hunter
School of Information Technology and Electrical Engineering, University of
Queensland, Brisbane, Qld., Australia
e-mail: jane@itee.uq.edu.au

Shan Jin
Communication Systems Group, Technische Universität Berlin, Sekr. EN 1,
Einsteinufer 17, 10587 Berlin, Germany
e-mail: shan@nue.tu-berlin.de

Yiannis Kompatsiaris
Multimedia Knowledge Laboratory, Centre for Research and Technology – Hellas,
Informatics and Telematics Institute, Thermi-Thessaloniki, Greece
e-mail: ikom@iti.gr

Wei-Hao Lin
School of Computer Science, Carnegie Mellon University, Pittsburgh, PA, USA
e-mail: whlin@cs.cmu.edu

Suzanne Little
CNR ISTI, Pisa, Italy
e-mail: suzanne.little@isti.cnr.it

Ralf Möller
Hamburg University of Technology, Hamburg, Germany
e-mail: r.f.moeller@tu-harburg.de

Phivos Mylonas
Image Video and Multimedia Laboratory, School of Electrical and Computer
Engineering, National Technical University of Athens, Athens, Greece
e-mail: fmylonas@image.ntua.gr

Bernd Neumann
University of Hamburg, Hamburg, Germany
e-mail: neumann@informatik.uni-hamburg.de

Carsten Saathoff
ISWeb – Information Systems and Semantic Web, University of Koblenz, Koblenz,
Germany
e-mail: saathoff@uni-koblenz.de

Amjad Samour
Communication Systems Group, Technische Universität Berlin, Sekr. EN 1,
Einsteinufer 17, 10587 Berlin, Germany
e-mail: samour@nue.tu-berlin.de

Ronald Schroeter
School of Information Technology and Electrical Engineering, University of
Queensland, Brisbane, Qld., Australia
e-mail: ronalds@itee.uq.edu.au

Thomas Sikora
Communication Systems Group, Technische Universität Berlin, Sekr. EN 1,
Einsteinufer 17, 10587 Berlin, Germany
e-mail: sikora@nue.tu-berlin.de

Michela Spagnuolo
Istituto di Matematica Applicata e Tecnologie Informatiche, Consiglio Nazionale
delle Ricerche, Genova, Italy
e-mail: spagnuolo @ge.imati.cnr.it

Steffen Staab
ISWeb – Information Systems and Semantic Web, University of Koblenz, Koblenz,
Germany
e-mail: staab@uni-koblenz.de

Michael G. Strinztis
Information Processing Laboratory, Electrical and Computer Engineering
Department, Aristotle University of Thessaloniki, Thessaloniki, Greece

Chrisa Tsinaraki
Laboratory of Distributed Multimedia Information Systems and Applications
(TUC/MUSIC), Technical University of Crete, Chania, Crete, Greece
e-mail: chrisa@ced.tuc.gr

David Vallet
Universidad Autónoma de Madrid, Madrid, Spain
e-mail: david.vallet@uam.es

Howard Wactlar
School of Computer Science, Carnegie Mellon University, Pittsburgh, PA, USA
e-mail: wactlarg@cs.cmu.edu

Rong Yan
Intelligent Information Management Department, IBM TJ Watson Research Center,
Hawthorne, NY, USA
e-mail: yanrong@gmail.com

List of Abbreviations

ACA	Audio content analysis
AJAX	Asynchronous JavaScript and XML
AO	Annotation ontology
AP	Average precision
API	Application programming interface
AR	Autoregressive
ARI	Adjusted Rand index
ASP	Audio spectrum projections
ASR	Automatic speech recognition
BIC	Bayesian information criterion
Bpm	Beats per minute
BPEL	Business process execution language
BSS	Blind source separation
CAD	Computer-aided design
CAM	Computer-aided manufacturing
CE	Concurrent engineering
CHMM	Continuous hidden markov models
CLD	Colour layout descriptor
CS	Classification schemes
CSD	Colour structure descriptor
CSG	Constructive solid geometry
CSP	Constraint satisfaction problem
DAML	DARPA agent markup language
DDL	Description definition language
DIA	Digital item adaptation
DIG	DL implementation group
DL	Description logics
DS	Description schemes
DSD	Divergence shape distance

DS-MIRF	Domain-specific multimedia indexing, retrieval and filtering
DTD	Document type definition
EOF	Empirical orthogonal function
EPA	Environmental protection authority
EXIF	Exchangeable image file format
FMA	Foundational model of anatomy
FN	False negative
FP	False positive
FSS	Feature subset selection
GCI	General concept inclusions
GLR	Generalised likelihood ratio
GMM	Gaussian mixture models
HMM	Hidden markov model
HSV	Hue saturation value
ICA	Independent component analysis
iff	if and only if
IR	Information retrieval
JPD	Joint probability distributions
KB	Knowledge base
KIM	Knowledge and information management
KLT	Karhunen Loeve transform
kNN	k nearest neighbour
LDA	Linear discriminant analysis
LEM	Laplacian eigenmaps
LLB	Locally fixed linear bound
LSA	Latent semantic analysis
LSCOM	Large-scale concept ontology for multimedia
LSI	Latent semantic indexing
LVCSR	Large vocabulary conversational speech recognition
MAP	Mean average precision
MatML	Materials markup language
MCA	Music content analysis
MDS	Multimedia description schemes
MFCC	Mel frequency cepstral coefficients

MI	Mutual information
MIR	Music information retrieval
ML	Maximum likelihood
MLE	Maximum likelihood estimation
MP7QL	MPEG-7 query language
MPEG	Moving picture experts group
MSO	Multimedia structure ontology
NIST	National institute of standards and technology
NLP	Natural language processing
NMF	Non-negative matrix factorization
ODRL	Open digital rights language
OIL	Ontology integration language
OMR	Optical music recognition
OOV	Out of vocabulary
OWL	Web ontology language
OWL DL	OWL with description logics
PCA	Principal component analysis
PER	Phone error rate
pLCA	Probabilistic local context analysis
PLP	Perceptual linear prediction
PP	Projection pursuit
PTDL	Probabilistic tiny DL
RDF	Resource description framework
RDFS	RDF schema
RMS	Root mean square
RSS	Really simple syndication
SBD	Shot boundary detection
SC	Spoken content
SCD	Scalable colour descriptor
SEC	Spatial event cube
SCI	Spoken content indexing
SDR	Spoken document retrieval
SMS	Spectral modelling synthesis
SOM	Self-organising maps
SOFC	Solid oxide fuel cell
SPARQL	RDF query language
STE	Short-time energy
SVD	Singular value decomposition
SVG	Scalable vector graphics

SVM	Support vector machine
SWRL	Semantic web rule language
SW	Semantic web
TGM	Thesaurus for graphic materials
TP	True positive
TREC	Text retrieval conference
TRECVID	Text retrieval conference video track
UBM	Universal background model
URI	Uniform resource identifier
VCV	Vowel consonant vowels
VDO	Visual description ontology
VH	Virtual human
VOCR	Video optical character recognition
VQ	Vector quantisation
VRML	Virtual reality modelling language
VSM	Vector space model
WER	Word error rate
wrt	with respect to
XHTML	eXtensible HyperText markup language
XML	eXtensible markup language
XSD	XML schema definition
XSL	eXtensible stylesheet language
ZCR	Zero crossing rate

Part I
Introduction

Part 1
Introduction

Chapter 1
Introduction to Semantic Multimedia

Yiannis Kompatsiaris and Paola Hobson

1.1 Introduction

Recent progress in hardware and communication technologies has resulted in a rapid increase in the amount of multimedia information available to users. The usefulness of multimedia applications is largely determined by the accessibility of the content, so new challenges are emerging in terms of storing, transmitting, personalising, querying, indexing and retrieval of the multimedia content. Some examples of such challenges include access by business users to multimedia content needed for their work, access by consumers to entertainment content in their home or when mobile, and sharing of content by both professional and private content owners. Clearly, a description and deeper understanding of the information at the semantic level is required (Chang 2002) in order to efficiently meet the requirements resulting from these challenges.

Attempts based on manual textual annotation, despite ensuring conceptual descriptions of a high level of abstraction, suffer from subjectivity of descriptions, thus creating a problem of interoperability and are extremely expensive in terms of labour and time resources. Hence, given the volume of information to deal with, it is imperative that the process of extracting (i.e. analysing) such semantic descriptions (i.e. annotations) takes place in an automatic manner, or with minimum human intervention. At the same time, interoperable description schemes must be used, since customised and application-dependent metadata description schemes do not ensure interoperability and reusability. Automatic techniques exploiting textual information associated with multimedia content (e.g. in Web pages or captions in video) can provide a solution only when such textual information exists, limited by the relevance of the text, by the efficiency of the linguistic analysis tools and, similarly with the manual case, by the subjectivity and polysemy of the description.

Y. Kompatsiaris
Centre for Research and Technology – Hellas, Informatics and Telematics Institute, Thermi-Thessaloniki, Greece
e-mail: ikom@iti.gr

Y. Kompatsiaris, P. Hobson (eds.), *Semantic Multimedia and Ontologies,*
© Springer Science+Business Media, LLC 2008

The limitations in terms of automation of the analysis and description processes provoke research into the direct exploitation of content-related (e.g. visual or audio) information. Moving from low-level perceptual features to high-level semantic descriptions that match human cognition became the final frontier in computer vision, and consequently in any multimedia applications targeting efficient and effective access to, and manipulation of, the available content. The early efforts targeting this so-called *semantic gap* formed what are known as content-based (analysis and) retrieval approaches, where focus is on extracting the most representative numerical descriptions and defining similarity metrics that emulate the human notion of similarity. Whilst low-level descriptors, metrics and segmentation tools are fundamental building blocks of any multimedia content manipulation technique, they evidently fail to fully capture, by themselves, the semantics of the audiovisual medium; achieving the latter is a prerequisite for reaching the desired level of efficiency in content manipulation and retrieval.

The limitations of such numerical-based methodologies, however, led to the investigation of ways to enhance their performance. Iterative approaches such as relevance feedback (Rui, Huang, Ortega and Mehrotra 1998), which puts the user in the loop to "teach" the system what is required, and incremental learning (Naphade and Smith 2003), which uses rules to self-learn, are two common such enhancements. However, the developed systems still could not meet realistic user needs, although some have proved particularly effective within certain application contexts, for example in Wu, Huang, Wang, Chiu and Chen (2007). As a result, research focus shifted to the exploitation of implicit and/or prior knowledge that could guide the process of analysis and semantics extraction. In other words, research efforts have concentrated on the semantic analysis of multimedia content, combining the aforementioned techniques with a priori domain-specific knowledge, so as to result in a high-level representation of multimedia content (Al-Khatib, Day, Ghafoor and Berra 1999). Domain-specific knowledge is utilised for guiding low-level feature extraction, high-level descriptor derivation and symbolic inference. Numerous approaches have been proposed building on this principle, exploiting various methods for modelling this knowledge, diverse representations and their consequent handling techniques. For example, see Tovinkere and Qian (2001) for description of a soccer events analysis method.

Depending on the adopted knowledge acquisition and representation process, two types of approaches can be identified in the relevant literature: implicit, realised by machine learning methods, and explicit, realised by model-based approaches. The usage of machine learning techniques has proved to be a robust methodology for discovering complex relationships and interdependencies between numerical image data and the perceptually higher level concepts. Moreover, these elegantly handle problems of high dimensionality. Among the most commonly adopted machine learning techniques are neural networks (NNs), hidden Markov models (HMMs), Bayesian networks (BNs), support vector machines (SVMs) and genetic algorithms (GAs) (Assfalg, Berlini, Del Bimbo, Nunziat and Pala 2005; Russell and Norvig 2003). On the other hand, model-based image analysis approaches make use of prior knowledge in the form of explicitly defined facts, models and rules, i.e. they provide a coherent semantic domain model to support "visual" inference in the specified context (Dasiopoulou, Mezaris, Kompatsiaris, Papastathis and Strintzis 2005; Hollink, Little and Hunter 2005). These facts, models and rules may connect semantic concepts with other concepts, or with low-level visual features.

The application of semantics to multimedia is further motivated by the need to ensure that the content can be used for current applications as well as be applicable to future applications. Explicit object models, rules and facts tie the application to a representation of the world which may become invalid in the future e.g. the presence of a typewriter as representing an office scene. Reference to standardised high-level semantics avoids the representation problem, and with appropriate abstraction, can support language independence.

In addition to persistence of the relevance of the metadata, consistent metadata is needed to ensure that usable applications can be developed. For example, in content personalisation, where available multimedia content is selected for presentation to a user according to their preferences and interests, it is very important for the personalisation system to be able to accurately match the user's requirements. This implies that the content should be suitably annotated such that there is no ambiguity, and its applicability can be determined by suitable automated processes. Clearly, standardised semantics are essential here, whereas informal, free-text annotations can lead to erroneous decisions.

Furthermore, in the real world, objects exist in a context. Representing context for multimedia applications is a research issue of great importance (Edmonds 1999), affecting the quality of the produced results, especially in the fields of multimedia retrieval, personalisation and analysis. The latter can be defined as a tightly coupled and constant interaction between low-level image analysis algorithms and high-level knowledge representation (Athanasiadis, Tzouvaras, Petridis, Precioso, Avrithis and Kompatsiaris 2005), an area where the role of context is crucial. In recent years, a number of different context aspects related to image analysis have been studied, and a number of different approaches to model context representation have been proposed (Zhao, Shimazu, Ohta, Hayasaka and Matsushita 1996).

As can be seen, there is a need for knowledge representation and processing in many multimedia applications or parts of the whole multimedia value chain (Fig. 1.1). This has led to an increasing convergence of research in the multimedia and knowledge domains, which we refer to as semantic multimedia. This knowledge may include components ranging from the subject matter of discourse to more general data such as about imaging, control strategy, etc. and may be used in equally diverse ways depending on the intended application such as personalised content summarisation, knowledge-assisted design, scientific modelling and semantics-based retrieval, as presented in the following chapters.

Among the possible domain knowledge representations, ontologies present a number of advantages, the most important being that they provide a formal framework for supporting explicit, machine-processable semantics definition, and they enable the derivation of implicit knowledge through automated inference. Ontologies are a representation of a shared understanding about a domain and form an important part of the emerging semantic web since the latter is based on ontologies

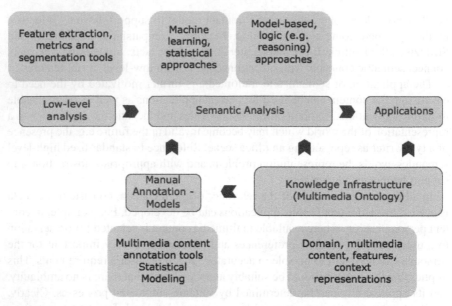

Fig. 1.1 Knowledge infrastructure plays an important role in the multimedia value chain analysis and applications

for enhancing (annotating) content with formal semantics. This enables autonomic agents to reason about Web content and to carry out more intelligent tasks on behalf of the user. Thus, ontologies are suitable for expressing multimedia content semantics so that annotation, automatic semantic analysis and further processing of the extracted semantic descriptions are allowed. Furthermore, ontologies provide a formal and appropriate framework for exploiting the generated semantic descriptions in context representation, retrieval, personalisation and related applications.

In this book, we provide a comprehensive treatment of semantic multimedia analysis, multimedia ontologies' development and applications from multiple perspectives, enabling the reader to gain understanding of the breadth of the emerging semantic multimedia research domain, including presentation of some of the fundamental theories underpinning the research. The following chapters integrate work from experts from the multimedia and the knowledge technology research communities, exploring how knowledge technologies can be exploited to create new multimedia applications, and how multimedia technologies can provide new contexts for the use of knowledge technologies.

We provide a step-by-step approach which takes the reader from the fundamental enabling technologies of ontologies, analysis and reasoning (Part II) to applications which have hitherto had less attention, such as personalisation of multimedia content and multidimensional applications (Part III). Finally, applications using alternative approaches to multimedia ontologies are also presented (Part IV).

1.2 Multimedia Ontologies

Multimedia standards, such as MPEG-7, as discussed in detail in Chapter 2, do not provide full support for the semantic descriptions of the content. For instance, in MPEG-7, semantic annotations are completely decoupled from low-level visual features. Moreover, semantic annotations can be modelled in multiple ways, leading to ambiguity and limited interoperability, rendering the development of tools retrieving and manipulating semantic interpretations of multimedia difficult. As such, although multimedia-related standards provide important functionalities for manipulation and transmission of objects and associated metadata, the representation and extraction of semantic descriptions and the annotation of the content with the corresponding metadata are out of the scope of these standards and are still left to the content manager. This fact is one of the main motivations for the ongoing intensive research efforts in the direction of semantic representation and automatic semantic annotation and exploitation of multimedia content using ontologies.

The complexity of content and structure that characterise multimedia objects, in combination with the need for high-level semantic analysis, has turned the ontology-driven representation of information related to and concerning multimedia content into a rather demanding process. For example, the main challenge in building a knowledge infrastructure for multimedia analysis and annotation is to link low-level multimedia properties such as spatio-temporal multimedia document structure and semantic concepts in a clean, extensible, effective and efficient manner. A consensus is emerging that there is a need for the development of highly focused, easy to use, comprehensible, and non-overlapping multimedia ontologies. They should be kept simple and small, addressing the substantial needs of the applications/systems that are going to use them. Modularity, clarity and unambiguousness should characterise them. Similarly, requirements hold for other applications as well such as retrieval, personalisation and context representation.

More specifically, a number of multimedia ontologies have been designed to serve one or more of these purposes:

- Annotation e.g. labelling or tagging of multimedia content;
- Analysis e.g. ontology-driven semantic analysis of multimedia content, for downstream annotation;
- Retrieval e.g. context-based retrieval of images or video from large archives;
- Personalisation e.g. filtering and recommendation of multimedia content according to user preferences;
- Algorithms and processes control e.g. ontologies used to model multimedia processes and procedures;
- Reasoning, which can be applied in various cases such as retrieval and personalisation for creating autonomous content applications.

When ontologies are used for media description and generally for the description of an information object, a clear distinction between annotations describing the information object and those concerning the multimedia document's content (e.g. semantic concepts depicted in an image) needs to be drawn. Furthermore, the ontologies need to describe and represent knowledge for either one or more of the following top-level hierarchical types of multimedia documents:

- image
- video
- 3D graphics
- audio
- audiovisual.

1.3 Multimedia Ontologies, Analysis and Reasoning – Theory

1.3.1 Multimedia Content Description Using Semantic Web Languages

Ontologies can be used for the representation of multimedia content structure. This refers to the structure of a multimedia document itself, depending on the type of document and the relations between different structural elements. For example, although a set of annotations of a video fragment may be structured along the same scene/sequence/shot hierarchy as the video itself, these characteristics seem to be an inadequate representation of a multimedia document. They need to be extended with spatial and temporal relations, topological information, and their combinations. Spatial relations are needed to describe how segments are placed and relate to each other in 2D space (e.g. "right and above"). Topological spatial relations are needed to describe how the spatial boundaries of the segments relate (e.g. "touch" or "overlap"). Temporal relationships among segments or events, providing information about the sequence in time, need to be represented when the multimedia object is of the type video. Spatio-temporal relations are closely related to partonomic relations as well. MPEG-7 multimedia description schemes (MDS) supports hierarchical structures for multimedia segment decomposition, along with spatial, temporal and spatio-temporal multimedia segment relations. Thus, in the design of an associated ontology, a large part of MPEG-7 could be appropriately captured, aligned and used. Another important requirement concerns the object localisation, i.e. the regions that correspond to semantic objects need to be described in terms of their location within the multimedia content.

Ontologies also model concepts and properties that describe audiovisual characteristics of objects, especially audio segments and visualisations in still images and videos, in terms of low-level features. Examples of such features are colour layout and colour histogram for visual objects. They also support multiple audiovisual descriptions per concept. This is because audiovisual characteristics of domain concepts, in the generic case, cannot be described using a single instance of the audiovisual descriptors in question. For example, while the net of a tennis racquet might be described in terms of its texture only once, its shape heavily depends on the viewing angle and occlusions (e.g. by the player in front of the net). The issue of low-level description representation touches upon a more generic issue, namely the need for support for basic and complex data types representation. Ontologies aligned to standards built on XML Schema, such as MPEG-7 or others, would have to embody the representation of basic data types, such as numeric types, dates, vector arrays, e.g. numerical vectors for the visual content ontology and so on. The use of feature matching algorithms on such data, as part of the reasoning process during knowledge-assisted analysis, makes this need quite essential.

Alignment to existing metadata standards is crucial in order, first, to avoid duplicate work, second, to benefit from existing artefacts, and third, to provide a viable solution – a tool upon which practical applications can be built. Alignment with existing metadata standards helps to ensure, to a significant extent, interoperability between different (or complementary) ontologies and data sharing between tools. As mentioned above, the MPEG-7 multimedia content description standard already provides tools for representing fragments such as colour, texture, shape and motion descriptors, although it suffers from serious limitations in terms of its expressive power with regard to semantic annotations and their own semantics.

In Part II of this book, we present four chapters containing fundamental theory relating to multimedia ontologies, analysis and reasoning. Chapter 2 describes the representation of multimedia content descriptions that are structured according to the MPEG-7 metadata description model and expressed using semantic web languages. The chapter addresses the limitations of the current MPEG-7 version (mainly a lack of explicit semantics) and the efforts made to move the MPEG-7 standard into the semantic web. Approaches for combining MPEG-7 and the web ontology language (OWL) are presented together with two use cases that show the benefits of the approaches, including semantic integration and retrieval in the music domain.

As explained in more detail in the next subsection of this chapter, understanding of the importance of generating a correspondence between domain-specific and low-level description vocabularies applied to multimedia, as well as the importance of exploiting a plurality of modalities for detecting cues useful to analysis, has recently revealed the possibility of using ontologies to drive the extraction of semantic descriptions. Chapters 3–5 of Part II of this book present recent research which is creating the basis for exploitation of knowledge in multimedia applications.

1.3.2 Multimedia Analysis and Reasoning

Despite intensive recent research, the automatic establishment of a correspondence between the low-level features and the semantic-level information (i.e. objects and events) needed to understand the content of the visual medium is a problem still far from being solved or adequately addressed (Chang 2002; Naphade and Huang 2002). Explicitly defined knowledge about objects and events of interest is generally not available for unrestricted domains. However, in well-structured domains such as sports, news and personal content, the necessary knowledge can easily be assembled for the finite number of objects and events of interest. Ontologies can be used in these cases for explicitly expressing domain knowledge, facilitating the further inference of additional knowledge based on rule-based processing of pre-existing knowledge.

Ontologies are the basis and foundation for new intelligent multimedia applications, but we need further tools in order to make these applications a reality, and additional tools are also needed to create commercially viable new businesses around these applications. In Chapters 3–5, of this book, we present techniques for analysing and reasoning on the content, based on frameworks similar to the ones described in Chapter 2.

Central to the realisation of automated and intelligent applications, reasoning enables formalisation of the media interpretation process. Chapter 3 presents new formal knowledge representation and reasoning techniques that can be used for the retrieval and interpretation of multimedia data. It is based on description logics (DLs) as the formal basis for ontology languages of the OWL family and on abductive reasoning for the interpretation framework described in the chapter. As a concrete example, the interpretation of images describing a sports event is considered.

Automated multimedia analysis tools will be described in Chapters 4 and 5, focusing on image and audio content, respectively. These tools are important enablers in making a wider range of information more accessible to intelligent search engines, real-time personalisation tools, and user-friendly content delivery systems. Such automated multimedia analysis tools, which add the semantic information to the content, are critical in realising the value of commercial assets e.g. sports, music and film-clip services, where manual annotation of multimedia content would not be economically viable, and are also applicable to users' personal content (e.g. acquired from video camera or mobile phone), where users generally do not have time to annotate all their content, or where the available user interface does not readily support highly intensive textual input. In order to achieve automated multimedia analysis, domain ontologies – which, in general, provide the concepts for semantic annotation – need to be extended with knowledge that would facilitate the interpretation of multimedia objects representing them. To explain this, we use an example. When analysing a news document, if the term "football" is found, then there is a higher probability that the terms "match", "game" and "player" exist in such a context. This type of knowledge, which refers to the co-relation and the co-occurrence of semantic entities within multimedia documents, has to do with the analysis context and can drive analysis tools to identify semantic objects with higher confidence.

More specifically, Chapter 4 presents an ontology-based framework for enhancing segment level annotations resulting from typical image analysis, through the exploitation of visual context and topological information. The formalisation of contextual information enables a first refinement of the input image analysis annotations, and the application of constraint reasoning brings further improvement, by ensuring the consistency of annotations, through the elimination of annotations violating the domain-topology semantics. Chapter 5 provides an extensive insight into audio content analysis techniques and their state of the art, and presents several recent systems as illustrations.

1.4 Applications of Semantic Multimedia

Applications of semantic multimedia, integrating ontologies, analysis and reasoning tools will be discussed in Part III of this book. As discussed above in Section 1.1, these applications are the motivators and drivers of the theory and tools which are presented in Part II of this book. Use of semantic frameworks and semantic multimedia tools bring efficiency savings to users, such as in automated annotation of content, but annotation is just one step in creation of a wide range of valuable applications including personalisation, knowledge-assisted authoring and intelligent retrieval.

Many users are overwhelmed by the choice of multimedia content which is available to them, and so would benefit from personalisation, where a system matches available content to the user's stated and learned preferences, thereby enabling content offerings to be closely targeted to the user's wishes. Given appropriate annotation of the content, sophisticated reasoning techniques can be used to create personalised summaries of content, which will be described in Chapter 6.

Chapter 7 presents research into application-specific multimedia ontology development applied to multidimensional applications. In particular, exciting work on semantic description of shapes will be discussed in the light of relevant applications in content authoring and retrieval. Chapter 8 continues the presentation of applications of semantic multimedia with emphasis on scientific applications and data modelling. Via illustration using case studies, the important assistance that semantic tools can provide in data-intensive applications will be shown.

1.5 Alternative Approaches to Multimedia Ontologies

Although ontologies play a significant role towards multimedia semantic analysis, there are alternative approaches which are being successfully applied, as shown in Part IV of this book. Chapter 9, dealing with multimedia content retrieval, describes multimedia clustering, search and retrieval research, which models the multimedia retrieval problem along the lines of text information retrieval techniques and also addresses the "curse of dimensionality" issue by presenting dimensionality reduction techniques. Chapter 10 examines the use of automatic semantic concept classifiers such as those related to people (face, anchor, etc.), acoustic (speech, music, significant pause), objects (image blobs, buildings, graphics), location (outdoors/indoors, cityscape, landscape, studio setting), genre (weather, financial, sports) and others. It provides first steps towards answering questions such as: What kinds of concepts are most useful? How many are needed? How accurate do they need to be? How can we use them to assist video retrieval? Answers to these questions can serve as guidelines for future work.

1.6 Conclusions

In the final Part of this book, we review the earlier chapters and comment on non-technical aspects of the multimedia semantic domain, including the user perspective, interoperability and standardisation. The work presented in Chapters 2–10 shows that recent research in semantic multimedia technologies can create beneficial opportunities for new multimedia applications development, since these add value to multimedia assets, which are important new commodities in today's information society. However, exploitation of opportunities by businesses and the ensuing benefits to users of these technologies require a holistic approach to the entire content value chain, via a systems-driven perspective. In Chapter 11, we discuss the benefits to both users and industry, as well as analyse some of the risks likely to impact commercial success, which include issues such as privacy and user satisfaction.

References

Al-Khatib, W., Day, Y.F., Ghafoor, A. and Berra, P.B. (1999) Semantic Modeling and Knowledge Representation in Multimedia Databases. *IEEE Transactions on Knowledge and Data Engineering*, 11(1), 64–80

Assfalg, J., Berlini, M., Del Bimbo, A., Nunziat, W. and Pala, P. (2005) Soccer Highlights Detection and Recognition using HMMs. IEEE International Conference on Multimedia and Expo (ICME), Amsterdam, The Netherlands, pp. 825–828

Athanasiadis, T., Tzouvaras, V., Petridis, K., Precioso, F, Avrithis, Y. and Kompatsiaris, I. (2005) Using a Multimedia Ontology Infrastructure for Semantic Annotation of Multimedia Content. 5th International Workshop on Knowledge Markup and Semantic Annotation (SemAnnot 2005) at the 4th International Semantic Web Conference (ISWC 2005), Galway, Ireland, November

Chang, S.-F. (2002) The Holy Grail of Content-Based Media Analysis. *IEEE Multimedia*, 9(2), 6–10

Dasiopoulou, S., Mezaris, V., Kompatsiaris, I., Papastathis, V.K. and Strintzis, M.G. (2005) Knowledge Assisted Semantic Video Object Detection. *IEEE Transactions, CSVT*, Special Issue on Analysis and Understanding for Video Adaptation, 15(10), 1210–1224

Edmonds, B. (1999) The Pragmatic Roots of Context. Proceedings of the 2nd International and Interdisciplinary Conference on Modeling and Using Context (CONTEXT-99), LNAI, Springer, Berlin, vol. 1688, pp. 119–132

Hollink, L., Little, S. and Hunter, J. (2005) Evaluating the Application of Semantic Inferencing Rules to Image Annotation. 3rd International Conference on Knowledge Capture (K-CAP05), Banff, Canada

Naphade, M.R. and T.S. Huang, T.S. (2002) Extracting Semantics from Audio-Visual Content: The Final Frontier in Multimedia Retrieval. *IEEE Transactions on Neural Networks*, 13(4), 793–810

Naphade, M.R. and Smith, J.R. (2003) Learning Visual Models of Semantic Concepts. ICIP (2), Barcelona, pp. 531–534

Rui, Y., Huang, T.S., Ortega, M., and Mehrotra, S. (1998) Relevance Feedback: A Power Tool for Interactive Content-Based Image Retrieval. *IEEE Transactions on Circuits and Systems for Video Technology*, 8(5), 644–655, September

Russell, S.J. and Norvig, P. (2003) Artificial Intelligence: A Modern Approach, 2nd ed., Prentice Hall, Upper Saddle River, NJ

Tovinkere, V. and Qian, R. (2001) Detecting Semantic Events in Soccer Games: Towards a Complete Solution. IEEE International Conference on Multimedia and Expo, Amsterdam, The Netherlands, pp. 1040–1043

Wu, Q., Huang, C., Wang, S., Chiu, W. and Chen, T. (2007) Robust Parking Space Detection Considering Inter-Space Correlation, Multimedia and Expo, 2007 IEEE International Conference on, July 2007, Beijing, China, pp. 659–662

Zhao, J., Shimazu, Y., Ohta, K., Hayasaka, R. and Matsushita, Y. (1996) An Outstandingness Oriented Image Segmentation and its Applications. Proceedings of the 4th International Symposium on Signal Processing and its Applications, vol. 1, pp. 45–48, Aug 1996

Part II
Multimedia Ontologies, Analysis and Reasoning – Theory

Chapter 2
Multimedia Content Description Using Semantic Web Languages

Roberto García, Chrisa Tsinaraki, Òscar Celma, and Stavros Christodoulakis

2.1 Introduction

During the last decades, digital media have revolutionised media reproduction. The availability of cheap consumer electronic devices that allow the consumption and management of digital multimedia content (e.g. MP3 players, digital cameras, DV camcorders, smart phones) has caused a media availability explosion. The amount of digital media that has been generated and stored, and which continues to be at an exponential rate, has already become unmanageable without fine-grained computerised support.

This, in combination with the media distribution break-up carried out by the World Wide Web and the emergence of advanced network infrastructures that allow for the fast, efficient, and reliable transmission of multimedia content, has formed an open multimedia consumption environment. Digital multimedia content services are provided in this environment, which offer high content quality, advanced interaction capabilities, media personalisation and adaptation according to the user preferences, and access conditions. Such an open environment will be successful only if it is based on standards that allow the services provided by different vendors to interoperate. The specification of different multimedia content description standards poses interoperability requirements and necessitates guidelines for semantic interoperability. These issues are discussed in detail in Tzouvaras and Pan (2007).

The dominant standard in multimedia content description is MPEG-7 (ISO MPEG Group), which provides rich general purpose multimedia content description capabilities, including both low-level features and high-level semantic description constructs. However, the lack of formal semantics in MPEG-7 makes the gap between low- and high-level descriptions difficult to cope with for the existing tools. Consequently, low-level features are common, as they can be easily extracted from the content, but there is a lack of high-level descriptions.

R. García
Human-Computer Interaction Research Group (GRIHO), Universitat de Lleida, Lleida, Spain
e-mail: rgarcia@diei.udl.cat

Y. Kompatsiaris, P. Hobson (eds.), *Semantic Multimedia and Ontologies,*
© Springer Science+Business Media, LLC 2008

Low-level approaches, based on signal analysis, are proving to be extremely limiting in making multimedia database systems accessible and useful to the end-users. These content-based descriptors lie far away from what the users recognise as media description means (Celma, Gómez, Janer, Gouyon, Herrera and García 2004). Consequently, recent research has begun to focus on bridging the semantic and conceptual gap that exists between the user and the computer – from content-based to high-level descriptions. One approach to overcome this gap is the use of knowledge-based techniques based on web ontologies. As formal and web-wide shared conceptualisations, ontologies facilitate automated integration and meaningful retrieval of multimedia – both content and metadata – from different sources.

Searching in digital libraries has been widely studied for several years, mostly focusing on retrieving textual information using text-based methods. These queries can be complemented and improved with advanced retrieval methods using content-based descriptors extracted from the audiovisual information by applying signal processing, even though some knowledge management and representation of the content is necessary. Moreover, from the service and content providers' point of view, multimedia metadata represents an added value to audiovisual assets, but then again manual annotation is a labour-intensive and error-prone task. Thus, managing audiovisual essence implies structuring its associated metadata using description schemes, taxonomies, and ontologies in order to organise a meaningful data knowledge representation.

In addition to the syntactic interoperation, which is achieved through the standards, semantic interoperation, which is achieved through the integration of domain knowledge expressed in the form of domain ontologies, is also needed for providing efficient retrieval and filtering services. The domain knowledge is subsequently utilised for supporting semantic personalisation, retrieval, and filtering and has been shown to enhance the retrieval precision (Tsinaraki, Polydoros and Christodoulakis 2007).

This chapter describes the representation of multimedia content descriptions that are structured according to the *MPEG-7* metadata description model and expressed using the Semantic Web languages. The rest of the chapter is structured as follows: Section 2.2 provides an overview of MPEG-7. The general purpose approaches for multimedia content description that are supported by the MPEG-7 standard are presented as well as the limitations of the current MPEG-7 version (mainly a lack of explicit semantics). Section 2.3 presents the existing web ontology languages, while Section 2.4 outlines the efforts made to move the MPEG-7 standard into the Semantic Web. In our case, this is accomplished by interpreting and expressing the informal MPEG-7 semantics using Semantic Web languages. An approach for mapping XML schema (Fallside 2001) constructs to OWL constructs (McGuinness and van Harmelen 2004) is presented in Section 2.5, while Section 2.6 presents two use cases that show the benefits of this approach, including semantic integration and retrieval in the music domain. An integrated ontological infrastructure for the semantic description of multimedia content is presented in Section 2.7. This infrastructure allows for combining the general purpose MPEG-7 constructs with domain and application-specific knowledge through the systematic representation of this knowledge in the form of *web ontology language* (*OWL*) domain and application ontologies integrated with the MPEG-7 semantics. The chapter conclusions are presented in Section 2.8.

2.2 Multimedia Content Description Using MPEG-7

MPEG-7, formally named *multimedia content description interface*, is an ISO/IEC standard developed by the Moving Picture Experts Group (MPEG), the committee that also developed the audiovisual standards: MPEG-1, MPEG-2, MPEG-4, and MPEG-21. MPEG-7 aims to create a standard for the description of the multimedia content. The main goal of the MPEG-7 standard is to provide structural and semantic description mechanisms for multimedia content (Salembier, Manjunath and Sikora 2002; Martínez 2004).

The MPEG-7 standard allows content description for audiovisual content, defining normative elements such as *descriptors*, *DescriptionSchemes*, and a *description definition language* (DDL). The DDL is the basic building blocks for the MPEG-7 metadata language. Descriptors are designed for describing different types of information; low-level audiovisual features, high-level semantic objects, content management, and information about storage media. Description schemes are used to group several descriptors (and description schemes) into structured semantic units using the DDL. Ideally, most descriptors corresponding to low-level features would be extracted automatically, whereas human intervention would be required for producing high-level descriptors.

The standard is divided into four main components: the DDL, the audio part, the visual part, and the information about how these elements are combined in a multimedia scenario – a set of multimedia description schemes that includes all the descriptors for capturing the semantic aspects of multimedia contents, e.g. places, actors, objects, events. Thus, the creation of MPEG-7 documents allows a user to query and retrieve (parts of) multimedia and audiovisual information.

In the rest of this section, we discuss media object information description in Section 2.2.1, text-based media description in Section 2.2.2, low-level feature-based media description in Section 2.2.3, semantic-based media description in Section 2.2.4, and MPEG-7 description retrieval in Section 2.2.5.

2.2.1 Media Object Information Description

Of special interest is part 5 of the MPEG-7 standard, named *MultimediaDescriptionSchemes* (MPEG-7 MDS, ISO/IEC 2003). This part includes a set of description tools dealing with generic features and multimedia descriptors. Figure 2.1 depicts all the components of the MDS. The basic elements component includes basic data types, such as media localisation, time format, and free text annotations. It includes, also, the classification schemes (CS) descriptors. CS descriptors define schemes for

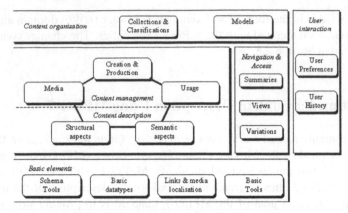

Fig. 2.1 Main elements of the MPEG-7 multimedia description schemes

classifying a subject area with a set of terms, organised into a taxonomy. Similar to the WordNet linguistic ontology, basic relationships among the taxonomy terms are available (e.g. narrow and broader terms, and synonyms).

Among the main components of the MDS are the *ContentManagement and description schemes*. The content management descriptors allow description of the life cycle of multimedia content, from its creation to its usage. They include media information to describe storage format, media quality, media location, etc. Moreover, the content management schemes allow gathering editorial data about the creation and production process of the content. The content description schemes describe the structural aspects (spatial, temporal, and media source structure of the multimedia content) and the semantic aspects.

In detail, the media object information consists of the following:

- The *media information*, which is captured in one of the *MediaInformation*, *MediaInformationRef*, and *MediaLocator* elements. The media information consists of the *media identification*, which allows the unique identification of the media object and its locator, and the *media profile*, which provides media-related information (including media format, quality).
- The *creation information*, which is captured in one of the *CreationInformation* and *CreationInformationRef* elements. The creation information consists of information about the media object *creation* (including title, creators, abstract), *classification* (including genre, subject, language) as well as information about *related material*.
- The *structural information*, which is captured in the *StructuralUnit* element and describes the role of the current multimedia object (segment) within the information context. Thus, the *StructuralUnit* may take values such as "scene", "shot", and "story".
- The *usage information*, which is captured in one of the *UsageInformation* and *UsageInformationRef* elements. The usage information consists of information

about the *rights* associated with the multimedia object, its *financial results*, its *availability*, and its *usage record*.

- Information regarding the importance of the multimedia content from specific *points of view*. This information is captured in the *PointOfView* element.
- The *relationships* of the multimedia content with other media or metadata items as well as the relationships of the semantic entities describing the multimedia content. This information is captured in the *Relation* element, which associates the media object descriptions with instances of the *RelationType* that represent relationships. A relationship may be directed or undirected and features a relationship *type*, the *target* and the *source* of the relationship, and the *strength* of the relationship. The standardised MPEG-7 relationship types are more than 100 and are classified into (a) basic relationship types (equals, inside, refines, etc.), which are specified in the *BaseRelation CS*; (b) graph node relationship types (identity, equivalent, etc.), which are specified in the *GraphRelation CS*; (c) spatial relationship types (over, below, north, etc.), which are specified in the *SpatialRelation CS*; (d) temporal relationship types (precedes, overlaps, contains, etc.), which are specified in the *TemporalRelation CS*; and (e) semantic relationship types (shows, agent, causer, etc.), which are specified in the *SemanticRelation CS*.
- The *matching hints* that allow expression of the criteria for matching the multimedia content with low-level audio and visual descriptors. This information is captured in the *MatchingHint* element.

As an example, consider the MPEG-7 image description of Fig. 2.2, where Chrisa is shown to write an article. The image description consists of the *MediaLocator* element, where the image location (http://www.music.tuc.gr/img01.jpg) is specified,

```
<Mpeg7 xmlns="urn:mpeg:mpeg7:schema:2001"
xmlns:xsi="http://www.w3.org/2001/XMLSchema-instance"
xsi:schemaLocation="urn:mpeg:mpeg7:schema:2001
C:\dbxml\mpeg7.xsd">
  <Description xsi:type="ContentEntityType">
   <MultimediaContent xsi:type="ImageType">
    <Image id="img1">
     <MediaLocator>
      <MediaUri>http://www.music.tuc.gr/img01.jpg</MediaUri>
     </MediaLocator>
     <CreationInformation>
      <Creation>
       <Title>Image showing Chrisa writing an article</Title>
      </Creation>
     </CreationInformation>
    </Image>
   </MultimediaContent>
  </Description>
</Mpeg7>
```

Fig. 2.2 MPEG-7 image description example

and the *CreationInformation* element, where the image title (image showing Chrisa writing an article) is specified in its *Title* element.

2.2.2 Text-Based Media Description

In this section, we describe the text-based multimedia content description capabilities that are provided by the MPEG-7 MDS (ISO/IEC 2003). The textual annotations are represented by the *TextAnnotation* element of the MPEG-7 segment descriptions. An MPEG-7 textual annotation consists of the following elements, each of which may occur an arbitrary number of times:

- The *FreeTextAnnotation* element, which represents free text annotations;
- The *StructuredAnnotation* element, which represents structured textual annotations in terms of *who* (people and animals), *what object*, *what action*, *where* (places), *when* (time), *why* (purpose), and *how*;
- The *KeywordAnnotation* element, which represents keyword annotations;
- The *DependencyStructure* element, which represents textual annotations with a syntactic parse based on dependency structures.

The confidence in the correctness of a textual annotation and its relevance to the multimedia object being described are represented, in the [0, 1] range, by the *confidence* and *relevance* attributes of the textual annotation.

As an example, consider the textual part of the MPEG-7 image description of Fig. 2.2, which is shown in Fig. 2.3. The textual annotation consists of a free text annotation (captured in the *FreeTextAnnotation* element) and a structured annotation (captured in the *StructuredAnnotation* element).

2.2.3 Low-Level Feature-Based Media Description

MPEG-7 (ISO MPEG Group) allows associating, in the MPEG-7 multimedia object descriptions, low-level visual and audio features with the media objects being described. According to the MPEG-7 MDS (ISO/IEC 2003), the MPEG-7

```
                         . . .
<TextAnnotation confidence="0.9" relevance="1">
 <FreeTextAnnotation>Chrisa writes an article</FreeTextAnnotation>
 <StructuredAnnotation>
  <Who><Name>Chrisa</Name></Who>
  <WhatObject><Name>Article</Name></WhatObject>
  <WhatAction><Name>Writes</Name></WhatAction>
 </StructuredAnnotation>
</TextAnnotation>
                         . . .
```

Fig. 2.3 Textual part of the MPEG-7 image description of Fig. 2.2

descriptions that describe (segments of) multimedia objects having a visual component (e.g. images, videos, audiovisual segments) may represent the visual features
of the described (segments of) multimedia objects through the *VisualDescriptor* and
the *VisualDescriptionScheme* elements using, respectively, visual descriptors and
visual description schemes. The MPEG-7 descriptions that describe (segments of)
multimedia objects having an audio component (e.g. audio segments, audiovisual
segments) may represent the audio features of the described (segments of) multimedia objects through the *AudioDescriptor* and the *AudioDescriptionScheme* elements
using, respectively, audio descriptors and audio description schemes (ISO/IEC
2001b). In the rest of this section, we will present the low-level feature-based
multimedia content description capabilities that are provided by MPEG-7, focusing
on the visual features.

A set of basic low-level descriptors are defined in the MPEG-7 visual, including
the basic *color descriptors*, the basic *texture descriptors*, the basic *shape descriptors*, and the basic *motion descriptors*.

MPEG-7 also provides supplementary textual structures for colour spaces, colour
quantisation, and multiple 2D views of 3D objects. It also allows for using static
(image) descriptors on video content and for the spatial as well as the temporal
localisation of media object descriptors.

2.2.4 Semantic-Based Media Description

In this section, we describe the semantic-based multimedia content description capabilities provided by the MPEG-7 MDS (ISO/IEC 2003). The semantic multimedia content descriptions are represented by the *Semantic* element of the MPEG-7
segments, where a set of semantic entities describing the segment content may
be defined or referenced. It has been shown in Tsinaraki, Polydoros, Kazasis and
Christodoulakis (2005) that the MPEG-7 semantic description capabilities allow,
in addition to the representation of semantic multimedia content descriptions, the
representation of domain ontologies using pure MPEG-7 constructs (details of this
methodology are provided in Section 2.7).

The semantic entities participating in MPEG-7 descriptions are instances of the
subtypes of the abstract type *SemanticBaseType*, which represent semantic entities
of specific types in a narrative world. The *AbstractionLevel* element of the *SemanticBaseType* specifies whether a semantic entity is abstract or concrete. *Abstraction-
Level* has one attribute, *Dimension*, of non-negative integer type. When *AbstractionLevel* is not present in a semantic description, the description refers to specific
audiovisual material. When *AbstractionLevel.Dimension*=0, it is a description of
a reusable semantic entity (e.g. the person Chrisa) that is referenced from every
segment where the entity appears. When *AbstractionLevel* has a non-zero *Dimension*, it specifies classes for the description of abstract semantic entities (e.g. the
Article semantic entity, with *AbstractionLevel.Dimension*=1, represents the class of
the articles). The subtypes of *SemanticBaseType* that represent different types of
semantic entities are the following:

- The *SemanticType*, which is a concrete type used for the description of collections of semantic entities;
- The *AgentObjectType*, which is a concrete type used for the description of the actors that appear in a segment. The actors are specified in the *Agent* element of *AgentObjectType*. Actors in general are represented using the subtypes of the abstract type *AgentType*. *PersonType*, *OrganizationType*, and *PersonGroupType* are the subtypes of *AgentType* and are used for the representation of persons (e.g. a student), organisations (e.g. a university), and groups of persons;
- The *ObjectType*, which is a concrete type used for the description of objects and object abstractions in the material world (e.g. a desk);
- The *EventType*, which is a concrete type used for the description of events that take place in a semantic world (e.g. writing);
- The *ConceptType*, which is a concrete type used for the description of concepts present in an audiovisual segment (e.g. cooperation);
- The *SemanticStateType*, which is a concrete type used for the description of a state of the world described in an audiovisual segment and the parametric description of its features (e.g. the average of a student's grades before and after an examination period);
- The *SemanticPlaceType*, which is a concrete type used for the description of a place in a semantic world (e.g. Crete);
- The *SemanticTimeType*, which is a concrete type used for the description of semantic time (e.g. New Year's Eve).

As an example, consider the semantic part of the MPEG-7 image description of Fig. 2.2, which is shown in Fig. 2.4.

Notice that the *ChrisaArticle* object is the result of the *Writes* event. The agent of the event is the person represented by the *Chrisa* semantic entity.

Semantic entity (abstract or concrete) definitions may occur in the context of either segment descriptions or independent semantic descriptions. The semantic entity definitions occurring in independent semantic descriptions may then be referenced from the segment descriptions they appear in. This is very useful both for the ontology classes and for the reusable semantic entities.

2.2.5 Retrieving Information from MPEG-7 Descriptions

The eXtensible Markup Language (XML) has been adopted as the format to represent MPEG-7 descriptors. Also the MPEG-7 DDL is an extension of the W3C XML schema. XML schema provides the means for defining the structure of XML documents, that is, simple and complex data types, type derivation and inheritance, element occurrence constraints, and, finally, namespace-awareness for element and attribute declarations. The MPEG-7 DDL extends the XML schema and covers the ability to define array and matrix data types, and provides specific temporal descriptions (by means of the *basicTimePoint* and *basicDuration* types).

```
                                    . . .
<Semantic>
  <Label><Name>Chrisa writes an article</Name></Label>
  <SemanticBase xsi:type="ObjectType" id="ChrisaArticle">
   <AbstractionLevel dimension="0"/>
   <Label><Name>Chrisa's Article</Name></Label>
  </SemanticBase>
  <SemanticBase xsi:type="AgentObjectType" id="Chrisa">
   <AbstractionLevel dimension="0"/>
   <Label><Name>Chrisa</Name></Label>
   <Agent xsi:type="PersonType">
    <Name>
     <GivenName>Chrisa</GivenName>
     <FamilyName>Tsinaraki</FamilyName>
    </Name>
   </Agent>
  </SemanticBase>
  <SemanticBase xsi:type="EventType" id="Writes">
   <AbstractionLevel dimension="0"/>
   <Label><Name>Writes</Name></Label>
   <Relation source="#Writes" target="#Chrisa"
type="urn:mpeg:mpeg7:cs:SemanticRelationCS:2001:agentOf"/>
   <Relation source="#Chrisa" target="#Writes"
type="urn:mpeg:mpeg7:cs:SemanticRelationCS:2001:agent"/>
   <Relation source="#ChrisaArticle" target="#Writes"
type="urn:mpeg:mpeg7:cs:SemanticRelationCS:2001:resultOf"/>
   <Relation source="#Writes" target="#ChrisaArticle"
type="urn:mpeg:mpeg7:cs:SemanticRelationCS:2001:result"/>
  </SemanticBase>
</Semantic>
                                    . . .
```

Fig. 2.4 Semantic part of the MPEG-7 image description of Fig. 2.2

The MPEG-7 XML schemas define 1182 elements, 417 attributes, and 377 complex types. The size of this standard makes it quite difficult to manage. Moreover, the use of XML technologies implies that a great part of the semantics remains implicit. Therefore, each time an MPEG-7 application is developed, semantics must be extracted from the standard and re-implemented.

The next two examples depict how to retrieve information from MPEG-7 MDS documents using the *XQuery* (Siméon, Chamberlin, Fernández, Boag, Florescu and Robie 2007) language and an XML database. The first example in Listing 1 shows an expression to retrieve MPEG-7 audiovisual segments containing any media information. The output is presented as simple HTML code, containing a link to the media file – with the title and type of file as the text link.

```
for $segment in//AudioVisualSegment
let $title:=$segment/CreationInformation/Creation/Title/text()
order by $title
return
 for $media in $segment/MediaInformation/MediaProfile
 let $file:=$media/MediaInstance/MediaLocator/MediaUri/text()
 let $type:=$media/MediaFormat/Content/Name/text ()
 return
  <a href="{$file}">{ $title," [",$type,"]" }</a>
```

Listing 1 *XQuery* expression to retrieving a list of multimedia items (title and format type)

```
for $creator in
/Mpeg7/Description/MultimediaContent/*/CreationInformation/
Creation/Creator
where
$creator/Role[@href="urn:opendrama:cs:SingerCS:%"]
and
$creator/Agent[@xsi:type="PersonType"]
order by $creator/Agent/Name/FamilyName
return
<agent>
{
let $completeName:= $creator/Agent/Name
let $name:= $completeName/GivenName/text()
let $surname:= $completeName/FamilyName/text()
return
 <singer> { $name," ",$surname }</singer>
}
{
let $completeName:= $creator/Character
let $name:= $completeName/GivenName/text()
let $surname:= $completeName/FamilyName/text()
return
 <character> { $name, " ",$surname }</character>
}
</agent>
```

Listing 2 *XQuery* example to retrieving the singers and the characters they play

The second example (Listing 2) shows an *XQuery* expression to retrieve all MPEG-7 person agents, whose role is *Singer,* and the characters they play. This query uses a taxonomy that defines different types of singers' roles (soprano, contralto, tenor, and bass).

The previous examples only illustrate one kind of difficulty derived from the use of just syntax-aware tools. In order to retrieve any kind of MPEG-7 *SegmentType* descriptions from an XML database, one must be aware of the hierarchy of segment types and implement an *XQuery* that covers any kind of multimedia segment (i.e. *Audio-VisualType, VideoSegmentType, AudioSegmentType*). On the other hand, once the hierarchy of segments is explicitly defined in an ontology (e.g. in OWL form), semantic queries benefit from the, now, explicit semantics. Therefore, a semantic query for *SegmentType* will retrieve all the subclasses without requiring additional efforts. This is necessary because although XML schemas capture some semantics of the domain they model, XML tools are based on syntax. The captured semantics remain implicit from the XML processing tools point of view. Therefore, when an *XQuery* searches for a *SegmentType*, the *XQuery* processor has no way to know that there are many other kinds of segment types that can appear in its place, i.e. they are more concrete kinds of segments. At this stage, a possible solution to avoid this is to use wildcards' syntax (see the second and fifth lines of Listing 2). However, this corresponds to a unconstrained generalisation, i.e. any element satisfies it and it is not possible to constrain it to just a kind of element, e.g. all the AudioVisualType subtypes.

Therefore, MPEG-7 constitutes a valuable starting point for more specific developments as it can be seen as an "upper-ontology" for multimedia. However, the lack of explicit semantics makes MPEG-7 very difficult for third-party entities to extend in an independent way. This lack of facilities for easy extension has been one of the main motivations to build solutions that make MPEG-7 semantics formal and thus easily machine-processable. Some solutions to this problem are detailed in Section 2.4.

2.3 Web Ontology Languages

The World Wide Web has changed the way people communicate with each other. Most of today's Web content is suitable for human consumption. Keyword-based engines have helped users to find the information they are seeking on the net. Yet, search engines present some limitations: the results are single web pages, results are highly sensitive to the vocabulary (semantically similar queries should return similar results), and usually there is a high recall and low precision of the result set (i.e. there is too much noise on the web page results) (Antoniou and van Harmelen 2004).

The main problem of the current Web, at this stage, is that the meaning of the content is not accessible by machines. Information retrieval and text processing tools are widely used, but there are still difficulties when interpreting sentences, or extracting useful information for users. The development of the Semantic Web, with machine-readable content, has the potential to revolutionise the current World Wide Web and its use.

2.3.1 Overview of the Semantic Web

The definition and vision that had Tim Berners-Lee (1999) is that the Semantic Web is an extension of the current Web in which information is given well-defined meaning, better enabling computers and people to work in cooperation. The Semantic Web is a vision: the idea of having data on the Web defined and linked in a way that it can be used by machines not just for display purposes but for automation, integration, and reuse of data across various applications (Berners-Lee, Hendler, and Lassila 2001; Shadbolt, Berners-Lee and Hall 2006).

The previous ideas and principles to enhance the Web are being put into practice under the guidance of the World Wide Web Consortium (W3C). The next statement presents their view:

> The semantic web is an extension of the current web in which information is given well-defined meaning, better enabling computers and people to work in cooperation. The mix of content on the web has been shifting from exclusively human-oriented content to more and more data content. The semantic web brings to the web the idea of having data defined and

linked in a way that it can be used for more effective discovery, automation, integration, and reuse across various applications. For the web to reach its full potential, it must evolve into a semantic web, providing a universally accessible platform that allows data to be shared and processed by automated tools as well as by people.

— W3C Semantic Web Activity Statement

The Semantic Web technologies have been arranged into a layered architecture. The key technologies include explicit metadata, ontologies, logic and inferencing, and intelligent agents. Each layer, from the bottom to the top, has an increasing level of complexity, yet it offers more expressivity.

The two base layers (unicode and URI, and the XML family) are inherited from the current Web. Section 2.2 already has presented some technologies relating to XML. The upper layers compose the Semantic Web, over the existing basic technologies. The next sections overview these layers, that is, the Resource Description Framework (RDF), the RDF Schema (RDFS), and the Web Ontology Language (OWL).

2.3.2 Resource Description Framework

The RDF (Brickley and Guha 2004) vocabulary is similar to other knowledge representation formalisms such as conceptual graphs (CG) or semantic nets. CG express meaning in a form that is logically precise, humanly readable, and computationally tractable. CG serve as an intermediate language for translating computer-oriented formalisms to and from natural languages. With a clear graphic representation, they serve as a readable – but formal – design and specification language. The next figure, Fig. 2.5, shows an example of a semantic net, which relates music bands, artists, and basic data.

Graph representation is a powerful tool for human understanding. However, in our context we need machine-processable representations.

The RDF vocabulary allows formally describing the previous example, and even serialising it using the XML language. RDF is, then, a data model for objects (resources) and the relations (properties) between them, and it provides simple

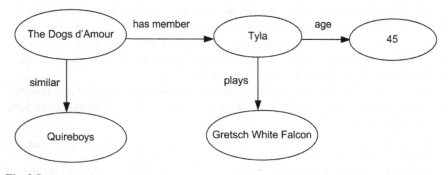

Fig. 2.5 A semantic net

semantics. A resource is an object, a thing we want to talk about. A resource has a URI (Uniform Resource Identifier). Properties are a special kind of resource that describe relations between resources (e.g. related with, age, plays). Properties are identified by URIs.

Statements assert the properties of resources. From a natural language point of view, a statement is composed of a *Subject–Predicate–Object* triple. From a more computer science point of view, this is equivalent to an *Object-Attribute-Value* triple, or in this context a *Resource-Property-Value* triple. A triple [x, P, y] is equal to a logical formula $P(x, y)$, where the binary predicate P relates the object x to the object y. Values can be either resources or literals (e.g. strings).

A possible statement could be, "Oscar Celma is the owner of the web page http://foafing-the-music.iua.upf.edu". This triple is equal to the graph statement, Fig. 2.6.

It is a directed graph, where the nodes correspond to the objects and the labelled arc is a property. The same statement can be represented in XML syntax (also known as RDF/XML):

```
<rdf:Description
 rdf:about="http://foafing-the-music.iua.upf.edu">
 <mydomain:owner>Oscar Celma</mydomain:owner>
</rdf:Description>
```

The rdf:Description makes a statement about the resource (a web page) http://foafing-the-music.iua.upf.edu. The property (*owner*) is used as a tag within the description, and the value is the content of the tag. Moreover, we can describe the person "Oscar Celma" by the resource with URL
http://www.mydomain.org/people/#44521:

```
<rdf:Description
 rdf:about="http://www.mydomain.org/people/#44521">
 <mydomain:name>Oscar Celma</mydomain:name>
 <mydomain:title>Associate Professor</mydomain:title>
</rdf:Description>
```

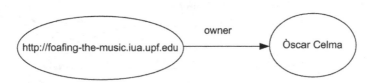

Fig. 2.6 Graph representation of a triple

In this case, the `rdf:Description` corresponds to two statements about the resource `http://www.mydomain.org/people/#44521` (the name, and the title of that person). Now, we can define a *course* that *is taughtby* that resource:

```
<rdf:Description
  rdf:about="http://www.tecn.upf.es/~ ocelma/edi2">
  <uni:courseName>Introduction to Databases</uni:courseName>
  <uni:creditsNumber>6</uni:creditsNumber>
  <uni:isTaughtBy rdf:resource="http://www.mydomain.org/people
     /#44521" />
</rdf:Description>
```

The resulting graph of the three previous examples is depicted in Fig. 2.7.

By now, we have defined a set of statements, but there are still no restrictions about them. For instance, we should state that the property *isTaughtBy* is only applied to courses (the subject) and professors (the object), or that an associate professor is a particular type of professor, with some restrictions (maximum number of hours, needs to hold a PhD, etc.). The RDF Schema vocabulary is intended to describe this information.

2.3.3 RDF Schema

RDF Schema (RDFS) (Manola and Milles 2004) is a vocabulary for describing properties and classes of RDF resources, and provides hierarchies of such properties and classes. The RDFS vocabulary allows definition of the semantics of the RDF statements.

As is common in other disciplines, to describe a particular domain one can use classes and properties. RDFS provides mechanisms to define a particular domain using classes (and properties), hierarchies, and inheritance. Classes model the entities (and their restrictions) of the domain, whereas properties provide relationships

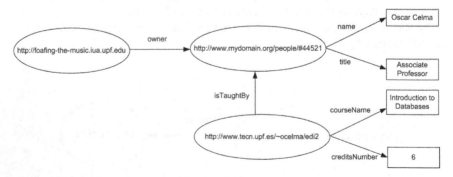

Fig. 2.7 Graph representation of the previous RDF statements

among the classes. Properties have a domain and range (similarly to mathematical functions), to impose restrictions on the values of the property. Yet there are some important missing features of RDFS:

- There are no local scope properties: *rdf:range* defines the range of a property for all classes. We cannot declare range restrictions that apply to some classes only;
- There is no disjointness of classes;
- Missing Boolean combinations of classes: union, intersection, and complement;
- No cardinality restrictions: restrictions on how many distinct values a property may or must take ("a person has two parents");
- No special characteristics of properties: transitive (greater than), unique (is mother of), and inverse (eats and is eaten by).

These limitations are solved in the OWL language, presented in the next section. To conclude this section, a simile can be established among the existing technologies on the current Web, and the ones proposed by the Semantic Web community: while the XHTML language makes the Web behave like a global book when viewed at the worldwide level, RDF and RDF Schema make it behave like a global database. Regarding the data structures, the basic RDF primitive is a directed graph, whereas the XML representation is based on a tree. Thus, an RDF graph is on its own basically unrestricted and more powerful in terms of expressiveness.

2.3.4 Ontology Vocabulary

An ontology is an explicit and formal specification of a conceptualisation (Gruber 1993). In general, an ontology describes formally a domain of discourse. The requirements for ontology languages are a well-defined syntax, a formal semantics, and a reasoning support that checks the consistency of the ontology, checks for unintended relationships between classes, and automatically classifies instances in classes.

The web ontology language (OWL) has a richer vocabulary description language for describing properties and classes than RDFS. OWL has relations between classes, cardinality, equality, characteristics of properties, and enumerated classes. The OWL is built on RDF and RDFS and uses RDF/XML syntax. OWL documents are, then, RDF documents.

The next example shows the definition of two classes:

```
<owl:Class rdf:ID="Singer">
 <rdfs:subClassOf rdf:resource="#Artist" />
</owl:Class>
<owl:Class rdf:ID="Song" />
```

Object property elements relate objects to other objects. For instance, "a singer *sings* songs".

```
<owl:ObjectProperty rdf:ID="sings">
 <rdfs:domain rdf:resource="#Singer"/>
 <rdfs:range rdf:resource="#Song"/>
</owl:ObjectProperty>
```

Data-type properties relate objects to data-type values. For example, the data property that denotes the age of an *Artist*:

```
<owl:DataProperty rdf:ID="age">
 <rdfs:domain rdf:resource="#Artist"/>
 <rdfs:range rdf:resource="&xsd;nonNegativeInteger"/>
<owl:DataProperty>
```

Property restrictions on classes are based on the use of rdfs:subclassOf. To say that class C satisfies certain conditions is equivalent to state that C is a subclass of C', where C' collects all objects that satisfy the conditions. For instance, a restriction on the kind of values the property can take:

```
<owl:Class rdf:about="#GuitarPlayer">
<rdfs:subClassOf>
 <owl:Restriction>
  <owl:onProperty rdf:resource="#plays"/>
  <owl:allValuesFrom rdf:resource="#Guitar"/>
 </owl:Restriction>
</rdfs:subClassOf>
</owl:Class>
```

Or cardinality restrictions (a *music band* comprises, at least, two members):

```
<owl:Class rdf:about="#Band">
 <rdfs:subClassOf>
   <owl:Restriction>
    <owl:onProperty rdf:resource="#hasMember"/>
    <owl:minCardinality ="&xsd;nonNegativeInteger">
    </owl:minCardinality>
   </owl:Restriction>
 </rdfs:subClassOf>
</owl:Class>
```

OWL offers some special properties, such as: *owl:TransitiveProperty* (e.g. "has better grade than", "is taller than", "is ancestor of"), *owl:SymmetricProperty* (e.g. "has same grade as", "is sibling of"), *owl:FunctionalProperty* (a property that has almost one value for each object, e.g. "age"), and *owl:InverseFunctionalProperty* (a property for which two different objects cannot have the same value, e.g. "socialSecurityNumber"). For example, a *playedwith* property is symmetric:

```
<owl:ObjectProperty rdf:ID="playedWith">
 <rdf:type rdf:resource="&owl;SymmetricProperty"/>
 <rdfs:domain rdf:resource="#Artist"/>
 <rdfs:range rdf:resource="#Artist"/>
</owl:ObjectProperty>
```

There are three different OWL sublanguages. Each sublanguage offers a level of expressivity. OWL Full is the most expressive of the three sublanguages. There are no special constraints about how the OWL primitives can be used. Therefore, the greatest level of expressivity of the language can be achieved. However, on the other hand, the language becomes undecidable, so efficient reasoning is not guaranteed.

OWL-DL is based on description logics. It has vocabulary partitioning, that is, any resource is allowed to be only a class, a data-type, a data-type property, an object property, an individual, a data value, or part of the built-in vocabulary. Also, there is explicit typing in OWL-DL, so the vocabulary partitioning must be stated explicitly.

Property separation implies that the following can never be specified for data type properties: *owl:inverseOf*, *owl:FunctionalProperty*, *owl:InverseFunctionalProperty*, and *owl:SymmetricProperty*. Additionally, there is a restriction for anonymous classes: they are only allowed to occur as the domain and range of either *owl:equivalentClass* or *owl:disjointWith* and as the range of *rdfs:subClassOf*.

These constraints on how OWL primitives are combined guarantee that to reason on OWL-DL expressions is decidable and tractable, i.e. it will terminate in a finite and a not too large amount of time. This is so because OWL-DL is in the family of description logics. Description logics allow the specification of a terminological hierarchy using a restricted set of first-order formulae. Restrictions ensure that description logics have nice computational properties, but the inference services are restricted to subsumption and classification. Subsumption means, given formulae describing classes, the classifier associated with certain description logic will place them inside a hierarchy. On the other hand, classification means that given an instance description, the classifier will determine the most specific classes to which the particular instance belongs.

Finally, OWL Lite has the same restrictions as OWL-DL plus it is not allowed to use *owl:oneOf*, *owl:disjointWith*, *owl:UnionOf*, *owl:complementOf*, or *owl:hasValue*. Regarding cardinality statements: only values 0 and 1 are possible. These additional constraints reduce even more the expressivity of the language but, on the other hand, make reasoning more efficient.

2.4 MPEG-7 Ontologies

As shown in Section 2.2, MPEG-7 allows for the semantic annotation of multimedia content and the systematic representation of domain knowledge using MPEG-7 constructs. The domain knowledge is usually expressed today in the form of domain ontologies, and several ontology description languages have been proposed, based on the OWL language presented in Section 2.3. Thus, it is expected both that many OWL domain ontologies will be developed and that many developers will be familiar with OWL and will use it for ontology definition. It is therefore very important for the multimedia community to have a methodology for the interoperability of OWL with MPEG-7 and for the integration of domain knowledge expressed in OWL within MPEG-7. This way, the MPEG-7 constructs will become Semantic Web objects and the Semantic Web tools (such as reasoners) and methodologies may be used with MPEG-7. This feature is useful for several applications, e.g. knowledge acquisition from multimedia content. In this section, we present the ontologies expressed in the Semantic Web languages that capture (fully or partially) the MPEG-7 semantics. As a consequence, although MPEG-7 is a standard, hence it enhances interoperability at least at the syntactic level, the several different ontological MPEG-7 representations are not standard, and are not compatible or interoperable with each other. Thus, a new interoperability issue appears, which is discussed in detail in the *Harmonization of Multimedia Ontologies activity* of the aceMedia project (2007) and Celma, Dasiopoulou, Hausenblas, Little, Tsinaraki and Troncy (2007).

Chronologically, the first efforts towards a semantic formalisation of MPEG-7 were carried out, during the MPEG-7 standardisation process, by Jane Hunter (1999). The proposal used RDF (Brickley and Guha 2004) and RDF Schema (Manola and Milles 2004) to formalise a small part of MPEG-7 and later incorporated some DAML+OIL constructs (McGuinness, Fikes, Hendler and Stein 2002) to further detail their semantics (Hunter 2001), where the DAML+OIL ontology definition language was used to partially describe the MPEG-7 MDS and visual metadata structures. The ontology has been recently translated into OWL. However, it continues to show one of its major shortcomings, the limited coverage of the MPEG-7 constructs.

Another proposal based on RDF/RDFS that captures the MPEG-7 visual has been presented in Simou, Tzouvaras, Avrithis, Stamou and Kollias (2005). The same shortcomings are observed due to the expressivity limitations of RDF/RDFS. Consequently, this ontology also provides limited support for the representation of MPEG-7 formal semantics.

An OWL full ontology that captures the whole MPEG-7 standard was presented in García and Celma (2005). This ontology has been automatically produced using the mappings from XML schema constructs to the OWL constructs, which are detailed in Section 2.5. This mapping is complemented with an XML to RDF one that makes it possible to map existing MPEG-7 data to RDF data based on the previous ontology.

The disadvantage of modelling the whole standard is that this ontology is OWL full, which means that computational completeness and decidability of reasoning are not guaranteed. However, this limitation is unavoidable due to the structure of the MPEG-7 standard XML schemas. The only way to avoid it, if all the semantics implicit in the schemas are formalised, is to restrict the ontology to just a part of the standard.

This is the approach of the OWL-DL ontology presented in Tsinaraki, Polydoros and Christodoulakis (2004b), which captures the full MPEG-7 MDS (including the classification schemes) and just the parts of the MPEG-7 visual and audio that are necessary for the complete representation of the MPEG-7 MDS. The ontology was manually developed, according to a methodology that allows the transformation of the XML schema constructs of MPEG-7 in OWL-DL.

The methodology consists of the following steps:

- The MPEG-7 simple data-types are imported from the XML schema syntax, as OWL does not directly support simple type definition.
- The MPEG-7 complex types are represented as OWL classes, which have the complex type names as identifiers. The attributes and the simple type elements (of type string, integer etc.) of the complex types are represented as OWL data type properties that have the OWL classes that represent the complex types as domain and the simple types as range. The complex type elements are represented as OWL object properties that have the OWL classes that represent the complex type as domain and the OWL classes that represent the element types as range (if the latter do not already exist, it is defined from scratch).
- For the representation of the subtype/supertype relationships that hold for a complex type, the following actions are performed: (a) If the complex type is a subtype of another complex type, the subclass relationship is represented using the OWL/RDF subclassing construct; and (b) If the complex type is a subtype of a simple type, a data-type property is defined that has as identifier "*type_name*Content", where *type_name* is the type of the supertype (e.g. string, integer). The data type property has the supertype as range and the OWL class that represents the complex type as domain.
- The XML schema restrictions are transformed to the analogous OWL constructs. Thus, a fixed attribute value is transformed to an OWL "hasValue" restriction, and the minOccurs/maxOccurs attributes are transformed to either simple cardinality restrictions (i.e. cardinality, minCardinality, and maxCardinality) or groups of cardinality restrictions, grouped using the OWL unionOf (in case of choices) and intersectionOf (in case of sequence) constructs.
- The MPEG-7 classification schemes are represented as individuals of the *ClassificationSchemeType* class, which represents the homonym MPEG-7 type that specifies the structure of the classification schemes.

The main advantage of the above methodology is that, thanks to the manual effort, an OWL-DL ontology has been produced, which accurately captures the semantics of the MPEG-7 constructs (including both the named and the unnamed – nested – ones).

2.5 Mapping Approach

The approach used to map XML schema constructs in the MPEG-7 standard to OWL constructs is based on a generic XML schema to OWL mapping combined with an XML to RDF translation. It has already shown its usefulness with other quite big XML schemas in the Digital Rights Management domain, such as MPEG-21 and ODRL (García, Gil and Delgado 2007), and also in the E-Business domain (García and Gil 2007).

The main contribution of this approach is that it exploits the great amount of metadata that has been already produced by the XML community. There are many attempts to move metadata from the XML domain to the Semantic Web. Some of them just model the XML tree using RDF primitives (Klein 2002). Others concentrate on modelling the knowledge implicit in XML language definitions, i.e. DTDs or the XML schemas, using Web ontology languages (Amann, Beer, Fundulak and Scholl 2002; Cruz, Xiao and Hsu 2004; Halevy, Ives, Mork and Tatarinov 2003). Finally, there are attempts to encode XML semantics integrating RDF into XML documents (Lakshmanan and Sadri 2003; Patel-Schneider and Simeon 2002).

None of the previous approaches facilitate an extensive transfer of XML metadata to the Semantic Web in a general and transparent way. Their main problem is that the implicit interpretation of XML schema in terms of RDF(S) and OWL semantics is not formalised when XML metadata instantiating this schema is mapped. Therefore, they do not benefit from XML semantics and produce RDF metadata almost as semantics-blind as the original XML. Or, on the other hand, they capture these semantics but they use additional ad hoc semantic constructs that produce less transparent metadata. Therefore, we have chosen the XML semantic reuse methodology (García 2006) implemented by the ReDeFer project. It combines an XML achema to Web ontology mapping, called XSD2OWL, with a transparent mapping from XML to RDF, XML2RDF. The ontologies generated by XSD2OWL are used during the XML to RDF step in order to generate semantic metadata that makes XML schema semantics explicit. Both steps are detailed next. To conclude, in order to improve the transfer from MPEG-7 XML metadata to the Semantic Web, there is also a simple MPEG-7 classification scheme to OWL mapping called CS2OWL. It maps MPEG-7 classification hierarchies, e.g. TV-anytime hierarchy of contents or formats, to an OWL hierarchy of classes.

2.5.1 XSD2OWL Mapping

The XML schema to OWL mapping is responsible for capturing the schema informal semantics. These semantics are derived from the combination of XML schema constructs. The mapping is based on translating these constructs to the OWL ones that best capture their meaning. These mappings are detailed in Table 2.1.

The XSD2OWL mapping is quite transparent and captures the semantics implicit in XML schema following the interpretations in Table 2.1. The same names used for

Table 2.1 XSD2OWL translations for the XML schema constructs and their interpretations in terms of the corresponding OWL constructs

XML schema	OWL	Shared semantics
element|attribute	rdf:Property owl:DatatypeProperty owl:ObjectProperty	Named relation between nodes or nodes and values
element@substitutionGroup	rdfs:subPropertyOf	Relation can appear in place of a more general one
element@type	rdfs:range	The relation range kind
complexType|group |attributeGroup	owl:Class	Relations and contextual restrictions package
complexType//element	owl:Restriction	Contextualised restriction of a relation
extension@base|restriction@base	rdfs:subClassOf	Package concretises the base package
@maxOccurs	owl:maxCardinality	Restrict the number of
@minOccurs	owl:minCardinality	occurrences of a relation.
None specified	owl:cardinality(1)	1 implicit if not specified
Sequence Choice	owl:intersectionOf owl:unionOf	Combination of relations in a context

XML constructs are used for the OWL ones, although in the new namespace defined for the ontology, XSD and OWL constructs names are identical. This usually produces uppercase-named OWL properties because the corresponding element name is uppercase, although this is not the usual convention in OWL.

Therefore, XSD2OWL produces OWL ontologies that make explicit the semantics of the corresponding XML schemas. The only caveats are the implicit order conveyed by *xsd:sequence* and the exclusivity of *xsd:choice*. For the first problem, *owl:intersectionOf* does not retain its operands' order; there is no clear solution that retains the great level of transparency that has been achieved. The use of RDF lists might impose order but introduces ad hoc constructs not present in the original metadata. Moreover, as has been demonstrated in practise, the element ordering does not contribute much from a semantic point of view. For the second problem, *owl:unionOf* is an inclusive union, and the solution is to use the disjointness OWL construct, *owl:disjointWith*, between all union operands in order to make it exclusive.

The XSD2OWL mapping has been applied to the MPEG-7 XML schemas producing the complete MPEG-7 ontology. This ontology has 2372 classes and 975 properties. The only adjustment that has been done to the automatically generated ontology is to resolve a name collision between an OWL class and an RDF property. This is due to the fact that XML has independent name domains for complex types and elements while OWL has a unique name domain for all constructs. Moreover, the resulting OWL ontology is OWL full because the XSD2OWL translator has been forced to employ *rdf:Property* for those *xsd:elements* that have both data type and object type ranges. Table 2.2 shows an example of an XML schema ComplexType mapping to the corresponding OWL class.

Table 2.2 XML schema to OWL mapping example (namespaces omitted for readability)

XML schema	OWL (abstract syntax)

```<complexType name="AudioType">```
  ```<complexContent>```
    ```<extension base=```
    ```"MultimediaContentType">```
    ```<sequence>```
    ```<element name="Audio" type=```
    ```"AudioSegmentType"/>```
    ```</sequence>```
    ```</extension>```
  ```</complexContent>```
```</complexType>```
	```Class (AudioType complete```
	  ```MultimediaContentType```
	  ```restriction(Audio```
	    ```allValuesFrom(AudioSegmentType)```
	    ```cardinality(1)))```

2.5.2 XML2RDF Mapping

Once all the XML schemas for the metadata under consideration are available as mapped OWL ontologies, it is time to map the XML metadata that instantiates them. The intention is to produce RDF metadata as transparently as possible. Therefore, a structure-mapping approach has been selected (Klein 2002). It is also possible to take a model-mapping approach (Tous, García, Rodríguez and Delgado 2005). XML model mapping is based on representing the XML information set using semantic tools. This approach is better when XML metadata is semantically exploited for concrete purposes. However, when the objective is semantic metadata that can be easily integrated, it is better to take a more transparent approach. Transparency is achieved in structure-mapping models because they only try to represent the XML metadata structure, i.e. a tree, using RDF. The RDF model is based on the graph so it is easy to model a tree using it.

Moreover, we do not need to worry about the loose semantics produced by structure mapping. We have formalised the underlying semantics into the corresponding ontologies and we will attach them to RDF metadata using the instantiation relation *rdf:type*.

The structure mapping is based on translating XML metadata instances to RDF ones that instantiate the corresponding constructs in OWL. The more basic translation is between relation instances, from *xsd:elements* and *xsd:attributes* to *rdf:Properties*. Concretely, owl:ObjectProperties for node to node relations and owl:DatatypeProperties for node to values relations. However, in some cases, it would be necessary to use *rdf: Properties* for *xsd:elements* that have both data type and object type values. Values are kept during the translation as simple types and RDF blank nodes are introduced in the RDF model in order to serve as source and destination for properties.

The resulting RDF graph model contains all that we can obtain from the XML tree. It is already semantically enriched, thanks to the *rdf:type* relation that connects each RDF property to the owl:ObjectProperty or owl:DatatypeProperty it instantiates. It can be enriched further if the blank nodes are related to the owl:Class that defines the package of properties and associated restrictions they contain, i.e. the corresponding *xsd:complexType*. This semantic decoration of the graph is formalised using *rdf:type* relations from blank nodes to the corresponding OWL classes.

At this point, we have obtained a semantics-enabled representation of the input metadata. The instantiation relations can now be used to apply OWL semantics to metadata. Therefore, the semantics derived from further enrichments of the ontologies, e.g. integration links between different ontologies or semantic rules, are automatically propagated to instance metadata, thanks to inference. We will show now how this mapping fits in the architecture for semantic multimedia metadata integration and retrieval.

However, before continuing to the next section, it is important to point out that these mappings have been validated in different ways. First, we have used OWL validators in order to check the resulting ontologies, not just the MPEG-7 ontology but also many others (García and Gil 2007; García, Gil and Delgado 2007). Second, our MPEG-7 ontology has been compared with handmade ontologies such as Jane Hunters' one (2001) and Tsinaraki et al.'s (2004b). This comparison has shown that our mapping captures all the semantics captured by these ontologies and even adds additional details not captured by them in order to get a full formalisation of the semantics in all the MPEG-7 XML schemas.

Finally, the two mappings have been tested in conjunction. Testing XML instances have been mapped to RDF, guided by the corresponding OWL ontologies from the used XML schemas, and then back to XML. Then, the original and derived XML instances have been compared using their canonical version in order to correct mapping problems.

2.6 Use Cases

Based on the previous XML to Semantic Web mapping, a system architecture that facilitates multimedia metadata integration and retrieval has been built. The architecture is sketched in Fig. 2.8. The MPEG-7 OWL ontology, generated by XSD2OWL, constitutes the basic ontological framework for semantic multimedia metadata integration and appears at the centre of the architecture. Other ontologies and XML schemas might be easily incorporated using the XSD2OWL module.

Semantic metadata can be directly fed into the system together with XML metadata, which is translated to semantic metadata using the XML2RDF module. XML MPEG-7 metadata has a great importance because it is commonly used for (automatically extracted) low-level metadata that constitutes the basic input of the system.

This framework has the persistence support of an RDF store, where metadata and ontologies reside. Once all metadata has been put together, the semantic integration can take place, as detailed in Section 2.6.1. Finally, from this

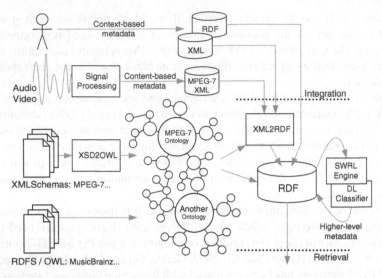

Fig. 2.8 Metadata integration and retrieval architecture

integrated space, higher-level metadata can be inferred and retrieved, as shown in Section 2.6.2.

2.6.1 Semantic Integration of Music Metadata

The problem of integrating heterogeneous data sources has grown in importance within the last years. One of the main reasons is the increasing availability of web-based data sources. Even within a single organisation, data from disparate sources must be integrated. Our approach to solve this problem is based on web ontologies. As we focus on the integration of multimedia assets, our base ontology is the MPEG-7 OWL ontology.

When multimedia metadata based on different schemes has to be integrated, the XML schemas are first mapped to OWL. Once this first step has been done, these schemas are easily integrated into the ontological framework using OWL semantic relations for equivalence and inclusion: *subClassOf*, *subPropertyOf*, *equivalent-Class*, *equivalentProperty*, *sameIndividualAs*, etc. These relationships capture the semantics of the data integration. Then, once metadata is incorporated into the system and semantically enhanced, the integration is automatically performed by applying inference.

Our study on metadata integration is based on three different schemas: MusicBrainz schema, *Foafing the Music* ontology, and a music vocabulary to describe performances. MusicBrainz is a community music metadatabase that attempts to create a comprehensive music information site. MusicBrainz schema is written in RDF and describes all the tracks, albums, and artists available in their

Table 2.3 MusicBrainz to MPEG-7 OWL ontology mappings

musicbrainz:Artist	⊆ mpeg7:CreatorType
Musicbrainz:Album	⊆ mpeg7:CollectionType
Musicbrainz:Track	⊆ mpeg7:AudioSegmentType
dc:author	⊆ mpeg7:Creator
Dc:title	⊆ mpeg7:Title
musicbrainz:sortName	⊆ mpeg7:Name
musicbrainz:duration	≡ mpeg7:MediaDuration

music repository. Their mappings to the MPEG-7 OWL ontology are shown in Table 2.3.

The *foafing the music* ontology describes (low-level) content-based descriptors extracted automatically from the audio itself. The mappings of this schema to the MPEG-7 OWL ontology are summarised in Table 2.4. An artist is defined as a subclass of the MPEG-7 creator type, a track is defined as a subclass of the MPEG-7 AudioSegment and the audio descriptor class describes the content-based properties of a track. This descriptor is linked with the MPEG-7 AudioDS type. Thus, all *foafing the music* descriptors' subclasses inherit the properties from the MPEG-7 audio descriptor scheme. To characterise the descriptors related with the tonality of a song, the *Foafing the Music* ontology defines some properties, such as mode and key. Finally, the ontology defines rhythm descriptors to describe the rhythm component of a track, e.g. metre and tempo.

The last of the three schemas, a music vocabulary to describe performances, is linked as well with the MPEG-7 OWL (see Table 2.5). This schema models – for example, in the classical music world – a concert with the conductor, performers, the whole programme, time schedule, etc. The most general class related with a music piece is the Musical_Unit, from which all types of performances are derived (e.g. an opera performance, a symphony, a movement of the symphony).

Decomposition of a musical unit is achieved by defining its sections, and we link it with the MPEG-7 AudioSegment. Finally, there is an Artist class, the superclass for all the agents of the performances, e.g. director, musician, singer. Therefore, we link the Artist class with MPEG-7 OWL, and, automatically (transitivity property of rdfs:subClassOf) all the subclasses are linked with the MPEG-7 OWL ontology.

Table 2.4 Foafing the music ontology to MPEG-7 OWL ontology mappings

foafingthemusic:Artist	⊆ mpeg7:CreatorType
foafingthemusic:name	≡ mpeg7:GivenName
foafingthemusic:Track	⊆ mpeg7:AudioSegmentType
foafingthemusic:title	≡ mpeg7:Title
foafingthemusic:duration	≡ mpeg7:MediaDuration
foafingthemusic:Descriptor	≡ mpeg7:AudioDSType
foafingthemusic:mode	≡ mpeg7:Scale
foafingthemusic:key	≡ mpeg7:Key
foafingthemusic:tempo	≡ mpeg7:Beat
foafingthemusic:meter	≡ mpeg7:Meter

Table 2.5 Music vocabulary ontology to MPEG-7 OWL ontology mappings

music:Music_Unit ⊆ mpeg7:AudioSegmentType
music:sections ≡ mpeg7:AudioSegment
music:Artist ⊆ mpeg7:CreatorType
music:key ≡ mpeg7:Key
music:meter ≡ mpeg7:Meter

Once these mappings are done, all the multimedia assets are integrated into the ontological framework; that is the MPEG-7 OWL linked with all the schemas. Now, querying the system for audio segments will retrieve information from all the different sources, transparently to the user.

2.6.2 Semantic Retrieval of Music Metadata

Retrieving multimedia assets in the proposed architecture can be easily achieved by using semantic query languages such as the SPARQL query language (Prud'hommeaux and Seaborne 2007). SPARQL can benefit from the semantics made explicit by the XSD2OWL and XML2RDF mappings. It can, as well, exploit the results of semantic rules for metadata integration in order to retrieve all the related multimedia information for a given query. In our case, SPARQL queries use the MPEG-7 OWL ontology "vocabulary" in order to integrate all data sources. Using the mappings explained in the previous section, a SPARQL query can acquire information from *MusicBrainz*, *Foafing the Music*, the classical music ontology, etc.

A typical scenario that shows the usefulness of the architecture proposed could be the following: an Internet crawler is looking for audio data (we may assume that it is searching for MP3 files) and it downloads all the files. Getting editorial and related information for these audio files can be achieved by reading the information stored in the ID3 tag. Unfortunately, sometimes there is no basic editorial information such as the title of the track, or the performer.

However, content-based low-level descriptors can be computed for these files, including its MusicBrainz fingerprint, a string that uniquely identifies each audio file based on its content. The example in Table 2.6 shows an RDF/N3 description for a track with the calculated tempo and fingerprint.

On the other hand, the MusicBrainz database has the editorial metadata – as well as the fingerprint already calculated – for more than 3 million tracks. For example, the RDF description of the song "Blowin' in the wind" composed by Bob Dylan in Table 2.7.

Table 2.6 Content-based metadata, tempo, and fingerprint

```
<http://example.org/track#1> a foafingthemusic:Track;
    foafingthemusic:tempo "122";
    musicbrainz:trmid "e3c41bc1-4fdc-4ccd-a471-243a0596518f".
```

Table 2.7 Editorial metadata, title, and author, plus fingerprint

```
<http://example.org/track#2> a musicbrainz:Track;
   dc:title "Blowin' in the wind";
   dc:author [musicbrainz:sortName "Bob Dylan"];
   musicbrainz:trmid "e3c41bc1-4fdc-4ccd-a471-243a0596518f".
```

A closer look at both examples should highlight that the two resources are sharing the same MusicBrainz's fingerprint. Therefore, it is clear that, using a simple rule (1), one can assert that both audio files are actually the same file, that is to say the same instance in terms of OWL, owl:sameIndividualAs.

```
mpeg7:AudioType(track1) ∧ mpeg7:AudioType(track2) ∧
musicbrainz:trmid(track1, trm1) ∧
musicbrainz:trmid(track2, trm2) ∧ (trm1 = trm2)        (1)
⇒ owl:sameIndividualAs (track1, track2)
```

From now on, we have merged the metadata from both sources and we have deduced that the metadata related with both tracks is in fact referring to the same track. This data integration (at the instance level) is very powerful as it can combine and merge context-based data (editorial, cultural, etc.) with content-based data (extracted from the audio itself).

Finally, issuing a SPARQL query that searches for all the songs composed by Bob Dylan that have a fast tempo retrieves a list of songs, including "Blowin' in the wind". Moreover, there is no need for metadata provenance awareness at the end-user level. As the example in Table 2.8 shows, all query terms are referred only to the MPEG-7 ontology namespace.

Table 2.8 SPARQL query for integrated metadata retrieval

```
PREFIX mpeg7:<http://rhizomik.net/ontologies/2005/03/Mpeg7-2001.
owl#>
SELECT ?title
WHERE {
   ?track   a                mpeg7:AudioSegmentType;
            mpeg7:Title       ?title;
            mpeg7:Beat        ?tempo;
            mpeg7:Creator     ?author.
   ?author mpeg7:Name         "Bob Dylan".
   FILTER (?tempo >= 60) }
ORDER BY ASC(?title)
```

2.7 An Integrated Ontological Infrastructure for the Semantic Description of Multimedia Content

In this section, we present the *DS-MIRF ontological infrastructure*, an integrated ontological infrastructure for the semantic description of multimedia content that allows for the systematic integration of domain knowledge within the MPEG-7 semantics. This infrastructure was developed in the context of the *DS-MIRF framework* (Tsinaraki et al. 2007), which facilitates the development of knowledge-based multimedia content services based on the MPEG-7/21 standards. The DS-MIRF ontological infrastructure can support different usage scenarios, which fall into two main categories:

- The usage scenarios where the DS-MIRF ontological infrastructure is used in order to guide MPEG-7-based semantic multimedia content annotation and/or semantic multimedia service provision on top of an OWL/RDF repository. In this case, the OWL/RDF semantic multimedia annotations are produced (manually, automatically, or semi-automatically), possibly after being enriched through the application of rule-based reasoning, and stored in the repository.
- The usage scenarios where the DS-MIRF ontological infrastructure is used in order to guide MPEG-7-based semantic multimedia content annotation and/or semantic multimedia service provision on top of a pure MPEG-7 repository. In this case, the OWL/RDF semantic multimedia annotations that are produced, possibly after being enriched through reasoning, are transformed into pure MPEG-7 descriptions and are then stored in the repository. This category of usage scenarios is extremely useful both for groups using pure MPEG-7 and for groups sharing pure MPEG-7 descriptions with their partners. Full support for this category of usage scenarios is provided by the DS-MIRF framework.

The ontological infrastructure of the DS-MIRF framework (depicted in Fig. 2.9) includes an *OWL-DL upper ontology*, *OWL-DL application ontologies*, and *OWL-DL domain ontologies*.

The *OWL-DL upper ontology* fully captures the semantics of the MPEG-7 MDS and the *MPEG-21 DIA architecture* (ISO/IEC 2004) and the parts of the MPEG-7 visual and audio that are necessary for the complete representation of the MPEG-7 MDS. This ontology includes the MPEG-7 OWL-DL ontology described in Section 2.4, extended with the MPEG-21 DIA architecture semantics in order to better support multimedia content personalisation and adaptation.

The *OWL application ontologies* either enhance, using OWL-DL syntax, the semantics of MPEG-7/21 so that the users find it easier to use MPEG-7/21 or allow using advanced multimedia content services that cannot be directly supported by MPEG-7/21. The application ontologies provide general purpose constructs that either are not available in MPEG-7/21 (for example, semantic user preferences) or are implied in the text of MPEG-7/21 but lacking in their syntax (for example, typed relationships).

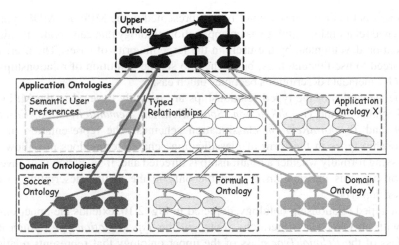

Fig. 2.9 The ontological infrastructure of the DS-MIRF framework

The *domain ontologies* systematically extend the upper ontology and the application ontologies with domain knowledge (for example, sports ontologies that extend the abstract semantic description capabilities of the MPEG-7 MDS).

In the rest of this section, we present the application ontologies that have been already integrated in the DS-MIRF ontological infrastructure (in Section 2.7.1), the methodology followed for domain knowledge representation in the form of OWL domain ontologies and their integration with the MPEG-7 semantics (in Section 2.7.2), and the DS-MIRF framework and the support it provides for pure MPEG-7 applications (in Section 2.7.3).

2.7.1 Application Ontologies

We outline in this section the application ontologies that have already been integrated in the DS-MIRF framework. These include (a) a *typed relationship* application ontology, which extends the MPEG-7 MDS in order to allow the full and systematic representation of typed relationships that are literally described in the MPEG-7 MDS text but their features are not fully captured in the MPEG-7 MDS syntax and (b) a *semantic user preference* application ontology that supports the semantic-based description of the desired multimedia content, which is not allowed in the MPEG-7 user preferences. The application ontologies are described in the following paragraphs.

2.7.1.1 Typed Relationship Application Ontology

The *typed relationship* application ontology assists the semantic multimedia content description. It extends the MPEG-7 MDS in order to allow the full and systematic representation of typed relationships that are literally described in the MPEG-7

MDS text but their features are not fully represented in the MPEG-7 MDS syntax. The typed relationship ontology is an application ontology that can greatly facilitate application development by the users in the large majority of cases. The users are not forced to use this ontology, but if they do so, the definition of relationships in MPEG-7 metadata descriptions becomes much easier.

The semantics of the typed relationships are partially covered in the MPEG-7 MDS syntax in the *GraphRelation, SpatialRelation, SemanticRelation, BaseRelation*, and *TemporalRelation* classification schemes. The representation of the relationship types in the form of classification scheme terms does not allow for expressing formally whether a relationship is directed and, if so, which is its inverse relationship; this information is available only in the textual description of the relationship type.

The typed relationship ontology, depicted in Fig. 2.10, extends the upper ontology with an OWL class hierarchy rooted in the *TypedRelationType* (which is a subclass of the *RelationType* class of the upper ontology that represents relationships). The direct subclasses of *TypedRelationType* are homonyms of the classification schemes where the relationship types are defined. Each of the subclasses of *TypedRelationType* has a number of subclasses, which correspond to the relationship types defined in the homonym classification scheme, together with the information literally described about them in the MPEG-7 MDS text. This information includes the type of the relationship, if it is directed or not and, in the latter case, its inverse relationship. The annotator that uses the typed relationship application ontology does not have to be aware of the textual description of the MPEG-7 MDS, since all the information is captured in the ontology.

The OWL classes of the typed relationship ontology formally capture all the information about the typed relationships that exist in the MPEG-7 MDS text. In fact, they express formally the semantics that exist in the textual descriptions of the different relationship types (for example, that the *before* relationship is directed and that the *after* relationship is its inverse).

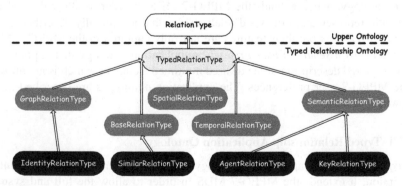

Fig. 2.10 The typed relationship ontology

2.7.1.2 Semantic User Preference Application Ontology

The *semantic user preference* application ontology allows the semantic-based description of the desired multimedia content in the user preferences. Such an extension of MPEG-7/21 is needed because the MPEG-7/21 user preference descriptions allow keyword-only descriptions of the semantics of the preferred content. As an example, consider a user who wishes to receive all the images that contain a teacher who gives a book to a student, as soon as such images are available. The current MPEG-7 search and filtering preference descriptions allow the users to describe the desired images using the keywords *teacher, student, gives,* and *book.* These user preference descriptions will provide, together with the images that contain a teacher who gives a book to a student, images that contain a student who gives a book to a teacher.

The application ontology is based on the semantic user preference model proposed in Tsinaraki and Christodoulakis (2007), which is also compatible with the MP7QL and allows for the explicit specification of the Boolean operators to be used in the different phases of multimedia content search and filtering. The semantic user preferences structured according to this model allow the accurate expression of the user preferences of a user who wishes to receive all the images that contain a teacher who gives a book to a student.

2.7.2 Domain Knowledge Representation and Integration with MPEG-7

The multimedia content description approaches, which have been implemented in MPEG-7 and have been described in Section 2.2, are general purpose and can be applied in any domain. In particular, the general purpose semantic description capabilities of MPEG-7 distinguish only events, agents (people, person groups, and organisations), places, states, times, objects, and concepts. On the other hand, the systematic integration of domain knowledge in the multimedia content descriptions has been shown to enhance the retrieval effectiveness of the multimedia content retrieval and filtering services built on top of them. We outline in this section a methodology for domain knowledge representation in OWL and its integration with MPEG-7 semantics (Tsinaraki et al. 2007; Tsinaraki, Polydoros and Christodoulakis 2004a). This methodology has been developed in the DS-MIRF framework for the definition and integration of domain ontologies in the DS-MIRF ontological infrastructure. Thanks to this methodology, OWL/RDF multimedia content descriptions can be defined that are structured according to MPEG-7 semantics and are also enhanced with domain knowledge.

According to this methodology, the domain-specific entities are represented as domain ontology classes. These classes are (direct or indirect) subclasses of the OWL classes that represent the subtypes of *SemanticBaseType* (*EventType, ObjectType, AgentObjectType, SemanticPlaceType, SemanticTimeType, Semantic-StateType,* and *ConceptType*) in the upper OWL-DL ontology defined in Tsinaraki

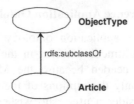

Fig. 2.11 RDF graph showing the *Article* class, which represents articles

et al. (2004b). This way, the knowledge captured in the domain ontologies is integrated with the MPEG-7 semantic model. As an example, the *Article* class (shown in Fig. 2.11), which represents the articles, should be defined as a subclass of the *ObjectType* class.

Features that are not present in the upper ontology class are represented as additional object or data type properties in its domain-specific subclass. For example, the number of pages of an article should be represented as a data type property of non-negative integer type in the domain of the *Article* class.

Additional constraints may be applied on the properties inherited from the ancestor classes, in order to guide the indexers to produce valid metadata (for example, the author of an article should have a name).

In addition, properties may be defined that permit the attachment of relationships to the allowed domain-specific entities only (for example, only persons are allowed to be related with articles as authors). These properties are subproperties of the *Relation* property of the *SemanticBaseType* class, which links semantic entities with relationships. The properties have as domain the union of the classes to which belong individuals that are capable of being sources of a typed relationship and the typed relationship class as range. The inverse property of the one defined previously is defined in the domain of the classes the individuals of which are capable of being targets of the typed relationship.

The methodology described above can be also used in order to integrate existing OWL domain ontologies in the MPEG-7 semantics. It has been tested in the DS-MIRF framework through the definition of domain ontologies for soccer and Formula 1 and their integration with the DS-MIRF ontological infrastructure.

2.7.3 The DS-MIRF Framework

The architecture of the DS-MIRF framework and the information flow between its components are depicted in Fig. 2.12.

The multimedia content *annotator* is a special type of user in the DS-MIRF framework that is responsible for the semantic annotation of multimedia documents. He uses a *multimedia annotation interface* that makes use of the ontological infrastructure of the DS-MIRF framework in order to support ontology-based semantic annotation of the multimedia content. The DS-MIRF framework ontologies are expressed in OWL; thus the result of the annotation process is an OWL description

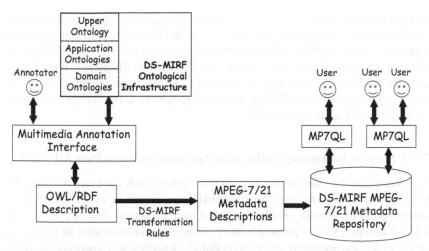

Fig. 2.12 The DS-MIRF framework – architecture and information flow

of the multimedia content. The OWL descriptions are then transformed, using the *DS-MIRF transformation rules* to standard *MPEG-7/21 metadata descriptions*. The MPEG-7/21 metadata are stored in the *DS-MIRF MPEG-7/21 metadata repository*, which is accessed by the end-users through application interfaces that are based on the *MPEG-7 query language* (*MP7QL*) (Tsinaraki and Christodoulakis 2007), a query language that has been developed in the context of the DS-MIRF framework for querying MPEG-7 multimedia descriptions.

In the following paragraphs, we will focus on the MP7QL query language and on the support for interoperation with applications using pure MPEG-7.

2.7.3.1 The MP7QL Query Language

The MP7QL query language has MPEG-7 as data model and allows for the querying of every aspect of an MPEG-7 multimedia content description, including semantics, low-level features, and media-related aspects. It also allows for the exploitation of domain knowledge encoded using pure MPEG-7 constructs. In addition, it allows the explicit specification of Boolean operators and/or preference values. The MP7QL queries may utilise the users' *filtering and search preferences* (*FASP*) and *usage history* as context, thus allowing for personalised multimedia content retrieval. The MP7QL has been expressed both in XML schema and in OWL-based syntax, in order to be applicable to all usage scenarios and working environments. The XML schema-based syntax of the MP7QL is used in the current implementation of the DS-MIRF framework.

General purpose languages, such as XQuery in the pure MPEG-7 environment and SPARQL in the Semantic Web environment, do not take into account the following peculiarities of the MPEG-7 description elements: (a) the MPEG-7 semantic model is expressed in a rather complex way; (b) the domain knowledge integrated in the semantic MPEG-7 descriptions is expressed in the document level; and (c) the low-level visual and audio features should be evaluated using specialised functions. Thus, in order to fully exploit the semantics of the MPEG-7 descriptions, a query language for querying MPEG-7 descriptions is needed, with clear, MPEG-7 specific semantics (instead of the generic semantics of XQuery and SPARQL). These semantics will also allow the optimisers to effectively perform consistency checking and first-level optimisation. The MP7QL fulfils the requirement for MPEG-7 semantics, as it has MPEG-7 as its data model.

2.7.3.2 Support for Interoperation with Applications Using Pure MPEG-7

Interoperation of the multimedia content descriptions with applications using pure MPEG-7 is achieved through the DS-MIRF transformation rules that allow the transformation of domain ontologies and semantic content descriptions to valid MPEG-7 descriptions. In particular, they allow the transformation of (a) domain ontologies defined according to the methodology described in Tsinaraki et al. (2005) into abstract MPEG-7/21 semantic descriptions; (b) OWL individuals that belong to the domain ontology classes into MPEG-7/21 semantic descriptions. The descriptions which are produced are valid MPEG-7/21 (parts of) documents.

During the metadata transformation from OWL to MPEG-7/21, the individuals representing MPEG-7/21 constructs are transformed into XML elements. The object properties are transformed into elements and the data-type properties are transformed into the constructs they represent in the original MPEG-7/21 schemas (attributes, elements, or simple values). In order to produce valid MPEG-7/21 descriptions, information regarding the MPEG-7/21 XML element order, the default values and the original MPEG-7/21 representation of the data type properties are needed. This information is kept in a mapping ontology and is utilised during both ontology and metadata transformations, as shown in Fig. 2.13.

The classes of the OWL domain ontologies and the OWL individuals belonging to them are both transformed into instances of the subtypes of *SemanticBaseType*. This way, the domain knowledge is represented in a way compatible with the domain knowledge expressed according to the methodology presented in Tsinaraki et al. (2005). The *AbstractionLevel* element of the *SemanticBaseType* and the MPEG-7 semantic relationships are used to capture the ontology semantics.

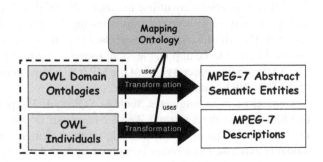

Fig. 2.13 OWL-MPEG-7 transformations in the DS-MIRF framework

An abstract semantic entity that represents a domain-specific class has a non-zero *AbstractionLevel.Dimension* and is related with the semantic entities that represent its subclasses through (a) a relationship of type *generalizes*, which has as source the semantic entity that represents the class and as target the semantic entity that represents the subclass, and (b) a relationship of type *specializes*, which has as source the semantic entity that represents the subclass and as target the semantic entity that represents the class. In addition, an abstract semantic entity that represents a class is related with each of the semantic entities representing the class individuals through pairs of *exemplifies/exemplifiedBy* relationships.

The data-type properties of the classes of the domain ontologies are transformed into *Property* elements and the object properties into pairs of *property/propertyOf* relationships.

The transformations outlined above allow the representation of the OWL class hierarchy and the preservation of the class properties. Several OWL axioms, especially the restrictions and the set operations, cannot be expressed in the pure MPEG-7 syntax. This feature does not allow the use of reasoning on top of the pure MPEG-7 descriptions, but it allows the systematic use of the domain knowledge that is expressed using MPEG-7 constructs. As a consequence, queries of the form "Give me the multimedia objects that show a teacher who gives a book to a student" can be expressed accurately, instead of searching in the textual parts of the MPEG-7 description elements (including the semantic ones) for the keywords *teacher*, *student*, *gives*, and *book*. The latter query is also ambiguous, as it will also return the multimedia objects where a student gives a book to a teacher. In addition, it may evaluate as teachers semantic entities that represent people who have worked as teachers for a while and the keyword *teacher* exists in the textual annotation of the semantic entities.

Another approach for domain knowledge representation is the definition of subtypes of the MPEG-7 types that represent semantic entities in order to represent domain-specific classes. The advantage of the utilisation of abstract semantic entities instead of subtypes of the semantic entity types for the representation of domain-specific classes is that this way, full compatibility with MPEG-7 is maintained so that all the tools and the applications that use pure MPEG-7 still work transparently with the MPEG-7 descriptions which are produced.

The ontological infrastructure of the DS-MIRF framework and the mechanisms that have been developed in the context of DS-MIRF for the support of interoperability between OWL domain ontologies and MPEG-7/21 support the semantic multimedia content description, which in turn allows the provision of advanced (semantic) multimedia content services. In particular, advanced retrieval services can be supported on top of the semantic multimedia annotations, which allow more accurate multimedia content retrieval. Accurate retrieval results in the better support of advanced services built on top of it, such as filtering and content-based personalisation. Such services are offered in the DS-MIRF framework based on the MP7QL language that supports personalised semantic retrieval and filtering on top of MPEG-7 multimedia content descriptions.

2.8 Conclusions

In this chapter, we have introduced the need for representing MPEG-7 constructs using Semantic Web languages. First, we presented in Section 2.2 the MPEG-7 standard and described the well-accepted general purpose approaches for multimedia content description that are supported by the MPEG-7 standard and their implementation in MPEG-7. Then, we have presented the Semantic Web languages in Section 2.3. The research efforts towards the expression of MPEG-7 using Semantic Web languages have been outlined in Section 2.4, followed by the mapping of the MPEG-7 constructs to OWL constructs in Section 2.5. The application of two of the MPEG-7 ontologies in real application environments have been presented next: (a) a case study for the music domain has been presented in Section 2.6, which has introduced the problems of annotating multimedia assets, integrating data from different sources, and retrieving music-related descriptors, and (b) an integrated ontological infrastructure for the semantic description of multimedia content which allows for combining the general purpose MPEG-7 constructs with domain and application-specific knowledge has been described in Section 2.7.

Both application scenarios show the benefits of the MPEG-7 formal semantics. MPEG-7 is a big standard, difficult to deal with, but the availability of some formal semantics facilitates the development of more advanced tools capable of dealing with its complexity.

References

The aceMedia project (2007) *Harmonization of Multimedia Ontologies Activity,* in aceMedia annual public report 2006.

Antoniou, G. and Harmelen, F. van. (2004) *A Semantic Web Primer.* The MIT Press, April.

Amann, B., Beer, C., Fundulak, I. and Scholl, M. (2002) *Ontology-Based Integration of XML Web Resources.* In Proceedings of the 1st International Semantic Web Conference (ISWC).

Berners-Lee, T. (1999) *Weaving the Web.* Texere Publishing Ltd., November.

Berners-Lee, T, Hendler, J. and Lassila, O. (2001) The semantic web. *Scientific American,* May.

Brickley, D. and Guha, R.V. (eds.) (2004) *RDF Vocabulary Description Language 1.0: RDF Schema.* W3C Recommendation.

Celma, O., Gómez, E., Janer, J., Gouyon, F., Herrera, P. and García, D. (2004) *Tools for Content-Based Retrieval and Transformation of Audio Using MPEG-7: The SPOffline and the MDTools.* Proceedings of 25th International AES Conference London, UK.

Celma O., Dasiopoulou S., Hausenblas M., Little S., Tsinaraki C. and Troncy R. (2007) *MPEG-7 and the Semantic Web.* W3C Multimedia Semantics Incubator Group (MMSEM-XG), XG deliverable.

Cruz, I., Xiao, H. and Hsu, F. (2004) *An Ontology-Based Framework for XML Semantic Integration.* In Proceedings of the Eighth International Database Engineering and Applications Symposium. Coimbra, Portugal (IDEAS'04).

Fallside, D. (2001) *XML Schema Part 0: Primer.* W3C Recommendation.

García, R. and Celma, O. (2005) *Semantic Integration and Retrieval of Multimedia Metadata.* In the Proceedings of the Knowledge Markup and Semantic Annotation Workshop, Semannot'05.

García, R. (2006) *A Semantic Web Approach to Digital Rights Management.* PhD thesis, Technologies Department, Universitat Pompeu Fabra.

García, R. and Gil, R. (2007) *Facilitating Business Interoperability from the Semantic Web*. In Proceedings of the 10th International Conference on Business Information Systems, BIS'07. Springer-Verlag, Lecture Notes in Computer Science, (4439):220–232.

García, R., Gil, R. and Delgado, J. (2007) *A Web Ontologies Framework for Digital Rights Management*. Journal of Artificial Intelligence and Law, 15(2):online first

Gruber, T. R. (1993) Towards principles for the design of ontologies used for knowledge sharing. In N. Guarino and R. Poli, editors, *Formal Ontology in Conceptual Analysis and Knowledge Representation*, Deventer, The Netherlands, Kluwer Academic Publishers.

Halevy, A., Ives, Z., Mork, P. and Tatarinov, I. (2003) *Piazza: Data Management Infrastructure for Semantic Web Applications*. In Proceedings of the 12th World Wide Web Conference. Budapest, Hungary, 556–567.

Hunter, J., (1999) *A proposal for an MPEG-7 description definition language*. Technical report, MPEG-7 AHG Test and Evaluation Meeting, Lancaster, UK

Hunter, J., (2001) *Adding Multimedia to the Semantic Web – Building an MPEG-7 Ontology*. In the Proceedings of the International Semantic Web Working Symposium (SWWS).

ISO/IEC (2001a) 15938-3:2001: Information Technology – Multimedia content description interface – Part 3 visual. Version 1.

ISO/IEC (2001b) 15938-4:2001: Information Technology – Multimedia content description interface – Part 4 audio. Version 1.

ISO/IEC (2003) 15938-5:2003: Information Technology – Multimedia content description interface – Part 5: Multimedia description schemes. First Edition.

ISO/IEC (2004) 21000-7:2004, Information Technology – Multimedia Framework (MPEG-21) – Part 7: Digital Item Adaptation.

Klein, M.C.A. (2002) *Interpreting xml Documents via an rdf Schema Ontology*. In Proceedings of the 13th International Workshop on Database and Expert Systems Applications (DEXA).

Lakshmanan, L. and Sadri, F. (2003) *Interoperability on XML Data*. In Proceedings of the 2nd International Semantic Web Conference (ICSW 03), pp. 146–163.

Manola, F. and Milles, E. (eds.) (2004) *RDF Primer*. W3C Recommendation.

Martínez, J. (ed.) (2004), *MPEG-7 Overview*, ISO/IEC JTC1/SC29/WG11 N6828, Palma de Mallorca, October.

McGuinness, D. L. and van Harmelen, F. (eds.) (2004) *OWL Web Ontology Language: Overview*. W3C Recommendation.

McGuinness, D.L., Fikes, R., Hendler, J. and Stein. L.A. (2002) *DAML+OIL: An Ontology Language for the Semantic Web*. IEEE Intelligent Systems, September–October, 17(5):72–80

Patel-Schneider, P. and Simeon, J. (2002) *The Yin/Yang Web: XML Syntax and RDF semantics*. In Proceedings of the 11th International World Wide Web Conference (WWW02), Honolulu, Hawaii, USA, 443–453.

Prud'hommeaux, R. and Seaborne A. (2007). *SPARQL Query Language for RDF*. W3C Working Draft, 26 March.

Salembier, P., Manjunath, B.S. and Sikora T. (eds.) (2002). *Introduction to MPEG 7: Multimedia Content Description Language*. Ed. Wiley.

Shadbolt, N., Berners-Lee, T. and Hall, W. (2006) *The Semantic Web Revisited*. IEEE Intelligent Systems, 21(3):96–101.

Siméon, J., Chamberlin, D., Fernández, M., Boag, S., Florescu, D. and Robie, J. (Eds) (2007) *XQuery 1.0: An XML Query Language*. W3C Recommendation, 23 January.

Simou, N., Tzouvaras, V., Avrithis, Y., Stamou, G. and Kollias, S. (2005) *A Visual Descriptor Ontology for Multimedia Reasoning*. In the Proceedings of the Workshop on Image Analysis for Multimedia Interactive Services (WIAMIS).

Tous, R., García, R., Rodríguez, E. and Delgado, J. (2005) *Arquitecture of a Semantic XPath Processor. Application to Digital Rights Management (DRM)*. In the Proceedings of E-Commerce and Web Technologies: 6th International Conference, EC-Web. Springer-Verlag, LNCS (3590):1–10

Tsinaraki, C. and Christodoulakis, S. (2007) *An MPEG-7 Query Language and a User Preference Model that allow Semantic Retrieval and Filtering of Multimedia Content*. ACM-Springer Multimedia Systems Journal, in Special Issue on Semantic Multimedia Adaptation and Personalization, (to appear)

Tsinaraki, C., Polydoros, P. and Christodoulakis, S. (2007) *Interoperability Support Between MPEG-7/21 and OWL in DS-MIRF*. Transactions on Knowledge and Data Engineering (TKDE), Special Issue on the Semantic Web Era, pp. 219–232.

Tsinaraki, C., Polydoros, P. and Christodoulakis, S. (2004a) *Integration of OWL Ontologies in MPEG-7 and TV-Anytime Compliant Semantic Indexing*. In the Proceedings of the 16th International Conference on Advanced Information Systems Engineering (CAISE), pp. 398–413.

Tsinaraki, C., Polydoros, P. and Christodoulakis, S. (2004b) *Interoperability Support for Ontology-Based Video Retrieval Applications*. In the Proceedings of the Conference on Image and Video Retrieval (CIVR), pp. 582–591.

Tsinaraki, C., Polydoros, P. Kazasis, F. and Christodoulakis, S. (2005) *Ontology-Based Semantic Indexing for MPEG-7 and TV-Anytime Audiovisual Content*. In Multimedia Tools and Application Journal (MTAP), Special Issue of on Video Segmentation for Semantic Annotation and Transcoding, 26, pp. 299–325, August.

Tzouvaras, V. and Pan, J. (2007) *Multimedia Annotation Interoperability Framework*. W3C Multimedia Semantics Incubator Group (MMSEM-XG) XG Deliverable.

Chapter 3
Ontology-Based Reasoning Techniques for Multimedia Interpretation and Retrieval

Ralf Möller and Bernd Neumann

3.1 Introduction

In this chapter, we show how formal knowledge representation and reasoning techniques can be used for the retrieval and interpretation of multimedia data. This section explains what we mean by an "interpretation" using examples of audio and video interpretation. Intuitively, interpretations are descriptions of media data at a high abstraction level, exposing interrelations and coherencies. In Section 3.2.3, we introduce description logics (DLs) as the formal basis for ontology languages of the OWL (web ontology language) family and for the interpretation framework described in subsequent sections. As a concrete example, we consider the interpretation of images describing a sports event in Section 3.3. It is shown that interpretations can be obtained by abductive reasoning, and a general interpretation framework is presented. Stepwise construction of an interpretation can be viewed as navigation in the compositional and taxonomical hierarchies spanned by a conceptual knowledge base.

What do we mean by "interpretation" of media objects? Consider the image shown in Fig. 3.1. One can think of the image as a set of primitive objects such as persons, garbage containers, a garbage truck, a bicycle, traffic signs, trees, etc. An interpretation of the image is a description which "makes sense" of these primitive objects. In our example, the interpretation could include the assertions "two workers empty garbage containers into a garbage truck" and "a mailman distributes mail" expressed in some knowledge representation language.

When including the figure caption into the interpretation process, we have a multimodal interpretation task which in this case involves visual and textual media objects. The result could be a refinement of the assertions above in terms of the location "in Hamburg". Note that the interpretation describes activities extending in time although it is only based on a snapshot. Interpretations may generally include

R. Möller
Hamburg University of Technology, Hamburg, Germany
e-mail: r.f.moeller@tu-harburg.de

Fig. 3.1 Street scene in Hamburg

hypotheses about things outside the temporal and spatial scope of the available media data.

An interpretation is a "high-level" description of media data in the sense that it involves terms which abstract from details at lower representation levels. This is typical for meaningful descriptions in human language and hence also a desirable goal for machine interpretation. Media interpretation is therefore often structured as a process computing higher level representations from lower level ones. Figure 3.2 shows the level structure of two early interpretation systems, the speech recognition system HEARSAY-II (Erman, Hayes-Roth, Lesser and Reddy 1980) and the image interpretation system VISIONS (Hanson and Riseman 1978).

The basic structure exemplified by each of the two systems also applies to interpretation systems in general: signal processing procedures first transform raw media

Fig. 3.2 Typical level structure of media interpretation systems exemplified by HEARSAY II and VISIONS. Signal processing (below *dotted line*) transforms the raw input signals into primitive media objects, various interpretation processes lead up to higher level interpretations

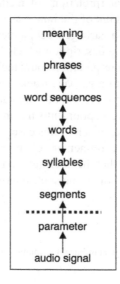
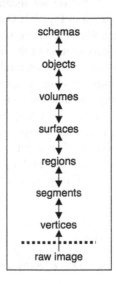

data into primitive media objects by low-level processing steps. Then higher level descriptions are determined based on the primitive media objects. The low-level processing steps are often called "analysis" (e.g. image analysis, speech analysis), the high-level steps constitute the interpretation process.

It is useful to view interpretation as a process which is both based on the general conceptual knowledge and the concrete contextual knowledge which an agent may possess. The term "contextual knowledge" covers specific prior knowledge relevant for the interpretation which the agent may possess (e.g. spatial and temporal context of a video clip) as well as the knowledge about the current task of the agent (e.g. recognizing criminal acts vs. recognizing sports events). The knowledge-based structure of an image sequence interpretation system is shown in Fig. 3.3.

The concepts represented in the conceptual knowledge base typically describe configurations of lower level entities forming some interesting higher level entity, for example a configuration of an athlete and a horizontal bar forming a "high jump" event. We call such concepts "aggregates" as they combine several components to a larger whole. Aggregates form a compositional hierarchy, in addition to the taxonomical hierarchy induced by logic-based concept definitions. In a description logic setting, an aggregate has the generic structure shown in Fig. 3.4 (Neumann and Möller 2006). An aggregate is defined by (1) inheritance from parent concepts, (2) roles relating the aggregate to parts, and (3) constraints relating parts to each other. Instantiations of aggregates are at the core of media interpretations.

In summary, interpretations have the following characteristics: they

- involve several objects;
- depend on the temporal or spatial relations between parts;
- describe the data in qualitative terms, omitting detail;
- exploit contextual information;
- include inferred facts, not explicit in the data;
- are based on conceptual knowledge about the application domain.

The chapter is structured as follows. We first describe how ontology-based information retrieval can be formalised using description-logic inference problems (Section 3.2). Introducing the necessary technical background, we demonstrate for what

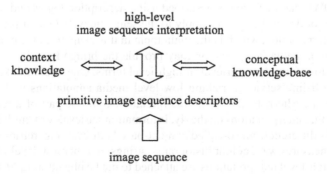

Fig. 3.3 Knowledge-based structure of a system for image sequence interpretation

$$Aggregate\_Concept \equiv Parent\_Concept_1 \sqcap \ldots \sqcap Parent\_Concept_n \sqcap$$
$$\exists_{\geq m_1} has PartRole. Part\_Concept_1 \sqcap$$
$$\cdots$$
$$\exists_{\geq m_k} has PartRole. Part\_Concept_k \sqcap$$
$$constraints\ between\ parts$$

Fig. 3.4 Generic structure of a definition for an aggregate concept (ontology design pattern)

purpose the output of media interpretation can be used, and, thereby, derive requirements for the media interpretation process. Then, in Section 3.3, the automatic construction of media interpretations is investigated. Techniques for dealing with uncertain and ambiguous interpretations are presented in Section 3.4. We conclude in Section 3.5.

In summary it is the purpose of this chapter to show that interpretations can be computed in a formal knowledge representation framework using various reasoning processes. This has multiple potential benefits. First, the complex computational process "media interpretation" is realised via standardised reasoning procedures, i.e. by programs which have been conceptually shown to meet correctness and completeness conditions, and have been implemented as reusable tools for a wide range of applications. Second, the terms by which interpretations are expressed are embedded in a sharable ontology which provides a transparent declarative representation with well-defined semantics. Furthermore, ontologies constitute resources not only for media interpretation but also for other tasks dealing with semantic content, such as information retrieval, communication, documentation, and various engineering processes.

3.2 Ontology-Based Information Retrieval

A task addressed in this chapter is information retrieval from the semantic web. Media data with semantic annotations will be an important part of the information provided by the semantic web. It is well known that the semantic web representation language OWL can be formally described using description logics and that reasoning services of description logics apply to the semantic web. One of those services is media interpretation, which is the main topic in this chapter. In the context of the semantic web, media interpretation may provide the bridge from low-level media annotation to information retrieval in high-level terms. One could think, for example, of an off-line service enriching low-level media annotations with high-level interpretations. Alternatively, media interpretation could be part of a retrieval service, providing interpretations on the fly. Information retrieval w.r.t. high-level interpretations is different from so-called content-based retrieval (e.g. retrieval based on similarity measures w.r.t. colour histograms, strings, or other low-level features). In our view, high-level interpretations are attached to media objects as metadata, which are specified using ontology languages.

3.2.1 Ontology Languages Based on Description Logics

Ontology languages of the OWL family, which provide the skeleton for research on information retrieval based on high-level media interpretations, are based on description logics. In this section, we introduce the logical basis of several ontology languages of the OWL family, define their semantics, and specify corresponding reasoning services. In the following subsections, we start with so-called expressive description logics (approximately corresponding to, but slightly more expressive than OWL Lite), introduce additional constructs afterwards (corresponding to OWL DL, OWL 1.1), and also specify other fragments of first-order logic, some of which have also been standardised by activities of the World Wide Web Consortium (W3C). For more details see Baader, Calvanese, McGuinness, Nardi, and Patel-Schneider (2003).

3.2.1.1 Expressive Description Logics: Syntax and Semantics

The DL $\mathcal{ALCQHI}_{R+}(\mathcal{D})^-$ which is also known as $\mathcal{SHIQ}$ is briefly introduced as follows. We assume five disjoint sets: a set of concept names C, a set of role names R, a set of feature names F, a set of individual names O and a set of names for (concrete) objects O_C. The mutually disjoint subsets P and T of R denote non-transitive and transitive roles, respectively ($R = P \cup T$). $\mathcal{ALCQHI}_{R+}(\mathcal{D})^-$ is introduced in Fig. 3.5 using a standard Tarski-style semantics with an interpretation $\mathcal{I}_D = (\Delta^\mathcal{I}, \Delta^\mathcal{D}, \cdot^\mathcal{I})$ where $\Delta^\mathcal{I} \cap \Delta^\mathcal{D} = \emptyset$ holds. A variable assignment α maps concrete objects to values in $\Delta^\mathcal{D}$.

In accordance with Baader and Hanschke (1991), we also define the notion of a concrete domain. A *concrete domain* $\mathcal{D}$ is a pair $(\Delta^\mathcal{D}, \Phi_\mathcal{D})$, where $\Delta^\mathcal{D}$ is a set called the domain, and $\Phi_\mathcal{D}$ is a set of predicate names. The interpretation function maps each predicate name P from $\Phi_\mathcal{D}$ with arity n to a subset $P^\mathcal{I}$ of $\Delta^n_\mathcal{D}$. Concrete objects from O_C are mapped to an element of $\Delta^\mathcal{D}$. We assume that $\perp_\mathcal{D}$ is the negation of the predicate $\top_\mathcal{D}$. A concrete domain $\mathcal{D}$ is called *admissible* iff the set of predicate names $\Phi_\mathcal{D}$ is closed under negation and $\Phi_\mathcal{D}$ contains a name $\top_\mathcal{D}$ for $\Delta^\mathcal{D}$, and the satisfiability problem $P_1^{n_1}(x_{11}, \ldots, x_{1n_1}) \wedge \ldots \wedge P_m^{n_m}(x_{m1}, \ldots, x_{mn_m})$ is decidable (m is finite, $P_i^{n_i} \in \Phi_\mathcal{D}$, n_i is the arity of P_i, and x_{jk} is a concrete object).

If $R, S \in R$ are role names, then $R \sqsubseteq S$ is called a *role inclusion axiom*. A *role hierarchy* $\mathcal{R}$ is a finite set of role inclusion axioms. Then, we define $\sqsubseteq^*$ as the reflexive transitive closure of $\sqsubseteq$ over such a role hierarchy $\mathcal{R}$. Given $\sqsubseteq^*$, the set of roles $R^\downarrow = \{S \in R \mid S \sqsubseteq^* R\}$ defines the *sub-roles* of a role R. R is called a super-role of S if $S \in R^\downarrow$. We also define the set $S := \{R \in P \mid R^\downarrow \cap T = \emptyset\}$ of *simple* roles that are neither transitive nor have a transitive role as sub-role. Due to undecidability issues, number restrictions are only allowed for simple roles (Horrocks, Sattler, Tessaris and Tobies 2000). In concepts, inverse roles R^{-1} (or S^{-1}) may be used instead of role names R (or S). In case of inverse roles being mentioned in number restrictions, the definition of "simple role" is more complex, but we neglect these details here.

If C and D are concepts, then $C \sqsubseteq D$ is a terminological axiom (*generalised concept inclusion* or *GCI*). $C \equiv D$ is used as an abbreviation for two GCIs $C \sqsubseteq D$ and

Syntax	Semantics
Concepts ($R \in R$, $S \in S$, and $f, f_i \in F$)	
A	$A^{\mathcal{I}} \subseteq \Delta^{\mathcal{I}}$ (A *is a concept name*)
$\neg C$	$\Delta^{\mathcal{I}} \setminus C^{\mathcal{I}}$
$C \sqcap D$	$C^{\mathcal{I}} \cap D^{\mathcal{I}}$
$C \sqcup D$	$C^{\mathcal{I}} \cup D^{\mathcal{I}}$
$\exists R.C$	$\{a \in \Delta^{\mathcal{I}} \mid \exists b \in \Delta^{\mathcal{I}} : (a, b) \in R^{\mathcal{I}} \wedge b \in C^{\mathcal{I}}\}$
$\forall R.C$	$\{a \in \Delta^{\mathcal{I}} \mid \forall b \in \Delta^{\mathcal{I}} : (a, b) \in R^{\mathcal{I}} \Rightarrow b \in C^{\mathcal{I}}\}$
$\exists_{\geq n} S.C$	$\{a \in \Delta^{\mathcal{I}} \mid \; \|\{x \mid (a, x) \in S^{\mathcal{I}}, x \in C^{\mathcal{I}}\}\| \geq n\}$
$\exists_{\leq m} S.C$	$\{a \in \Delta^{\mathcal{I}} \mid \; \|\{x \mid (a, x) \in S^{\mathcal{I}}, x \in C^{\mathcal{I}}\}\| \leq m\}$
$\exists f_1, \ldots, f_n . P$	$\{a \in \Delta^{\mathcal{I}} \mid \exists x_1, \ldots, x_n \in \Delta^{\mathcal{D}} : (a, x_1) \in f_1^{\mathcal{I}} \wedge \ldots \wedge (a, x_n) \in f_n^{\mathcal{I}} \wedge$ $(x_1, \ldots, x_n) \in P^{\mathcal{I}}\}$
$\forall f_1, \ldots, f_n . P$	$\{a \in \Delta^{\mathcal{I}} \mid \forall x_1, \ldots, x_n \in \Delta^{\mathcal{D}} : (a, x_1) \in f_1^{\mathcal{I}} \wedge \ldots \wedge (a, x_n) \in f_n^{\mathcal{I}} \Rightarrow$ $(x_1, \ldots, x_n) \in P^{\mathcal{I}}\}$
Roles and Features	
R	$R^{\mathcal{I}} \subseteq \Delta^{\mathcal{I}} \times \Delta^{\mathcal{I}}$
f	$f^{\mathcal{I}} : \Delta^{\mathcal{I}} \to \Delta^{\mathcal{D}}$ (features are partial functions)

(a)

$\| \cdot \|$ denotes the cardinality of a set, and $n, m \in \mathbb{N}$ with $n > 1$, $m > 0$.

(b)

Axioms	
Syntax	Satisfied if
$R \in T$	$R^{\mathcal{I}} = (R^{\mathcal{I}})^{+}$
$R \sqsubseteq S$	$R^{\mathcal{I}} \subseteq S^{\mathcal{I}}$
$C \sqsubseteq D$	$C^{\mathcal{I}} \subseteq D^{\mathcal{I}}$

(c)

Assertions ($a, b \in O$, $x, x_i \in O_C$)	
Syntax	Satisfied if
$a : C$	$a^{\mathcal{I}} \in C^{\mathcal{I}}$
$(a, b) : R$	$(a^{\mathcal{I}}, b^{\mathcal{I}}) \in R^{\mathcal{I}}$
$(a, x) : f$	$(a^{\mathcal{I}}, \alpha(x)) \in f^{\mathcal{I}}$
$(x_1, \ldots, x_n) : P$	$(\alpha(x_1), \ldots, \alpha(x_n)) \in P^{\mathcal{I}}$
$a = b$	$a^{\mathcal{I}} = b^{\mathcal{I}}$
$a \neq b$	$a^{\mathcal{I}} \neq b^{\mathcal{I}}$

Fig. 3.5 Syntax and semantics of $\mathcal{ALCQHI}_{R^+}(\mathcal{D})^{-}$

$D \sqsubseteq C$. A finite set of terminological axioms $\mathcal{T}_{\mathcal{R}}$ is called a *terminology* or *TBox* w.r.t. to a given role hierarchy $\mathcal{R}$. The reference to $\mathcal{R}$ is omitted in the following if we use $\mathcal{T}$. An *ABox* $\mathcal{A}$ is a finite set of assertional axioms as defined in Fig. 3.5c.

An interpretation $\mathcal{I}$ is a *model* of a concept C (or *satisfies* a concept C) iff $C^{\mathcal{I}} \neq \emptyset$ and for all $R \in R$ it holds that iff $(x, y) \in R^{\mathcal{I}}$ then $(y, x) \in (R^{-1})^{\mathcal{I}}$. An interpretation $\mathcal{I}$ is a model of a TBox $\mathcal{T}$ iff it satisfies all axioms in $\mathcal{T}$ (see Fig. 3.5b). An interpretation $\mathcal{I}$ is a model of an ABox $\mathcal{A}$ w.r.t. a TBox $\mathcal{T}$ iff it is a model of $\mathcal{T}$ and satisfies all assertions in $\mathcal{A}$ (see Fig. 3.5c). Different individuals are mapped to different domain objects (unique name assumption).

Reasoning about objects from other domains (so-called concrete domains, e.g. for real numbers) is very important for practical applications, in particular, in the context of the semantic web. For instance, one might want to express intervals for integer values ("the price range is between 200 and 300 Euro"), state the relationship between the Fahrenheit and Celsius scales, or describe linear inequalities ("the total price for the three goods must be below 60 Euro"). In Baader and Hanschke (1991), the description logic $\mathcal{ALC}(\mathcal{D})$ is investigated and it is shown that, provided a decision procedure for the concrete domain $\mathcal{D}$ exists, the logic $\mathcal{ALC}(\mathcal{D})$ is decidable. Unfortunately, adding concrete domains to expressive description logics such as $\mathcal{ALCNH}_{R^+}$ Haarslev and Möller (2000) might lead to undecidable inference problems. In Haarslev, Möller, and Wessel (2001), it has been shown that $\mathcal{ALCNH}_{R+}$ extended by a limited form of concrete domains leads to decidable inference problems. This is achieved by disallowing so-called feature chains in $\mathcal{ALCNH}_{R+}(\mathcal{D})^-$. It is easy to see that the same pragmatic approach can also be applied to very expressive DLs. By analogy to $\mathcal{ALCNH}_{R+}(\mathcal{D})^-$, the description logic $\mathcal{ALCQHI}_{R+}(\mathcal{D})^-$ extends the logic $\mathcal{ALCQHI}_{R+}$ or $\mathcal{SHIQ}$ (Horrocks, Sattler, Tessaris and Tobies 2000) with concrete domains.

An important property of the language $\mathcal{SHIQ}$ is that the subsumption hierarchy of the *TBox* part $\mathcal{T}$ of a *knowledge base* $(\mathcal{T}, \mathcal{A})$ is stable w.r.t. additions to the *ABox* part $\mathcal{A}$ (i.e. subsumption relations between concepts cannot be introduced by adding assertions to the ABox). In the case of multiple knowledge bases $(\mathcal{T}, \mathcal{A}_1), \ldots, (\mathcal{T}, \mathcal{A}_n)$, for query answering on any of the ABoxes $\mathcal{A}_i$, one can reuse computations done so far for the TBox $\mathcal{T}$ (e.g. indexing computations). This is due to the stability of the subsumption relationships between concepts, since they depend only on axioms in the TBox $\mathcal{T}$. This important property is lost when introducing *nominals*, which are described in the next subsection.

3.2.1.2 Very Expressive Description Logics

A *nominal* (the letter $\mathcal{O}$ in a language name indicates the presence of nominals) is a singleton concept, syntactically represented as $\{o\}$ and semantically interpreted as $\{o\}^{\mathcal{I}} = \{o^{\mathcal{I}}\}$. Thus, *nominals* stand for concepts with exactly one individual in contrast to concepts which stand for a set of individuals. This allows the use of individuals in concept definitions, for instance, as names for specific persons, countries, etc., leading to the situation in which there is no longer a difference between TBoxes and ABoxes. OWL DL is a language that supports nominals.

$\mathcal{SROIQ}$ (Horrocks, Kutz and Sattler 2006) is one of the most expressive DL languages whose decidability has been proved. On top of $\mathcal{SHIQ}$ plus nominals, $\mathcal{SROIQ}$ allows for more expressivity concerning roles, where besides a TBox and an ABox, an *RBox* is introduced to include role statements, allowing for:

1. *complex role inclusion axioms* of the form $R \circ S \sqsubseteq R$ and $S \circ R \sqsubseteq R$ where R is a role and S is a simple role.
2. *disjoint roles*
3. *reflexive, irreflexive, and antisymmetric roles*
4. *negated role assertions*
5. *universal role*
6. *local expressivity* to allow concepts of the form $\exists R.\text{Self}$.

$\mathcal{SROIQ}$ represents the logical basis of OWL 1.1 plus datatypes and datatypes restrictions $\mathcal{SROIQ}(D^+)$. In Horrocks et al. (2006), a tableau algorithm is presented, proving that $\mathcal{SROIQ}$ is decidable if some restrictions concerning the so-called cyclicity of role axioms are obeyed.

As observed in previous sections, decidability is a characteristic that should be preserved by ontology languages and which has caused expressivity restrictions.

This is one of the reasons why rules are gaining interest as an option to overcome expressivity limitations in DLs.

A relevant proposal to extend DL languages (more specifically, the syntactic variant OWL DL) with rules is the rule language called SWRL (semantic web rule language). SWRL uses OWL DL or OWL Lite as the underlying DL language to specify a KB. The syntax of SWRL is also based on XML. For brevity, however, we prefer a mathematical notation and define a rule as an axiom of the form

$$P_1(X_1, \ldots, X_{n_1}), \ldots, P_k(X_{n_1}, \ldots, X_{n_k}) \leftarrow$$
$$Q_1(Y_{1,1}, \ldots, Y_{1,m_1}), \ldots, Q_j(Y_{j,1}, \ldots, Y_{j,m_j})$$

such that P_{i_k} and Q_{i_j} are names and X_i mentioned in the head (left-hand side of the $\leftarrow$ constructor) as well as $Y_{i,j}$ (in the body on the right-hand side) stand for variable names (or variables for short). Variables in the head must also be mentioned in the body. Predicate terms in a rule body are called (rule) atoms.

The semantics of SWRL rules is defined as follows. An interpretation satisfies a rule of the above form if it satisfies the first-order predicate

$$\forall X_1, \ldots, X_{n_1}, Y_{1,1}, \ldots, Y_{1,m_1}, \ldots, Y_{j,1}, \ldots, Y_{j,m_j} :$$
$$Q_1(Y_{1,1}, \ldots, Y_{1,m_1}) \wedge \ldots \wedge Q_j(Y_{j,1}, \ldots, Y_{,m_j}) \rightarrow$$
$$P_1(X_1, \ldots, X_{n_1}) \wedge \ldots \wedge P_k(X_{n_1}, \ldots, X_{n_k})$$

The extension of OWL DL with SWRL rules is known to be undecidable if predicate names are mentioned in the ontology (TBox) (Motik, Sattler and Studer 2005). Various decidable fragments of OWL DL with SWRL rules exist.

In order to add rules and still preserve decidability, a variant of SWRL can be used, the so-called *DL-safe* rules (Motik et al. 2005). DL-safe rules are rules of the above form and are formally defined as follows.

Suppose a set of concept names N_c, a set of abstract and concrete role names $N_{R_a} \cup N_{R_c}$. A DL atom is of the form C(x) or R(x,y), where $C \in N_C$ and $R \in N_{R_a} \cup N_{R_c}$. Rule atoms may be DL atoms or atoms as defined above. A rule r is called safe if each of its variables also occurs in a non-DL atom in the rule body. All rules must be safe. Additionally, in the ABox, assertions of the following form are allowed: $P(ind_1, \ldots, ind_n)$ where P is a name for a predicate used in a non-DL atom. The assertions are called *facts* (rules with empty bodies). Thus, in practice, the safety restriction introduced for DL-safe rules means that rules are applied to ABox individuals only. Note, however, that DL-safe rules are not trigger rules, they have a first-order semantics (and hence, e.g. the law of contraposition holds, etc.).

In order to support the recognition of events in image sequences (see Section 3.3.4), rules with time variables will be used as part of a specific query language (see Section 3.2.2). We assume that assertions involving time variables such as, e.g. "ind_1 approaching ind_2 from t_1 to t_2" are generated by low-level image sequence analysis processes. The results are added to an ABox as so-called temporal propositions.

A *temporal proposition* is a syntactic structure of the following form:

$$P_{[t_1,t_2]}(ind_1, \ldots, ind_n)$$

where t_i denotes an element of a linear temporal structure $\Theta \subseteq \mathbb{N}$, ind_i with $i \in \{1, \ldots, n\}$ denotes an individual, and $P \in Preds$.

The semantics for rules with time intervals is different from DL-safe rules, and formally defined as follows. Let $\Theta \subseteq \mathbb{N}$ be a linear temporal structure. A temporal interpretation $\mathcal{I}_T$ is a tuple $(\Delta, \cdot^{\mathcal{I}}, \Theta, \Im)$ such that, in addition to the standard components of an interpretation, $\Im$ is an injective mapping from the temporal structure Θ to a set of standard Tarskian interpretation functions as used in previous sections.

A temporal interpretation $\mathcal{I}_T = (\Delta, \cdot^{\mathcal{I}}, \Theta, \Im,)$ satisfies a GCI or an ABox assertion if the standard part $(\Delta, \cdot^{\mathcal{I}})$ satisfies the GCI or the ABox assertion. The remaining components are used for defining satisfiability of temporal propositions. A temporal interpretation $\mathcal{I}_T$ satisfies a temporal proposition $P_{[t_1,t_2]}(ind_1, \ldots, ind_n)$ if the predicate is true for all time points in the non-empty interval $[t_1, t_2]$. Hence, we assume that temporal propositions are durative, i.e. the proposition holds for all non-empty subintervals (cf. Neumann and Novak 1983) for a more detailed analysis). More formally:

$$\mathcal{I}_T \models P_{[t_1,t_2]}(ind_1, \ldots ind_n)$$

if for all $\theta \in \Theta$, $|\Theta| > 1$, it holds that if $t_1 \leq \theta \leq t_2$, then $(ind_1^{\Im(\theta)}, \ldots, ind_n^{\Im(\theta)}) \in P^{\Im(\theta)}$. As usual, a temporal interpretation that satisfies a temporal proposition is called a *temporal model* for this term. A temporal interpretation which satisfies a GCI or an ABox assertion is called a (temporal) model for the GCI or ABox assertion, respectively. An Abox with a set of temporal propositions such as $\{move\_forward_{[10,20]}(ind_1), move\_backward_{[10,20]}(ind_1)\}$ should be inconsistent, but this requires (TBox) knowledge about the disjointness of predicates *move_forward* and *move_backward* for all time points. We ignore these issues here.

Temporal propositions are relevant for queries with time variables, which are described in Section 3.2.2.

3.2.2 Introduction to Basic Reasoning Problems

3.2.2.1 Standard Inference Services

In the following, we define standard inference services for description logics.

A *concept* C is called *consistent* (w.r.t. a TBox $\mathcal{T}$) if there exists a model of C (that is also a model of $\mathcal{T}$ and $\mathcal{R}$). An *ABox* $\mathcal{A}$ is *consistent* (w.r.t. a TBox $\mathcal{T}$) if $\mathcal{A}$ has model $\mathcal{I}$ (which is also a model of $\mathcal{T}$). A *knowledge base* $(\mathcal{T}, \mathcal{A})$ is called *consistent* if there exists a model for $\mathcal{A}$ which is also a model for $\mathcal{T}$. A concept, ABox, or knowledge base that is not consistent is called *inconsistent*.

A concept D *subsumes* a concept C (w.r.t. a TBox $\mathcal{T}$) if $C^{\mathcal{I}} \subseteq D^{\mathcal{I}}$ for all interpretations $\mathcal{I}$ (that are models of $\mathcal{T}$). If D subsumes C, then C is said to be *subsumed by* D.

For the definitions above, corresponding decision problems are defined as usual. In order to solve these problems, practical description logic systems implement algorithms as so-called inference services. Besides services for the basic decision problems introduced above, DL inference servers usually provide some additional inference services. A basic reasoning service is to compute the subsumption relationship between every pair of concept names mentioned in a TBox (i.e. elements from C). This inference is needed to build a hierarchy of concept names w.r.t. specificity. The problem of computing the most-specific concept names mentioned in $\mathcal{T}$ that subsume a certain concept is known as computing the *parents* of a concept. The *children* are the most-general concept names mentioned in $\mathcal{T}$ that are subsumed by a certain concept. We use the name *concept ancestors* (*concept descendants*) for the transitive closure of the parents (children) relation. The computation of the parents and children of every concept name is also called *classification* of the TBox. Another important inference service for practical knowledge representation is to check whether a certain concept name occurring in a TBox is inconsistent. Usually, inconsistent concept names are the consequence of modelling errors. Checking the consistency of all concept names mentioned in a TBox without computing the parents and children is called a TBox *coherence check*.

If the description logic supports full negation, consistency and subsumption can be mutually reduced to each other since D subsumes C (w.r.t. a TBox $\mathcal{T}$) iff $C \sqcap \neg D$ is inconsistent (w.r.t. $\mathcal{T}$), and C is inconsistent (w.r.t. $\mathcal{T}$) iff C is subsumed by $\bot$ (w.r.t. $\mathcal{T}$). Consistency of concepts can be reduced to ABox consistency as follows: A concept C is consistent (w.r.t. a TBox $\mathcal{T}$) iff the ABox $\{a:C\}$ is consistent (w.r.t. $\mathcal{T}$).

An individual i is an *instance* of a concept C (w.r.t. a TBox $\mathcal{T}$ and an ABox $\mathcal{A}$) iff $i^{\mathcal{I}} \in C^{\mathcal{I}}$ for all models $\mathcal{I}$ (of $\mathcal{T}$ and $\mathcal{A}$). For description logics that support full negation for concepts, the instance problem can be reduced to the problem of deciding if the ABox $\mathcal{A} \cup \{i : \neg C\}$ is inconsistent (w.r.t. $\mathcal{T}$). This test is also called *instance checking*. The most-specific concept names mentioned in a TBox $\mathcal{T}$ that an individual is an instance of are called the *direct types* of the individual w.r.t. a knowledge base $(\mathcal{T}, \mathcal{A})$. The direct type inference problem can be reduced to subsequent instance problems (see e.g. Baader, Franconi, Hollunder, Nebel, and Profitlich, (1994) for details).

An ABox $\mathcal{A}'$ is *entailed* by a TBox $\mathcal{T}$ and an ABox $\mathcal{A}$ if all models of $\mathcal{T}$ and $\mathcal{A}$ are also models of $\mathcal{A}'$. For ABox entailment we write $\mathcal{T} \cup \mathcal{A} \models \mathcal{A}'$.

ABox entailment can be reduced to query answering. An ABox $\mathcal{A}'$ is entailed by a TBox $\mathcal{T}$ and an ABox $\mathcal{A}$ if for all assertions α in $\mathcal{A}'$ it holds that the boolean query $\{() \mid \alpha\}$ returns *true*. Query answering is discussed in the next subsection.

TBox inference services are provided by the systems CEL (Baader, Lutz and Suntisrivaraporn 2006), Fact++ (Tsarkov and Horrocks 2006), KAON2 (Hustadt, Motik and Sattler 2004), Pellet (Sirin and Parsia 2006), QuOnto (Calvanese, De Giacomo, Lembo, Lenzerini and Rosati 2005), and RacerPro (Haarslev and Möller 2001). At the time of this writing, only the latter four systems support ABox inference services.

3.2.2.2 Retrieval Inference Services

For practical applications, another set of inference services deals with finding individuals (or roles) that satisfy certain conditions.

The *retrieval* inference problem is to find all individuals mentioned in an ABox that are instances of a certain concept C. The set of *fillers* of a role R for an individual i w.r.t. a knowledge base $(\mathcal{T}, \mathcal{A})$ is defined as $\{x \mid (\mathcal{T}, \mathcal{A}) \models (i, x) : R\}$ where $(\mathcal{T}, \mathcal{A}) \models ax$ means that all models of $\mathcal{T}$ and $\mathcal{A}$ also satisfy ax. The set of *roles* between two individuals i and j w.r.t. a knowledge base $(\mathcal{T}, \mathcal{A})$ is defined as $\{R \mid (\mathcal{T}, \mathcal{A}) \models (i, j) : R\}$.

In practical systems such as RacerPro, there are some auxiliary queries supported: retrieval of the concept names or individuals mentioned in a knowledge base, retrieval of the set of roles, retrieval of the role parents and children (defined analogously to the concept parents and children, see above), retrieval of the set of individuals in the domain and in the range of a role, etc. As a distinguishing feature to other systems, which is important for many applications, we would like to emphasise that RacerPro supports multiple TBoxes and ABoxes. Assertions can be added to ABoxes after queries have been answered. In addition, RacerPro and Pellet also provide support for retraction of assertions in particular ABoxes. The system Pellet can reuse previous computations.

Grounded Conjunctive Queries

In addition to the basic retrieval inference service described above (*concept-based instance retrieval*), more expressive query languages are required in practical applications. Well established is the class of conjunctive queries.

A *conjunctive query* consists of a *head* and a *body*. The head lists variables for which the user would like to compute bindings. The body consists of query atoms (see below) in which all variables from the head must be mentioned. If the body contains additional variables, they are seen as existentially quantified. A query answer is a set of tuples representing bindings for variables mentioned in the head. A query is written $\{(X_1, \ldots, X_n) \mid atom_1, \ldots, atom_m\}$.

Query atoms can be *concept* query atoms $(C(X))$, *role* query atoms $(R(X, Y))$, *same-as* query atoms $(X = Y)$ as well as so-called *concrete domain* query atoms. The latter are introduced to provide support for querying the concrete domain part of a knowledge base and will not be covered in detail here.

In the literature (e.g. Horrocks, Sattler, Tessaris and Tobies 2000; Glimm, Horrocks, Lutz and Sattler 2007; Wessel and Möller 2006), two different semantics for these kinds of queries are discussed. In *standard* conjunctive queries, variables (in the head and in query atoms in the body) are bound to (possibly anonymous) domain objects. A system supporting (unions of) grounded conjunctive queries is QuOnto.

In so-called *grounded* conjunctive queries, variables are bound to named domain objects (object constants). However, in grounded conjunctive queries the standard semantics can be obtained (only) for so-called tree-shaped queries by using existential restrictions in query atoms. Due to space restrictions, we cannot discuss the details here. In the following, we consider only (unions of) grounded conjunctive queries, which are supported by KAON2, RacerPro, and Pellet.

Complex queries are built from query atoms using boolean constructs for conjunction (indicated with comma), union ($\vee$), and negation ($\backslash$). Note that the latter refers to atom negation not concept negation and, for instance, negation as failure semantics is assumed in Wessel and Möller (2005). In addition, a *projection* operator π is supported in order to reduce the dimensionality of an intermediate tuple set. This operator is particularly important in combination with negation (complement). These operators are only supported by RacerPro (for details see Wessel and Möller 2005).

In practical applications, it is advantageous to name subqueries for later reuse, and practical systems, such as RacerPro, support this for grounded conjunctive queries with non-recursive rules of the following form.

$$P(X_1, \ldots, X_{n_1}) \leftarrow A_1(Y_1),$$
$$\ldots$$
$$A_l(Y_l),$$
$$R_1(Z_1, Z_2),$$
$$\ldots$$
$$R_h(Z_{2h-1}, Z_{2h}).$$

The predicate term to the left of $\leftarrow$ is called the head and the rest is called the body, which, informally speaking, is seen as a conjunction of predicate terms. All variables in the head must be mentioned in the body, and rules must be non-recursive (with the obvious definition of non-recursivity). Since rules must be non-recursive, there is no need to specify the semantics of rules because subsequent replacements (with well-known variable substitutions and variables renaming) of query atoms with their rule-defined body is possible (unfolding). For instance, unfolding an atom $P(X_1, \ldots, X_{n_1})$ results in a term $\pi(X_1, \ldots, X_{n_1}) : A_1(Y_1), \ldots A_l(Y_l), R_1(Z_1, Z_2), \ldots R_h(Z_{2h-1}, Z_{2h})$. If there are multiple rules (definitions) for the same predicate P, corresponding disjunctions are generated. We do not discuss these details here, however.

It should be noted that answering queries in DL systems goes beyond query answering in relational databases. In databases, query answering amounts to model checking (a database instance is seen as a model of the conceptual schema). Query answering w.r.t. TBoxes and ABoxes must take all models into account, and thus requires deduction. The aim is to define expressive but decidable query languages. Well-known classes of queries such as *conjunctive queries* and *unions of conjunctive queries* are topics of current investigations in this context.

A tuple $(ind_1, \ldots, ind_n)$ is in the result set of a grounded conjunctive query

$$\{(X_1, \ldots, X_n) \mid A_1(Y_1),$$
$$\ldots$$
$$A_l(Y_l),$$
$$R_1(Z_1, Z_2),$$
$$\ldots$$
$$R_h(Z_{2h-1}, ZW_{2h})\}$$

if the variable substitution $[X_1 \leftarrow ind_1, \ldots, X_n \leftarrow ind_n]$ can be extended such that additional substitutions for all other variables in the body can be found such that the resulting query atoms after applying the substitution are satisfied in all models of the ontology (TBox and ABox). Hence, given a variable substitution, grounded conjunctive queries can be reduced to standard inference problems, which are discussed above. For unions and projections, the semantics is slightly more complicated, and we refer to Wessel and Möller (2006). Although, for brevity, in this chapter, we use a mathematical notation for conjunctive queries, there exist proposals for conjunctive queries in the XML-based DIG 2.0 format (Turhan, Bechhofer, Kaplunova, Liebig, Luther, Möller, Noppens, Patel-Schneider, Suntisrivaraporn and Weithöner 2006). In addition, another XML-based format called OWL-QL has been proposed, and practical query answering systems are available (e.g. Kaplunova, Kaya and Möller 2006).

Queries w.r.t. Temporal Propositions:

In order to support event recognition in an ontology-based media interpretation system, we introduced temporal propositions. For queries over ABoxes that also contain temporal propositions, rules with time intervals can be defined. Suppose three disjoint sets of names *Preds*, *TimeVars*, and *Vars* neither of which is a subset of the names mentioned in the axioms of the ontology. Then, a *rule with time intervals* has the following structure:

$$P_{[T_0, T_1]}(X_1, \ldots, X_{n_1}) \leftarrow Q_{1[T_2, T_3]}(Y_{1,1}, \ldots, Y_{1,m_1}),$$
$$\ldots$$
$$Q_{k[T_{2k}, T_{2k+1}]}(Y_{k,1}, \ldots, Y_{k,m_k}),$$
$$A_1(Z_1),$$
$$\ldots$$
$$A_l(Z_l),$$
$$R_1(W_1, W_2),$$
$$\ldots$$
$$R_h(W_{2h-1}, W_{2h}).$$

where the $T_i \in$ *TimeVars* are temporal variables and $X_i, Y_{j,k}, Z_l, W_h \in$ *Vars* are (not necessarily disjoint) variables that are bound to individuals mentioned in the ABox, $P, Q_i \in$ *Preds*, and A_j, R_k are concept names and role names, respectively. In a similar way as for conjunctive queries introduced above, all variables in the head must be mentioned in the body, and rules must be non-recursive. Thus, queries w.r.t. time variables are unfolded, similar to rules for defined queries.

A *conjunctive query with time variables* is an expression of the following form:

$$\{(X_1, \ldots, X_n)_{[T_1, T_2]} \mid Q_{1[T_2, T_3]}(Y_{1,1}, \ldots, Y_{1,m_1}),$$

$$\ldots$$

$$Q_{k[T_{2k}, T_{2k+1}]}(Y_{k,1}, \ldots, Y_{k,m_k}),$$
$$A_1(Z_1),$$

$$\ldots$$

$$A_l(Z_l),$$
$$R_1(W_1, W_2),$$

$$\ldots$$

$$R_h(W_{2h-1}, W_{2h})\}$$

Note that the variables X_i, $Y_{i,j}$, Z_i, and W_i are not necessarily disjoint. A tuple $(ind_1, \ldots, ind_n)_{[t_1, t_2]}$ is a potential solution of a grounded unfolded temporal conjunctive query (temporal query for short) if the variable substitution $[X_1 \leftarrow ind_1, \ldots, X_n \leftarrow ind_n, T_1 \leftarrow t_1, T_2 \leftarrow t_2]$ can be extended with additional assignments for all other variables in the body such that the resulting query atoms after applying the substitution are satisfied in all temporal models of the ontology (TBox and ABox). The result set for a temporal query comprises all tuples $(ind_1, \ldots, ind_n)_{[(t_{1_{min}}, t_{1_{max}}), (t_{2_{min}}, t_{2_{max}})]}$ such that there exists no other potential solution $(ind_1, \ldots, ind_n)_{[t_1, t_2]}$ with $t_1 < t_{1_{min}}$ or $t_1 > t_{1_{max}}$ or $t_2 < t_{2_{min}}$ or $t_2 > t_{2_{max}}$.

Algorithms for answering queries involving rules with time variables have been published in Neumann and Novak (1983) and Neumann (1985). The algorithms are implemented as inferences only in the RacerPro description logic system. In addition to the original Prolog-style approach in Neumann (1985), conjunctive query atoms for ABoxes are provided for queries with time variables.

3.2.2.3 Non-standard Inference Services

Many inference services different from those mentioned above have been introduced in the literature (non-standard inference services). We discuss only one non-standard inference service, namely abduction, which is relevant for the media interpretation processes described below (Elsenbroich, Kutz and Sattler 2006).

The *abduction* inference service aims to construct a set of (minimal) explanations Δ for a given set of assertions Γ such that Δ is consistent w.r.t. to the ontology $(\mathcal{T}, \mathcal{A})$ and satisfies:

1. $\mathcal{T} \cup \mathcal{A} \cup \Delta \models \Gamma$ and
2. If Δ' is an ABox satisfying $\mathcal{T} \cup \mathcal{A} \cup \Delta' \models \Gamma$, then $\Delta' \models \Delta$ (Δ is least specific).

This inference service is used in Section 3.3 as the basis for formalising the derivation of annotations (metadata) for media objects. The annotations describe high-level interpretations of media objects. Furthermore, they can be used to retrieve the media objects from which they are derived. Often, the names in Δ and Γ are predefined (and are called abducibles and observables, respectively).

3.2.3 Retrieval of Media Objects

An application scenario for automatically derived interpretations of media objects is information retrieval, for instance, in the semantic web. Interpretations are seen as annotations of media objects and can be practically represented in RDF or OWL format. In our view, annotations describe "real-world" objects and events. It is not the goal to merely "classify" images and attach keywords but to construct a high-level interpretation of the content of a media object. The former approach has a limited applicability if examples such as Fig. 3.1 are considered and queries for, e.g. media objects with a mailman have to be answered. The goal of this section is to motivate the use of Aboxes for describing media content in contrast to using just keywords (or concept names) for classifying media objects. Details about how description logics can be used for media retrieval based on description logics have been published in Möller, Haarslev and Neumann (1998), see also subsequent works of, Di Sciascio, Donini and Mongiello (1999), Di Sciascio, Donini and Mongiello (2000) and Schober, Hermes and Herzog (2005). In a more general setting, Sebastiani (1994) deals with description logic and information retrieval.

A set of media objects with annotations attached to each media object can be made available via a web server with standard application server technology. We assume that the web server provides a query interface (for instance, using the XML-based DIG 2.0 or OWL-QL query language, see Section 3.2.2). For readability reasons, however, here we use ABoxes for content descriptions, and employ a mathematical notation for queries. Details about XML-based multimedia content descriptions and MPEG-7 have been described in Chapter 2 of this book.

Using the example from Fig. 3.1, we sketch how media interpretations are used to implement a media retrieval system. Fig. 3.6 illustrates the main ideas about annotations for media objects using ABoxes (we omit the TBox for brevity). It would have been possible to more appropriately describe the role which the parts play in the events (in the sense of case frames). We omit the discussion of these issues here for brevity, however, and use a "generic" role $hasPart$. It is also possible to use another "aggregate" $street\_scene_1$ for combining the garbage collection and mail delivery events.

A query which might be posed in an information system is shown in Fig. 3.7. As a result, the inference system returns the tuple $(mail\_deliv_1, bicycle_1)$, and in order to show the image (and highlight the area with the bicycle), the associated URL names can be retrieved (see also Fig. 3.7). The form $value(x)$ returns a unique binding for a variable (in this case a string) if it exists, and $\emptyset$ otherwise. In case of $URLQuery_1$, the answer is $(url_1,$ "http://www.img.de/image-1.jpg").

$$
\begin{aligned}
mailman_1 &: Mailman \\
bicycle_1 &: Bicycle \\
mail\_deliv_1 &: MailDeliv \\
(mail\_deliv_1, mailman_1) &: hasPart \\
(mail\_deliv_1, bicycle_1) &: hasPart \\
(mail\_deliv_1, url\_1) &: hasURL \\
(mailman_1, url\_2) &: hasURL \\
(bicycle_1, url\_3) &: hasURL \\
(url\_1) &: =\text{"http://www.img.de/image-1.jpg"} \\
(url\_2) &: =\text{"http://www.img.de/image-1.jpg\#(200,400)/(300/500)"} \\
(url\_3) &: =\text{"http://www.img.de/image-1.jpg\#(100,400)/(150/500)"} \\
garbageman_1 &: Garbageman \\
garbageman_2 &: Garbageman \\
garbagetruck_1 &: Garbage\_Truck \\
gc_1 &: Garbage\_Collection \\
(gc_1, garbageman_1) &: hasPart \\
(gc_1, garbageman_2) &: hasPart \\
(gc_1, garbagetruck_1) &: hasPart \\
(gc_1, url\_4) &: hasURL \\
&\cdots
\end{aligned}
$$

Fig. 3.6 An ABox representing the annotation of the image in Fig. 3.1. The predicate $=_{string}$ stands for a one-place predicate $p(x)$ which is true for $x = string$

The result of $URLQuery_2$ is defined analogously. The URLs can be used to actually retrieve the image data. Subsequent queries w.r.t. the annotation individuals $mail\_deliv_1$ and $bicycle_1$ are certainly possible. We do not discuss details here, however. In summary, it should be clear now, how annotations with metadata are used in an ontology-based information retrieval system.

With axioms such as

$$Mailman \sqsubseteq Postal\_Employee$$
$$Mailman \equiv Postman$$

a query for a *Postal_Employee* or a *Postman* will also return the media object shown in Fig. 3.1. In general, all benefits of description logic reasoning carry over to query answering in an information retrieval system of the kind sketched above.

It is easy to see that annotations such as the ones shown in Fig. 3.6 can be set up such that the URLs are tied to the ABox individuals comprising the high-level descriptions. In particular, one can easily imagine a situation in which there exist multiple interpretations of an image, which results in multiple annotations being

$$
\begin{aligned}
ImageQuery_1 &:= \{(X, Y) \mid MailDeliv(X), Bicycle(Y), hasPart(X, Y)\} \\
URLQuery_1 &:= \{(X, value(X)) \mid hasURL(mail\_deliv_1, X)\} \\
URLQuery_2 &:= \{(X, value(X)) \mid hasURL(bicycle_1, X)\}
\end{aligned}
$$

Fig. 3.7 Query for "a mail delivery with a bicycle" and subsequent queries for retrieving the URLs w.r.t. the result for $ImageQuery_1$

associated with an image. In addition, it is obvious that a repository of media objects together with their annotations (metadata) gives rise to one or more ABoxes that are managed by the ontology-based information system. Not so obvious is how metadata can be automatically derived since manual annotation is too costly in almost all practical scenarios. The derivation of metadata representing high-level interpretation of media content is discussed in the next section. Querying as discussed in this section refers to metadata (Aboxes) but not directly to media content. Processes for the automatic derivation of metadata, however, do refer to media content, and as we will see later, a set of given queries can indeed influence media interpretation.

3.3 Automatic Construction of Metadata for Media Objects

In this section, we will discuss how media objects can be automatically interpreted. We start with images, continue with text, and finally discuss image sequence interpretation. A first attempt to understand fusion of information gained w.r.t. different modalities is presented afterwards.

3.3.1 Image Interpretation

An ontology in a description logic framework is seen as a tuple consisting of a TBox and an ABox. In order to construct a high-level interpretation, the ABox part of the ontology is extended with some new assertions describing individuals and their relations. These descriptions are derived by media interpretation processes using the ontology (we assume the ontology axioms are denoted in a set Σ).

Interpretation processes are set up for different modalities, still images, videos, audio data, and texts. In this section, we discuss the interpretation process using an example interpretation for still images. The output is a symbolic description represented as an ABox. This ABox is the result of an abduction process (see Hobbs, Stickel, Appelt and Martin 1993; Shanahan 2005 for a general introduction). In this process, a solution for the following equation is computed: $\Sigma \cup \Delta \models \Gamma$. The solution Δ must satisfy certain side conditions (see Section 3.2.2).

In Fig. 3.8 an example from the athletics domain is presented. Assuming it is possible to detect a horizontal bar bar_1, a human $human_1$, and a pole $pole_1$ by image analysis processes, the output of the analysis phase is represented as an ABox Γ. Assertions for the individuals and (some of) their relations detected by analysing Fig. 3.8 are shown in Fig. 3.9. We are aware of the fact that crisp object recognition might be hard to achieve. Therefore, in Section 3.4, we develop an approach that deals with uncertainty in this respect.

In order to continue the interpretation example, we assume that the ontology contains the axioms shown in Fig. 3.10 (the ABox of the ontology is assumed to be empty). If we compare with the aggregate design patterns shown in Fig. 3.4, axioms for both, *Pole_Vault* as well as *High_Jump*, contain parent concepts and

Fig. 3.8 Still image displaying a pole vault event

restrictions for parts. However, in Fig. 3.10 there are no constraints between part objects. Therefore, the conditions mentioned on the right-hand side are only necessary and not sufficient conditions as in Fig. 3.4. For expressing constraints between parts in an aggregate (at least three objects are involved), description logics are not expressive enough (only the two-variable fragment of first-order logic is captured). Thus, some additional mechanism is required without jeopardizing decidability. In order to capture constraints among aggregate parts, we assume that the ontology is extended with DL-safe rules (rules that are applied to ABox individuals only, see Section 3.2.1). In Fig. 3.11, a set of rules for the athletics example is specified. Note that the spatial constraints *touches* and *near* for the parts of a *Pole_Vault* event (or a *High_Jump* event) are not imposed by the TBox in Fig. 3.10. Thus, rules are used to represent additional knowledge. Since spatial relations depend on the specific "subphases" of the events, corresponding clauses are included on the right-hand sides of the rules. For instance, a jumper as part of a *High_Jump* is near the bar if the image shows a *High_Jump* in the jump phase. Later, in the context of fusion discussed in Section 3.3.5, we will see how information about the phase (e.g. $HJ\_InJumpPhase$)

Fig. 3.9 An ABox Γ representing the result of the image analysis phase

$$pole_1 : Pole$$
$$human_1 : Human$$
$$bar_1 : Horizontal\_Bar$$
$$(bar_1, human_1) : near$$
$$(human_1, pole_1) : touches$$

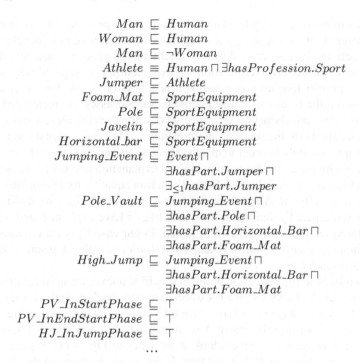

$$Man \sqsubseteq Human$$
$$Woman \sqsubseteq Human$$
$$Man \sqsubseteq \neg Woman$$
$$Athlete \equiv Human \sqcap \exists hasProfession.Sport$$
$$Jumper \sqsubseteq Athlete$$
$$Foam\_Mat \sqsubseteq SportEquipment$$
$$Pole \sqsubseteq SportEquipment$$
$$Javelin \sqsubseteq SportEquipment$$
$$Horizontal\_bar \sqsubseteq SportEquipment$$
$$Jumping\_Event \sqsubseteq Event \sqcap$$
$$\exists hasPart.Jumper \sqcap$$
$$\exists_{\leq 1} hasPart.Jumper$$
$$Pole\_Vault \sqsubseteq Jumping\_Event \sqcap$$
$$\exists hasPart.Pole \sqcap$$
$$\exists hasPart.Horizontal\_Bar \sqcap$$
$$\exists hasPart.Foam\_Mat$$
$$High\_Jump \sqsubseteq Jumping\_Event \sqcap$$
$$\exists hasPart.Horizontal\_Bar \sqcap$$
$$\exists hasPart.Foam\_Mat$$
$$PV\_InStartPhase \sqsubseteq \top$$
$$PV\_InEndStartPhase \sqsubseteq \top$$
$$HJ\_InJumpPhase \sqsubseteq \top$$
$$\ldots$$

Fig. 3.10 A tiny example TBox Σ for the athletics domain

as captured in an image is related to the spatio-temporal knowledge of the image sequence modality.

In the following, we assume that rules such as those shown in Fig. 3.11 are part of the TBox Σ.

$$touches(Y, Z) \leftarrow Pole\_Vault(X),$$
$$PV\_InStartPhase(X),$$
$$hasPart(X, Y), Jumper(Y),$$
$$hasPart(X, Z), Pole(Z).$$
$$near(Y, Z) \leftarrow Pole\_Vault(X),$$
$$PV\_InEndStartPhase(X),$$
$$hasPart(X, Y), Horizontal\_Bar(Y),$$
$$hasPart(X, Z), Jumper(Z).$$
$$near(Y, Z) \leftarrow High\_Jump(X),$$
$$HJ\_InJumpPhase(X),$$
$$hasPart(X, Y), Horizontal\_Bar(Y),$$
$$hasPart(X, Z), Jumper(Z).$$
$$\ldots$$

Fig. 3.11 Additional restrictions for *Pole_Vault* and *High_Jump* in the form of rules

In order to provide a high-level interpretation, i.e. to provide a description of the image content in the form of high-level aggregates, we assume that spatial relations between certain objects detected by low-level analysis processes are not arbitrary. In order to construct an interpretation, an explanation is computed why it is the case that a jumper touches a pole and is near a horizontal bar. Such explanations are considered the results of image interpretation processes. As mentioned above, the idea is to use the abduction inference service for deriving these kinds of (minimal) explanations (in the sense of interpretations). Minimal explanations might be extended appropriately in order to match expectations and task context.

We start with the computation of a minimal explanation in our athletics scenario. For this purpose, we slightly modify the abduction equation by taking into consideration that initially the ABox does not need to be empty. Thus, we divide Γ (see Fig. 3.9) into a part Γ_2 that the agent would like to have explained, and a part Γ_1 that the interpretation agent takes for granted. In our case Γ_2 is $\{(bar_1, human_1) : near, (human_1, pole_1) : touches\}$ and Γ_1 is $\{pole_1 : Pole, human_1 : Human, bar_1 : Horizontal\_Bar\}$.

Coming back to the abduction problem specified above, we need solution(s) for the equation $\Sigma \cup \Delta \cup \Gamma_1 \models \Gamma_2$. In other words, given the background ontology Σ from Figs. 3.10 and 3.11, a query as derived from Γ_2 should return $true$ (see Fig. 3.12).

Obviously, this is not the case if Δ is empty. In order to see how an appropriate Δ could be derived, let us have a look at the rules in Fig. 3.11. In particular, let us focus on the rules for $Pole\_Vault$ first. If we apply the rules to the query in a backward chaining way (i.e. from left to right) and unify corresponding terms, we get variable bindings for Y and Z. The "unbound" variable X of the corresponding rules is instantiated with fresh individuals (e.g. pv_1 and pv_2). Since the parts and their relations can be explained with one aggregate, it is reasonable to assume that only one event provides a complete explanation, i.e. only one individual pv_1 is used (Occam's Razor). Then, a possible solution Δ for the abduction equation can be derived. Δ is shown in Fig. 3.13.

Note that due to the involvement of $human_1$ in the pole vault event, $human_1$ is now seen as an instance of $Jumper$, and, due to the TBox, also as an $Athlete$. Thus, information from high-level events also influences information that is available about the related parts. With queries for $Jumpers$, the corresponding media

Fig. 3.12 Query representing Γ_2

$$Q_1 := \{() \mid near(bar_1, human_1), \\ touches(human_1, pole_1)\}$$

Fig. 3.13 One possible solution of the abduction equation

$$pv_1 : Pole\_Vault \\ pv_1 : PV\_InStartPhase \\ pv_1 : PV\_InEndStartPhase \\ human_1 : Jumper \\ (pv_1, human_1) : hasPart \\ (pv_1, bar_1) : hasPart \\ (pv_1, pole_1) : hasPart$$

objects would not have been found otherwise. Thus, recognizing high-level events is of utmost importance in information retrieval systems (and pure content-based retrieval does not help).

Considering the GCIs involving *Pole_Vault* in the TBox shown in Fig. 3.10, it becomes apparent that for a pole vault, there also exists a foam mat which is not found by the image analysis module. Maybe it is not visible or the analysis just could not detect it. In the latter situation, one could somehow adapt the image analysis processes and start a feedback loop. This feedback from the image interpretation module (high level) to the image analysis module (low level) is subject to ongoing research and will be covered in more detail in Section 3.3.6. The assertions concerning the relation *hasPart* and the phases derived by the rule are included in the interpretation result. Thus, the output of the interpretation phase in our example is the ABox shown in Fig. 3.14.

The example discussed here covers the interpretation of still images. It is necessary, however, to keep in mind that each media object might consist of multiple modalities, each of which will be the basis of modality-specific interpretation results (ABoxes). In order to provide for an integrated representation of the interpretation of media objects as a whole, these modality-specific interpretation results must be appropriately integrated. A cornerstone of this integration process will be to determine which modality-specific names refer to the same domain object. This will be discussed in later sections. In the following, both modality-specific and media-specific ABoxes will be called interpretation ABoxes. In a specific context, ambiguities should not arise.

So far we have discussed an example where there is one unique explanation (and, hence, one unique interpretation). However, this need not necessarily be the case. In Fig. 3.15 an example is presented that might lead to two different interpretations. For example, we assume that the ABox in Fig. 3.16 is produced by the image analysis component.

For the interpretation process, we assume the same ontology as above. It is easy to see that we can get two explanations by the abduction process (see Figs. 3.17 and 3.18). Note that new names which might refer to the same domain object are used in each explanation.

$$pole_1 : Pole$$
$$human_1 : Human$$
$$bar_1 : Horizontal\_Bar$$
$$(bar_1, human_1) : near$$
$$(human_1, pole_1) : touches$$
$$pv_1 : Pole\_Vault$$
$$pv_1 : PV\_InStartPhase$$
$$pv_1 : PV\_InEndStartPhase$$
$$human_1 : Jumper$$
$$(pv_1, human_1) : hasPart$$
$$(pv_1, bar_1) : hasPart$$
$$(pv_1, pole_1) : hasPart$$

Fig. 3.14 An ABox representing the result of the image interpretation phase

Fig. 3.15 Image displaying a snapshot of a high jump or pole vault (where the pole is outside the image)

$$bar_2 : Horizontal\_Bar$$
$$human_2 : Human$$
$$(bar_2, human_2) : near$$

Fig. 3.16 An ABox Γ representing the result of the analysis of the image in Fig. 3.15

Continuing the example, it might be the case that for some images, the ontology does not contain relevant axioms or rules. In this case, the interpretation result, i.e. the result of solving the abduction problem $\Sigma \cup \Delta \cup \Gamma_1 \models \Gamma_2$ will be degenerate because, due to missing axioms or rules in Σ, Δ must necessarily be equal to Γ_2 in order to solve the equation. As an example of such a situation we can discuss an interpretation of Figs. 3.8 or 3.15 without the rules from Fig. 3.11 and the GCIs for *Pole_Vault* and *High_Jump* in Fig. 3.10. The degenerate interpretation result is shown (as Γ) in Fig. 3.9. An annotation based on such a degenerate interpretation will certainly not support queries such as $\{(x) \mid Pole\_Vault(x) \vee High\_Jump(x)\}$.

In Fig. 3.19, a pole vault is shown. Suppose the ABox shown in Fig. 3.20 is generated by image analysis processes. Compared to Fig. 3.16, there is only one

Fig. 3.17 An ABox representing the first result of the image interpretation process

$$human_2 : Human$$
$$bar_2 : Horizontal\_Bar$$
$$(bar_2, human_2) : near$$
$$hj_2 : High\_jump$$
$$hj_2 : HJ\_InJumpPhase$$
$$human_2 : Jumper$$
$$(hj_2, human_2) : hasPart$$
$$(hj_2, bar_2) : hasPart$$

$$human_2 : Human$$
$$bar_2 : Horizontal\_Bar$$
$$(bar_2, human_2) : near$$
$$pv_2 : Pole\_Vault$$
$$pv_2 : PV\_InEndStartPhase$$
$$human_2 : Jumper$$
$$(pv_2, human_2) : hasPart$$
$$(pv_2, bar_2) : hasPart$$

Fig. 3.18 An ABox representing the second result of the image interpretation process

additional assertion, the assertion for the pole. If we apply the abduction process in a naive way, the result will also be two interpretation ABoxes as shown above (one for a pole vault and one for a high jump). In the high jump event, the pole is just ignored (and erroneously considered as "noise"). As the abduction process is defined now, there is no reason to explain the pole since up to now only the spatial relations are put into Γ_2 and hence are "explained". The example demonstrates that also assertions about single objects have to be put into Γ_2 in order to avoid spurious effects.

3.3.2 Towards an Abduction Procedure

The interpretation example presented so far exhibits several interesting characteristics which will now be discussed in greater generality.

First, it is important to note that, in general, interpretations do not logically follow from the data and the knowledge base. Visual or audio data are inherently ambiguous, and multiple interpretations may be possible. Hence deductive reasoning is not adequate. Rather, media data must be seen as a causal consequence of some real-

Fig. 3.19 Image displaying a snapshot of a pole vault (where the pole is partially outside the image)

$$bar_3 : Horizontal\_Bar$$
$$jumper_3 : Human$$
$$pole_3 : Pole$$
$$(bar_3, jumper_3) : near$$

Fig. 3.20 An ABox Γ representing the result of the analysis of the image in Fig. 3.19

world scenario which is to be described by an interpretation. For example, natural images are caused by projecting 3D scenes, and interpretations of the images should provide descriptions of the underlying 3D scenes. Furthermore, media data may be sparse, describing only parts of a scenario. For example, Fig. 3.15 is just a snapshot of a complete high jump occurrence. Obviously, sparse data may be ambiguous and interpreted in several ways, in this case as a high jump or a pole vault event.

In the example, the causal relationship between high-level concepts (such as *Pole_Vault(X)*) and relations between low-level data (such as near(Y, Z)) is represented by rules because description logics are not expressive enough for these kinds of constraints. In some case, however, there might be axioms in the Tbox that provide necessary conditions (see, e.g. the axiom for Athlete in Fig. 3.10). These axioms are more general than corresponding rules (they apply to all domain objects, not only to objects for which there is a name in the Abox). A rule such as

> *Athlete(X)* ← *Human(X)*
> *hasProfession(X,Y)*
> *Sport(Y)*

might be implicitly derived from the axiom. This approximation process might take into account a set of externally defined abducibles in order to limit the number of axioms to be considered for the abduction operation. Details of the approximation process are subject to further research. Using rules for sufficient conditions is one way to enable backward chaining from low-level data to high-level explanations. In general, such rules should also be available for all conjunctive constituents of a high-level concept in order to enable backward chaining along multiple paths. For instance, the following concept inclusion (see Fig. 3.10)

> *High_Jump* $\sqsubseteq$ *Jumping_Event* $\sqcap$
> $\exists hasPart.Horizontal\_Bar$ $\sqcap$
> $\exists hasPart.Foam\_Mat$

should give also rise to the rules

> *Jumping_Event(X)* ← *High_Jump(X)*
> *Horizontal_Bar(X)* ← *High_Jump(Y)*,
> $hasPart_{Bar}(Y, X).$
> *Foam_Mat(X)* ← *High_Jump(Y)*,
> $hasPart_{Mat}(Y, X).$

where $hasPart_C$ represents a relation (or role) that associates a high jump instance with a part instance of concept C (the role $hasPart_C$ is range-restricted to C). In this case, there is no simple syntactic transformation for exploiting the GCI for $High\_Jump$ in the abduction process. A possible explanation for the data

$$bar_1 : Horizonal\_Bar$$

could be generated by the rule which states that a $Horizontal\_Bar$ can be part of a $High\_Jump$. Hence, a high jump aggregate can be generated to which bar_1 is associated via the function $hasPart_{Bar}$. Similar arguments and rules derived from the Tbox will lead to a pole vault aggregate as another (minimal) explanation for a bar in a picture (without the pole being shown). If, additionally, there is a pole as in Fig. 3.19, and it is mentioned in the analysis ABox, e.g.

$$pole_1 : Pole$$

then, unfortunately, a high jump does provide an explanation for the bar (neglecting the pole). Thus if we require the process to explain the existence of objects, spurious interpretations such as "a high jump with some arbitrary pole" (see Fig. 3.20) can be avoided. This has been discussed in the literature as the principle of consilience (Hobbs, Stickel, Martin and Edwards 1988; Hobbs, Stickel, Appelt and Martin 1990).

It is evident that interpretation by abduction can in general be achieved by exploiting the *hasPart* structure of concepts and explaining data as part of a larger whole. It is therefore useful to view possible interpretation steps within the compositional hierarchy of aggregate concepts (Neumann and Weiss 2003). Figure 3.21 shows a compositional hierarchy for the domain of sports events, based on and extending the example TBox in Fig. 3.10. Given the media data shown in Fig. 3.8, the compositional hierarchy exposes all aggregate concepts which could explain the data.

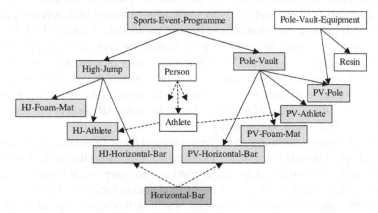

Fig. 3.21 Compositional hierarchy induced by hasPart roles in aggregate concepts. The *dotted arrows* indicate specialisation relations

In order to provide additional support for an explanation, it may also be useful to follow *hasPart* arcs from aggregates to parts. For instance, to verify a pole vault, one may check whether the media data includes a pole.

Besides the compositional hierarchy, the taxonomical hierarchy can also be exploited for generating explanations. For example, $athlete_1$: *Athlete* may not have been recognised, and $moving\_object_1$: *Person* is included in the media data instead. In this case, it proves useful to explore a possible specialization of *Person* which would then lead to interesting aggregate concepts.

In summary, possible explanations can be generated by navigating from data to higher level concepts by

- aggregate instantiation,
- aggregate expansion, and
- instance specialisation.

These considerations can be used to guide the knowledge-modelling process and might help to find appropriate rules for the abduction process described above.

As already shown by Reiter and Mackworth (1990) and further elaborated in Schröder (1999), image interpretation can also be formally described as constructing a partial model. "Model" is used here in the logical sense and means a mapping from the symbols of logical formulae into a real-world domain such that the formulae are true. A partial model can be constructed by a computer (which has no direct access to the real-world domain) by building the model on top of the primitive media data which are taken to map into the intended real-world objects. As opposed to interpretation by abduction, interpretation by model construction does not focus on the data but aims at constructing a symbolic description of some real-world scenario consistent with the data.

As pointed out in Section 3.1, the scope of an interpretation depends also on the task and other contextual information. However, the logical formalisation in terms of model construction gives no clue as to what to include and what not to include in an interpretation as long as the interpretation is consistent and entails the data. One way to restrict interpretations is by introducing a notion of dependency and by requiring that the interpretation should depend on the data. This can be formalised by considering the compositional hierarchy formed by aggregate concepts. We say that a concept depends on data D if it is a predecessor of some element of D or a successor of a predecessor. This notion of dependency is the same as in Bayesian networks with causality arcs corresponding to the hasPart relations in the figure. In Fig. 3.21, it is assumed that *Horizontal_Bar* is the data. All concepts dependent on *Horizontal_Bar* are depicted in light grey.

The dependency definition can be further refined by distinguishing between necessary and optional parts (expressed by cardinality restrictions for the *hasPart* roles). If, for example, a sports event has all its parts as optional parts, it would make little sense to include a *High_Jump* as part of the explanation for a *Pole_Vault*.

Restricting interpretations to assertions which in this sense depend on the data appears to be useful for many interpretation tasks. However, one can also conceive of tasks where non-dependent assertions may be interesting, for example providing

$$object_1 : Event$$
$$object_2 : Horizontal\_Bar$$
$$object_3 : Athlete$$
$$object_3 : Famous$$
$$(object_1, object_2) : precedes$$
$$(object_1, object_3) : precedes$$

Fig. 3.22 Interpretation ABox produced by shallow text analysis

further explanations for some of the hypothesised instances. In any case, a task-based control of the scope of an interpretation remains necessary.

3.3.3 Shallow Text Interpretation

Another modality which might provide additional information for media interpretation is "text". There exists a large amount of publications about natural language understanding, text interpretation, information retrieval from text, etc. We cannot give a survey of all trends and current research results here. However, using an example, we show how the technique of abduction introduced in the previous section can be used to provide interpretation ABoxes. The goal of the example discussed in this subsection is to demonstrate the feasibility of the general approach for multimedia interpretation. Abduction for natural language interpretation is investigated in much more detail in Hobbs et al. (1988). Abduction is even used to formalise discourse understanding. No decidable representation formalism is used, however.

Our example assumes that standard techniques from information retrieval approaches are applied ("shallow text processing"). Consider the sentences "A new world record in this year's event was missed. The remaining famous athlete touched the crossbar and failed 2.40 m." We assume that the ABox shown in Fig. 3.22 is generated by low-level text analysis components. For the nouns, individuals are generated as instances of appropriate concepts (we suppose a mapping from word to concepts is taken from a gazetteer e.g. "crossbar" $\rightarrow$ *Horizontal_Bar*). The role *precedes* represents the fact that there exists a linear precedence between corresponding nouns across adjacent sentence boundaries. In our example, the athlete and the crossbar are mentioned in the sentence immediately after the sentence with the event.

Note that in Fig. 3.22 for the word "famous" there is no new object generated. The word "famous" is used as an adjective here, and this can be easily detected even by shallow text-processing techniques. For generating an interpretation ABox, we assume that the *precedes* assertions are to be explained (Γ_2), whereas the first four assertions are taken for granted (Γ_1). The query

$$Q_2 := \{() \mid precedes(object_1, object_2), precedes(object_1, object_3)\}$$

$$object_1 : High\_Jump$$
$$(object_1, object_2) : hasPart$$
$$(object_1, object_3) : hasPart$$

Fig. 3.23 Addendum to the interpretation ABox shown in Fig. 3.22

represents Γ_2 in a similar way as discussed in Section 3.3.1. The goal is to compute a Δ that explains the "surface relation" *precedes* with a "semantically deep relation" such as *hasPart*. We assume that the TBox Σ is extended with the axiom

$$precedes(X, Y) \leftarrow hasPart(X, Y)$$

The role *hasPart* represents a domain-specific relation, whereas the role *precedes* represents an "abstraction" of this role. With the verbalisation technique in our example, there is no explicit part relation mentioned in the text. The part of relation is expressed by corresponding associations in the text (linear precedence and local connectedness). The deep domain-specific interpretation is induced by abduction, and hence, as a result, the abduction process returns the Δ shown in Fig. 3.23. Together with Fig. 3.22, an interpretation ABox can be constructed (the "modality-specific" assertions for the role *precedes* might be removed if appropriate). It is obvious that *hasPart* might not be the only deep interpretation. In order to keep the discussion focussed, we do not discuss further possibilities, but we keep in mind that possible alternatives might be ruled out later on due to results in fusion (see Section 3.3.5). In addition, it should be mentioned that even in shallow text interpretation, for instance, the tense of detected verbs could be taken into consideration and so a more linguistic-based precedence relation could be established. The example we discussed here illustrates the general principles, however.

3.3.4 Image Sequence Interpretation

In contrast to still images, events in image sequences have a temporal extension that has to be appropriately considered for constructing media interpretations. In order to detect high-level events such as "high jump", event predicates are described using rules with time variables. For high jump events, we sketch the rule design pattern in Fig. 3.24. In our approach we suppose that basic events can be detected by image analysis processes. Basic events are described with temporal propositions (being added to an interpretation ABox by low-level processes). An example is shown in Fig. 3.25.

In order to actually recognise events for particular individuals which satisfy restrictions w.r.t. the ontology, the query language for temporal propositions introduced in Section 3.2.2 is applied. An example for a query involving events and time intervals is shown below.

$$\{(X)_{[T_1, T_2]} \mid High\_Jump\_Event_{[T_1, T_2]}(X, Y)\}$$

$$High\_Jump\_Event_{[T_1,T_2]}(X,Y) \leftarrow accelerate\_horizontally_{[T_1,T_3]}(Y),$$
$$vertical\_upward\_movement_{[T_3,T_4]}(Y),$$
$$turn_{[T_4,T_5]}(Y),$$
$$vertical\_downward\_movement_{[T_5,T_2]}(Y).$$
$$Jumper(Y),$$
$$High\_Jump(X),$$
$$hasPart(X,Y),$$

Fig. 3.24 Rule with time intervals for recognizing high-jump events

To answer a query, two steps have to be carried out. First, an assignment α for query variables (i.e. X in the query shown above) has to be found such that the body predicate terms and atoms are satisfied. Second, the goal is to determine lower bound and upper bound values for the temporal variables (T_1, T_2 in the example) such that the temporal propositions in the query body are satisfied. The result of the example query is $(event_1)_{[(219,223),(229,230)]}$. Thus, for all $T_1 \in (219,223)$ and $T_2 \in (229,230)$ and for all remaining temporal variables in the body of the rule in Fig. 3.24, there exist values such that all predicate terms in the body are satisfied with the assignment $\alpha(X) \rightarrow event_1$.

If a high jump event is expected but the query for the high jump event (see above) returns *false*, then abduction can be used to determine what has to be added to the interpretation ABox. For instance, the temporal proposition

$$accelerate\_horizontally_{[219,224]}(moving\_object_1)$$

might probably be missing, and will be added by abduction such that the answer will be *true* and the high-jump event is "explained". It might also be the case that the image sequence analysis determined a mutilated partial basic event such as

$$accelerate\_horizontally_{[219,223]}(moving\_object_1)$$

instead. In this case, abduction would just add the proposition as in the case before. However, in this case, we prefer that a near-miss is recognised, and believe that a "repair" operation for the assertion in the analysis ABox should be proposed.

$$accelerate\_horizontally_{[219,224]} \ (moving\_object_1)$$
$$vertical\_upward\_movement_{[224,226]} \ (moving\_object_1)$$
$$turn_{[226,228]} \ (moving\_object_1)$$
$$vertical\_downward\_movement_{[228,230]} \ (moving\_object_1)$$
$$moving\_object_1 : \quad Jumper$$
$$event_1 : High\_Jump$$
$$(event_1, moving\_object_1) : \quad hasPart$$

Fig. 3.25 Abox assertions for basic events (temporal propositions) that are detected by image sequence analysis components. In addition, three standard assertions possibly extracted from other sources (e.g. images and text) are added

3.3.5 Formalisation of Fusion

In the preceding subsections, we have discussed how an interpretation ABox can be constructed for different modalities. The main idea of the approach is to use abduction and a decision procedure for determining which assertions of the analysis ABox computed by low-level analysis processes have to be explained. We did not investigate the latter decision procedure in this chapter, however.

In Fig. 3.26, three interpretation pipelines for the modalities "image", "text", and "video" are shown. (see also Fig. 3.3 details of the "processing pipelines" for "audio" and "image"). Let us assume that interpretation ABoxes have been computed in the "Interpretation" phase (see Fig. 3.26). Actually, for every modality, there might be multiple interpretation ABoxes representing multiple possibilities for high-level interpretations.

One of the problems to be solved if information from different modalities has to be combined is the *identification problem*, which is the problem of determining equality assertions in order to declare co-references of different identifiers (individuals in an ABox) to the same domain objects. This problem is also relevant for single modalities (see e.g. Gabsdil, Koller and Striegnitz 2001 for the text modality) but obviously is particularly important for multiple modalities. Heuristics, such as having the same direct types, will lead a fusion process to generate assumptions for individual equality assertions. The overall goal is to minimise the number of different domain objects (principle of Occam's Razor).

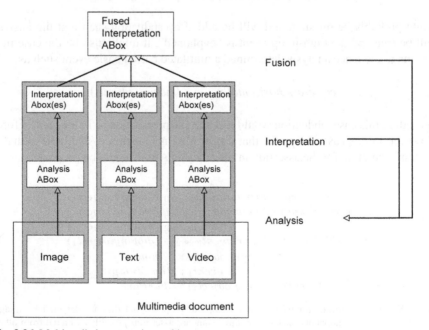

Fig. 3.26 Multimedia interpretation architecture

In the interpretation ABoxes for different modalities, individuals are mentioned that might refer to the same domain object. For instance, in the multimedia document about high jump events which we used for the discussion above, there may be an image from which hj_2 and $human_2$ are extracted (see Fig. 3.17). Let us assume, the image has a caption which gives rise to $object_3$ (see Fig. 3.22). In addition, there could be a video from which an individual $event_1$ is extracted (see Fig. 3.25). In this example, there are three different interpretation ABoxes (see Fig. 3.26). Fusing these ABoxes means to construct a combined interpretation ABox. We assume that during this process, the following questions arise. Could it be the case that hj_2 and $event_1$ are names for the same event? In addition, is it reasonable to assume that $human_2$ and $object_3$ are identical? In order to test whether these assumptions do not lead to an inconsistency, the following assertions are added to the ABox.

$$hj_2 = event_1$$
$$human_2 = object_3$$

In both events, the same jumper must be involved because, due to the TBox (see Fig. 3.10), at most one *Jumper* must participate in a *Jumping_Event* (a parent of *High_Jump*). The resulting ABox is consistent (the unique name assumption is not applied, see Section 3.2.1). However, from a logical point of view, adding the above-mentioned equality assertions is not really motivated. The resulting ABox stays consistent but why should an agent assume object identity in this case? In the same spirit as we argued above, there must be a motivation for adding assertions (in the sense of assumptions). In the abduction example for constructing interpretation ABoxes that we have discussed above, adding assertions allows the agent to prove certain entailments (assumptions serve as explanations for the Γ_2 assertions). In other words, queries are answered with *true*. We believe that similar mechanisms are required for a formalisation of the fusion process. The key insight is that fusing objects will allow the agent to answer certain queries, too. Consider the following example.

$$H J\_Occurs_{[T_1,T_2]}(X) \leftarrow High\_Jump(X),$$
$$H J\_InJumpPhase(X),$$
$$hasPart(X, Y),$$
$$Jumper(Y),$$
$$vertical\_upward\_movement_{[T_1,T_3]}(Y),$$
$$turn_{[T_3,T_4]}(Y),$$
$$vertical\_downward\_movement_{[T_4,T_2]}(Y).$$

Under the assumption that hj_2 and $event_1$ denote the same domain object, we can query the knowledge base about temporal information about a high jump event with a famous athlete.

$$Q_3 := \{(X)_{[T_1,T_2]} \mid H J\_Occurs_{[T_1,T_2]}(X), hasPart(X, Y), Famous(Y)\}.$$

The result $(hj_2)_{[(224,225),(229,230)]}$ cannot be derived without fusing the information from multiple modalities. The query result would have been the empty set if it was not possible to prove that for $event_1$ the predicate $HJ\_InJumpPhase$ holds. This is possible due to the equality assertion $hj_2 = event_1$ (see above). Thus, fusion is motivated in this case.

Up to now it is unclear how to formalise what kinds of queries are important in a certain situation. In other words, we do not formalise what questions to ask and assume that this is represented by "context knowledge" as indicated in Fig. 3.3. Context knowledge is induced by a feedback-loop from higher level processes, which are not investigated in this work. However, feedback can also occur between analysis and interpretation. This is discussed in the next section.

3.3.6 Relating Analysis and Interpretation

Looking at the image shown in Fig. 3.8 and the corresponding analysis ABox given in Fig. 3.9, it becomes clear that the foam mat is not detected in this example. Even in the interpretation ABox (Fig. 3.14), there is no explicit name for a foam mat involved in the pole vault event. However, due to the TBox underlying the interpretation process (see Fig. 3.10), a foam mat must exist implicitly. In other words, in all models of the interpretation ABox, the pole vault individual pv_1 is associated with a foam-mat object. If this is made explicit, feedback might be given to the analysis module (see Fig. 3.26), which might use specifically parameterised image analysis techniques to then localise a foam mat in the image. In general, the more objects are made explicit in the analysis and interpretation ABoxes, the better is the interpretation. Let us assume that in the example an assertion $f_1 : Foam\_Mat$ is added to the analysis ABox, maybe together with spatial relations to the other objects localised in the scene. Then, the interpretation process will reuse the previously generated pole vault object pv_1 and associates it with f_1 appropriately such that the following is added:

$$f_1 : Foam\_Mat$$
$$(pv_1, f_1) : hasPart.$$

The derivation of a complete (fused) interpretation ABox can be seen as a bootstrap process. In case the foam mat is not visible in the image, the interpretation might be considered as less plausible for a high jump event. With the help of the distinction between domain and picture objects, and a theory for dealing with uncertainty, this can be formalised as shown in the next section.

3.4 Uncertain and Ambiguous Interpretations

Interpretations are generally ambiguous and not clearly defined with respect to a task. When constructing an explanation for media data, one often has the choice between alternatives. For example, given the limited knowledge base in Fig. 3.10, the image in Fig. 3.15 can be interpreted both as *Pole_Vault* or *High_Jump*. In the course of a stepwise interpretation, there can be many more decision points where multiple choices are available. For example, a *High_Jump* or *Pole_Vault* may be part of a *Training_Event* or *Sports_Event*. As humans, we seem to exploit our experiences for such decisions and prefer the most likely choice given all we know about the domain and the current scenario. Hence it appears natural to provide a probabilistic model for the uncertainty of logically ambiguous choices. In this section, we sketch a probabilistic model which is intended to guide choices in the logic-based interpretation process presented so far.

3.4.1 Towards a Probabilistic Preference Measure

The task of the probabilistic model is illustrated in Fig. 3.27. In this figure, we distinguish between the concepts describing real-world objects and concepts describing the corresponding media objects, a distinction which we omitted so far to simplify the presentation. All media-object concept names are marked with the suffix "pict" and describe the properties of pictures taken from the corresponding real-world objects. This way it can be explained, for example, that a real-world pole vault requires a pole but that a picture of a pole vault may not show a pole.

Figure 3.27 illustrates the interpretation step, where the media object *Horizontal-Bar-Pict* must be explained. *Pole_Vault* and *High_Jump* are both

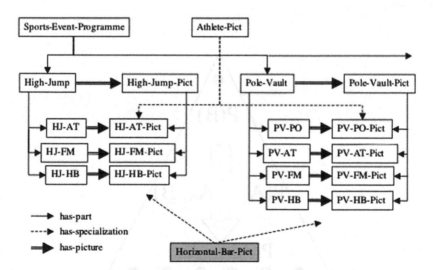

Fig. 3.27 Aggregate concepts relating a high jump and a pole vault to corresponding media object concepts. The *Horizontal-Bar-Pict* can be interpreted as an instance of a high-jump-horizontal-bar picture (*HJ-HB-Pict*) or of a pole-vault-horizontal-bar picture (*PV-HB-Pict*)

logically possible, hence this is a point where a probabilistic preference measure should help.

The basic idea is to provide an estimate of how likely *Horizontal-Bar-Pict* is a high jump picture (i.e. an instance of $HJ - HB - Pict$) or a pole vault picture (i.e. an instance of $PV - HB - Pict$). For this, we need probability distributions such that the probabilities of one or another aggregate having a media object as part can be compared and the most probable choice can be made.

We take a frequentist approach and want the probabilities to reflect the statistics of the domain, including the statistics of corresponding media objects. Determining these statistics is, of course, a formidable task. But the example illustrates that estimates of the frequency of occurrence of pole vault pictures without pole as opposed to the frequency of occurrence of high jump pictures may very well tip the balance for one interpretation rather than the other.

To compute such estimates, we invoke Bayes net technology. We consider concepts as random variables with probability distributions which govern the likelihood of instantiations which satisfy the concept. A general approach to constructing Bayes nets for first-order logic expressions is presented in Russell and Norvig (2003, p. 519ff.). For details see also Koller and Pfeffer (1997, 1998), Pfeffer, Koller, Milch and Takusagawa (1999). Our approach exploits the fact that aggregates are the concepts of interest for an interpretation task and dependencies between objects can effectively be encapsulated in aggregates. This limits probabilistic dependencies and provides for efficient propagation mechanisms.

To show this, consider a probabilistic model for the interpretation task in Fig. 3.27. We propose that each aggregate is described by a structure shown in Fig. 3.28.

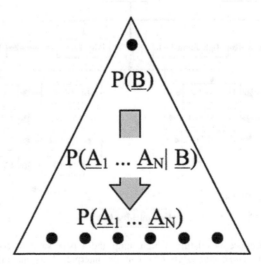

Fig. 3.28 Probabilistic structure of an aggregate. Internal properties $\underline{A}_i$ represent parts, external properties $\underline{B}$ represent the aggregate as a whole

In the aggregate structure, we distinguish between an internal probabilistic description $P(\underline{A_1}, \underline{A_2}, \ldots, \underline{A_N})$ of the parts (each represented by properties $\underline{A_i}$ and depicted as a node at the bottom of Fig. 3.28) and an external, abstracted description $P(\underline{B})$ which is used to represent the aggregate as part of higher level aggregates in the compositional hierarchy. $P(\underline{A_1}, \underline{A_2}, \ldots, \underline{A_N})$ follows from $P(\underline{B})$ by means of the conditional probability distribution $P(\underline{A_1} \ldots \underline{A_N}|\underline{B})$ which specifies the internal probabilistic structure of the aggregate.

For the time being, we consider all constituents of a high jump event, including the pictures taken thereof, as parts of an aggregate *High-Jump* and do not go into details about the internal dependency structure between real-world concepts and pictures thereof. Similarly, the pole vault event is modelled as an aggregate *Pole-Vault*, and both are parts of a higher level aggregate *Sports-Event-Programme*. The structure of an aggregate hierarchy induced by this aggregate structure is shown in Fig. 3.29.

In order to provide a preference measure, we must be able to compute the effect of evidence for one node on the probabilities of other nodes. It is not obvious under which conditions this can be done based on the joint probability distributions (JPDs) of the individual aggregates as specified in Fig. 3.29. The following requirements ensure that the compositional hierarchy constitutes an abstraction hierarchy where a complete JPD encompassing all aggregates can in principle be computed from the individual JPDs.

Let X be any node, $parts(X) = Y_1 \ldots Y_N$ its parts, and $succ(X)$ all its successor nodes in the aggregate hierarchy. Then for a compositional hierarchy to be an abstraction hierarchy, we require that

$$P(\underline{X}|succ(\underline{X})) = P(\underline{X} \mid \underline{Y_1} \ldots \underline{Y_N}). \tag{3.1}$$

Aggregate properties do not depend on details below the part properties.

$$P(succ(\underline{Y_i}) \mid \underline{Y_1} \ldots \underline{Y_N}) = P(succ(\underline{Y_i}) \mid \underline{Y_i}). \tag{3.2}$$

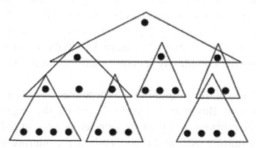

Fig. 3.29 Structure of aggregate hierarchy induced by aggregate structure. The quasi-tree structure reflects abstraction properties and allows for efficient probabilistic inferences

Part properties only depend on the properties of the corresponding mother aggregate, not on correlations the mother aggregate may have as a part in a higher level aggregate.

$$P(succ(\underline{Y}_1 \ldots \underline{Y}_N) \mid \underline{Y}_1 \ldots \underline{Y}_N) = \prod_{i=1}^{N} P(succ(\underline{Y}_i) \mid \underline{Y}_1 \ldots \underline{Y}_N). \qquad (3.3)$$

Parts of different aggregates are statistically independent given their mother aggregates.

From (3.2) and (3.3) it follows that

$$P(succ(\underline{Y}_1 \ldots \underline{Y}_N) \mid \underline{Y}_1 \ldots \underline{Y}_N) = \prod_{i=1}^{N} P(succ(\underline{Y}_i) \mid \underline{Y}_i). \qquad (3.4)$$

These requirements agree well with intuitions of an abstraction hierarchy. If they are fulfilled, one can show that the JPD of the aggregate hierarchy can be written as

$$P(\underline{Z}_0 \ldots \underline{Z}_M) = P(\underline{Z}_0) \prod_{i=1}^{M} P(parts(\underline{Z}_i) \mid \underline{Z}_i) \qquad (3.5)$$

where $Z_i, i = 0 \ldots M$ are all nodes of the hierarchy and Z_0 is the root node (representing the general aggregate "any scene").

Hence for an abstraction hierarchy, the JPD of the complete hierarchy is defined by the product of all conditional aggregate JPDs similar to a Bayes net. Furthermore, Equation (3.5) applies also to branches of the abstraction hierarchy. Hence, probabilities within a branch can be compared without considering the rest of the hierarchy. For example, in the interpretation task shown in Fig. 3.27, only the probabilities below the node Sports-Events-Programme have to be evaluated for choosing the most probable interpretation of Horizontal-Bar-Pict. After making the choice, Horizontal-Bar-Pict is entered into the probabilistic structure as evidence and other probabilities must be updated. Again, this can be restricted to the relevant branch of the compositional hierarchy. Updating can be performed by propagation procedures similar to those in tree-shaped Bayes nets. On the other hand, for updates within an aggregate no simplifying dependency structure can be assumed in general, and a Bayes net representing the internal probability structure need not be tree-shaped. This higher complexity remains local, however, due to the abstraction property.

The approach for exploiting conditional independencies discussed above allows for the construction of Bayesian networks based on the aggregate structure of domain objects. The purpose is to provide a preference measure for multiple interpretations arising naturally from abduction, and for the interpretation steps leading to such interpretations. Different from several other marriages between probabilities and logics (e.g. as discussed in the following section), our approach does not require a reinterpretation of description logic formulas but fills the space left open by multiple abduction solutions, ambiguous object classifications, and qualitative predicates over quantitative values. In consequence, there is no conceptual conflict in combining this probabilistic preference measure with a description logic framework. Combinations of description logics with approaches for modelling uncertainty are investigated in the next section.

3.4.2 Related Work About Uncertainty and Description Logics

Modelling uncertainty in the context of description logics has been a topic of research for many years. An overview of such extensions to classical description logics is presented in Baader, Küsters and Wolter (2003). The research is oriented to the work of modelling uncertain knowledge on the basis of first-order structures (Nilsson 1986; Bacchus 1990; Halpern 1990). The fundamental view of the approaches based on description logics is such that it should also be possible to represent the degree of overlap between concepts (and not only subsumption or disjunction) through probabilities. Furthermore, it should also be possible to formulate uncertainty about the structure of objects. Initial approaches considered primarily probabilistic knowledge at the conceptual level, this means, at the level of the TBox (Heinsohn 1994). Also knowledge representation for single objects and their relations from a probabilistic view were studied (Jaeger 1994), such that structural uncertainty could potentially be modelled. Along with early research results about decidability of very expressive logics (e.g. OWL DL), proposals for the modelling of uncertain knowledge were given.

In Giugno and Lukasiewicz (2002), a probabilistic description logic language was studied, in which it is possible to formulate, in addition to probabilistic knowledge at the conceptual level (i.e. TBox), also assertional probabilistic knowledge (i.e. ABbox) about concepts and role instances. In this language (P-$\mathcal{SHOQ}$), there is no longer a separation between TBox and ABox for the modelling of uncertainty. Its underlying reasoning formalism is based on probabilistic lexicographic entailment by Lehmann (1995). Lexicographic entailment is based on default logic and makes use of model creation to look for preferred minimal models, where the minimal verifying (resp. falsifying) model determines entailment (resp. non-entailment). In Giugno and Lukasiewicz (2002) the work of Lehmann (1995) is extended from propositional logic to first-order logic, furthermore Giugno and Lukasiewicz (2002) generalise classical interpretations to probabilistic interpretations by adding a probability distribution over the abstract domain and by interpreting defaults as statements of high conditional probability. For example, in Lehmann (1995), a default like $P(bird/fly) \geq 1 - \varepsilon$ is in (Giugno and Lukasiewicz 2002) a conditional constraint like $l \leq P(fly|bird) \leq u$. The work of Giugno and Lukasiewicz (2002) allows representation of probabilistic knowledge in a description logic language with high expressivity.

It is important to observe that the semantics used in the different approaches do not differ much (for example w.r.t. (Jaeger 1994) and (Giugno and Lukasiewicz

2002)). An approach for the modelling of uncertain structures for a less expressive language is presented in Dürig and Studer (2005). However, no specific inference algorithms are known for this approach. An important step for the practical use of description logics with probabilities occurred with the integration of Bayesian networks in P-CLASSIC (Koller, Levy and Pfeffer 1997), nevertheless very strong disadvantages were obtained: for number restrictions, the supremum limits must be known and separate Bayesian networks are necessary to consider role fillers. Along with this problem, the probabilistic dependencies between instances must also be modelled. This problem was overcome in (Koller and Pfeffer 1998) – however not in the context of description logics but with a frame-based approach, in which the treatment of default values is given without formal semantics. The main idea in Koller and Pfeffer (1998) is the view of considering role fillers as nodes in Bayes network which have CPTs (conditional probability tables) associated to them as generalised number restrictions in the sense of description logics. Related studies followed in Pfeffer et al. (1999).

Complementary to the P-CLASSIC approach, another approach called PTDL (Yelland 2000) was developed for probabilistic modelling with the use of first-order structures. In this approach, the Bayesian network theory is considered as the basis reference for further extensions, instead of (classical) description logics. The Bayesian network nodes represent function values and an individual is associated to other nodes through these function values. The approach in Yelland (2000) avoids some disadvantages of P-CLASSIC, but it offers minimal expressivity on the side of description logics. In context with very expressive description logics, another approach (Ding and Peng 2004; Ding, Peng and Pan 2005) was presented for the integration of Bayes networks. Algorithms for deduction over probabilistic first-order structures were developed by Poole (2003). Poole observes that the existing approaches (e.g. Koller and Pfeffer 1998; Pfeffer et al. 1999) only consider individuals that are explicitly named. Qualitative probabilistic matching with hierarchical descriptions was studied (Smyth and Poole 2004). It allows for a variation of the level of abstraction.

Previous studies have investigated the combination of Datalog and description logics (so-called description logic programs) (Nottelmann and Fuhr 2004; Lukasiewicz 2005a, 2005b; Nottelmann and Fuhr 2006). Approaches for information retrieval with probabilistic Datalog are presented in Fuhr (1995, 2000). In this area, work on learning from Datalog predicates with uncertainty is also relevant (Nottelmann and Fuhr 2001).

Modelling vagueness to capture notions of imprecise knowledge has been intensively studied (Straccia 2001; Tresp and Molitor 1998; Yen 1991), such that existing knowledge representation formalisms like first-order logic can be extended to represent vague concepts (e.g. hot, cold) which are not entirely true or false, but rather have a truth value between true and false. Fuzzy logic, with a basis in fuzzy set theory, allows the modelling of vagueness, and its fundamental view is that the classical ideas of satisfiability and subsumption are modified such that concepts are satisfiable to a certain degree, or a concept subsumes another to a certain degree.

In Tresp and Molitor (1998), a tableau-like method for computing the degree of subsumption between two concepts in the language $\mathcal{ALC}_{fm}$ was presented. In (Yen 1991) work on extending description logics with fuzzy features is presented for the language FL^-, in which it is possible to determine subsumption, but not possible to determine whether an individual is an instance of a concept with a certain probability. In (Straccia 2001), the use of fuzzy logic is highlighted in the context of multimedia information retrieval, in which images are semantically annotated with fuzzy statements. Recently, more expressive fuzzy description logics have been investigated (Stoilos, Stamou, Tzouvaras, Pan and Horrocks 2005a, 2005b; 2005c; Pan, Stoilos, Stamou, Tzouvaras and Horrocks 2006; Stoilos, Straccia, Stamou and Pan 2006; Stoilos, Stamou and Pan 2006).

At the time of this writing, details of a probabilistic (and fuzzy) inference scheme for media interpretation in a local context are still being investigated in ongoing research. One of the open questions is how to trade off precision (which may not be vital for a preference measure) against computational effort (which may be unacceptable if all dependencies in a large knowledge base have to be considered).

3.4.3 Probabilities, Description Logics, Abduction, and Logic Programming

While Hobbs et al. (1993) and Shanahan (2005) use first-order logic for text and image/video interpretation, with description logics, we use a decidable knowledge representation formalism with well-tested implementations that are known to be efficient for many typical-case inputs. The use of logical rules and backward chaining for implementing an abduction algorithm as described in Section 3.3 is also investigated in the area of logic programming (Kakas, Kowalski and Toni 1992; Poole 1993a; Poole 1992; Kakas and Denecker 2002; Flach and Kakas 2000). In our approach, however, predicate names in rules are defined w.r.t. ontologies represented as description logic Tboxes, and thus we use another expressive fragment of first-order logic. In the context of information retrieval, user queries can be answered regarding user-specified Tboxes. In the previous sections, we have argued that probabilistic reasoning would really add to the application scenario of information retrieval that we have used in this chapter. In Sebastiani (1994) a proposal is made for using probabilistic description logics for information retrieval. No system implementation has been developed, though.

In the previous section, we have discussed related work for integrating probabilistic and description logic reasoning. Only recently, however, abduction has been investigated in the context of description logics (Colucci, Noia, Sciascio, Mongiello and Donini 2004). However, in this work, abduction is considered for concepts, not Aboxes and queries. Due to the best of our knowledge, abduction has not yet been considered in the context of probabilistic description logics. Interesting input to this research is provided by abduction in probabilistic logic programming (Charniak and Goldman 1991; Poole 1993b).

3.5 Conclusions

In this chapter, a formal account of media interpretation has been presented. It has been shown that results from media analysis processes can be appropriately enriched with high-level descriptions using automatic processes. Thus, applications which require access to high-level descriptions can be supported, for example, retrieval of media in a semantic web context. The central idea is to use abduction and deduction in concert to construct high-level descriptions for characterizing media content. It should be emphasised that the architecture not just describes an algorithm that constructs the descriptions but formalises the description generation in a meaningful way. High-level descriptions are constructed to explain assertions from media analysis. The same holds also for the way we tackle the fusion problem. In its current state, our architecture does not specify which assertions are taken to be explained (and which queries are constructed or selected in the case of fusion). This is seen as an even higher level process and is left for future work.

It has also been shown that the crisp logical framework should be supported by probabilistic preference measures in order to provide the most desirable interpretations. We have made a first contribution towards a probabilistic preference measure which can be used to rank different interpretations.

Acknowledgments This work is partially supported by the EU-funded projects BOEMIE (Bootstrapping Ontology Evolution with Multimedia Information Extraction, IST-FP6-027538) and TONES (Thinking ONtologiES, IST-FP6-007603). We would like to thank all members of the BOEMIE project for providing examples about the sports domains that we use here to demonstrate insights about media interpretation and reasoning. In particular, we would like to mention Sofia Espinosa, Atila Kaya, and Sylvia Melzer.

References

Baader, F., Calvanese, D., McGuinness, D., Nardi, D. and Patel-Schneider, P.F., eds (2003), *The Description Logic Handbook: Theory, Implementation and Applications*, Cambridge University Press.

Baader, F., Franconi, E., Hollunder, B., Nebel, B. and Profitlich, H.-J. (1994), An empirical analysis of optimization techniques for terminological representation systems or: Making KRIS get a move on, *Applied Artificial Intelligence. Special Issue on Knowledge Base Management* 4, 109–132.

Baader, F. and Hanschke, P. (1991), A Schema for Integrating Concrete Domains into Concept Languages, '*in Proceedings of the 12th International Joint Conference on Artificial Intelligence (IJCAI'91)*', pp. 452–457.

Baader, F., Küsters, R. and Wolter, F. (2003), Extensions to description logics, *in* Baader, Calvanese, McGuinness, Nardi and Patel-Schneider (2003), chapter 6, pp. 219–261.

Baader, F., Lutz, C. and Suntisrivaraporn, B. (2006), CEL—a polynomial-time reasoner for life science ontologies, *in* U. Furbach and N. Shankar, eds, '*Proceedings of the 3rd International Joint Conference on Automated Reasoning (IJCAR'06)*', Vol. 4130 of *Lecture Notes in Artificial Intelligence*, Springer-Verlag, pp. 287–291.

Bacchus, F. (1990), *Representing and Reasoning with Probabilistic Knowledge: A Logical Approach to Probabilities*, The MIT Press, Cambridge.

Calvanese, D., De Giacomo, G., Lembo, D., Lenzerini, M. and Rosati, R. (2005), DL-Lite: Tractable description logics for ontologies, *in* 'Proceedings of the 20th National Conference on Artificial Intelligence (AAAI 2005)', pp. 602–607.

Charniak, E. and Goldman, R. (1991), Probabilistic abduction for plan recognition, Technical report, Brown University, Providence, RI, USA.

Colucci, S., Noia, T. D., Sciascio, E. D., Mongiello, M. and Donini, F. M. (2004), Concept abduction and contraction for semantic-based discovery of matches and negotiation spaces in an e-marketplace, *in* 'ICEC '04: Proceedings of the 6th International Conference on Electronic Commerce', ACM Press, New York, NY, USA, pp. 41–50.

Di Sciascio, E., Donini, F. M. and Mongiello, M. (1999), A description logic for image retrieval, *in* 'Proceedings of the 6th Congress of the Italian Association for Artificial Intelligence on Advances in Artificial Intelligence', number 1792 *in* 'Lecture Notes in Computer Science', Springer, pp. 13–24.

Di Sciascio, E., Donini, F. and Mongiello, M. (2000), Semantic indexing in image retrieval using description logic, *in* 'Proceedings of the 22nd International Conference on Information Technology Interfaces (ITI 2000)', pp. 125–132.

Ding, Z. and Peng, Y. (2004), A probabilistic extension to ontology language OWL, *in* 'Proceedings of the 37th Hawaii International Conference on System Sciences (HICSS)'.

Ding, Z., Peng, Y. and Pan, R. (2005), BayesOWL: Uncertainty modeling in semantic web ontologies, *in* 'Soft Computing in Ontologies and Semantic Web', Springer & Hidelberg.

Dürig, M. and Studer, T. (2005), Probabilistic abox reasoning: Preliminary results, *in* 'Proceedings of the International Description Logics Workshop', pp. 104–111.

Elsenbroich, C., Kutz, O. and Sattler, U. (2006), A case for abductive reasoning over ontologies, *in* 'Proceedings OWL: Experiences and Directions', Athens, Georgia, USA, November 10–11'.

Erman, L. D., Hayes-Roth, F., Lesser, V. R. and Reddy, D. R. (1980), 'The hearsay-ii speech-understanding system: Integrating knowledge to resolve uncertainty', *ACM Computing Surveys* **12**(2), 213–253.

Flach, P. and Kakas, A., eds (2000), *Abduction and Induction: Essays on their Relation and Integration*, Kluwer Academic Publishers, USA.

Fuhr, N. (1995), Probabilistic datalog: a logic for powerful retrieval methods, *in* 'Proceedings of SIGIR-95: 18th ACM International Conference on Research and Development in Information Retrieval', pp. 282–290.

Fuhr, N. (2000), 'Probabilistic datalog: Implementing logical information retrieval for advanced applications', *Journal of the American Society of Information Science* **51**(2), 95–110.

Gabsdil, M., Koller, A. and Striegnitz, K. (2001), Building a text adventure on description logic, *in* 'International Workshop on Applications of Description Logics', CEUR Electronic Workshop Proceedings.

Giugno, R. and Lukasiewicz, T. (2002), P-SHOQ(D): A probabilistic extension of SHOQ(D) for probabilistic ontologies in the semantic web, *in* 'JELIA '02: Proceedings of the European Conference on Logics in Artificial Intelligence', Springer-Verlag, pp. 86–97.

Glimm, B., Horrocks, I., Lutz, C. and Sattler, U. (2007), Conjunctive query answering for the description logic $\mathcal{SHIQ}$, *in* 'Proceedings of the Twentieth International Joint Conference on Artificial Intelligence IJCAI-07', AAAI Press.

Haarslev, V. and Möller, R. (2000), Expressive ABox reasoning with number restrictions, role hierarchies, and transitively closed roles, *in* 'Proceedings of the 7th International Conference on the Principles of Knowledge Representation and Reasoning (KR 2000)', pp. 273–284.

Haarslev, V. and Möller, R. (2001), RACER System Description, *in* 'Proceedings of the International Joint Conference on Automated Reasoning (IJCAR 2001)', Vol. 2083 of *Lecture Notes in Computer Science*, Springer, pp. 701–705.

Haarslev, V., Möller, R. and Wessel, M. (2001), The description logic $\mathcal{ALCNH}_{R+}$ extended with concrete domains: A practically motivated approach, in 'Proceedings of the International Joint Conference on Automated Reasoning (IJCAR 2001)', pp. 29–44.

Halpern, J. (1990), An analysis of first-order logics of probability, Artificial Intelligence 46(3), 311–350.

Hanson, A. and Riseman, E. (1978), VISIONS: A computer system for interpreting scenes, in A. Hanson and E. Riseman, eds, 'Computer Vision Systems', Academic Press, New York, pp. 303–333.

Heinsohn, J. (1994), Probabilistic description logics, in R. L. de Mantaras and D. Poole, eds, 'Proceedings of the 10th Conference on Uncertainty in Artificial Intelligence', Morgan Kaufmann, Seattle, Washington, pp. 311–318.

Hobbs, J. R., Stickel, M., Appelt, D. and Martin, P. (1993), Interpretation as abduction, Artificial Intelligence 63, 69–142.

Hobbs, J. R., Stickel, M. E., Appelt, D. and Martin, P. (1990), Interpretation as Abduction, Technical Report 499, AI Center, SRI International, Menlo Park, California.

Hobbs, J. R., Stickel, M., Martin, P. and Edwards, D. D. (1988), Interpretation as abduction, in '26th Annual Meeting of the Association for Computational Linguistics: Proceedings of the Conference', Buffalo, New York, pp. 95–103.

Horrocks, I., Kutz, O. and Sattler, U. (2006), The even more irresistible $\mathcal{SROIQ}$, in 'Proceedings of the 10th International Conference on Principles of Knowledge Representation and Reasoning (KR 2006)', AAAI Press, pp. 57–67.

Horrocks, I., Sattler, U., Tessaris, S. and Tobies, S. (2000), How to decide query containment under constraints using a description logic, in 'Proceedings of the 7th International Conference on Logic for Programming and Automated Reasoning (LPAR)', Vol. 1955 of Lecture Notes in Computer Science, Springer, pp. 326–343.

Horrocks, I., Sattler, U. and Tobies, S. (2000), Reasoning with individuals for the description logic $\mathcal{SHIQ}$, in D. McAllester, ed., 'Proceedings of the 17th International Conference on Automated Deduction (CADE 2000)', Vol. 1831 of Lecture Notes in Computer Science, Springer, pp. 482–496.

Hustadt, U., Motik, B. and Sattler, U. (2004), Reducing $\mathcal{SHIQ}$-Description Logic to Disjunctive Datalog Programs, in 'Proceedings of the 9th International Conference on the Principles of Knowledge Representation and Reasoning (KR 2004)', pp. 152–162.

Jaeger, M. (1994), Probabilistic reasoning in terminological logics, in 'Proceedings of the 4th International Conference on the Principles of Knowledge Representation and Reasoning (KR'94)', pp. 305–316.

Kakas, A. C., Kowalski, R. A. and Toni, F. (1992), 'Abductive logic programming', Journal of Logic and Computation 2(6), 719–770.

Kakas, A. and Denecker, M. (2002), Abduction in logic programming, in A. Kakas and F. Sadri, eds, 'Computational Logic: Logic Programming and Beyond. Part I', number 2407 in 'LNAI', Springer, pp. 402–436.

Kaplunova, A., Kaya, A. and Möller, R. (2006), First experiences with load balancing and caching for semantic web applications, Technical report, Institute for Software Systems (STS), Hamburg University of Technology, Germany.

Koller, D., Levy, A. and Pfeffer, A. (1997), P-CLASSIC: A tractable probabilistic description logic, in 'Proceedings of the 14th National Conference on Artificial Intelligence (AAAI'97)', AAAI Press/The MIT Press, pp. 390–397.

Koller, D. and Pfeffer, A. (1997), Object-oriented Bayesian networks, in 'Proceedings of the 13th Annual Conference on Uncertainty in AI (UAI)', pp. 302–313. Winner of the Best Student Paper Award.

Koller, D. and Pfeffer, A. (1998), Probabilistic frame-based systems, in 'Proceedings of the 15th National Conference on Artificial Intelligence (AAAI)', Madison, Wisconsin'.

Lehmann, D. J. (1995), Another perspective on default reasoning, Annals of Mathematics and Artificial Intelligence 15(1), 61–82.

Lukasiewicz, T. (2005a), Probabilistic description logic programs, in 'Proceedings of ECSQARU', pp. 737–749.

Lukasiewicz, T. (2005b), Stratified probabilistic description logic programs, in 'Proceedings of ISWC-URSW', pp. 87–97.

Möller, R., Haarslev, V. and Neumann, B. (1998), Semantics-based information retrieval, in 'Proceedings IT&KNOWS-98: International Conference on Information Technology and Knowledge Systems, 31. August- 4. September, Vienna, Budapest', pp. 49–62.

Motik, B., Sattler, U. and Studer, R. (2005), Query answering for OWL-DL with rules, Journal of Web Semantics 3(1), 41–60.

Neumann, B. (1985), Retrieving events from geometrical descriptions of time-varying scenes, in J. Schmidt and C. Thanos, eds, 'Foundations of Knowledge Base Management – Contributions from Logic, Databases, and Artificial Intelligence', Springer, New York, pp. 443–452.

Neumann, B. and Möller, R. (2006), On scene interpretation with description logics, in H. Christensen and H.-H. Nagel, eds, 'Cognitive Vision Systems: Samping the Spectrum of Approaches', number 3948 in 'LNCS', Springer, pp. 247–278.

Neumann, B. and Novak, H.-J. (1983), Event models for recognition and natural language description of events in real-world image sequences, in 'Proceedings of the 8th International Joint Conference on Artificial Intelligence (IJCAI'83)', pp. 724–726.

Neumann, B. and Weiss, T. (2003), Navigating through logic-based scene models for high-level scene interpretations, in 3rd International Conference on Computer Vision Systems - ICVS 2003, Springer, pp. 212–22.

Nilsson, N. (1986), Probabilistic logic, Artificial Intelligence 28, 71–87.

Nottelmann, H. and Fuhr, N. (2001), Learning probabilistic datalog rules for information classification and transformation, in 'In Proceedings CIKM', pp. 387–394.

Nottelmann, H. and Fuhr, N. (2004), pDAML+OIL: A probabilistic extension to DAML+OIL based on probabilistic datalog, in 'Proceedings Information Processing and Management of Uncertainty in Knowledge-Based Systems'.

Nottelmann, H. and Fuhr, N. (2006), Adding probabilities and rules to OWL Lite subsets based on probabilistic datalog, International Journal of Uncertainty, Fuzziness and Knowledge-Based Systems 14(1), 17–41.

Pan, J. Z., Stoilos, G., Stamou, G., Tzouvaras, V. and Horrocks, I. (2006), f-swrl: A fuzzy extension of swrl, Data Semantics, special issue on Emergent Semantics 4090, 28–46.

Pfeffer, A., Koller, D., Milch, B. and Takusagawa, K. (1999), SPOOK: A system for probabilistic object-oriented knowledge representation, in 'Proceedings of the Fifteenth Annual Conference on Uncertainty in Artificial Intelligence (UAI-99)', pp. 541–550.

Poole, D. (1992), Logic programming, abduction and probability, in 'Proceedings of the International Conference on Fifth Generation Computer Systems (FGCS'92),', pp. 530–538.

Poole, D. (1993a), 'Logic programming, abduction and probability: a top-down anytime algorithm for estimating prior and posterior probabilities', New Generation Computing 11(3–4), 377–400.

Poole, D. (1993b), Probabilistic horn abduction and bayesian networks, Artificial Intelligence 64(1), 81–129.

Poole, D. (2003), First-order probabilistic inference, in 'Proceedings International Joint Conference on Artificial Intelligence IJCAI-03', pp. 985–991.

Reiter, R. and Mackworth, A. (1990), 'A logical framework for depiction and image interpretation', Artificial Intelligence 41, 125–155.

Russell, S. J. and Norvig, P. (2003), Artifical Intelligence: A Modern Approach, Prentice Hall New Jersey, 2nd edition.

Schober, J.-P., Hermes, T. and Herzog, O. (2005), Picturefinder: Description logics for semantic image retrieval, in 'IEEE International Conference on Multimedia and Expo (ICME)', pp. 1571–1574.

Schröder, C. (1999), Bildinterpretatation durch Modellkonstruktion: Eine Theorie zur rechnergestützten Analyse von Bilder, PhD thesis, Universität Hamburg.

Sebastiani, F. (1994), A Probabilistic Terminological Logic for Modelling Information Retrieval, *in* W. Croft and C. v. Rijsbergen, eds, *'Proceedings of the 17th Annual International ACM SIGIR Conference on Research and Development in Information Retrieval'*, Springer-Verlag, Dublin, Ireland, pp. 122–130.

Shanahan, M. (2005), 'Perception as abduction: Turning sensor data into meaningful representation', *Cognitive Science* **29**, 103–134.

Sirin, E. and Parsia, B. (2006), Pellet System Description, *in* *'Proceedings of the 2006 Description Logic Workshop (DL 2006)'*, CEUR Electronic Workshop Proceedings.

Smyth, C. and Poole, D. (2004), Qualitative probabilistic matching with hierarchical descriptions, *in* *'Proceedings Knowledge Representation and Reasoning (KR&R 2004)'*.

Stoilos, G., Stamou, G. and Pan, J. (2006), Handling imprecise knowledge with fuzzy description logic, *in* *'International Workshop on Description Logics (DL 06), Lake District, UK'*.

Stoilos, G., Stamou, G., Tzouvaras, V., Pan, J. and Horrocks, I. (2005*a*), The fuzzy description logic f-shin, *in* *'International Workshop on Uncertainty Reasoning For the Semantic Web'*.

Stoilos, G., Stamou, G., Tzouvaras, V., Pan, J. and Horrocks, I. (2005*b*), A fuzzy description logic for multimedia knowledge representation, *in* *'Proceedings of the International Workshop on Multimedia and the Semantic Web'*.

Stoilos, G., Stamou, G., Tzouvaras, V., Pan, J. and Horrocks, I. (2005*c*), Fuzzy owl: Uncertainty and the semantic web, *in* *'International Workshop of OWL: Experiences and Directions, Galway'*.

Stoilos, G., Straccia, U., Stamou, G. and Pan, J. Z. (2006), General concept inclusions in fuzzy description logics, *in* *'17th European Conference on Artificial Intelligence (ECAI 06)*, Riva del Garda, Italy'.

Straccia, U. (2001), Reasoning within fuzzy description logics, *Journal of Artificial Intelligence Research* **14**, 137–166.

Tresp, C. B. and Molitor, R. (1998), A description logic for vague knowledge, *in* *'Proceedings of the 13th European Conference on Artificial Intelligence (ECAI'98)'*, pp. 361–365.

Tsarkov, D. and Horrocks, I. (2006), FaCT++ Description Logic Reasoner: System Description, *in* *'Proceedings of the International Joint Conference on Automated Reasoning* (IJCAR 2006)'. To appear.

Turhan, A.-Y., Bechhofer, S., Kaplunova, A., Liebig, T., Luther, M., Möller, R., Noppens, O., Patel-Schneider, P., Suntisrivaraporn, B. and Weithöner, T. (2006), DIG 2.0 – towards a flexible interface for description logic reasoners, *in* B. C. Grau, P. Hitzler, C. Shankey and E. Wallace, eds, *'OWL: Experiences and Directions 2006'*.

Wessel, M. and Möller, R. (2005), A High performance semantic web query answering engine, *in* I. Horrocks, U. Sattler and F. Wolter, eds, *'Proceedings International Workshop on Description Logics'*.

Wessel, M. and Möller, R. (2006), A flexible DL-based architecture for deductive information systems, *in* G. Sutcliffe, R. Schmidt and S. Schulz, eds, *'Proceedings IJCAR-06 Workshop on Empirically Successful Computerized Reasoning (ESCoR)'*, pp. 92–111.

Yelland, P. Y. (2000), An alternative combination of Baysian networks and description logics, *in* 'Proceedings of the 7th International Conference on the Principles of Knowledge Representation and Reasoning (KR 2000)', pp. 225–234.

Yen, J. (1991), Generalizing term subsumption languages to fuzzy logic, *in* 'Proceedings of the 12th International Joint Conference on Artificial Intelligence (IJCAI'91)', pp. 472–477.

Chapter 4
Introducing Context and Reasoning in Visual Content Analysis: An Ontology-Based Framework

Stamatia Dasiopoulou, Carsten Saathoff, Phivos Mylonas, Yannis Avrithis, Yiannis Kompatsiaris, Steffen Staab, and Michael G. Strinztis

4.1 Introduction

The amount of multimedia content produced and made available on the World Wide Web, and in professional and, not least, personal collections, is constantly growing, resulting in equally increasing needs in terms of efficient and effective ways to access it. Enabling smooth access at a level that meets user expectations and needs has been the holy grail in content-based retrieval for decades as it is intertwined with the so-called *semantic gap* between the features that can be extracted from such content through automatic analysis and the conveyed meaning as perceived by the end users. Numerous efforts towards more reliable and effective visual content analysis that target the extraction of user-oriented content descriptions have been reported, addressing a variety of domains and applications, and following diverse methodologies. Among the reported literature, knowledge-based approaches utilising explicit, a priori, knowledge constitute a popular choice aiming at analysis methods decoupled from application-specific implementations. Such knowledge may address various aspects including visual characteristics and numerical representations, topological knowledge about the examined domain, contextual knowledge, as well as knowledge driving the selection and execution of the processing steps required.

Among the different knowledge representations adopted in the reported literature, ontologies, being the key enabling technology of the Semantic Web (SW) vision for knowledge sharing and reuse through machine processable metadata, have been favoured in recent efforts. Indicative state-of-the-art approaches include, among others, the work presented in Little and Hunter (2004), and Hollink, Little and Hunter (2005), where ontologies have been used to represent objects of the

S. Dasiopoulou
Multimedia Knowledge Laboratory, Centre for Research and Technology Hellas, Informatics and Telematics Institute, Thermi-Thessaloniki, Greece
e-mail: dasiop@iti.gr

Y. Kompatsiaris, P. Hobson (eds.), *Semantic Multimedia and Ontologies,*
© Springer Science+Business Media, LLC 2008

examined domain and their visual characteristics in terms of MPEG-7 descriptions, and the ontological framework employed in Maillot and Thonnat (2005) that employs domain knowledge, visual knowledge in terms of qualitative descriptions, and contextual knowledge with respect to image capturing conditions, for the purpose of object detection. Furthermore, in Dasiopoulou, Mezaris, Kompatsiaris, Papastathis and Strintzis (2005), ontologies combined with rules have been proposed to capture the processing steps required for object detection in video, while in the approaches presented in Schober, Hermes and Herzog (2004) and Neumann and Möller (2004), the inference services provided by description logics (DLs) have been employed over ontology definitions that link domain concepts and visual characteristics.

In this chapter, we propose an ontology-based framework for enhancing segment-level annotations resulting from typical image analysis, through the exploitation of visual context and topological information. The concepts (objects) of interest and their spatial topology are modelled in RDFS (Brickley and Guha 2004) ontologies, and through the use of reification, a fuzzy ontological representation is achieved, enabling the seamless integration of contextual knowledge. The formalisation of contextual information enables a first refinement of the input image analysis annotations utilising the semantic associations that characterise the context of appearance. For example, in an image from the beach domain, annotations corresponding to concepts such as *Sea* and *Sand* are favoured contrary to those referring to concepts such as *Mountain* and *Car*. The application of constraint reasoning brings further improvement, by ensuring the consistency of annotations, through the elimination of annotations violating the domain topology semantics, such as the case of the *Sky*-annotated segment on the left of the *Sea*-annotated segment in Fig. 4.1.

Thereby, as illustrated in Fig. 4.1, the image analysis part is treated as a black box that provides initial annotations on top of which the proposed context analysis and constraint reasoning modules perform to provide for more reliable content descriptions. The only requirement with respect to the image analysis is that the produced annotations come with an associated degree of confidence. It is easy to see that such a requirement is not restricting but instead reflects the actual case in image analysis, where due to the inherent ambiguity, the similarities shared among different objects, and the different appearances an object may have, it is hardly possible to obtain unique annotations (labels) for each of the considered image segments. Consequently, under such a framework, the advantages brought are threefold:

- Arbitrary image analysis algorithms can be employed for acquiring an initial set of annotations, without the need for specialised domain-tuned implementations, and integrated for achieving more complete and robust content annotations.
- The context-aware refinement of the degrees renders the annotations more reliable for subsequent retrieval steps, as the confidence is strengthened for the more plausible annotations and lowered for the less likely ones, while false annotations are reduced through the application of constraint reasoning.
- The use of ontologies, apart from allowing the sharing of domain knowledge and providing a common vocabulary for the resulting content annotations (labels),

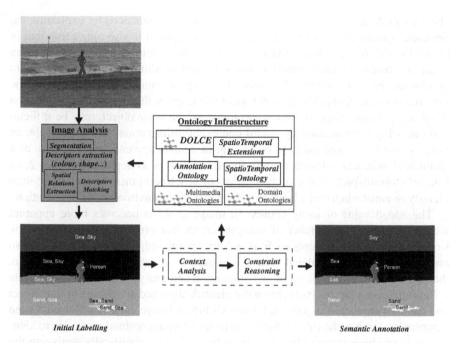

Fig. 4.1 Ontology-based framework introducing context and constraint reasoning in image analysis

ensures smooth communication among the different modules involved and facilitates interoperability with respect to future extensions with additional modules.

The rest of the chapter is organised as follows. Section 4.2 presents relevant work in terms of utilising visual context and constraint reasoning approaches in semantic image analysis, while in Section 4.3, the proposed framework is described, including the specification and design of the ontology infrastructure. Section 4.4 details the modelling and ontological representation of context of appearance and presents the methodology for readjusting the initial degrees of confidence, while Section 4.5 describes the application of constraint reasoning for the purpose of consistent image labelling. Experimental results and evaluation of the proposed framework are presented in Section 4.6, while Section 4.7 concludes the chapter.

4.2 Relevant Work

4.2.1 Context in Image Analysis

In semantic content-based image search and retrieval, research has shifted beyond low-level colour, texture, and shape features in pursuit of more effective methods of content access at the level of the meaning conveyed. Towards this goal, context plays a significant role as it allows performance to be enhanced by exploiting the semantic correlation between the considered concepts. It is also rather true that in the real world, objects always exist in a context. In principle, a single image taken in an unconstrained environment is not sufficient to allow a computer algorithm or a human being to identify the object. However, a number of cues based on the statistics of our everyday visual world are useful to guide this decision. Identification of an object in an image, or a close-up image of the same object, may be difficult without being accompanied by useful contextual information. As an example, an image of a cow is more likely to be present in a landscape environment, such as a green field, whereas a desk is usually found indoors, or as depicted in Fig. 4.2, an isolated close-up picture of a kitchen gadget or beach equipment is more difficult to identify or enrol when considered out of the rest of the environmental information.

The added value of using context in image analysis becomes more apparent when considering the number of analysis errors that often occur because of the similarities in visual features such as colour, texture, edge characteristics, and so on of the concepts considered. The advantages of context utilisation overwhelm the required effort increase on object annotation and analysis, provided a moderate balance, between the efforts spent on the identification and annotation of one object and the total amount of objects annotated within an image, will be followed. Given a particular domain, the rule of thumb, in order to obtain optimal results, is to identify a set of characteristic objects to be annotated, after statistically analysing the objects' co-occurrence in a subset of the entire dataset (e.g. 20% of the images).

A number of interesting enhanced analysis efforts have been reported including, among others, the exploitation of co-occurrence information for the detection of natural objects in outdoor images (Vailaya and Jain 2000; Naphade, Kozintsev and Huang 2002). In Luo, Singhal and Zhu (2003), a spatial context-aware object detection system is presented that combines the output of individual object detectors into a composite belief vector for the objects potentially present in an image. In Murphy, Torralba and Freeman (2003), scene context is proposed as an extra source of global

Fig. 4.2 Isolated object vs.
object in context   Isolated object   Object in context

information to assist in resolving local ambiguities, while in Boutell (2006), three types of context are explored for the scene classification problem, namely spatial, temporal, and image capture condition context in the form of camera parameters, also examined in Boutell and Luo (2005). Context information in terms of a combination of a region index and a presence vector has been proposed in Le Saux and Amato (2004) for scene classification.

The aforementioned efforts indicate the shift witnessed towards utilising available contextual information in multimedia analysis. However, contrary to natural language processing (NLP), where the use of context has been investigated thoroughly (Wiebe, Hirst and Horton 1996), the respective efforts in the field of multimedia analysis are in a very early stage. The formal model of context semantics and its application as described in Section 4.4 aims to contribute with a generic methodology towards introducing and benefiting from contextual knowledge.

4.2.2 Constraint Reasoning in Image Analysis

Constraint reasoning has a long history, starting with the system SKETCHPAD (Sutherland 1963) in the early 1960s. Later, Waltz formalised the notion of constraints in order to solve the problem of deriving a 3D interpretation of 2D line drawings as the *scene labelling problem* (Waltz 1975). Haralick and Shapiro formulated this problem even more generally as the labelling of image segments based on automatic low-level processing techniques (Haralick and Shapiro 1979). However, this original work was mainly formal, introducing the consistent labelling problem as a general set of problems, while in the approach proposed in this chapter we provide a concrete instantiation of the scene labelling problem, deployed in a real application setting. As discussed in the following, only a few other approaches exist that employ constraint reasoning to introduce explicit knowledge about spatial arrangements of real-life objects into the image interpretation process.

In Kolbe (1998), constraint reasoning techniques are employed for the identification of objects in aerial images. One main aspect of the presented study is the handling of over-constrained problems. An over-constrained problem is a constraint satisfaction problem in which not all constraints can be satisfied simultaneously. In traditional constraint reasoning, this would mean that no solution exists and the problem is consequently unsolvable. Several techniques were proposed to solve such over-constrained problems, providing solutions that are close to optimal. Kolbe specifically introduces a solving technique based on an information theory-based evaluation measure. However, Kolbe uses, in addition, specialised constraints between the image parts that render the proposed techniques less applicable to more generic domains.

In Hotz and Neumann (2005), a configuration system is adopted to provide high-level scene interpretations. The system is evaluated on table-laying scenes, i.e. scenes where a table is laid and where the table is monitored by a camera. The goal is to identify the purpose the table is laid for, e.g. *"Dinner for Two"*,

"Breakfast". Hotz and Neumann use well-defined domain models based on the spatial arrangements of the concepts found within the given domain to introduce reasoning into this task. The underlying interpretation of the spatial knowledge is also based on the notion of constraints on variable assignments, although the terminology of constraint reasoning is not used. The whole approach does not focus solely on the application of spatial knowledge, but also on the inference of higher level knowledge and the scene-specific interpretation of the image. However, again the problem is extremely specific and relies on very well-defined domain models that are unlikely to exist for broad domains such as the ones of "holiday" or "family" images.

Finally, an interesting approach is presented in Srihari and Zhang (2000), where images are annotated semi-automatically and a user can manually prune the search space by specifying hints such as "An L-shaped building in the upper left corner". A constraint reasoner is employed to enforce the user hints. Obviously, this approach uses the constraints in an ad hoc manner, and not as a domain model, which is the case of the framework proposed in this chapter.

4.3 Ontology Infrastructure

The proposed ontology-based framework aims to serve as a generic, easy-to-extend knowledge-based framework for enhancing available semantic image analysis annotations through context-aware refinement and spatial consistency checking. As such, the intended usage purpose imposes certain requirements with respect to the knowledge infrastructure that constitutes the proposed framework's backbone, which reflect on the representation and engineering choices.

The first requirement refers to the need for smooth communication among the involved modules while preserving the intended semantics. This practically means that the annotations and the employed contextual and spatial knowledge have to be captured and represented in such a way as to promote clean semantics and facilitate exchange. The ontology languages that emerged within the Semantic Web initiative constitute promising candidates as, due to their relation with logic and particularly DLs, they provide well-defined semantics, while their XML-based syntax enhances exchange across different applications. Among the available languages, OWL DL constitutes the optimal choice with respect to expressivity and complexity trade-off. However, as described in the following sections, the expressivity requirements of the proposed framework restrict in subclass and domain/range semantics, thus not justifying the use of OWL DL or Lite. Additionally, the need for incorporating fuzziness into the representation on the one hand and the lack of a formal notation for accomplishing this on the other renders reification the only viable choice, which in turn would cancel out the inference capabilities the adoption of OWL DL would bring. For these reasons, the RDFS language was chosen for the employed knowledge infrastructure.

An additional aspect relates to the kind of knowledge that needs to be captured. Given that image analysis and annotation relate both to domain-specific aspects, i.e. the specific domain concepts and relations, and to media-related ones, i.e. the structure of the labelled image, the corresponding knowledge infrastructure needs to capture the knowledge of both aspects in an unambiguous, machine-processable way. For the multimedia-related knowledge, the MPEG-7 specifications (Sikora 2001) have been followed, as it constitutes the main standardisation effort towards a common framework for multimedia content description. Another important requirement relates to the need for enabling extensibility in terms of incorporating image analysis annotations that adhere to possibly different models of the domain or media-related knowledge. To enable the smooth harmonisation between such annotations, a reference point is needed so that the corresponding intended meanings, i.e. ontological commitments, can be disambiguated and correctly aligned. Consequently, the use of a core ontology through its rigorous axiomatisation provides the means to handle more effectively terminological and conceptual ambiguities.

As illustrated in Fig. 4.1, the developed knowledge infrastructure follows a modular architecture where different ontologies are utilised to address the different types of knowledge required. Appropriate multimedia ontologies have been developed to describe the structure and low-level features of multimedia content, which are harmonised with the corresponding domain ontologies via the use of a core ontology. The latter has been extended to cover the concrete spatiotemporal relations required when analysing such content. Finally, a dedicated ontology has been developed to provide the vocabulary and structure of the generated annotations. In the following, we briefly overview the role of each of the ontologies. For further details, the reader is referred to Bloehdorn, Petridis, Saathoff, Simou, Tzouvaras, Avrithis, Handschuh, Kompatsiaris, Staab and Strintzis (2005).

4.3.1 Core Ontology

The role of the core ontology in this framework is threefold: (i) to serve as a starting point for the engineering of the rest of the ontologies, (ii) to serve as a bridge allowing the integration of the different ontologies employed, i.e. by providing common attachment points, and (iii) to provide a reference point for comparisons among different ontological approaches. In our framework, we utilise DOLCE (Gangemi, Guarino, Masolo, Oltramari and Schneider 2002), which was explicitly designed as a core ontology. DOLCE is minimal in the sense that it includes only the most reusable and widely applicable upper-level categories, and rigorous in terms of axiomatisation, as well as extensively researched and documented.

4.3.2 SpatioTemporal Extensions Ontology

In a separate ontology, we have extended the dolce:Region concept branch of DOLCE to accommodate topological and directional relations between regions. Directional spatial relations describe how visual segments are placed and relate to each other in 2D or 3D space (e.g. left and above), while topological spatial relations describe how the spatial boundaries of the segments relate (e.g. touches and overlaps). In a similar way, temporal relations have been introduced following Allen interval calculus (e.g. meets, before).

4.3.3 Visual Descriptor Ontology

The visual descriptor ontology (VDO) models properties that describe visual characteristics of domain objects. VDO follows the MPEG-7 visual part (ISO/IEC 2001), with some modification so as to translate the XML schema and datatype definitions into a valid RDFS representation.

4.3.4 Multimedia Structure Ontology

The multimedia structure ontology (MSO) models basic multimedia entities from the MPEG-7 MDS (ISO/IEC 2003). More specifically, the MSO covers the five MPEG-7 multimedia content types, i.e. image, video, audio, audiovisual, and multimedia, and their corresponding segment and decomposition relation types. Apart from the definition of classes (properties) reflecting the MPEG-7-defined descriptions, additional classes (relations) have been introduced to account for descriptions perceived semantically distinct, but treated ambiguously in MPEG-7 (such as the concept of frame).

4.3.5 Annotation Ontology

The annotation ontology (AO) provides the schema for linking multimedia content items to the corresponding semantic descriptions, i.e. for linking image regions to domain concept and relation labels. Furthermore, it is the AO that models the uncertainty with respect to the extracted labelling and allows the association of a degree of confidence to each label produced by the analysis.

4.3.6 Domain Ontology

In the presented multimedia annotation framework, the domain ontologies are meant to model the semantics of real-world domains that the content belongs to, such as sports events or personal holiday images. They serve a dual role: (i) they provide the vocabulary to be used in the produced annotations, thus providing the domain conceptualisation utilised during retrieval, and (ii) they provide the spatial and contextual knowledge necessary to support the context-aware and constraint reasoning refinements. As aforementioned, each domain ontology is explicitly aligned to the

DOLCE core ontology, ensuring thereby interoperability between different domain ontologies possibly used by different analysis modules.

4.4 Context Analysis

4.4.1 Ontology-Based Contextual Knowledge Representation

It should be rather clear by now that ontologies are suitable for expressing multimedia content semantics in a formal machine-processable representation that allows manual or automatic analysis and further contextual processing of the extracted semantic descriptions. Amongst all possible ways to provide an efficient knowledge representation, we propose one that relies on concepts and their relationships. In general, we may formalise domain ontologies as follows:

$$O = \{C, \{R\}\}, \text{ where } R : C \times C \to \{0, 1\} \tag{4.1}$$

where O is a domain ontology, C is a subset of the set of concepts described by the domain ontology, and R is a possible semantic relation amongst any two concepts that belong to C. In general, semantic relations describe specific kinds of links or relationships between any two concepts. In the crisp case, a semantic relation either relates ($R = 1$) or does not relate ($R = 0$) a pair of concepts with each other.

In addition, for a knowledge model to be highly descriptive, it must contain a large number of distinct and diverse relations among its concepts. A major side effect of this approach is the fact that available information will then be scattered among them, making each one of them inadequate to describe a context in a meaningful way. Consequently, relations need to be combined to provide a view of the knowledge that suffices for context definition and estimation. In this work, we utilise three types of relations, whose semantics are defined in the MPEG-7 standard, namely the *specialisation* relation Sp, the *part* relation P, and the *property* relation Pr.

The last point to consider when designing such a knowledge model is the fact that real-life data often differ from research data. Real-life information is, in principal, governed by uncertainty and fuzziness, thus herein its modelling is based on *fuzzy* relations. For the problem at hand, the above set of commonly encountered crisp relations can be modelled as fuzzy relations and can be combined for the generation of a meaningful fuzzy taxonomic relation, which will assist in the determination of context. Consequently, to tackle such complex types of relations, we propose the following "fuzzification" of the previous domain ontology definition:

$$O_F = \{C, \{r_{pq}\}\}, \text{ where } r_{pq} = F(R) : C \times C \to [0, 1] \tag{4.2}$$

where O_F defines a "fuzzified" domain ontology, C is again a subset of all possible concepts it describes, and r_{pq} denotes a fuzzy semantic relation amongst two concepts $p, q \in C$. In the fuzzy case, a fuzzy semantic relation relates a pair of concepts p, q with each other to a given degree of membership, i.e. the value of r_{pq} lies within the [0, 1] interval. More specifically, given a universe U, a crisp set C is described by a membership function $\mu_C : U \rightarrow \{0, 1\}$ (as already observed in the crisp case for R), whereas according to Klir and Yuan (1995), a fuzzy set F on C is described by a membership function $\mu_F : C \rightarrow [0, 1]$. We may describe the fuzzy set using the widely applied sum notation (Miyamoto 1990):

$$F = \sum_{i=1}^{n} c_i/w_i = \{c_1/w_1, c_2/w_2, \ldots, c_n/w_n\} \qquad (4.3)$$

where $n = |C|$ is the cardinality of set C and concept $c_i \in C$. The membership degree w_i describes the membership function $\mu_F(c_i)$, i.e. $w_i = \mu_F(c_i)$, or for the sake of simplicity, $w_i = F(c_i)$. As in Klir et al., a fuzzy relation on C is a function $r_{pq} : C \times C \rightarrow [0, 1]$ and its inverse relation is defined as $r_{pq}^{-1} = r_{qp}$. Based on the relations r_{pq} and for the purpose of image analysis, we construct the following relation T with use of the corresponding set of fuzzy relations Sp, P, and Pr:

$$T = Tr^t(Sp \cup P^{-1} \cup Pr^{-1}). \qquad (4.4)$$

Based on the roles and semantic interpretations of Sp, P, and Pr, as they are defined in the MPEG-7 MDS (ISO/IEC 2003), it is easy to see that Equation (4.4) combines them in a straightforward and meaningful way, utilising inverse functionality where it is semantically appropriate, i.e. where the meaning of one relation is semantically contradictory to the meaning of the rest on the same set of concepts. The set of the above relations is either defined explicitly in the domain ontology or is considered to be a superset of the set defined in the latter. Most commonly encountered, a domain ontology includes some relations between its concepts that are all of the *SubclassOf* type, and consequently, we extend it by defining additional semantic relations. The transitive closure relation extension Tr^t is required in both cases, in order for T to be taxonomic, as the union of transitive relations is not necessarily transitive, as discussed in Akrivas, Wallace, Andreou, Stamou and Kollias (2002).

The representation of this concept-centric contextual knowledge model follows the resource description framework (RDF) standard (Becket and McBride 2004) proposed in the context of the Semantic Web. RDF is the framework in which Semantic Web metadata statements can be expressed and represented as graphs. Relation T can be visualised as a graph, in which every node represents a concept and each edge between two nodes constitutes a contextual relation between the respective concepts. Additionally, each edge has an associated membership degree, which represents the fuzziness within the context model. A sample graph derived from the motor-sports domain is depicted in Fig. 4.3.

Representing the graph in RDF is a straightforward task, since the RDF structure itself is based on a similar graph model. Additionally, the *reification* technique (Brickley and Guha 2004) was used in order to achieve the desired expressiveness

Fig. 4.3 Graph
representation example –
motor-sports domain

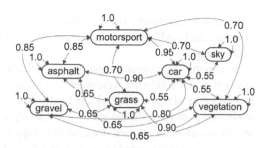

and obtain the enhanced functionality introduced by fuzziness. Representing the membership degree associated with each relation is carried out by making a statement about the statement, which contains the degree information. Representing fuzziness with such reified statements is a novel but acceptable way, since the reified statement should not be asserted automatically. For instance, having a statement such as *Motor-sportsScene part Car*, which means that a car is part of a motor-sports scene, and a membership degree of 0.75 for this statement does obviously not entail that a car is always a part of a motor-sports scene. A small illustrative example is provided in Table 4.1 for an instance of the specialisation relation Sp. As defined in the MPEG-7 standard, $Sp(x, y) > 0$ means that the meaning of x "includes" the meaning of y; the most common forms of specialisation are subclassing, i.e. x is a generalisation of y, and thematic categorisation, i.e. x is the thematic category of y. In the example, the RDF subject *wrc* (World Rally Championship) has *specialisationOf* as an RDF predicate and *rally* forms the RDF object. Additionally, the proposed reification process introduces a statement about the former statement on the *specialisationOf* resource, by stating that 0.90 is the membership degree to this relation.

4.4.2 Visual Context Analysis

Since visual context is acknowledged to be a difficult notion to grasp and capture (Mylonas and Avrithis 2005), we restrict it herein to the notion of ontological context, as the latter is defined on the "fuzzified" version of traditional ontologies presented in Section 4.4.1. From a practical point of view, we consider context as

Table 4.1 Fuzzy relation representation: RDF reification

```
<rdf:Description rdf:about="#s1">
<rdf:subject rdf:resource="&dom;wrc"/>
<rdf:predicate rdf:resource="&dom;specialisationOf"/>
<rdf:object> rdf:resource="&dom;rally"</rdf:object>
<rdf:type rdf:resource="http://www.w3.org/1999/02/22-rdf-syntax-ns#Statement"/>
<context:specialisationOf rdf:datatype="http://www.w3.org/2001/XMLSchema#float">0.90<
   /context:specialisationOf>
</rdf:Description>
```

information depicted by specific domain concepts that are identified and whose relations are analysed based on the utilised data set and not by external factors, such as EXIF metadata.

In a more formal manner, the problem that this work attempts to address is summarised in the following statement: the visual context analysis algorithm readjusts in a meaningful way the initial label confidence values produced by the prior steps of multimedia analysis. In designing such an algorithm, contextual information residing in the aforementioned domain ontology is utilised. In general, the notion of context is strongly related to the notion of ontologies since an ontology can be seen as an attempt towards modelling real-world (fuzzy) entities, and context determines the intended meaning of each concept, i.e. a concept used in different contexts may have different meanings. In this section, the problems to be addressed include how to meaningfully readjust the initial membership degrees and how to use visual context to influence the overall results of knowledge-assisted image analysis towards higher performance.

Based on the mathematical background described in the previous sections, we introduce the algorithm used to readjust the degree of membership $\mu_a(c)$ of each concept c in the fuzzy set of candidate labels $L_a = \sum_{i=1}^{|C|} c_i/\mu_a(c_i)$ associated with a region a of an image in an image scene. Each specific concept $k \in C$ present in the application domain's ontology is stored together with its relationship degrees r_{kl} to any other related concept $l \in C$.

Another important point to consider is the fact that each concept has a different probability of appearing in the scene. A flat context model (i.e. relating concepts only to the respective scene type) would not be sufficient in this case. We model a more detailed graph where ideally concepts are all related to each other, implying that the graph relations used are in fact transitive. As can be observed in Fig. 4.3, every concept participating in the contextualised ontology has at least one link to the root element. Additional degrees of confidence exist between any possible connections of nodes in the graph, whereas the root motor-sports element could be related either directly or indirectly with any other concept. To tackle cases where more than one concept is related to multiple concepts, the term context relevance $cr_{dm}(k)$ is introduced, which refers to the overall relevance of concept k to the root element characterising each domain dm. For instance, the root element of the motor-sports domain is concept $c_{motorsports}$. All possible routes in the graph are taken into consideration, forming an exhaustive approach to the domain, with respect to the fact that all routes between concepts are reciprocal.

An estimation of each concept's degree of membership is derived from direct and indirect relationships of the concept with other concepts, using a meaningful compatibility indicator or distance metric. Depending on the nature of the domains provided in the domain ontology, the best indicator could be selected using the *max* or the *min* operator, respectively. Of course the ideal distance metric for two concepts is again one that quantifies their semantic correlation. For the problem at hand, the *max* value is a meaningful measure of correlation for both of them. A simplified example derived again from the motor-sports domain ontology, assuming that the

Fig. 4.4 Graph representation example – compatibility indicator estimation

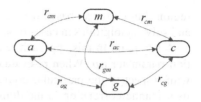

only available concepts are *motorsports* (the root element – denoted as *m*), *asphalt* (*a*), *grass* (*g*), and *car* (*c*), is presented in Fig. 4.4 and summarised in the following: let concept *a* be related to concepts *m*, *g*, and *c* directly with: r_{am}, r_{ag}, and r_{ac}, while concept *g* is related to concept *m* with r_{gm} and concept *c* is related to concept *m* with r_{cm}. Additionally, *c* is related to *g* with r_{cg}. Then, we calculate the value for $cr_{dm}(a)$:

$$cr_{dm}(a) = \max\{r_{am}, r_{ag}r_{gm}, r_{ac}r_{cm}, r_{ag}r_{cg}r_{cm}, r_{ac}r_{cg}r_{gm}\}. \tag{4.5}$$

The general structure of the degree of membership re-evaluation algorithm is as follows:

1. Identify an optimal normalisation parameter np to use within the algorithm's steps, according to the considered domain(s). The np is also referred to as domain similarity, or dissimilarity, measure and $np \in [0, 1]$.
2. For each concept *k* in the fuzzy set L_a associated with a region in a scene with a degree of membership $\mu_a(k)$, obtain the particular contextual information in the form of its relations to the set of any other concepts: $\{r_{kl} : l \in C, l \neq k\}$.
3. Calculate the new degree of membership $\mu_a(k)$ associated with the region, based on np and the context's relevance value. In the case of multiple concept relations in the ontology, when relating concept *k* to more than one concept, rather than relating *k* solely to the "root element" r^e, an intermediate aggregation step should be applied for *k*: $cr_k = \max\{r_{kr^e}, \ldots, r_{km}\}$. We express the calculation of $\mu_a(k)$ with the recursive formula:

$$\mu_a^n(k) = \mu_a^{n-1}(k) - np(\mu_a^{n-1}(k) - cr_k) \tag{4.6}$$

where *n* denotes the iteration used. Equivalently, for an arbitrary iteration *n*,

$$\mu_a^n(k) = (1 - np)^n \cdot \mu_a^0(k) + (1 - (1 - np)^n) \cdot cr_k \tag{4.7}$$

where $\mu_a^0(k)$ represents the original degree of membership.

In practice, typical values for *n* reside between 3 and 5. Interpretation of the above equations implies that the proposed contextual approach will favour confident degrees of membership for a region's concept in contradistinction to non-confident or misleading degrees of membership. It will amplify their differences, while on the other hand it will diminish confidence in clearly misleading concepts for a specific region. Furthermore, based on the supplied ontological knowledge, it will clarify and solve ambiguities in cases of similar concepts or difficult-to-analyse regions.

A key point in this approach remains the definition of a meaningful normalisation parameter np. When re-evaluating this value, the ideal np is always defined with respect to the particular domain of knowledge and is the one that quantifies its semantic correlation to the domain. Application of a series of experiments on a training set of images for every application domain results in the definition of an np corresponding to the best overall evaluation score values for each domain. Thus, the proposed algorithm readjusts in a meaningful manner the initial degrees of membership, utilising semantics in the form of the contextual information that resides in the constructed "fuzzified" ontology.

4.5 Constraint Reasoning to Eliminate Ambiguities in Labelled Images

So far, the initial labelling provides a hypothesis set of labels for each segment, that is computed based on the low-level features extracted from the specific segment. Each label is associated with a degree of confidence, indicating how likely the label is to be depicted. The context algorithm introduces global context into the labelling by readjusting the degrees for each label. In this section, we will discuss the application of spatial knowledge to the initially labelled image, with the goal to identify a final and spatially consistent labelling. The spatial knowledge will be represented by a set of spatial constraints, and the initially labelled image will be transformed into a *constraint satisfaction problem (CSP)*, which will be solved using standard constraint reasoning techniques.

4.5.1 Constraint Satisfaction Problems

Informally, a constraint satisfaction problem (CSP) consists of a number of variables and a number of constraints. A variable is defined by its domain, i.e. the set of values that can be assigned to the variable, and a constraint relates several variables and thereby restricts the legal assignments of values to each of the involved variables. *Constraint reasoning* is the process of computing a solution to the given CSP, i.e. an assignment of values to the variables that satisfy all the given constraints on the variable.

In Fig. 4.5, a simple CSP is depicted, containing three variables x, y, and z and three constraints. The domains of x, y, and z are $D(x) = \{1, 2, 3\}$, $D(y) = \{2, 3, 4\}$, and $D(z) = \{2, 3\}$. The constraints are $x = y$, $x = z$, and $y = z$, so that in a solution to the problem, the values of x, y, and z must be equal.

Formally, a CSP consists of a set of variables $V = \{v_1, \ldots, v_k\}$ and a set of constraints $C = \{c_1, \ldots, c_l\}$. Each variable v_i has an associated domain $D(v_i) = \{l_1, \ldots, l_m\}$, which contains all values that can be assigned to v_i. Each

Fig. 4.5 A simple constraint satisfaction problem

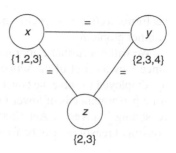

constraint c_j is a relation on the domains of a set of variables, $v_1, \ldots, v_r \in V$, such that a constraint c_j is defined as $c_j \subseteq D(v_1) \times \cdots \times D(v_r)$. The constraint is said to be solved iff both $c_j = D(v_1) \times \cdots \times D(v_r)$ and c_j is non-empty. A CSP is solved iff both all of its constraints are solved and no domain is empty and failed iff it contains either an empty domain or an empty constraint.

A variety of techniques have been proposed to solve constraint satisfaction problems, and they are usually collected under the name *constraint reasoning*. One can distinguish between two major types of solving techniques: consistency techniques and search methods. Consistency techniques try to simplify subproblems of a given CSP. However, a CSP that is locally consistent, i.e. where each relevant subproblem is consistent, is not necessarily (and in fact usually not) globally consistent. As an example consider *arc consistency*. Arc consistency only considers one constraint at a time. The constraint is said to be arc consistent if for each assignment of a domain value to a variable of the constraint, assignments to all other related variables exist that satisfy the constraint. This variable is said to have support in the other domains. A CSP is arc consistent if each of its constraints is arc consistent.

Now, in the example of Fig. 4.5, the domain of x, y, and z would all be reduced to $\{2, 3\}$ by an arc consistency algorithm. One can easily verify this, since an assignment of 1 to x would in every case violate the constraint $x = y$, since 1 is not a member of $D(y)$, and the same is true for an assignment $y = 4$, which has support neither in $D(x)$ nor in $D(z)$.

Local consistency can remove values from the domains of variables that will never take part in a solution. This can already be useful in some scenarios, but usually one searches for a concrete solution to a given CSP, i.e a unique assignment of values to variables that satisfy all the given constraints. As we can see from the example, an arc consistent CSP does not provide this solution directly. Obviously, assigning an arbitrary value from the remaining domains will not yield a valid solution. For instance, the assignment $x = 2$, $y = 2$, $z = 3$ only uses values from the arc consistent domains, but it is not a solution.

Therefore, in order to compute a concrete solution, search techniques are employed, such as backtracking. Often local consistency checks and search are integrated in hybrid algorithms, which prune the search space during search using local consistency notions and thus provide an improved runtime performance. However, solving CSPs efficiently is highly problem specific, and a method that performs well for a specific problem might have a much worse performance in another problem.

We will not further elaborate on local consistency notions and search techniques since they are out of the scope of this chapter. We assume that standard methods are employed to solve the constraint satisfaction problems we generate and that run-time performance is of lower priority. In general, a good introduction to constraint reasoning is given in Apt (2003). An overview of recent research in the field of constraint reasoning can be found in the survey presented in Bartak (1999).

4.5.2 Image Labelling as a Constraint Satisfaction Problem

In order to disambiguate the region labels using a constraint reasoning approach, we have to

1. represent the employed knowledge as constraints and
2. transform a segmented image into a CSP.

Spatial relations provide an important means to interpret images and disambiguate region labels. Although heuristic, they give very valuable hints on what kind of object is depicted in a specific location. So, one would never expect a car depicted in the sky, or in the context of our framework, one would not expect the sky to be depicted below the sea in a beach image. Obviously, in order to use spatial knowledge for this kind of multimedia reasoning, the core elements are the spatial relations between the regions and the knowledge about the expected spatial arrangements of objects (i.e. labels) in a given domain.

It is obvious that, projected on the terminology of CSPs, the regions will become variables of the resulting CSP and that the spatial relations will be modelled as constraints on those variables. In the following section, we will first discuss how to define spatial constraints and then, in the subsequent section, introduce the transformation of an initially labelled image into a CSP.

4.5.2.1 Spatial Constraints

The purpose of a spatial constraint is to reduce the number of labellings for a number of segments that are arranged in a specific spatial relationship. In other words, if a segment is above another segment, we want to make sure that the lower segment only gets the label *Sky* if the upper one has a compatible label, such as *Sky* or *Cloud*. We will therefore define for each *spatial relation* that we want to consider a corresponding *spatial constraint type* that encodes the valid labellings as tuples of allowed labels. We will also call this set of tuples the domain of the constraint type. The concrete *spatial constraint* that is instantiated between a set of variables will then be formed by the intersection of the constraint type domain and the cross-product of the relevant variable domains.

Let SR now be the set of spatial relations under consideration and $r_t \in SR$ be a spatial relation of type t. Furthermore, O is the set of all possible labels of a given application domain. We then define the domain of a spatial constraint type t to be $D(t) \subseteq O^n$, with n being the arity of the spatial relation. Obviously, each tuple in the domain of the constraint type is supposed to be a valid arrangement of labels for the spatial relation of type t.

Now, let $V := \{v_1, \ldots, v_n\}$ be a set of variables related by a spatial relation $r_t \in SR$ and $D(t)$ the corresponding domain for the spatial relation. A constraint c_V^t of type t on the set of variables V is now defined as $c_V^t := D(t) \cap (D(v_1) \times \cdots \times D(v_n))$. Apparently, c_V^t now is a relation on the variable domains containing only those tuples that are allowed for the spatial relation r_t.

Currently, we only consider two types of spatial relations: relative and absolute. Relative spatial relations are binary and derived from spatial relations that describe the relative position of one segment with respect to another, such as *contained-in* or *above-of*. Absolute spatial constraints are derived from the absolute positions of segments on the image, such as *above-all*, and which are apparently unary constraints.

4.5.2.2 Transformation

In order to describe the transformation of an initially segmented and labelled image, we will shortly introduce some formal notions. Let a labelled image be a tuple $I = (S, SR)$, where S is the set of segments produced by the initial segmentation and SR is the set of spatial relations extracted by the spatial extraction module. For each segment $s \in S$, the hypothesis set of initial labels is denoted as $ls(s)$. The set of all possible labels is named O and $ls(s) \in O$ must hold. Each spatial relationship $r_t \in SR$ is of type t and has an associated domain of $D(t)$.

Transforming a labelled image into a CSP is now a straightforward process. For each segment, a variable is created and the hypotheses sets become the domains of the variables. For each spatial relation, a constraint with the corresponding type is added. In the following, we will formalise the transformation.

Let $I = (S, SR)$ be a labelled image as introduced above; then the algorithm to transform I into a corresponding CSP is as follows:

1. For each segment $s \in S$ create a variable v^s.
2. For the newly created variable v^s, set the domain to $D(v^s) = ls(s)$.
3. Let SR be the set of all spatial relations defined in the domain knowledge, then add for each spatial relation $r_t \in SR$ between a number of segments $s_1, \ldots, s_n \in S$ a constraint $c_{\{v_1, \ldots, v_n\}}^t$ to the CSP, where $v_1, \ldots, v_n$ are the variables created from $s_1, \ldots, s_n$.

The result is a CSP conforming to what was introduced in Section 4.5.1. Standard constraint reasoning techniques can be used to solve the CSP, and because of the finiteness of the problem, all solutions can be computed. The latter property is quite useful, since the degree of confidence produced during the initial labelling, which is currently not employed during the constraint reasoning, can afterwards be used to rank the solutions according to the labels' degrees. If only one solution would be computed, one would have to accept the first one found.

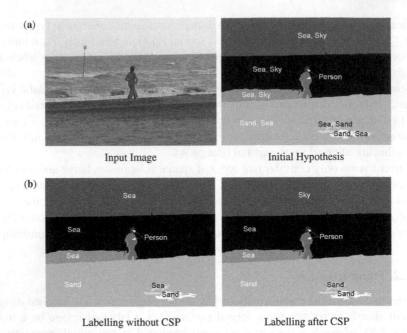

Fig. 4.6 Example of CSP application

An example is depicted in Fig. 4.6, where the input image, the initial set of hypotheses, the corresponding labelling that would have been produced without constraint reasoning, and the labelling after the constraint reasoning are depicted. Please note that for the initial labelling, the labels with the highest score are kept for each segment. It is easy to see that two errors were made by the segment classification. The topmost segment was labelled as *Sea* instead of *Sky* and one of the small segments within the sand region was labelled with *Sea*. After applying the constraint reasoning, both erroneous labels have been corrected. For the topmost segment, the absolute spatial relation *above-all* restricts the segment to the label *Sky* and the second wrong label was corrected using the *contained-in* constraint that does not allow a *Sand* segment to contain a *Sea* segment.

4.6 Experimental Results and Evaluation

In this section, we present experimental results and evaluation of the enhancement achieved by the application of the proposed context analysis and constraint reasoning modules over typical image analysis. As aforementioned, under the proposed framework, image analysis is treated as a black box, and different implementations can be used interchangeably. In the presented experimentation, we followed the approach presented in Petridis, Bloehdorn, Saathoff, Simou, Dasiopoulou, Tzouvaras, Handschuh, Avrithis, Kompatsiaris and Staab (2006) for two main reasons:

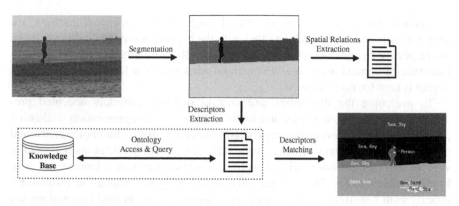

Fig. 4.7 Image analysis architecture

(i) the presented approach is quite generic, not making use of domain-specific implementation and tuning that would boost performance, and (ii) the produced annotations adhere to the proposed framework ontology infrastructure, thus making the application of the framework straightforward, without the need for an intermediate aligning step to harmonise the annotations' semantics with the corresponding framework.

The overall architecture of the analysis used for experimentation is illustrated in Fig. 4.7. First segmentation is applied to partition the image into a set of segments. Subsequently, for each of the resulting segments, the dominant colour, homogeneous texture, and region shape descriptors are extracted, and additionally, the spatial relations between adjacent segments are estimated. Initial sets of graded hypotheses, i.e. sets of labels with associated degrees of confidence, are generated for each image segment through the computation of matching distances between each segment's descriptors and the prototypical values defined for the considered domain objects. These prototypical values are created using the M-OntoMat-Annotizer tool, which enables users to annotate segments with concepts from a given ontology and then extract selected descriptors, thus allowing the linking of low-level visual features to domain concepts (Petridis, Bloehdorn, Saathoff, Simou, Dasiopoulou, Tzouvaras, Handschuh, Avrithis, Kompatsiaris and Staab 2006).

For the experimentation, a set of 150 images from the beach domain has been assembled, 30 of which were used as the training set for estimating the parameter values required for context analysis, as well as to statistically induce the initial fuzzy values of relations utilised within the context ontology. The resulting 120 images have first undergone the aforementioned analysis in order to obtain the corresponding initial annotation (labelling). Then, the proposed framework was applied. First, the context analysis module, exploiting the domain concepts' associations and the information extracted through training, readjusts the annotations' degrees of confidence towards more meaningful values. Secondly, the constraint reasoner, applying the spatial rules on the contextually refined labels results in the removal of those that violate the domain spatial topology. To quantify the performance of image analysis, and allow us to measure the enhancement brought by the proposed framework, we keep for each image segment the label with the highest degree of confidence from the respective hypotheses set as the analysis results. Similarly, to measure the performance of context analysis and constraint reasoning, the label with the highest degree is kept for each segment.

To overcome the difficulties and cost in defining generally accepted pre-annotated segmentation masks and avoid getting into a segmentation evaluation process, a grid-based evaluation approach has been followed. This choice is justified by the given evaluation context as well, since contrary to applications that require very accurate object boundaries detection, it allows a certain tolerance for these kinds of inaccuracies. More specifically, in the proposed evaluation framework, ground truth construction and comparison against the examined annotations are both performed at block level. The grid size is selected with respect to the desired degree of evaluation precision: the smaller the block size, the greater the accuracy attained. To evaluate an annotation, the corresponding annotated mask is partitioned according to the selected grid size, and the annotations within each block are compared to the ground truth.

To quantify the performance, we adopted the precision and recall metrics from the information retrieval (IR) field. For each domain concept, *precision* (p) defines the proportion of correctly annotated segments cf over all the number of segments annotated with that concept f, while *recall* (r) is the proportion of correctly annotated segments over the number of segments depicting that concept in reality c. To determine the overall performance per concept, all c, f, and cf for each of the respective concepts are added up, and using the above formulae, overall precision and recall values are calculated. Additionally, the *F-measure* was used to obtain a single metric. The *F-measure* is the harmonic mean of precision and recall, i.e. $F = 2pr/(p + r)$, and contrary to the arithmetic mean, it gets large only if both precision and recall are large. In the case that a concept was not depicted in an image at all, all three values are set to 0, so that they do not influence the overall computation. Furthermore, objects that appear in the test images but do not belong to the supported set of concepts have not been taken into account, since they do not add to assessing the proposed modules performance.

In the current experimentation, six concepts have been considered, namely *Cliff*, *Person*, *Plant*, *Sand*, *Sea*, and *Sky*. In Table 4.2, the precision (p), recall (r), and *F-measure* (f) are given for the examined test images with respect to sole image analysis, image analysis followed by context analysis, and image analysis followed by constraint reasoning respectively, while in Table 4.3, the integrated performance is shown. From the obtained results, one easily notes that in almost all cases, precision and recall improve. The actual percentage of the gained performance improvement differs with respect to the concept considered, as each concept bears less or more semantic information. For example, a lower improvement is observed with respect to the concept *Person*, as due to over- and under-segmentation phenomena the effects of the transition from 2D to 3D, and its generic context of appearance a region depicting a *Person* may validly appear almost in any configuration with respect to the rest of the domain concepts. Observing the integrated context

Table 4.2 Evaluation results for the beach domain (where IA, CTX and CSP stand for image analysis, context, and constraint reasoning, respectively)

Concept	IA			IA+CTX			IA+CSP		
	p	r	f	p	r	f	p	r	f
Cliff	0.09	0.20	0.12	0.30	0.94	0.46	0.47	0.40	0.44
Person	0.56	0.40	0.47	1.00	0.07	0.14	0.61	0.40	0.48
Plant	0.35	0.77	0.48	0.72	0.26	0.38	0.85	0.89	0.87
Sand	0.82	0.80	0.81	0.90	0.95	0.92	0.81	0.94	0.87
Sea	0.87	0.58	0.70	0.90	0.83	0.86	0.87	0.49	0.63
Sky	0.86	0.89	0.87	0.94	0.94	0.94	0.80	0.95	0.87
AVG	0.73	0.73	0.73	0.84	0.85	0.84	0.77	0.75	0.76

Table 4.3 Evaluation results for the beach domain for the combined application of context and constraint reasoning over image analysis

	IA+CTX+CSP		
Concept	p	r	f
Cliff	0.38	0.94	0.54
Person	1.00	0.14	0.25
Plant	0.82	0.48	0.61
Sand	0.90	0.97	0.93
Sea	0.90	0.86	0.88
Sky	0.95	0.91	0.93
AVG	0.86	0.86	0.86

analysis and constraint reasoning results, it is noted that the latter adds only a little to the attained performance, compared to when combined with image analysis only. However, given the set of concepts currently supported and the inaccuracies of the segmentation, this is an expected outcome. Having a broader set of concepts from different and possibly partial overlapping domains (in terms of concepts included) would lower the context refinement accuracy and would make more evident the role of spatial consistency for disambiguation.

4.7 Conclusions and Further Discussions

In this chapter, we have proposed an ontology-based framework for enhancing semantic image analysis through the refinement of initially available annotations by means of explicit knowledge about context of appearance and spatial constraints of the considered semantic objects. Following the proposed framework, one can smoothly integrate independent analysis modules benefiting from the knowledge sharing facilities provided by the use of ontologies and from the sole dependency of context analysis and constraint reasoning from the available knowledge that decouples them from the actual analysis. Consequently, the main contributions of the proposed framework can be summarised as follows: (i) the formal representation of context of appearance semantics in an ontology compliant way that facilitates its integration within knowledge-based multimedia analysis, and a methodology for its application; (ii) the adoption of a constraint problem solving methodology within the semantic image annotation domain for addressing topological knowledge; and (iii) the proposed framework that supports its applicability and extensibility to different image analysis applications.

Future directions include further investigation of the proposed framework using more concepts, thereby making available additional knowledge, i.e. more spatial constraints and contextual associations. More specifically, with respect to the constraint reasoner, a fuzzified extension is under investigation in order to provide greater flexibility and better scalability to broader domains. Introducing such uncertainty support will enable the handling of situations that cannot be adequately modelled in the provided domain knowledge, and for which the current crisp implementation may fail to provide a solution, i.e. none of the values may satisfy the constraints. Another appealing characteristic of using a fuzzy CSP approach is that preferences among certain solutions can be captured, as for instance solutions where the sea is above the sand. Furthermore, since the manual definition of constraints for large numbers of concepts is infeasible and error-prone, a heuristic approach towards a more efficient acquisition needs to be investigated. With respect to contextual knowledge modelling and utilisation, an interesting future aspect refers to the exploration of additional semantic associations between the concepts that participate in a domain and the interdependencies that emerge from overlapping sets of concepts between different domains. Finally, experimentation with alternative analysis modules or their combination would provide useful and concrete insight into the proposed framework contribution in real applications scenarios.

Acknowledgments The work presented in this chapter was partially supported by the European Commission under contract FP6-001765 aceMedia.

References

Akrivas, G., Wallace, M., Andreou, G., Stamou, G. and Kollias, S. (2002) *Context – Sensitive Semantic Query Expansion*. In: Proceedings of the IEEE International Conference on Artificial Intelligence Systems (ICAIS), Divnomorskoe, Russia.

Apt, K. (2003) *Principles of Constraint Programming*. In: Cambridge University Press, Cambridge.

Bartak, R. (1999) *Constraint Programming: In Pursuit of the Holy Grail*. In: Proceedings of Week of Doctoral Students (WDS99), pp. 555–564.

Becket, D. and McBride, B. (2004) *RDF/XML Syntax Specification, W3C Recommendation, 10 February*.

Bloehdorn, S., Petridis, K., Saathoff, C., Simou, N. Tzouvaras, V., Avrithis, Y., Handschuh, S., Kompatsiaris, I., Staab, S. and Strintzis. M.G. (2005) *Semantic Annotation of Images and Videos for Multimedia Analysis*. In: Proceedings of the 2nd European Semantic Web Conference (ESWC), Heraklion, Greece.

Boutell, M. (2006) *Exploiting Context for Semantic Scene Classification*. In: Technical Report 894 (Ph.D. Thesis), University of Rochester.

Boutell, M. and Luo, J. (2005) *Beyond Pixels: Exploiting Camera Metadata for Photo Classification*. In: Pattern Recognition 38(6).

Brickley, D. and Guha, R.V. (2004) *RDF Schema Specification 1.0, W3C Recommendation, 10 February*.

Dasiopoulou, S., Mezaris, V., Kompatsiaris, I., Papastathis, V.K., and Strintzis, M.G. (2005) *Knowledge-Assisted Semantic Video Object Detection*. In: IEEE Transactions on Circuits and Systems for Video Technology, vol. 15, no 10, pp. 1210–1224.

Gangemi, A., Guarino, N., Masolo, C., Oltramari, A. and Schneider, L. (2002) *Sweetening Ontologies with DOLCE*. In: Knowledge Engineering and Knowledge Management. Ontologies and the Semantic Web, Proceedings of the 13th International Conference on Knowledge Acquisition, Modeling and Management (EKAW), Siguenza, Spain.

Haralick, R.M. and Shapiro, L.G. (1979) *The Consistent Labeling Problem: Part I*. In: IEEE Transactions on Pattern Analysis and Machine Intelligence, vol. 1, pp. 173–184.

Hollink, L., Little, S. and Hunter, J. (2005) *Evaluating the Application of Semantic Inferencing rules to Image Annotation*. In: K-CAP, pp. 91–98.

Hotz, L. and Neumann, B. (2005) *Scene Interpretation as a Configuration Task*. In: Künstliche Intelligenz, pp. 59–65.

ISO/IEC (2001) 15938-3:2001: *Information Technology – Multimedia Content Description Interface – Part 3 visual*. Version 1.

ISO/IEC (2003) 15938-5:2003: *Information Technology – Multimedia Content Description Interface – Part 5: Multimedia Description Schemes*. First Edition.

Klir G., Yuan, B. (1995) *Fuzzy Sets and Fuzzy Logic, Theory and Applications*. In: New Jersey, Prentice Hall.

Kolbe. T.H. (1998) *Constraints for Object Recognition in Aerial Images – Handling of Unobserved Features*. In: Lecture Notes in Computer Science, vol. 1520.

Le Saux, B., Amato, G. (2004) *Image Classifiers for Scene Analysis*. In: International Conference on Computer Vision and Graphics (ICCVG), Warsaw, Poland.

Little, S. and Hunter, J. (2004) *Rules-By-Example – A Novel Approach to Semantic Indexing and Querying of Images*. In: International Semantic Web Conference (ISWC), pp. 534–548.

Luo, J., Singhal, A., and Zhu, W. (2003) *Natural Object Detection in Outdoor Scenes Based on Probabilistic Spatial Context Models*. In: Proceedings of IEEE International Conference on Multimedia and Expo (ICME), pp. 457–461.

Maillot, N. and Thonnat, M. (2005) *A Weakly Supervised Approach for Semantic Image Indexing and Retrieval*. In: CIVR, pp. 629–638.

Miyamoto, S. (1990) *Fuzzy Sets in Information Retrieval and Cluster Analysis*. In: Kluwer Academic Publishers, Dordrecht, Boston, London.

Mylonas, Ph. and Avrithis, Y. (2005) *Context modeling for multimedia analysis and use*. In: Proceedings of 5th International and Interdisciplinary Conference on Modeling and Using Context, Paris, France.

Murphy, P., Torralba, A., and Freeman, W. (2003) *Using the forest to See the Trees: a Graphical Model Relating Features, Objects and Scenes*. In: Advances in Neural Information Processing Systems 16 (NIPS), Vancouver, BC, MIT Press.

Naphade, M., Kozintsev, I. and Huang, T.S. (2002) *Factor Graph Framework for Semantic Indexing and Retrieval in Video*. In: IEEE Transactions on Circuits Systems Video Technology, vol. 12, no 1, pp. 40–52.

Neumann, B. and Möller, R. (2004) *On Scene Interpretation with Description Logics*. In: Technical report FBI-B-257/04, University of Hamburg, Computer Science Department.

Petridis, K., Anastasopoulos, D., Saathoff, C., Timmermann, N., Kompatsiaris, I., and Staab, S. (2006) *M-OntoMat-Annotizer: Image Annotation. Linking Ontologies and Multimedia Low-Level Features*. In: 10th International Conference on Knowledge-Based and Intelligent Information and Engineering Systems (KES 2006), Bournemouth, UK, October.

Petridis, K. Bloehdorn, S., Saathoff, C., Simou, N., Dasiopoulou, S., Tzouvaras, V., Handschuh, S., Avrithis, Y., Kompatsiaris, I., and Staab, S. (2006) *Knowledge Representation and Semantic*

Annotation of Multimedia Content. IEE Proceedings on Vision Image and Signal Processing, Special issue on Knowledge-Based Digital Media Processing, Vol. 153, No. 3, pp. 255–262, June.

Schober, J.P, Hermes, T. and Herzog, O. (2004) *Content-Based Image Retrieval by Ontology-based Object Recognition.* In: Proceedings of the KI-2004 Workshop on Applications of Description Logics (ADL), Ulm, Germany.

Sikora, T. (2001) *The MPEG-7 Visual Standard for Content Description – an Overview.* In: Special Issue on MPEG-7, IEEE Transactions on Circuits and Systems for Video Technology, 11/6:696–702, June.

Srihari, R.K. and Zhang, Z. (2000) *Show&Tell: A Semi-Automated Image Annotation System.* In: IEEE MultiMedia, vol. 7, no 3, pp. 63–71.

Sutherland, I.E. (1963), *Sketchpad: A Man-Machine Graphical Communication System.* In: PhD thesis, Massachusetts Institute of Technology.

Vailaya, A. and Jain, A. (2000) *Detecting Sky and Vegetation in Outdoor Images.* In: Proceedings of SPIE, vol. 3972, January.

Waltz, D. (1975) *Understanding Line Drawings of Scenes with Shadows.* In: The Psychology of Computer Vision,McGraw-Hill, Winston, Patrick Henry, New York.

Wiebe, J., Hirst, G., and Horton, D. (1996) *Language Use in Context.* In: Communications of the ACM, 39(1), pp. 102–111.

Chapter 5
Audio Content Analysis

Juan José Burred, Martin Haller, Shan Jin, Amjad Samour, and Thomas Sikora

5.1 Introduction

Since the introduction of digital audio more than 30 years ago, computers and signal processors have been capable of storing, modifying and transmitting sound signals. Before the advent of the Internet, compression technologies and digital telephony, such systems were aimed at the highest possible reproduction quality from physical media, or constrained to very specialised voice recognition or security systems. The first set of widespread techniques aimed at the extraction of semantics from audio were automatic speech recognition (ASR) systems. In the last couple of years, large-scale, online distribution of high-quality audio has become a reality, widening the type of sounds to be analysed to music and any other kind of sounds, and shifting computers to the central position on the user side of the audio distribution chain. This has mainly been motivated by the advances in audio compression algorithms, especially the enormously successful MP3, and in network technologies.

Audio content analysis (ACA), i.e. the automatic extraction of semantic information from sounds, arose naturally from the need to efficiently manage the growing collections of data and to enhance man–machine communication. ACA typically delivers a set of numerical measures from the audio signals, called audio features, that offer a compact and representative description. Such measures are usually called low-level features to denote that they represent a low level of abstraction. Although the classification is not strict, it is possible to consider as low-level features the measures most directly tied to the shape of the signal in the time or spectral domain, and which are mostly applicable to any kind of audio. Mid- and high-level features provide information more easily processed and usable by humans like phonemes, words or prosody in the case of speech or melody, harmony and structure in the case of music. To ensure interoperability, both low- and mid-level features can be

J.J. Burred
Communication Systems Group, Technische Universität Berlin, Sekr. EN 1, Einsteinufer 17, 10587 Berlin, Germany
e-mail: burred@nue.tu-berlin.de

Y. Kompatsiaris, P. Hobson (eds.), *Semantic Multimedia and Ontologies,* 123
© Springer Science+Business Media, LLC 2008

conveyed as metadata by standardised syntactical formalisations, the most important of which is the audio part of the MPEG-7 standard (ISO/IEC 2002), based on the XML mark-up language.

As a demanding pattern recognition problem, most ACA systems are still in the development and testing stage, with the exception of speech recognition systems. However, the advent of collaborative filtering methods and of semantic web technologies in the last couple of years allows us to envisage effective multimedia information retrieval systems that combine social and cultural metadata (i.e. the context) with the signal-related features (the content). Fixed taxonomies are evolving into dynamic ontologies that can encompass metadata from very heterogeneous sources; syntactic languages such as XML are evolving into semantic languages such as OWL (web ontology language). Sound data plays a crucial role in this paradigm shift since it represents both the most natural way of human communication (speech) and the most powerful digital entertainment industry (music). Several online services that are solely based on cultural or manually annotated metadata, and which will be mentioned later in the chapter, are enjoying a huge success to the present date. The current challenge is to combine that information with the features delivered by ACA in such a way that both robustness and usability are enhanced.

The role of ACA within the emerging semantic technologies is thus twofold. On the one hand, it implements itself a powerful set of applications such as speech recognition, speaker segmentation, or music analysis, which solve specific needs of semantical access. On the other hand, it constitutes the basis of the bottom-up approach to overcome the semantic gap by defining a mapping between physical features and ontologic knowledge representations. The latter aspect has only recently been addressed, and little work has been done with generalised audio in this context. One of the few works that follow an ontological approach to generalised audio (i.e. speech, music, or noise) is the one by Nakatani and Okuno (1998). In this case, an ontology has been used to integrate different systems for stream segregation. More specific cases, like recommendation systems based on music ontologies, have gained more attention and will be briefly addressed in the corresponding sections.

The present chapter provides an extensive insight into ACA techniques and their state of the art, and presents several recent systems as illustration. After a brief general overview (Section 5.2), this chapter follows the blocks in Fig. 5.1. The *audio classification and segmentation* stage (Section 5.3) recognises the different audio types contained in a general audio signal and their temporal borders. The following analysis techniques are adapted to audio content. For a speech signal, speaker segmentation or spoken content indexing can be applied. *Speaker segmentation* (Section 5.4) identifies speaker change points and speaker identities. *Spoken content indexing and spoken document retrieval* (Section 5.5) are used to extract the text or even sub-word units from speech signals and use these metadata for retrieval tasks. *Music content analysis* (Section 5.6) techniques are applied for music signals. The chapter concludes (Section 5.7) with a summarisation and an outlook on further research directions in the field of audio content analysis.

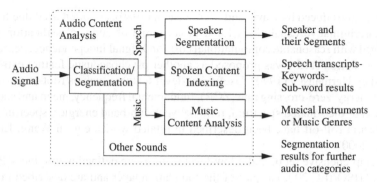

Fig. 5.1 Audio content analysis

5.2 Overview of Audio Content Analysis

In a general ACA system using supervised machine learning techniques, the following four stages can be identified: feature extraction, temporal feature integration, dimension reduction, training/testing and late information fusion, as shown in Fig. 5.2. Feature extraction and training/testing are the two essential and mandatory parts, whereas feature integration, dimension reduction, and information fusion are optional. The following sections will introduce the mentioned building blocks.

5.2.1 Feature Extraction

ACA is based on the successive extraction of feature vectors (patterns) from the original signals within time intervals of a given duration. The length of such an analysis frame should be chosen in such a way that the extracted features remain reasonably constant within it and is usually in the range of tens of milliseconds (which is referred to as *short-time* rate). Most audio features are extracted on a short-time basis, even if they can be later subjected to temporal integration over longer time windows, as it will be explained later.

A wide variety of low-level audio features have been proposed. It is not the scope of the present chapter to address feature extraction in detail; instead, we will briefly mention some of the most important ones. The Mel frequency cepstral coefficients

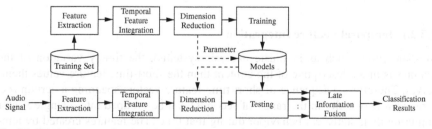

Fig. 5.2 Block diagram of a general audio content analysis system

(MFCCs), introduced by Davis and Mermelstein (1980), are often used due to their good discriminative capabilities for a broad range of audio classification tasks, combined with reasonable computational costs and signal independence. Perceptual linear prediction (PLP) was proposed as another psychoacoustic feature extraction method by Hermansky (1990). Useful low-level features such as root-mean-square (RMS) energy, zero-crossing rate (ZCR), fundamental frequency, mean and standard deviation of the squared spectrum, ratio between sub-band energies, spectrum flux, and spectral roll-off have been described in related works, e.g. in Wang, Liu and Huang (2000).

A comprehensive set of audio low-level features are defined within the MPEG-7 standard (ISO/IEC 2002) as part of the foundation layer and are described in more detail in Kim, Moreau and Sikora (2005). This set comprises basic (waveform, power), basic spectral (envelope, centroid, spread and flatness), signal parameter (fundamental frequency, harmonicity), timbral temporal (log attack time, temporal centroid), timbral spectral (harmonic spectral centroid, deviation, spread, variation and spectral centroid), and spectral basis (spectrum projection and basis) descriptors as well as a silence descriptor. The first amendment of the MPEG-7 audio part (ISO/IEC 2004) introduces additional audio low-level features (background noise level, relative delay, balance, DC offset, cross-channel correlation, and bandwidth) for the audio signal quality on an audio segment level.

5.2.2 Information Fusion

Information fusion techniques combine different sources of information for a new representation or for decision-making. Following Sanderson and Paliwala (2004), these techniques can be subdivided into three categories: pre-mapping (early fusion), midst-mapping and post-mapping (late fusion). Temporal feature integration can be seen as a pre-mapping of short-time features into measures regarding the long-term properties. Also, the concatenation of feature vectors from different feature extraction methods is a pre-mapping technique. The midst-mapping technique, however, performs feature fusion later during the classification process. This technique addresses the problem of fusion of features coming from different modalities with different temporal resolutions. Finally, late information fusion or post-mapping takes place after the classification. Both early and late information fusion techniques are addressed in the following two sections.

5.2.2.1 Temporal Feature Integration

In some cases (such as in music analysis systems), the timely variation of the features is more descriptive of the content than the short-time feature values themselves. Therefore, a sequence of short-time feature vectors spanning a certain *texture window* (usually in the range of seconds) can be grouped into a single vector capturing their statistical behaviour during that time. The features created by temporally integrating short-time feature vectors are called *sub-features*.

One simple example of feature integration is to compute the mean and variance of each short-time feature during the texture window and to define the new sub-feature vector with their values. More sophisticated techniques include using the coefficients of an autoregressive (AR) model as sub-features, or multivariate techniques accounting also for the correlation between different features (Meng and Shawe-Taylor 2005).

5.2.2.2 Late Information Fusion

Late information fusion techniques combine the results of different classifiers for decision-making. Depending on the classifier type, the results can be either hard decisions or a set of confidence values. In the former case, decision fusion methods are used together with hard decisions for specific classes. This includes majority voting, combination of ranked lists and the application of AND or OR operations. In the latter case, opinion fusion (also known as score fusion or expert fusion) techniques can be applied to confidence values yielded by different classifiers.

5.2.3 Dimension Reduction

A well-known phenomenon in pattern recognition, the *curse of dimensionality*, states that increasing the number of features used for classification (i.e. the dimensionality of the feature space), with the corresponding increase in computational requirements, does not necessarily result in higher classification accuracies. Occasionally, it can even produce worse results (see Chapter 9). To avoid this, some systems include a dimension reduction step prior to classification, which should have as little influence on the classification accuracy as possible. Dimension reduction is usually performed either by automatic feature subset selection (FSS) algorithms or by adaptive linear transforms such as principal component analysis (PCA), which is optimal for representation or compression purposes, or linear discriminant analysis (LDA), optimal for classification purposes. In the case of FSS, a subset of features is selected out of the initial set of features according to a certain objective function. In the transformation case, the original features are combined as a weighted sum to create new ones with enhanced discriminative capabilities. Typically, in audio applications, a reduction of 1/4 to 1/3 of the original dimensionality can be achieved without significantly affecting the performance, although this can greatly vary depending on the features and classifier used.

5.2.4 Machine Learning: Supervised Classification and Clustering

Pattern classification can be either supervised or unsupervised. Supervised classification works on the basis of a predefined class taxonomy. The term *supervised* denotes that the algorithm developer must rely on a training database, i.e. a collection of feature vectors that must have been previously labelled manually, and that he will use to derive the decision process involved in the classification. This *training* can be done, e.g. by estimating the parameters of the probability distribution which is assumed to model the classes (parametric methods), or, more generally, by partitioning the sample space into class regions delimited by decision boundaries. Then, the classification rule is applied to unknown incoming feature vectors to assign class membership. Examples of supervised systems include speaker verification, speech recognition, music genre classification and musical instrument classification. Many standard methods of pattern recognition are used within audio applications, including *k-nearest neighbour* (*k*-NN) classifiers, *Gaussian mixture models* (GMM), *support vector machines* (SVM), *hidden Markov models* (HMM) and neural networks. The interested reader is referred to Duda, Hart and Stork (2000) or Theodoridis and Koutroumbas (2006).

Figure 5.3 shows an example of a generic supervised audio classification process using temporal feature integration. The short-time features extracted from the audio signal (here are shown, as an example, root-mean-square energy, spectral centroid and flatness) are measured statistically over longer texture windows (in the range of seconds) in order to capture long-term behaviours. These measurements form the elements of a feature vector. In the feature space, the unlabelled input vector (denoted in the figure by the question mark) is assigned a class according to its position relative to decision boundaries, which are derived from a collection of labelled vectors (shown here for two different classes as dark and light points) during the training process.

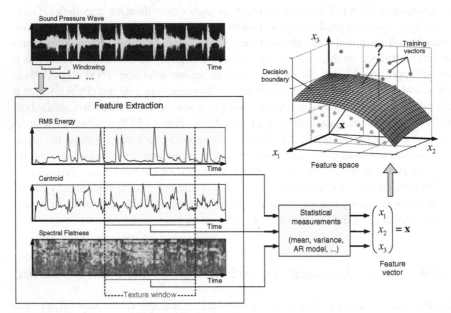

Fig. 5.3 Supervised classification with temporal feature integration. The example shows RMS energy, spectral centroid and spectral flatness as features

In the case of unsupervised classification, also called *clustering*, there is no predefined taxonomy, and the algorithm groups sound examples following some similarity measure. The input to these systems is an unlabelled set of sound samples, and an iterative algorithm creates clusters in a similarity space, where each point represents a sample and the distance between points the grade of measured similarity. Appropriate techniques in this context include *k-means clustering*, *hierarchical clustering* and *self-organising maps* (SOM). Applications include speaker segmentation, query by example scenarios and music recommendation systems. Hierarchical clustering will be addressed in Section 5.4 in the context of its application to speaker segmentation.

5.3 General Audio Classification and Segmentation

5.3.1 General Audio Signals and Source Separation

A general audio signal can be conceived as a mixture produced by an arbitrary and unknown number of superposed audio sources. The signal is recorded with an arbitrary number of microphones and can be represented with digitised samples in a multi-channel setup. Such a general audio signal can obviously contain different types of audio (e.g. music and/or speech). These signals can be pure or a mixture of different audio types. Furthermore, the audio type or the mixture of audio types can change over time. These changes can be abrupt or gradual.

This raises the question of which audio types appear and when in the audio signal. The question implicitly assumes that we are only interested in specific audio types instead of recognising the underlying audio sources of the signal. Here, the problem is simplified for general audio classification and segmentation using supervised machine learning techniques where the audio types are known in advance. Audio analysis techniques can be applied independently for each channel or else the channels can be pre-processed with source separation techniques. Source separation aims at extracting the underlying audio events from a mixture and is therefore useful for audio classification and segmentation. Furthermore, the separation of audio sources is important in the context of music content analysis and will be discussed in Section 5.6.2.

5.3.2 Audio Classification and Segmentation: The Starting Point of ACA

The starting point of audio content analysis for a general time-dependent audio signal is the temporal segmentation of this signal in segments belonging to different types of audio. Later in this chapter, the types are referred to as audio classes or categories. Audio classification techniques recognise the audio category of the identified segments. Since some audio analysis techniques are more useful for specific categories of audio signals, the results of classification can be used to steer the further analysis process. Therefore, general audio classification and segmentation can be seen as a pre-processing step, as shown in Fig. 5.1. Then, the segments can be analysed with content-adapted techniques such as spoken content indexing or speaker segmentation for speech segments, musical content analysis for music segments and other specialised techniques for other audio categories.

However, audio classification and segmentation does not only partition an audio signal into speech or music segments. For subsequent content analysis or semantic techniques, it is useful to recognise as many different audio categories as possible, e.g. recognition of different environmental sounds. To this end, the audio classification method needs a trained model for each audio category of interest.

5.3.3 Different Approaches for Audio Classification and Segmentation

Methods for audio classification and segmentation can be distinguished with respect to the order of classification and segmentation and the techniques used in each stage. Three different approaches are possible here.

The first approach segments an audio signal initially, so that only segment boundaries are identified. Only the succeeding classification method recognises the most probable class membership for these segments. The second approach classifies at first parts of the audio signal. Then, the segmentation method determines the segment boundaries, based on the prior classification results. Classification and segmentation is achieved jointly in the third approach, e.g. with HMM and Viterbi decoding.

All three approaches work with a certain temporal granularity. For instance, such granularities could be analysis frames with a duration of tens of milliseconds, longer-term windows with a duration of more than one second including several frames or even a complete audio file. Finer temporal granularities have less feature vectors available for classification than coarser granularities and class assignments might be less correct. Thus, there exists a trade-off between temporal precision of segmentation and precision of classification results for each segment.

Techniques for temporal segmentation can be further categorised into four different approaches (Chen and Gopalakrishnan 1998; Kim, Moreau and Sikora 2005): energy-, metric-, model-based, and hybrid. The energy-based segmentation method measures the energy of an audio signal for the detection of silence. Metric-based segmentation approaches identify segment boundaries at the maxima of distances between succeeding windows. Such distances will be addressed in more detail in Section 5.4.2. Model-based segmentation methods use supervised classification techniques. Here, the different audio categories are known in advance. Therefore, the partitioning of an audio stream in meaningful units with similar properties can be performed without and with prior knowledge about the audio content. The combination of metric- and model-based segmentation techniques is referred to as hybrid segmentation. Here, after an initial metric-based segmentation, unsupervised clustering algorithms are used to identify possible audio classes, and in the final pass, model-based segmentation methods use trained models of these clusters.

5.3.4 Music/Speech Discrimination

Research by Saunders (1996) and Scheirer and Slaney (1997) inspired many succeeding works aimed at the discrimination between music and speech. Saunders (1996) presents a Gaussian classifier using statistical measures based on the zero-crossing rate (ZCR) and short-time energy (STE). Scheirer and Slaney (1997) examine 13 features with classification techniques such as GMM and k-NN. As features, they use 4-Hz modulation energy, low-energy frame percentage, spectral roll-off point, spectral centroid, spectral flux, ZCR, and others. Five features are determined with temporal feature integration. Carey, Parris and Lloyd-Thomas (1999) compare several features together with GMM as classification method for music/speech discrimination. They compare MFCCs, amplitude, pitch, ZCR and their delta (differential) values. Their experiments show that cepstral coefficients and the corresponding delta values give the best performance along with GMM classification. Arias, Pinquier and André-Obrecht (2005) use MFCC features and compare GMM with SVM as classification techniques. They found that SVMs obtain slightly better results for fewer training data in comparison with GMM, which achieve slightly better results for large amounts of training data.

5.3.5 Sound Classification

Several works deal with general sound classes such as environmental sounds, background noises, foley, animal sounds, speech sounds and non-speech utterances. They have to deal with small differences in the characteristics of features between two different sounds. For higher numbers of audio categories it is of interest to have a unified framework and not to have methods that are heavily dependent on specific audio categories. Therefore, the sound classification approach as combination of feature extraction and classification techniques has to capture the properties of sound that are significant for the recognition of different sounds and, at the same time, be general enough for such varied audio categories.

Goldhor (1993) compares linear frequency cepstral coefficients and MFCCs for the recognition of 23 environmental sounds with maximum likelihood (ML) classification. Wold, Blum, Keislar and Wheaton (1996) propose statistical measures such as means, variances and autocorrelations of perceptual features such as loudness, pitch, brightness, bandwidth, and harmonicity. Pfeiffer, Fischer and Effelsberg (1996) use biologically inspired features for sound classification of gunshot, cry, and explosion. Foote (1997) uses MFCCs and energy as features to construct a learning tree vector quantiser. Timbre and rhythm features are used along with HMM classifiers by Zhang and Kuo (1999b). Hierarchical combination of an audio classification/segmentation stage with a few classes and a fine-level sound classification is proposed by Zhang and Kuo (1999a). Logarithmic values from the amplitude spectrum are used with HMM classifiers for the classification of 10 sound classes. Guo, Zhang and Li (2001) compare the machine-learning techniques AdaBoost and SVM for perceptual features such as total power, sub-band powers, brightness, bandwidth, pitch and MFCCs.

Casey (2001) proposes a framework for sound recognition that uses decorrelated, dimension-reduced log-spectral features along with HMM classification for classes such as speech, explosions, laughter and several musical instruments. This framework leads to the MPEG-7 sound recognition tools (ISO/IEC 2002), where those features are referred to as MPEG-7 audio spectrum projections (ASP).

Xiong, Radhakrishnan, Divakaran and Huang (2003) compare MPEG-7 ASP with PCA and MFCC features for six sports-related categories with HMM classifiers. Reported results are similar for both feature extraction methods. Kim, Burred and Sikora (2004) make a further comparison for MPEG-7 ASP vs. MFCC features. For the computation of ASP, the three basis decomposition algorithms PCA, ICA and non-negative matrix factorisation (NMF) are used. They obtained 90.4% recognition accuracy for 12 sound classes using MPEG-7 ASP with PCA and 93.2% for MFCCs, both with 13 dimensions. The main finding for these sound recognition experiments is that MFCC features outperform MPEG-7 ASP features for the continuous hidden Markov model (CHMM).

5.4 Speaker Segmentation

The automatic segmentation and classification of an audio stream according to speaker identities is increasingly gaining in importance. This process is useful in the task of automatic transcription and indexing of broadcast news or movie audio data, speaker adaptation techniques for advanced speech recognition systems, and speaker tracking in multimedia data processing. Previous research on speaker segmentation has mainly focused on the three directions mentioned in Section 5.3.3: metric-based segmentation, model-based segmentation, and hybrid segmentation (Kim, Moreau and Sikora 2005). In Chen and Gopalakrishnan (1998) and Delacourt and Wellekens (2000), model selection-based segmentation approaches are investigated. The audio stream is segmented at the maxima of the distance between neighbouring windows placed in evenly spaced time intervals. In Gauvain, Lamel and Adda (1998) and Sönmez, Heck and Weintraub (1999), alternative model-based approaches using GMM and HMM were investigated. For every speaker in the audio recording, a model is trained and then maximum likelihood selection is performed to find the best time-aligned speaker sequence. In Yu, Seide, Ma and Chang (2003) and Kim, Moreau and Sikora (2005), it is shown that a hybrid algorithm which combines metric-based and model-based techniques works significantly better than all other approaches. A two-stage real-time speaker change detection approach for broadcast news was proposed in Wu, Lu and Zhang (2003). In the "pre-segmentation" stage, a universal background model (GMM-UBM) is used to categorise feature vectors into three sets: reliable speaker-related set, doubtful speaker-related set, and unreliable speaker-related set. Potential speaker change boundaries are detected based on a distance measure. In the "refinement" stage, incremental speaker adaptation is applied so that the potential speaker change boundaries can be confirmed and refined. Although a lot of work has been done in utilising information from audio analysis (speaker change detection, speaker recognition) for scene segmentation (Liu, Wang and Chen 1998), shot clustering (Taskiran, Albiol, Torres and Delp 2004) and news browsing (Qi, Gu, Jiang, Chen and Zhang 2000), there are few systems (Samour, Karaman, Goldmann and Sikora 2007) that exploit video information to support audio segmentation.

This section will mainly concentrate on the most common techniques for segmenting speech signals into speaker segments according to their identity. Due to its importance to speaker segmentation, the next section will give a short overview about hierarchical clustering methods.

5.4.1 Hierarchical Clustering

A basic process of hierarchical clustering which develops a correspondence between any hierarchical clustering system and a particular type of distance measure was introduced in Johnson (1967). Hierarchical clustering can be categorised into two types: *agglomerative (bottom–up)* and *divisive (top–down)*.

At the initial stage of agglomerative clustering, each entity is assigned to a single cluster, so that the distance between clusters is equal to the distance between the items they contain. At the next step, the algorithm merges the closest pair of clusters according to a distance metric to build a bigger cluster. This step is repeated until all entities of the entire data are merged into one single cluster. The divisive methods consider the entire data as one cluster and split iteratively the object of this cluster into finer groups. To determine if two clusters are sufficiently similar to be linked together, a linkage rule is needed, which can be of one of the following types:

- *Single linkage (minimum method)*: The distance between two clusters is considered to be equal to the shortest distance from any member of one cluster to any member of the other cluster.
- *Complete linkage (maximum method)*: The distance between two clusters is considered to be equal to the distance between their farthest members.
- *Average linkage*: The average distance is calculated from the distance between each member in a cluster and all other members in another cluster. The closest pair is merged together to form the new cluster. A variation on average-link clustering is the UCLUS method by D'Andrade (1978), which uses the median distance.
- *Centroid linkage*: This variation uses the group centroid as the average. The centroid is defined as the centre of gravity of the cloud of points.

The result of hierarchical clustering is generally represented as a dendrogram (tree), which summarises each operation (fusion or division) during the analysis steps. For speaker segmentation tasks, an agglomerative clustering algorithm is often used in order to cluster the speaker segments that are previously detected by the change point detection.

5.4.2 Metric-Based Speaker Segmentation

Metric-based segmentation consists of two main modules: change point detection and clustering. In the first, the distance (dissimilarity) between two adjacent windows that contain the acoustic feature vectors is computed. The acoustic features (see Section 5.2.1) are extracted prior to the speaker change detection and they are assumed to follow some probability density (usually Gaussian). The speech within the two windows is considered to be spoken by the same speaker if the distance between these windows is small. Otherwise, if the distance exceeds a predefined threshold, the speech could be considered as being spoken by different speakers. In the clustering module, the segments produced by the change point detection are merged together if they contain speech from the same speaker. The dissimilarity between two clusters is calculated using a distance measure. The clustering procedure creates different clusters as output that ideally contain only one speaker. The overall procedure of metric-based segmentation is depicted in Fig. 5.4.

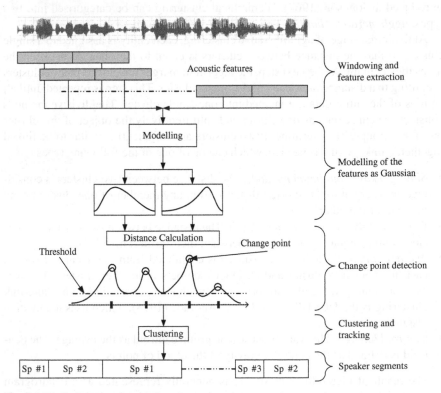

Fig. 5.4 Block diagram of metric-based segmentation

A variety of metric-based algorithms has been investigated in the literature. These algorithms differ in the kind of distance measure they use, the way of evaluation and thresholding of the distance values, and the choice of the window size. The most popular distances used for speaker segmentation are symmetric Kullback-Leibler distance (KL2), divergence shape distance (DSD), generalised likelihood ratio (GLR), Mahalanobis distance, Bhattacharyya distance, and Gish distance. The latter is a variation of the GLR distance and was presented in Gish and Schmidt (1994) and Gish, Siu and Rohlicek (1991).

Consider two contiguous sequences (windows) of short-time feature vectors with different sizes $X_1 = \{x_1 \ldots x_i\}$ and $X_2 = \{x_{i+1} \ldots x_N\}$, where N is the number of feature vectors within both windows, and assume that the feature sequences X_1 and X_2 are n-variate Gaussian distributed, $X_1 \sim N(\Sigma_{X_1}, \mu_{X_1})$, $X_2 \sim N(\Sigma_{X_2}, \mu_{X_2})$. The distance measures mentioned above can be then used to calculate the dissimilarity between those two audio sequences. As an example, the KL2 distance has been used by Siegler, Jain, Raj and Stern (1997), Lu and Zhang (2002a,b), Campbell (1997), Jørgensen, Mølgaard and Hansen (2006) and Hung, Wang and Lee (2000). The DSD, which is a simplification of the Kullback-Leibler distance, was presented in Campbell (1997) to reduce the sensitivity of the distance to various environment conditions.

To improve the thresholding, which is important to detect potential speaker change points, an automatic threshold setting method and some heuristic rules were proposed in the work of Lu and Zhang (2002b). It is defined as

$$\text{Th}_i = \frac{\alpha}{N} \sum_{n=0}^{N} D(i - n - 1, i - n) \tag{5.1}$$

where N is the number of previous distances used for predicting the threshold and α is an amplifier coefficient.

GLR is used (Mori and Nakagawa 2001; Delacourt and Wellekens 2000; Liu and Kubala 1999; Adami, Kajarekar and Hermansky 2002; Nakagawa and Suzuk 1993) to decide whether the null hypothesis H_0 (no speaker turn) or H_1 (speaker turn at time t) is true. For the actual computation of the likelihoods, one multivariate full-covariance Gaussian model is estimated on each of the windows and on the union of two windows. The null hypothesis H_0 is preferred for a high GLR value, otherwise H_1 is favoured so that a speaker turn is detected at time t. Finally, Campbell (1997), Pietquin, Couvreur and Couvreur (2001) and Hung et al. (2000) use the Mahalanobis and Bhattacharyya distances as dissimilarity measures.

The metric-based methods have the advantage of low computation cost, and thus are suitable for real-time applications (Cheng and Wang 2003). However, they have the following drawbacks:

- It is difficult to decide an appropriate threshold.
- Each acoustic changing point is detected only by its neighbouring acoustic information.

- To deal with homogeneous segments of various lengths, the window length is usually short (typically 2 s), so the feature vectors could be insufficient to obtain robust distance statistics.

5.4.3 Model-Selection-Based Speaker Segmentation

The Bayesian information criterion (BIC) is a parametric model-selection method which was first proposed by Schwarz (1978) to solve the problem of selecting a set of candidate models with differing complexities, i.e. different number of parameters and components, to fit an observed data set. The aim of modelling data is to maximise the likelihood of the training data. This can be achieved by increasing the model's complexity. However, if the model is created with a very high complexity, this may cause over-fitting. The BIC method is widely used for unsupervised speaker segmentation and clustering. To apply BIC to speaker segmentation, acoustic features (e.g. MFCCs) are extracted typically every 20 ms from the incoming audio stream. The basic problem is to find all the possible audio frames with a speaker turn. With the assumption that a window X of consecutive feature vectors $\{x_1 \ldots x_N\}$ is drawn from an independent multivariate Gaussian process and contains at most one speaker change point at $i \in (1, N)$, the segmentation problem can be then cast as a model selection problem between the following two models: $M1$, where $X = \{x_1 \ldots x_N\}$ is drawn from a single Gaussian, and $M2$ where $X_1 = \{x_1 \ldots x_i\}$ is drawn from one Gaussian while $X_2 = \{x_{i+1} \ldots x_N\}$ from another Gaussian. The variations of the BIC values between the two models is given by

$$\Delta \text{BIC}_i = -\frac{N_X}{2} \log |\Sigma_X| + \frac{N_{X_1}}{2} \log |\Sigma_{X_1}| + \frac{N_{X_2}}{2} \log |\Sigma_{X_2}| + \lambda D, \quad (5.2)$$

where Σ_X, Σ_{X_1} and Σ_{X_2} are the covariance matrices of the whole window X, the subset X_1 and the subset X_2, respectively, and λ is the penalty weight to compensate for cases of small sample size N_X, N_{X_1} and N_{X_2} are the number of acoustic vectors in the complete sequence, the subset X_1 and the subset X_2, respectively, with the penalty

$$D = \frac{1}{2} \left(d + \frac{d(d+1)}{2} \right) \log(N_X), \quad (5.3)$$

where d is the dimension of the acoustic feature vectors. The ith frame is a good candidate segment boundary if $\Delta \text{BIC}_i > 0$. The final change point decision can be made via maximum likelihood estimation (MLE).

In Chen and Gopalakrishnan (1998), if there is no change point detected, the window will grow in size to have more robust distance statistics. Otherwise, a new window is started from the detected change point. This scheme is extremely computationally expensive and therefore is not suitable for real-time applications. An extension of this system was proposed by Tritschler and Gopinath (1999) and Zhou and Hansen (2000). A variable window scheme and some heuristics were applied to the BIC framework while Hotelling's T^2-statistics were used to preselect the candidate change point boundary before applying BIC to make the segmentation decision. It was shown that an improvement in the final algorithm speed by an order of 100 can be achieved. Two-pass techniques that take advantage of metric-based methods and model selection-based methods were introduced in Delacourt and Wellekens (2000). Metric-based segmentation was used in combination with a thresholding process to detect the change points. Then BIC was used in the second pass to confirm or discard the previously detected change points. The literature alludes to the threshold independence, robustness and optimality of BIC in comparison with metric-based methods. It should be noted, however, that it is hard to choose an applicable and generally valid λ for different audio files and acoustic conditions. BIC can be also used as a similarity measure in order to apply the bottom-up hierarchical clustering, as has been described in Section 5.4.1.

5.4.4 Model-Based Speaker Segmentation

Model-based segmentation is realised by using classical classification methods (see Section 5.2.4). It is divided into a training step to build a set of models for different speakers from a predefined training corpus and a testing (classification) step to classify the incoming audio stream according to the generated models. First, the incoming audio stream is split into smaller acoustic frames in order to apply feature extraction (Section 5.2.1). A sliding window containing a sequence of the extracted acoustic features is used for the segmentation. The content of the sliding window is then classified as one of the predefined acoustic classes by using maximum likelihood selection. Segmentation can be made at the location where a change in the acoustic class occurs. The boundaries between the classes are used as segment boundaries. A general scheme of model-based segmentation is shown in Fig. 5.5. Most model-based algorithms are based on GMM, HMM, SVM, and vector quantisation (VQ). In Mori and Nakagawa (2001), VQ distortion was used as the segmentation criterion. A codebook was created by a VQ algorithm; the VQ distortion is then calculated between the model and an utterance.

An HMM-based segmentation scheme was proposed by Wilcox, Chen, Kimber and Balasubramanian (1994), in which an HMM network was used in the case of known speakers while an agglomerative clustering algorithm was applied in the case of unknown speakers. In the work of Sugiyama, Murakami and Watanabe (1993), a similar system was proposed. The segmentation of an unknown number of speakers was made using an ergodic HMM-based technique. The output probability was obtained for the clustering step by assuming the number of speakers to be known. Another system based on HMM was studied in Cohen and Lapidus (1996), which was limited to discriminate between only two speakers in a telephone conversation. A segmentation scheme based on SVM was described in Kartik, Satish and Sekhar (2005). Positive (data around the speaker change points) and negative (data

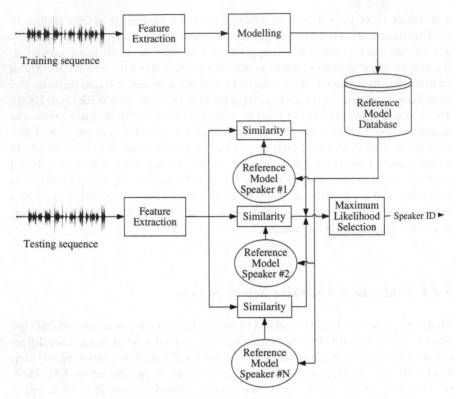

Fig. 5.5 General scheme of model-based speaker segmentation

between the speaker change points) examples are used in training an SVM for speaker change detection. Model-based approaches are robust and more accurate in comparison with other segmentation techniques. The disadvantage of model-based methods is that they require prior information to generate the speaker models. Furthermore, the training step is an iterative procedure which make these algorithms very time-consuming.

5.4.5 Hybrid Speaker Segmentation

The basic idea of hybrid speaker segmentation (Kemp, Schmidt, Westphal and Waibel 2000; Yu et al. 2003; Kim, Moreau and Sikora 2005) is to combine metric-based or model-selection-based approaches with model-based techniques. Model-based methods achieve a very high level of segment boundary precision, while metric-based methods yield better recall (for the definitions of recall and precision, see Section 5.4.7). Hybrid segmentation aims at reducing false alarms caused by metric-based segmentation. We evaluated the system presented in Kim, Moreau and Sikora (2005) with exactly the same database and implementation. After many experiments and tuning of the threshold values for the different used metrics, we achieved at least a maximum value for the F_1-measure (5.4.7) of 87%, while (Kim, Moreau and Sikora 2005) reported an F_1-measure of 98.1%. Although the optimal threshold value was selected, we did not achieve the same result of Kim. Without any tuning of the threshold, an F_1-measure of about only 64% could be achieved for the various data sets. The setting of the threshold value depends on the data sets used for the segmentation. Bad selection of the threshold value would directly affect the precision and recall values, and in consequence the result of the clustering. That leads to the creation of incorrect models for the individual speakers. Thus, the re-segmentation (model-based segmentation) results will be negatively affected. Therefore, hybrid segmentation can only provide good results if the speaker change detection provides reliable results.

5.4.6 Multimodal Speaker Segmentation

A lot of work has been done in utilising information from audio analysis (speaker change detection, speaker recognition) for scene segmentation (Liu et al. 1998), shot clustering (Taskiran et al. 2004) and news browsing (Qi et al. 2000). In Samour et al. (2007), two approaches (see Fig. 5.6) were proposed that consider temporal

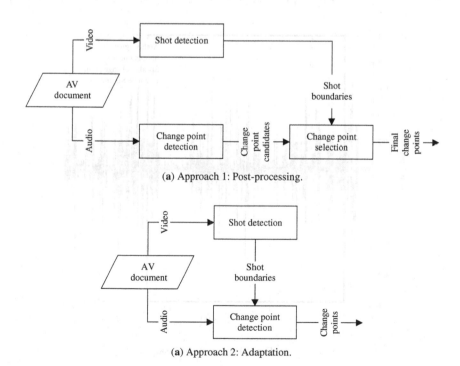

Fig. 5.6 Multimodal speaker change detection

information from video for improving the audio-based speaker change detection. Speaker change points often coincide with shot boundaries, especially in edited AV data (broadcast news, discussions).

Figure 5.6(a) depicts the first method which operates as a post-processing step using the output of each module (*speaker change detection* and *shot boundary detection* (SBD)). With the assumption that the results of the modules yield a low miss-detection rate (false negative rate) and high false alarm rate (false positive rate), the purpose of this system is to reduce the false positive number of speaker change points as much as possible.

The temporal distance between all detected change points $C = \{c_1, c_2, \ldots, c_M\}$ and all detected shot boundaries $S = \{s_1, s_2, \ldots, s_N\}$ is computed. A temporal threshold Th_d is set according to the maximum delay between shot boundaries and speaker change points for this kind of edited video material. The available change point with the smallest distance to the shot boundary within the scope of the predefined Th_d is declared as a potential change point. This idea is illustrated in Fig. 5.7(a), which shows an example including shot boundaries, change points, and the corresponding distances.

This approach naturally exhibits some disadvantages. If the SBD does not detect a shot boundary near a change point, it is automatically rejected. This may lead to a larger number of false negatives within the final set of change points. On the other hand, if the SBD is very sensitive, more false positives may be accepted.

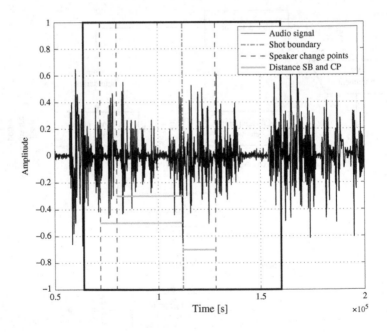

(a) Example for post-processing.

Fig. 5.7 Examples of multi-modal speaker change detection

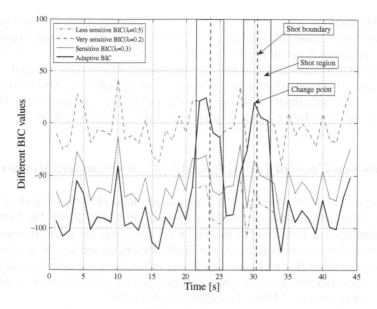

(**b**) Example for adaptation.

Fig. 5.7 (continued)

In the second approach (see Fig. 5.6(b)), the results of the SBD directly influence the speaker change detection by adapting the BIC used for measuring the similarity between two segments. The idea is to make BIC more sensitive in regions (±2 s) around shot boundaries and less sensitive in regions out of shot boundaries. This is achieved by adapting the penalty term λ within BIC. For regions around shot boundaries, a smaller λ_S is chosen, while otherwise a larger $\lambda_{\overline{S}}$ is used. The advantage of this approach is that it may detect change points near shot boundaries as well as between them. It influences only the sensitivity of the change point detection based on the shot boundaries.

5.4.7 Evaluation Measures

Evaluation of segmentation results is based on standard measures derived from a confusion matrix. To obtain the confusion matrix, the set of automatically detected change points $A = \{a_1, a_2, \ldots, a_N\}$ is compared to the set of manually annotated change points $G = \{g_1, g_2, \ldots, g_M\}$, also known as "ground truth". The temporal distance d_{ij} between each detected change point a_i and each annotated change point g_j is calculated. Since the change point detection operates in discrete steps, it is possible that detected change points have slightly different positions as annotated change points. Thus, a small window around an annotated change point is searched for possible matches with detected change points. Out of multiple detected change points within this window, the closest change point is considered as a true positive

(TP). All others are counted as false positives (FP). Annotated change points without any match are considered as false negatives (FN). Based on the obtained confusion matrix, precision P, recall R and F_1-measure can be calculated.

Precision describes the ratio between the number of correctly detected change points and all detected change points, while recall describes the ratio between the number of correctly detected change points and all relevant change points. The F_1-measure combines both by assigning equal importance to each of them.

5.5 Spoken Content Indexing and Spoken Document Retrieval

Spoken content (SC) is the semantic information contained in spoken parts in audio streams of multimedia documents (Kim, Moreau and Sikora 2005). The extraction of spoken content metadata has become a key challenge for the development of efficient methods to index/retrieve multimedia documents and for the development of concise multimedia ontologies for efficient information management and access by both users and computers. A syntax for description of spoken content is specified in the audio part of the MPEG-7 standard (ISO/IEC 2002).

Spoken content indexing (SCI) could be performed manually. Obviously, this highly accurate method does not suit the huge volume of currently available data. ASR systems which transcribe the digital speech signal into a sequence of pre-defined symbols can be used as an alternative to such manual methods. Although research in ASR is already about five decades old, it was not until the last few years that it has become a feasible technology for commercial applications. Nowadays, ASR algorithms are widely employed in human–machine, dictation, automatic phone and data-mining systems (Coden, Brown and Srinivasan 2001). This section concerns the application of SCI within the field of spoken document retrieval (SDR).

After the description of the basic principles and structure of an ASR system, the following types of ASR will be discussed in Section 5.5.1: connected word recognition, large-vocabulary conversational speech recognition (LVCSR), sub-word recognition, and keyword spotting. The common evaluation criteria will be introduced.

In Section 5.5.2, we review the basic structure of an SDR system and then discuss four different SDR approaches, including word-based, sub-word-based, phoneme-based and combined-index-unit approach. These four different SDR approaches will be compared using common SDR performance measures.

5.5.1 Spoken Content Indexing

Figure 5.8 shows a generic ASR process. Basically, ASR consists of the following three main components:

- *Feature extraction*: A set of useful measurements or features are extracted at a fixed short-time rate, typically once every 10–20 ms, from the input digitised speech signal.

- *Modelling/classification*: A characterisation of the sources of variability (phonetic, acoustic and within-speaker variability).
- *Decoding*: The representation is matched against a set of predefined acoustic models, each of which represents one of the recognisable symbols. The most likely candidates determine the output sequence of symbols.

The main principles and definitions related to the ASR components described above are briefly introduced in the following.

At the stage of feature extraction, short-term cepstral features, the most popular acoustic features in ASR systems, are extracted from the digitised speech signal. These features reduce the model complexity while keeping the most relevant information. There are two common sets of cepstral coefficients typically used in this context: MFCCs and the cepstral coefficients derived from PLP analysis. Both methods were introduced in Section 5.2.1. For ASR, PLP analysis has been verified by some researchers to be more robust in the presence of background noise (Kershaw, Robinson and Renals 1996; Woodland, Gales, Pye and Valtchev 1996).

Due to the sources of variability associated with the signal, ASR is a very demanding task. The representative signal variabilities include phonetic, acoustic, within-speaker and cross-speaker variabilities (Cole, Mariani, Uszkoreit, Zaenen and Zue 1998). Phonetic variabilities concern the acoustic differences of the phonemes, which depend on the context in which they appear. At the word boundaries, especially, contextual variations can be quite dramatic. Acoustic variabilities are the result of the changing of environment as well as the variance of the position and characteristics of the transducer. Within-speaker variabilities indicate changes in the speaker's physical and emotional states, speaking rate and voice quality. Finally, changes in the socio-linguistic background, dialect and vocal tract size, and shape can be summarised as cross-speaker variabilities (Cole et al. 1998).

The modelling/classification step of an ASR system tries to model the variabilities mentioned before in several ways. Hermansky (1990) has developed representations that emphasise perceptually important speaker-independent features of the signal and de-emphasise speaker-dependent characteristics. The speaker variability is typically modelled using statistical techniques applied to large amounts of data. Speaker adaptation algorithms are employed to adapt speaker-independent acoustic models to those of the current speaker. The phonetic variabilities of the signal are often compensated by means of training separate models for phonemes in different contexts, the so-called context-dependent acoustic modelling.

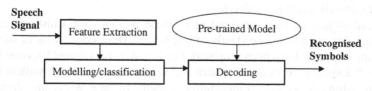

Fig. 5.8 Schematic description of automatic speech recognition

The decoding procedure tries to determine the most probable sequence of units knowing the acoustic features. An HMM is trained for each recognisable unit. Once the HMMs have been trained, acoustic observations can be matched against them using the Viterbi algorithm (Rabiner and Juang 1993), which aims at determining the sequence of HMM states that best matches the sequence of acoustic vectors, the so-called best alignment. At the end of the decoding process, the output transcription of the input signal consists of a sequence of models with the best score.

5.5.1.1 Different Types of ASR Approaches

ASR approaches can be classified according to their complexity into five categories: connected word recognition, large-vocabulary continuous speech recognition (LVCSR), sub-word recognition, keyword spotting and ontology-based SCI applications. The remainder of this section considers each of these approaches in more detail.

Connected word recognition aims at recognising a sequence of words spoken in a connected or fluent manner. The deployment of a fixed syntactic network strongly restrains the authorised sequences of output symbols. An HMM model is constructed for each vocabulary word. The acoustic representation of the input speech signal is matched against whole word patterns using connected word pattern matching algorithms to give a set of candidate strings. With confidence measures, the unreasonable candidates are eliminated and the most likely digit strings are the output resulting from this process. Due to the word modelling, this approach is only appropriate with recognition tasks involving a small vocabulary and is impracticable with large vocabularies.

LVCSR aims at transcribing the input digital speech signal into normal text. Instead of the whole-word modelling, words are modelled by the concatenation of sub-lexical HMMs. The deployment of sub-lexical HMM reduces the size of acoustic HMMs dramatically. However, an additional dictionary is required to provide the sub-lexical transcription of every vocabulary word. After feature extraction, Viterbi decoding is used to find the word candidates with the best matching score. A dictionary is required to build whole-word models from trained sub-lexical acoustic HMMs. After whole-word matching, a further language model detects the sequence of word candidates which are grammatically well formed and meaningful. The main problem that the LVCSR must deal with is the occurrence of out-of-vocabulary (OOV) words. An OOV word is usually substituted by a vocabulary word or a sequence of vocabulary words which is most acoustically similar to it. Several research efforts have been dedicated to detect OOV words, but the precision of such methods is still not satisfying.

Instead of normal text, sub-word recognition provides sub-word transcription of spoken documents, independently of any lexical knowledge. A lot of sub-word recognition systems have been proposed. For instance, Larson and Eickeler (2003) have built a syllable recognition system and Glass, Chang and McCandless (1996) built an automatic phonetic transcription system. In their work, the phones are extracted by means of the SUMMIT system Zue, Glass, Goodine, Phillips and Seneff (1990).

A keyword spotting application detects a predefined set of keywords in speech streams. The main problem in this case is how to model the irrelevant speech between keywords. The so-called filler models are often constructed to deal with this problem. There are two main types of filler models. One of them uses HMM filler models which are trained for each distinct "non-keyword" event, including silence, environmental noise, OOV speech (Wilpon, Rabiner and Lee 1990). The other uses a more flexible solution to model non-keyword speech by means of an unconstrained phone loop that recognises phonetic sequences without any lexical constraint (Rose 1995). A predefined threshold value is set on the acoustic score of each keyword candidate during the decoding process to decide whether the word candidates are hits or not. The value of the threshold must be chosen considering the desired trade-off between the number of missed words and false alarms.

An SCI system can make multimedia ontologies more concise. At the same time, the embedding of prior knowledge can also improve SCI performance significantly. To that end, ontology-based SCI applications, such as the one proposed by Gurevych and Porzel (2003), use knowledge-based scores to identify the best speech recognition hypotheses. Using the high-level knowledge encoded in the ontology, the competing speech recognition hypotheses are evaluated in terms of their semantic coherence.

5.5.1.2 Common ASR Performance Measurements

Word error rate (WER) is the most common measure for the evaluation of ASR performance. The output of an ASR system could be a best hypothesised sequence of recognisable units, N-best list or lattice. The measurement of the ASR system performance is generally performed on the best hypothesis. The main problem of performance evaluation is that the recognised transcription has a different length than the reference sequence. Therefore, the WER is derived using the Levenshtein distance which solves the problem by first aligning the recognised word sequence with the sequence using dynamic string alignment. The WER is defined as sum of the substitutions, deletions and insertions divided by the correct sentence length (Lee 1989).

5.5.2 Spoken Document Retrieval

Spoken document retrieval (SDR) is "concerned with retrieving spoken documents in response to a written or spoken query" (Crestani 2003). Figure 5.9 shows the structure of a typical spoken document retrieval system. An SDR system accepts written or spoken queries and returns a ranked spoken document list. It generally consists of two stages: indexing and retrieval.

The indexing tools transcribe the spoken or text queries and spoken documents into text or phonetic representations. Based on the representations, the retrieval tools compute a similarity score for each document according to the query. This score is used later to rank the document. Finally, a decreasingly sorted document list will be returned as the result of retrieval.

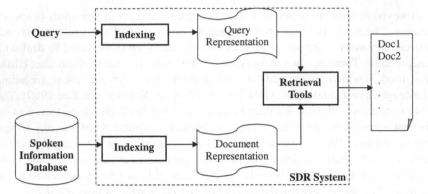

Fig. 5.9 Schematic view of a spoken document retrieval (SDR) system

Some relevant concepts in this context are the following:

- *Representation*: a textual format transcription consisting of indexing terms.
- *Indexing term*: term used by indexing tools. It can be a word, phone, etc.
- *Acoustic model*: a recognisable unit used by a speech recognition system.

ASR tools are usually employed as indexing tools to transcribe the digital spoken signal into transcription consisting of recognisable units. The retrieval procedure tries to detect the query-relevant section in the recognised transcription. The performance of SDR is influenced by the "term miss-recognition problem", i.e. the recognition errors of the ASR system (Crestani 2003). Therefore, the performance of the ASR system employed has a significant influence on the effectiveness of the SDR. Usually, the quality of an ASR system is affected by the following factors:

- *Recording environment*: background noise is present or not,
- *Speech variability*: the temporal and acoustic properties of the same spoken text vary from one recording to another,
- *Speech type*: continuous speech or isolated spoken words,
- *Number of distinct units to recognise*: a large set of recognisable units increases computation complexity,
- Amount and quality of training data needed to train both acoustic models and language models,
- Number and gender of different speakers. Every speaker has his or her own individual speaking speed and pronunciation.

5.5.2.1 Different Types of SDR Approaches

Many spoken document retrieval approaches have been developed recently. According to the type of employed speech recogniser, they can be classified into four categories: word-based approaches, sub-word-based approaches, phone- or phoneme-based approaches, combined approaches and ontology-based SDR applications.

Word-based SDR approaches rely on a word recognition system that transcribes a spoken document into a sequence of words. Text retrieval algorithms can then be used to find relevant information. The SDR system for British and North American broadcast news presented by Renals (1999), the online spoken document retrieval system SpeechFind presented by Zhou and Hansen (2002) and the English radio news retrieval application presented by James (1995) are based on this approach. The main advantage is that classical text retrieval techniques can be employed. However, in order to make the word recogniser have a low word error rate, a huge training set must be used to infer the word models. Moreover, the recognition vocabulary is restricted, which leads to the restriction of the query vocabulary.

Sub-word-based approaches use sub-word units as indexing terms, such as the vowels–consonants–vowels (VCV) features presented by Schaeuble and Glavitsch (1994). A VCV feature is a sequence of three concatenated vowels or consonants. For example, the word "information" has three VCV features: "info", "orma" and "atio". A set of suitable VCV features are extracted from a text collection using an algorithm which selects features based on a statistical selection criterion. The SDR approach presented by Glavitsch (1995) is an example. He extracted about 1000 VCV units directly from text and trained an acoustic model for each one. Compared with word-based approaches, these types of methods decrease the number of recognition units without significantly reducing their descriptive power, which is crucial for effective retrieval. The recognisable units are extracted directly from text without considering the acoustic properties of the indexing terms.

Phone/phoneme-based approaches use phones or phonemes as indexing terms. Phones are defined by acoustic properties. Phonemes are more general sound units. A phoneme recognition system transcribes the digital speech signal into a sequence of phonemes (Ng and Zue 1998; Ferrieux and Peillon 1999). Phoneme-based approaches are classified into two groups:

- Retrieval based on vector space model (VSM) and N-gram extraction
- Keyword spotting through phone string matching techniques

Contrary to the word-based approaches, these types of approaches have no restriction on the query vocabulary, that is to say they perform "open vocabulary retrieval". Furthermore, the number of different phones used in one particular language is generally less than 100. Phoneme recognition can also be performed considerably faster than LVCSR systems. The main drawback of these approaches is the high error rate of phoneme recognition. The phone error rate (PER) depends on the quality and amount of training data.

It is possible to combine different indexing sources (Ng 2000). One representative example of this type of combined approaches is an application of the traditional information retrieval techniques to spoken documents, which was presented by James (1995). This application combined word recognition with phone recognition in a complete recognition system in which the phone recogniser is only used to spot the out-of-vocabulary words. This combination improves the retrieval effectiveness of a spoken document retrieval system but needs more training data and more efforts for building the two recognisers, which makes the system very computationally expensive.

Logan (Logan, Prasangsit and Moreno 2003) proposed an ontology-based SDR application by fusion of semantic and acoustic information. This approach combines probabilistic latent semantic analysis with phonetic indexing. The final ranking of the hits is yielded by a linear combination of both acoustic and semantic scores.

5.5.2.2 Common SDR Performance Measurements

The retrieval performance is evaluated using the ranked document list returned by the retrieval procedure. Two common evaluation measures, precision and recall, which were already defined in Section 5.4.7, are used. In the context of SDR, true positives (TP) is the number of relevant documents. The number of all retrieved documents is the sum of TP and false positives (FP), and the number of all relevant documents in the collection is the sum of TP and false negatives (FN).

Usually, the precision–recall curve is used to evaluate the ranked document list by plotting precision against recall after each new document is added to the retrieval list. The plot normalisation proposed by TREC 2001 (Vorhees and Harman 2001) is used to interpolate the precision values to 11 standard recall levels $[0.0, 0.1, \ldots, 1.0]$. The precision and recall depend on the number of documents included in the n-best retrieved document list.

It is sometimes difficult to compare the performance of different retrieval systems using precision–recall curves. In this case, a single performance measure called mean average precision (mAP) is usually employed (Harman 2000). This value is obtained by averaging the precision values across all recall points. The mAP value can be interpreted as the area under the precision–recall curve. However, the mAP value is a single number, and much performance information may be hidden. Two retrieval systems with different precision–recall curves can have the same mAP (the area under the precision–recall curve is the same). Therefore, generally both of them are used, i.e. the precision–recall curve and the mAP, to evaluate the performance of a system.

Experiments have been made to compare the performance of different phone-based SDR approaches on a German application (Moreau, Jin and Sikora 2005). The embedded German phone recogniser consists of 32 German phonemes HMM models trained on Verbmobil I (a large collection of spontaneous speech from different speakers) and obtained a phone error rate (PER) of 43% on the VM14.1 corpus. Both text and spoken queries were tested on data from the PhonDat corpora (PhonDat 1 and 2), consisting of short sentences read by different speakers. For text and clean-spoken queries, the string matching methods (SM) (with $mAP = 47.4\%$) proved significantly more effective than retrieval based on VSM n-grams $(mAP = 39.9\%)$. However, VSM and N-gram methods (with $mAP = 21.4\%$) were shown to be more robust than SM (with $mAP = 19.8\%$) with noise-spoken queries.

5.6 Music Content Analysis

The music industry is experiencing a drastic transformation in order to adapt itself to the unstoppable future paradigm of network distribution. It is widely accepted that in the years to come, the biggest part of the business will rely on commercial online music services. Until now, most music searches on the Internet were based on textual information manually attached to the files or contained in centralised metadata databases such as Grace, note (www.gracenote.com) or freedb (www.freedb.org), and music browsers were in fact just text retrieval systems. In the last couple of years, a new generation of music services have appeared, which additionally take into account user feedback or an analysis of their music listening habits, a technique called *collaborative filtering*. This approach allowed new services such as online music discovery and recommendation, some of which have been very successful (e.g. Last.fm, www.last.fm).

Another trend consists of enriching such metadata with information describing the music signals themselves, i.e. semantic or content-based metadata. The Pandora music recommendation service (www.pandora.com) provides an example; it is based on a database of more than 400 features manually annotated for each song or musical work. It is obvious that in such a context, a robust music content analysis (MCA) system capable of performing this task automatically can be of extremely high value. Apart from networked music navigation, other areas will also benefit from MCA techniques, such as management of local or private music libraries and archives, musicological research, musical education, intelligent signal processing, structured audio coding and digital rights management.

Needless to say, the challenge of linking the low- and mid-level features delivered by MCA to the human understanding and expectations on the other side of the semantic gap applies in the music context as well. However, the highly structured nature of music, the large number of music consumers participating in collaborative services and the commercial interest of music companies can turn music websites into the first robust and feasible services of the semantic web (Celma, Herrera and Serra 2006). The first of such experimental systems aims at combining editorial and cultural metadata (following the distinction by Pachet (2005)) with acoustic or content-based metadata under the scope of a common ontology, a topic that has been addressed in Chapter 2. Examples of music ontologies include the one defined for the *Foafing the Music* system described in that chapter and in Celma (2006), and the one by Abdallah, Raimond and Sandler (2006), both based on OWL.

In general, MCA can be performed on music available in symbolic or in acoustic form. Symbolic representations of music include printed notation and, in the computer domain, music representation languages, which encode notation in detail (such as MusicXML or GUIDO) and music interface protocols, consisting of a series of time-stamped events (such as MIDI or OpenSound Control). These computer descriptions can be entered manually, automatically generated (as in algorithmic composition) or retrieved from scanned printed music by means of optical music recognition (OMR). Music in acoustic form is fed into the computer as a digitised waveform.

The very different nature of both kinds of input calls for two specific sets of techniques for performing content analysis (see Fig. 5.10). *Symbolic MCA* relies on methods similar to the ones used in the automatic semantic or syntactic analysis of text, but thoroughly adapted in order to deal with the more complex relationship between acoustical events and musical meaning. In this case, all the processing is done in the symbolic domain, and therefore no audio signal processing is required.

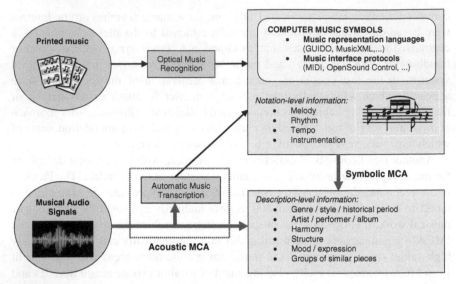

Fig. 5.10 Overview of music content analysis (MCA)

Acoustic MCA systems must obtain information from the audio signals proper and, like other audio content analysis, machine listening or computer audition systems, are based on the extraction of signal features that are considered relevant for the desired application. Automatic music transcription is the bridge between the acoustical and symbolic domains and itself constitutes an important acoustic MCA application.

Although it is computationally far more demanding than symbolic MCA, acoustic MCA has dramatically gained in importance in recent years. This is because the music material to which most people have access is in raw, audio form (recorded music, compressed files on the Internet, TV or radio broadcasting, etc.). There are also hybrid systems in which the acoustic input is transcribed into symbolic form and further processed symbolically. This section concentrates on the signal processing aspects of content extraction and thus covers the acoustic MCA problem.

MCA is very closely related to the field of music information retrieval (MIR) (Downie 2003). In fact, both terms are often understood as synonyms. There are however, some subtle differences. Traditionally, information retrieval refers to the set of techniques for implementing searches of user queries in a certain database. In a musical context, the online search scenario mentioned above is the paradigmatic example of MIR, where the queries can be of many different forms (query by humming, singing, whistling, playing, tapping, traditional textual queries, query by example, etc.), and the output is an ordered list of database entries sorted by similarity. The term MCA is used here to denote the analytic stage of MIR, i.e. the actual content extraction from the music signals or symbols regardless of if it will be used in a database querying application or not. However, it should be noted that these definitions are not strict and are used flexibly and interchangeably within the research community.

5.6.1 Feature Extraction for Music Signals

Many short-time, low-level features intended for general audio are also useful to describe music signals. These include energy and zero-crossing features, basic spectral shape features, such as spectral centroid, roll-off and flatness, and psychoacoustically motivated features such as MFCCs. For music signals, short-time frames in the range between 10 and 100 ms ensure enough local stationarity.

Several works (Tzanetakis and Cook 2002; Meng and Shawe-Taylor 2005) have demonstrated the special importance of feature integration (see Section 5.2.2) for music analysis, which comes from the fact that almost each musical parameter (pitch, tempo, dynamics, structure) evolves within a time horizon much longer than a few milliseconds. Usually, music texture windows are in the range of several seconds (mid-term feature extraction), or even cover the whole song or music file (song- or file-level feature extraction).

Apart from such general purpose feature extraction and integration techniques, some special characteristics of music signals call for the definition of music-specific features. For some applications, such as management of a sound sample database, it is required to work with individual notes, recorded separately. In this case, it is possible to design features aimed at an accurate description of the timbral characteristics based on a dynamic representation of the spectral content over the duration of each note. The detection of spectral peaks corresponding to sinusoidal components of the sound is crucial in this context, and their relative frequency position and amplitude values, and the changes in time thereof, are the factors that most influence our perception of timbre.

If the partials are located at integer multiples of the fundamental frequency, the sound is harmonic and we perceive it as having a definite pitch. Acoustical instruments never produce a perfectly harmonic spectrum; however, wind instruments and string instruments with thin and moderately stiff strings (such as guitars, violins and harps) come very close to ideal harmonicity. Stiffer and/or thicker materials, such as piano strings or xylophone bars, have the effect of displacing the frequency position of the partials from that corresponding to the harmonics. This displacement is greater the higher the partial frequency is. Such a moderate inharmonicity contributes to the timbral quality of these instruments; however, a clear pitch assignment is still possible. The higher the degree of inharmonicity, the less definite will be our pitch perception (and the more difficult will be its automatic extraction using objective features). A stronger source of inharmonicity is the complex vibration patterns produced by membranes, plates or bells. In this case, new partials, which are not related to a fundamental frequency, are introduced. Again, according to the degree of inharmonicity, we can distinguish a specific pitch (e.g. timpani), perceive a compound of pitches (gongs, bells) or not perceive any pitch at all (cymbals, snare drum). In the latter case, the spectrum consists of very closely located partials and comes close to a noise spectrum.

However, it is the relative amplitude values of the partials (i.e. the *spectral envelope*) that mostly help when distinguishing between different musical instruments. Some instruments feature formants in a similar way to the human voice, produced by the resonances of the resonating body. Furthermore, physical characteristics of the instrument can greatly constrain the nature of the partials (e.g. the internal cylindrical shape of the clarinet suppresses the even harmonics).

All these considerations demonstrate the value of a detailed analysis of the spectral partials, which can be performed by signal analysis techniques such as spectral peak detection and partial tracking. Such an analysis yields a data matrix containing the amplitude, frequency position and phase of each partial. This information can be directly used as feature for content analysis tasks, with appropriate pre-processing (and possibly dimension reduction). Another possibility is to define features compactly describing the amplitude and/or frequency relationships of the partials as some scalar quantity. This is the case of the MPEG-7 harmonic features, such as harmonic spectral spread and harmonic spectral centroid.

To further improve the model, the sinusoidal analysis data can be used to resynthesise a deterministic signal consisting of only sinusoidal components (the *sinusoidal* or *deterministic part* of the signal), which can be then subtracted from the original signal, yielding a noise-like residual (the *noise* or *stochastic part* of the signal). This residual can be modelled by frame-wise fitting the noise spectrum to a certain filter frequency response and keeping the coefficients as features. By means of this analysis, a powerful and flexible model of the signal is obtained, called *sinusoidal plus noise model*, which is the basis of the spectral modelling synthesis (SMS) framework (Serra 1997). An extension thereof, called transient modelling synthesis (TMS) (Verma, Levine and Meng 1997), uses an explicit model of note *transients*, which are the pulse-like, non-harmonic segments occurring in the attack phase of a note, or in the transitions between consecutive notes.

When working on a higher abstraction level, and with real musical recordings, rather than with isolated notes, it is possible to take into consideration music semantics and structure to design higher-level features describing melody, harmony, rhythm, etc. as an alternative to integrating low-level features with the above-mentioned methods. An important example is *chroma features*, which group the pitch occurrences within a music excerpt into the 12-pitch classes corresponding to the tempered chromatic scale, or to any other partition of the octave, obtaining a robust, octave-independent harmonic description that has successfully been used for structure analysis, chord and tonality recognition and song cover identification (Gómez 2006). A wide selection of mid- and high-level features have been standardised within MPEG-7 audio (ISO/IEC 2002) and its two amendments (ISO/IEC 2004; ISO/IEC 2006).

Rhythmic analysis can be also performed at several semantic levels. On the lowest level, *tempo extraction* consists of measuring the repetition interval of the main pulsating beat and is the basis of *beat tracking* systems. Tempo is usually given in beats per minute (bpm), and its extraction is commonly based on using autocorrelation functions to measure periodicity. A more sophisticated analysis is offered by the *beat spectrum* (Foote 2001) or *beat histogram* (Tzanetakis and Cook 2002) approaches, which yield a measure of beat periodicities as a function of bpm, allowing an insight into internal metric subdivisions and sub-beats. The beat spectrum/histogram can be either directly used as a feature or taken as the basis for more compact measurements, such as overall rhythmic regularity, amplitudes or bpm ratios of subbeats, energy. On an even higher abstraction level, authors like Klapuri (2004) analyse rhythmic characteristics at a hierarchy of metric layers (metric refers to the organisation of beats and sub-beats into measures and their subdivisions, i.e. the time signature).

5.6.2 Automatic Music Transcription and Source Separation

To automatically extract the music score from a digital music signal is an extraordinarily demanding task. There exist robust systems for pitch detection and transcription of single instruments or melodies, and some success has been achieved with polyphonic content of two or three voices. However, when it comes to a larger degree of polyphony, the problem remains unsolved, and it is a matter of debate whether it can be achieved in the near future. The problem mostly resides in the overlapping of spectral partials belonging to different voices or instruments. The degree of overlapping will be higher with simple tonal relationships such as unisons, octaves and fifths, which are the basis of most types of music. Other difficulties are the *tonal fusion* that occurs when several instruments play a voice together, which is then perceived as a single sound entity, as well as temporal overlaps in rhythmically regular music, which hinder the detection of simultaneous transients or onsets.

One straightforward approach to polyphonic transcription would be to separate the polyphonic excerpts to their constituent voices, e.g. using blind source separation (BSS) or unmixing techniques, and then perform monophonic transcription on each of the voices. However, many of the above-mentioned difficulties apply here as well. In particular, the relationship between the number of recorded channels (mixtures) and the number of musical instruments present in the mixtures is a critical factor in source separation. It is actually possible to obtain good results using independent component analysis (ICA) if there are at least as many mixtures as instruments, but this is very rarely the case in music recordings, where the most common format is still stereo. Thus, in a musical context, *under-determined separation* is needed, meaning there are fewer mixtures available (usually one or two) than instruments or voices playing. Some advances have been obtained in under-determined music separation by exploiting spatial cues, by using highly sparse signal representations or by designing sophisticated instrument-related source models (for a recent overview of techniques, see O'Grady, Pearlmutter and Rickard (2005). Another difficulty is the common presence of reverberation or artificial sound effects, which increase the degree of spectral, temporal or spatial overlapping.

In any case, up to now there is no separation algorithm that is able to segregate voices with enough accuracy and generality. Therefore, polyphonic music transcription has tried to circumvent the separation problem by concentrating on multipitch analysis, which often relies on the extraction of a sinusoidal model consisting of partial tracks such as SMS, and on the subsequent detection of strong frequency components and harmonic structures as a good indication of the musical notes played (Klapuri 2004). Other approaches use basis decomposition methods on the spectrogram, with the aim of revealing structural information that more clearly hints to the played notes. As an example, Smaragdis and Brown (2003) use non-negative matrix factorisation (NMF), a decomposition method similar to ICA, on the magnitude spectrogram to transcribe polyphonic piano sounds.

5.6.3 Music Classification and Clustering

Music classifiers seek to assign a certain category such as musical genre, a label describing its mood or expression content, the composer or performers to a music fragment. An example of an application is musical instrument classification, which can be either trained on a database of isolated notes or on solo melodies. All the considerations about classifiers mentioned in Section 5.2 apply here as well. Additionally, informative and accurate timbral descriptions are vital for this purpose, and in many cases, timbral features intended for general audio do not describe spectral content with enough detail to assure reasonable performance. For instance, partial-based timbral descriptions are far more accurate than general purpose timbre features such as MFCCs, which are based on a rough approximation to the spectral envelope.

In Burred, Röbel and Rodet (2006), a comparison between MFCCs and a partial-based timbre model was performed in the context of instrument detection from isolated notes, obtaining an accuracy of 60.37% correct classifications with MFCCs and of 94.86% with partial-based features in a database of 1098 samples and five types of instruments. Figure 5.11 shows the corresponding trained models as prototype curves, each one corresponding to the time-varying mean of a Gaussian process, projected in a dimension-reduced space whose bases were obtained by applying PCA to the partials of the original data. Such a space can be interpreted as a *timbre space*, in which each point corresponds to a spectral envelope, and thus to a timbre, and a curve corresponds to the variation in time of a spectral envelope. Apart for being useful for classification, such a visual representation allows a non-categorical characterisation and comparison mechanism for instrumental timbre. Other pattern recognition methods usually applied to instrument classification include PCA for dimension reduction and GMM, SVM and kNN for class assignment. A comprehensive overview on the topic can be found in Herrera, Peeters and Dubnov (2003).

Music genre classification has also attracted great attention from researchers since it is surely the most natural way for a user to browse for a certain title in a database, be it an online service, a sound archive or a retail shop, as well as for the database manager to organise it. Unlike in the case of instrument classification, establishing the ground-truth labelling for the training examples is not a trivial process since musical genres are of an inherently fuzzy and subjective nature and are understood in many different ways. When designing an appropriate taxonomy for automatic genre classification, it must be taken into account, on the one hand, how far is it possible to describe the different genres according to objective criteria which

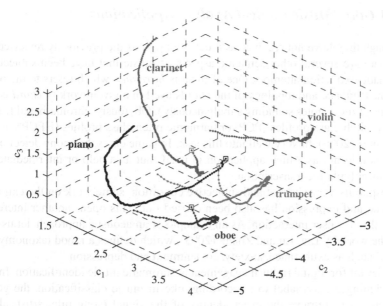

Fig. 5.11 Timbre space representation of a musical instrument database. Each curve corresponds to a trained instrument class. Each point in the space corresponds to a spectral envelope shape and thus to a different timbre

can be handled by signal processing methods. On the other hand, the success of such an application will strongly depend on how it can meet the expectations of a wide range of users with different opinions about musical categories.

Up to now, genre classifiers are feasible with around 3–10 broad genres, such as pop, rock, jazz, classical, dance. Participants to the genre classification task of the MIREX audio description contest (MIREX 2006) obtained classification accuracies up to 77.75% when using a 10-genre database of 1515 files and up to 86.92% when using a 6-genre database of 1414 files. Popular features used for this task include general measures of spectral shape (spectral centroid, roll-off, flatness, etc.), measures of the energy profile, statistical measures of the music signal in the time, Fourier or wavelet domains and MFCCs. It is also possible to take advantage of the transcription-related analysis to obtain higher level descriptions of melody, harmony, rhythm, etc. to further help differentiating genres. Usual classifiers include GMM, HMM, SVM and neural networks. Feature integration plays a specially important role here (Meng and Shawe-Taylor 2005) since it captures mid- and long-term characteristics related to rhythm or structure.

Instead of assigning predefined genres, music clustering systems group music pieces according to timbral or perceptual similarity. This can be used as the basis for a music recommendation system or as an intuitive graphical interface to navigate through a large music database. An example of such a kind of interface is "Islands of Music" by Pampalk (2006), in which the music database is represented as a three-dimensional archipelago whose islands correspond to clusters of similar pieces.

5.6.4 Other Music Content Analysis Applications

Although they have not received as much attention as the previously reviewed topics, there are several other semantic aspects of music that have been subjected to automatic extraction attempts. One of them is *harmony*, which refers to the organisation, sequence and topology of the chords used in a given work (a *chord* is a set of three or more notes sounding simultaneously). Obviously, chroma-based features such as pitch class profiles (PCP) or harmonic pitch class profiles (HPCP), as used by Gómez (2006), fit very well into this task. In some cases, harmony detection has been viewed not as a final application in itself, but as a help or intermediate step towards polyphonic transcription.

Despite its very abstract and subjective condition, some work on the extraction of mood and expression has also been carried out. This opens another interesting possibility for user interaction. As an example of an acoustic approach, let us mention the work by Liu, Lu and Zhang (2003), which defines a mood taxonomy with classes such as exuberance, anxiety, contentment and depression.

Relevant for digital rights management is automatic music identification. Instead of assigning a class label to a recording, like in music classification, the goal in this case is to retrieve the exact identity of the signal (song title, artist, album) taking the unknown recording as input. Therefore, it must rely on a previously created database of individual descriptions for each sound subject to identification. Important techniques in this field are *audio watermarking* and *audio fingerprinting*. An introductory overview can be found in Venkatachalam, Cazzanti, Dhillon and Wells (2004).

Finally, an emerging research field worth mentioning is that of automatic musical structure detection, which is aimed at detecting repetitions, solo passages, modulations, transitions, etc. Applications include archiving, automated analysis of musical form and *audio summarisation* or *thumbnailing* (Chai and Vercoe 2003). A typical usage scenario is to automatically locate the chorus of pop songs, usually their most recognisable part, to present them as example excerpts in an online music distribution service.

5.7 Summary and Concluding Remarks

This chapter provided a comprehensive overview of computational methods aimed at extracting semantics from audio signals. We addressed separately the specific needs and challenges each different type of sound (speech, music, general sounds) calls for. General audio classification and segmentation is the starting point of audio content analysis. Here, the audio signal is segmented into segments belonging to different types of audio and the recognised type is assigned to the segment. Depending on the type, further content-adapted techniques can be applied. The task of general audio classification and segmentation is challenged by the diverse nature of general audio signals.

Speaker segmentation partitions speech audio streams containing more than one speaker according to their identities. The most commonly used methods yield good results under certain acoustic and environmental conditions. In real-world applications, the speech audio streams are recorded at various places with different devices. Therefore, they have naturally different characteristics and acoustic conditions. The analysis of video content may provide useful temporal and spatial information for detecting speaker changes. The combination of the two modalities from both audio and visual domains makes the speaker segmentation applications more general and more robust against changes in the acoustic condition.

Spoken content indexing (SCI) extracts directly semantic information from speech segments of an audio stream. Automatic speech recognition (ASR) is the key technology for spoken content indexing and has achieved significant advances in the past decades. A short review of the state-of-the-art ASR technologies has been given. Spoken document retrieval (SDR) takes advantage of indexed spoken documents and enables the user to retrieve sought parts in the speech segments of an audio stream. To this end, many approaches have been developed. Even though SDR approaches using combined index sources provide the best performances, it is still not a viable technology for commercial applications. However, SDR methods using independent index sources could be the most efficient ones in the future, helped by decreasing storage costs and growing computational power.

Finally, the challenges of music content analysis are not only technical, but to a great extent also social. The huge variety of music styles and the lack of cultural agreement about them make the generalisation and robustness of a system performance difficult, and labelling of training databases an unavoidably biased task. Furthermore, music databases available to researchers for training purposes are scarce in comparison with real-world catalogues, often due to copyright issues. The solution for the future seems to be to design hybrid systems that combine, under a common ontology, audio analysis with user feedback, as well as with automatic gathering of related metadata via search engines or online resources, and whose trained models, decision rules or cluster topologies are adaptive and constantly updated with such information.

References

Abdallah, S., Raimond, Y. and Sandler, M. (2006), An ontology-based approach to information management for music analysis systems, *in* 'Proceedings of the 120th Convention of the Audio Engineering Society'.

Adami, A. G., Kajarekar, S. S. and Hermansky, H. (2002), A new speaker change detection method for two-speaker segmentation, *in* 'Proceedings of the ICASSP', Vol. 4, pp. 3908–3911.

Arias, A., Pinquier, J. and André-Obrecht, R. (2005), Evaluation of classification techniques for audio indexing, *in* 'Proceedings of the EUSIPCO'.

Burred, J. J., Röbel, A. and Rodet, X. (2006), An accurate timbre model for musical instruments and its application to classification, *in* 'Proceedings of the First Workshop on Learning the Semantics of Audio Signals (LSAS)', pp. 22–32.

Campbell, J. P. (1997), 'Speaker recognition: A tutorial', *Proc. IEEE* **85**(9), 1437–1462.

Carey, M. J., Parris, E. S. and Lloyd-Thomas, H. (1999), A comparison of features for speech, music discrimination, *in* 'Proceedings of the ICASSP', Vol. 1, pp. 149–152.

Casey, M. (2001), 'MPEG-7 sound-recognition tools', *IEEE Trans. Circ. Syst. Video Tech.* **11**(6), 737–747.

Celma, Ò. (2006), Foafing the music: Bridging the semantic gap in music recommendation, *in* 'Proceedings of the 5th International Semantic Web Conference', Vol. 4273 of *LNCS*, pp. 927–934.

Celma, Ò., Herrera, P. and Serra, X. (2006), Bridging the music semantic gap, *in* 'Proceedings of the ESWC 2006 Workshop on Mastering the Gap: From Information Extraction to Semantic Representation'.

Chai, W. and Vercoe, B. (2003), Structural analysis of musical signals for indexing and thumbnailing, *in* 'Proceedings of the 3rd ACM/IEEE-CS Joint Conference on Digital Libraries', pp. 27–34.

Chen, S. S. and Gopalakrishnan, P. S. (1998), Speaker, environment and channel change detection and clustering via the bayesian information criterion, *in* 'Proceedings of the DARPA Speech Recognition Workshop'.

Cheng, S.-s. and Wang, H.-M. (2003), A sequential metric-based audio segmentation method via the bayesian information criterion, *in* 'Proceedings of the EUROSPEECH', pp. 945–948.

Coden, A., Brown, E. W. and Srinivasan, S., eds (2001), *Proceedings of the ACM SIGIR 2001 Workshop on Information Retrieval Techniques for Speech Applications*, Vol. 2273 of *LNCS*, Springer, New York.

Cohen, A. and Lapidus, V. (1996), Unsupervised speaker segmentation in telephone conversations., *in* 'Proceedings of the Nineteenth Convention of Electrical and Electronics Engineers', pp. 102–105.

Cole, R. A., Mariani, J., Uszkoreit, H., Zaenen, A. and Zue, V., eds (1998), *Survey of the state of the art in Human Language Technology*, Cambridge University Press, Cambridge.

Crestani, F. (2003), 'Combination of similarity measures for effective spoken document retrieval', *J. Inform. Sci.* **29**(2), 87–96.

D'Andrade, R. (1978), U-statistic hierarchical clustering, *in* 'Psychometrika', Vol. 43, pp. 59–68.

Davis, S. B. and Mermelstein, P. (1980), 'Comparison of parametric representations for monosyllabic word recognition in continuously spoken sentences', *IEEE Trans. Acoust., Speech, Signal Process.* **28**(4), 357–366.

Delacourt, P. and Wellekens, C. J. (2000), 'DISTBIC: A speaker-based segmentation for audio data indexing', *Speech Comm.* **32**(1), 111–126.

Downie, J. S. (2003), 'Music information retrieval', *Annu. Rev. Inform. Sci. Tech.* **37**, 295–342.

Duda, R. O., Hart, P. E. and Stork, D. G. (2000), *Pattern Classification*, Wiley Interscience, New York.

Ferrieux, A. and Peillon, S. (1999), Phoneme-level indexing for fast and vocabulary-independent voice/voice retrieval, *in* 'Proceedings of the ESCA ITRW on Accessing Information in Spoken Audio', pp. 60–63.

Foote, J. (2001), The beat spectrum: A new approach to rhythm analysis, *in* 'Proceedings of the ICME', pp. 881–884.

Foote, J. T. (1997), Content-based retrieval of music and audio, *in* C.-C. Jay Kuo et al., ed., 'Proceedings of the Electronic Imaging', Vol. 3229, pp. 138–147.

Gauvain, J.-L., Lamel, L. and Adda, G. (1998), Partitioning and transcription of broadcast news data, *in* 'Proceedings of the ICSLP', Vol. 5, pp. 1335–1338.

Gish, H. and Schmidt, M. (1994), 'Text-independent speaker identification', *IEEE Signal Process Mag.* **11**(4), 18–32.

Gish, H., Siu, M.-H. and Rohlicek, R. (1991), Segregation of speakers for speech recognition and speaker identification., *in* 'Proceedings of the ICASSP', pp. 873–876.

Glass, J., Chang, J. and McCandless, M. (1996), A probabilistic framework for feature-based speech recognition, *in* 'Proceedings of the ICSLP', Vol. 4, pp. 2277–2280.

Glavitsch, U. (1995), A first approach to speech retrieval, Technical Report 238, ETH Zrich, Institute of Information Systems.

Goldhor, R. S. (1993), Recognition of environmental sounds, *in* 'Proceedings of the ICASSP', Vol. 1, pp. 149–152.

Gómez, E. (2006), Tonal Description of Music Audio Signals, PhD thesis, Universitat Pompeu Fabra, Barcelona, Spain.

Guo, G., Zhang, H.-J. and Li, S. Z. (2001), Boosting for content-based audio classification and retrieval: An evaluation, *in* 'Proceedings of the ICME', pp. 1200–1203.

Gurevych, I. and Porzel, R. (2003), Using knowledge-based scores for identifying best speech recognition hypothesis, *in* 'Proceedings of the ISCA ITRW on Error Handling in Spoken Dialog Systems', pp. 77–81.

Harman, D. (2000), 'Overview of the sixth text retrieval conference (trec-6)', *Inform. Process. Manag.* **36**(1), 3–35.

Hermansky, H. (1990), 'Perceptual linear predictive (PLP) analysis of speech', *J. Acoust. Soc. Am.* **87**(4), 1738–1752.

Herrera, P., Peeters, G. and Dubnov, S. (2003), 'Automatic classification of musical instrument sounds', *J. New. Music Res.* **32**(1), 3–21.

Hung, J.-W., Wang, H.-M. and Lee, L.-S. (2000), Automatic metric-based speech segmentation for broadcast news via principal component analysis, *in* 'Proceedings of the ICSLP', Vol. 4, pp. 121–124.

ISO/IEC (2002), '15938-4:2002 – Information technology – Multimedia content description interface – Part 4: Audio'.

ISO/IEC (2004), '15938-4:2002/amd 1:2004 – Information technology – Multimedia content description interface – Part 4: Audio, Amendment 1: Audio extensions'.

ISO/IEC (2006), '15938-4:2002/amd 2:2006 – Information technology – Multimedia content description interface – Part 4: Audio, Amendment 2: High-level descriptors'.

James, D. (1995), The application of classical information retrieval techniques to spoken documents, PhD thesis, University of Cambridge, UK.

Johnson, S. C. (1967), 'Hierarchical clustering schemes', *Psychometrika* **32**(3), 241–254.

Jørgensen, K. W., Mølgaard, L. L. and Hansen, L. K. (2006), Unsupervised speaker change detection for broadcast news segmentation, *in* 'Proceedings of the EUSIPCO'.

Kartik, V., Satish, D. S. and Sekhar, C. C. (2005), Speaker change detection using support vector machines, *in* 'Proceedings of the ISCA ITRW on Non-linear Speech Processing', pp. 130–136.

Kemp, T., Schmidt, M., Westphal, M. and Waibel, A. (2000), Strategies for automatic segmentation of audio data, *in* 'Proceedings ICASSP', Vol. 3, pp. 1423–1426.

Kershaw, D., Robinson, A. and Renals, S. (1996), The 1995 abbot hybrid connectionist-hmm large-vocabulary recognition system, *in* 'Proceedings of the ARPA Speech Recognition Workshop', pp. 93–98.

Kim, H.-G., Burred, J. J. and Sikora, T. (2004), How efficient is MPEG-7 for general sound recognition?, *in* 'Proceedings AES 25th International Conference'.

Kim, H.-G., Ertelt, D. and Sikora, T. (2005), Hybrid speaker-based segmentation system using model-level clustering, *in* 'Proceedings of the ICASSP', Vol. 1, pp. 745–748.

Kim, H.-G., Moreau, N. and Sikora, T. (2005), *MPEG-7 Audio and Beyond: Audio Content Indexing and Retrieval*, John Wiley & Sons, New York.

Klapuri, A. (2004), Signal Processing Methods for the Transcription of Music, PhD thesis, Tampere University of Technology, Tampere, Finland.

Larson, M. and Eickeler, S. (2003), Using syllable-based indexing features and language models to improve german spoken document retrieval, *in* 'Proceedings of the EUROSPEECH', pp. 1217–1220.

Lee, K.-F. (1989), *Automatic Speech Recognition*, Kluwer Academic Publishers, chapter Appendix I.2, p. 147.

Liu, D. and Kubala, F. (1999), Fast speaker change detection for broadcast news transcription and indexing, *in* 'Proceedings of the EUROSPEECH', Vol. 3, pp. 1031–1034.

Liu, D., Lu, L. and Zhang, H.-J. (2003), Automatic mood detection from acoustic music data, *in* 'Proceedings of the ISMIR'.

Liu, Z., Wang, Y. and Chen, T. (1998) , 'Audio feature extraction and analysis for scene segmentation and classification', *J. VLSI Signal Process.* **20**(1/2), 61–79.

Logan, B., Prasangsit, P. and Moreno, P. (2003), Fusion of semantic and acoustic approaches for spoken document retrieval, *in* 'Proceedings of the ISCA Workshop on Multilingual Spoken Document Retrieval', pp. 1–6.

Lu, L. and Zhang, H. J. (2002a) , Real-time unsupervised speaker change detection, *in* 'Proceedings of the ICPR', Vol. 2, pp. 358–361.

Lu, L. and Zhang, H. J. (2002b) , Speaker change detection and tracking in real-time news broadcasting analysis., *in* 'Proceedings of the ACM International Conference on Multimedia', pp. 602–610.

Meng, A. and Shawe-Taylor, J. (2005) , An investigation of feature models for music genre classification using the support vector classifier, *in* 'Proceedings of the ISMIR', pp. 604–609.

MIREX (2006), 'Music information retrieval evaluation exchange'. http://www.music-ir.org/mirex2006/ (last checked February 2007).

Moreau, N., Jin, S. and Sikora, T. (2005), Comparison of different phone-based spoken document retrieval methods with text and spoken queries, *in* 'Proceedings of the EUROSPEECH', pp. 641–644.

Mori, K. and Nakagawa, S. (2001), Speaker change detection and speaker clustering using VQ distortion for broadcast news speech recognition, *in* 'Proceedings of the ICASSP', Vol. 1, pp. 413–416.

Nakagawa, S. and Suzuk, H. (1993), A new speech recognition method based on VQ-distortion and HMM, *in* 'Proceedings of the ICASSP', Vol. 2, pp. 676–679.

Nakatani, T. and Okuno, H. (1998), Sound ontology for computational auditory scene analysis, *in* 'Proceedings of the National Conference on Artificial Intelligence (AAAI)', pp. 1004–1010.

Ng, K. (2000), Information fusion for spoken document retrieval, *in* 'Proceedings ICASSP', Vol. 6, pp. 2405–2408.

Ng, K. and Zue, V. W. (1998), Phonetic recognition for spoken document retrieval, *in* 'Proceedings ICASSP', Vol. 1, pp. 325–328.

O'Grady, P. D., Pearlmutter, B. A. and Rickard, S. T. (2005), 'Survey of sparse and non-sparse methods in source separation', *Int. J. Imag. Syst. Tech.* **15**(1), 18–33.

Pachet, F. (2005), Musical metadata and knowledge management, *in* D. Schwartz, ed., 'Encyclopedia of Knowledge Management', Idea Group, pp. 672–677.

Pampalk, E. (2006), Computational Models of Music Similarity and their Application in Music Information Retrieval, PhD thesis, Technische Universitt Wien.

Pfeiffer, S., Fischer, S. and Effelsberg, W. (1996), Automatic audio content analysis, *in* 'Proceedings 4th ACM International Multimedia Conference', pp. 21–30.

Pietquin, O., Couvreur, L. and Couvreur, P. (2001), Applied clustering for automatic speaker-based segmentation of audio material, *in* 'JORBEL', Vol. 41, pp. 69–81.

Qi, W., Gu, L., Jiang, H., Chen, X. and Zhang, H. (2000), Integrating visual, audio and text analysis for news video, *in* 'Proceedings of the ICIP', Vol. 3, pp. 520–523.

Rabiner, L. and Juang, B.-H. (1993), *Fundamentals of Speech Recognition*, Prentice Hall.

Renals, S. (1999), The THISL spoken document retrieval project, *in* 'Proceedings IEEE International Conference on Multimedia Computing and Systems (MCS)', Vol. 2, pp. 1049–1051.

Rose, R. (1995), 'Keyword detection in conversational speech utterances using hidden markov model based continuous speech recognition', *Comput. Speech Lang.* **9**(4), 309–333.

Samour, A., Karaman, M., Goldmann, L. and Sikora, T. (2007), Video to the rescue of audio: Shot boundary assisted speaker change detection, *in* 'Proceedings of the Electronic Imaging', Vol. 6506.

Sanderson, C. and Paliwala, K. K. (2004), 'Identity verification using speech and face information', *Digit. Signal Process.* **14**(5), 449–480.

Saunders, J. (1996), Real-time discrimination of broadcast speech/music, *in* 'Proceedings of the ICASSP', Vol. 2, pp. 993–996.

Schaeuble, P. and Glavitsch, U. (1994), Assessing the retrieval effectiveness of a speech retrieval system by simulating recognition errors, *in* 'Proceedings Workshop on Human Language Technology', pp. 370–372.

Scheirer, E. and Slaney, M. (1997), Construction and evaluation of a robust multifeature speech/music discriminator, *in* 'Proceedings of the ICASSP', Vol. 2, pp. 1331–1334.

Schwarz, G. (1978), Estimation the dimension of a model, *in* 'Annals of Statistics', Vol. 6, pp. 461–464.

Serra, X. (1997), Musical sound modeling with sinusoids plus noise, *in* C. Roads, S. T. Pope, A. Piccialli and G. D. Poli, eds, 'Musical Signal Processing', Swets & Zeitlinger The Netherlands, pp. 91–122.

Siegler, M. A., Jain, U., Raj, B. and Stern, R. M. (1997), Automatic segmentation, classification and clustering of broadcast news audio, *in* 'Proceedings of the DARPA Speech Recognition Workshop', pp. 97–99.

Smaragdis, P. and Brown, J. C. (2003), Non-negative matrix factorization for polyphonic music transcription, *in* 'Proceedings of the WASPAA', pp. 177–180.

Sönmez, K., Heck, L. and Weintraub, M. (1999), Speaker tracking and detection with multiple speakers, *in* 'Proceedings of the EUROSPEECH', Vol. 5, pp. 2219–2222.

Sugiyama, M., Murakami, J. and H.Watanabe (1993), Speech segmentation and clustering based on speaker features, *in* 'Proceedings of the ICASSP', Vol. 2, pp. 395–398.

Taskiran, C., Albiol, A., Torres, L. and Delp, E. (2004), Detection of unique people in news programs using multimodal shot clustering, *in* 'Proceedings of the ICIP', Vol. 1, pp. 697–700.

Theodoridis, S. and Koutroumbas, K. (2006), *Pattern Recognition*, Elsevier, The Netherlands.

Tritschler, A. and Gopinath, R. (1999), Improved speaker segmentation and segments clustering using the bayesian information criterion., *in* 'Proceedings of the EUROSPEECH', pp. 679–682.

Tzanetakis, G. and Cook, P. (2002), 'Musical genre classification of audio signals', *IEEE Trans. Speech Audio Process.* **10**(5), 293–302.

Venkatachalam, V., Cazzanti, L., Dhillon, N. and Wells, M. (2004), 'Identification of sound recordings', *IEEE Signal Process. Mag.* **21**(2), 92–99.

Verma, T., Levine, S. and Meng, T. (1997), Transient modeling synthesis: A flexible analysis/synthesis tool for transient signals, *in* 'Proceedings of the International Computer Music Conference (ICMC)', pp. 164–167.

Vorhees, E. and Harman, D., eds (2001), *NIST Special Publication 500-250: 10th Text Retrieval Conference (TREC)*, chapter Common Evaluation Measures, pp. A14–A23.

Wang, Y., Liu, Z. and Huang, J.-C. (2000), 'Multimedia content analysis using both audio and visual clues', *IEEE Signal Process. Mag.* **17**(6), 12–36.

Wilcox, L., Chen, F., Kimber, D. and Balasubramanian, V. (1994), Segmentation of speech using speaker identification, *in* 'Proceedings of the ICASSP', pp. 161–164.

Wilpon, J., Rabiner, L. and Lee, C.-H. (1990), 'Automatic recognition of keywords in unconstrained speech using hidden markov models', *IEEE Trans. Acoust., Speech, Signal Process.* **38**, 1870–1878.

Wold, E., Blum, T., Keislar, D. and Wheaton, J. (1996), 'Content-based classification, search, and retrieval of audio', *IEEE Multimedia* **3**(3), 27–36.

Woodland, P., Gales, M., Pye, D. and Valtchev, V. (1996), The HTK large vocabulary recognition system for the 1995 ARPA H3 task, *in* 'Proceedings of the ARPA Speech Recognition Workshop', pp. 99–104.

Wu, T., Lu, L. and Zhang, H.-J. (2003), UBM-based real-time speaker segmentation for broadcasting news, *in* 'Proceedings of the ICASSP', Vol. 2, pp. 193–196.

Xiong, Z., Radhakrishnan, R., Divakaran, A. and Huang, T. S. (2003), Comparing MFCC and MPEG-7 audio features for feature extraction, maximum likelihood HMM and entropic prior HMM for sports audio classification, *in* 'Proceedings of the ICASSP', Vol. 5, pp. 628–31.

Yu, P., Seide, F., Ma, C. and Chang, E. (2003), An improved model-based speaker segmentation system, *in* 'Proceedings of the EUROSPEECH', pp. 2025–2028.

Zhang, T. and Kuo, C.-C. (1999a), Hierarchical classification of audio data for archiving and retrieving, *in* 'Proceedings of the ICASSP', Vol. 6, pp. 3001–3004.

Zhang, T. and Kuo, C.-C. J. (1999b), Classification and retrieval of sound effects in audiovisual data management, *in* 'Proceedings of the Asilomar Conference on Signals, Systems, and Computers', Vol. 1, pp. 730–734.

Zhou, B. and Hansen, J. (2002), Speechfind: An experimental on-line spoken document retrieval system for historical audio archives, *in* 'Proceedings of the ICSLP', Vol. 3, pp. 1969–1972.

Zhou, B. and Hansen, J. H. L. (2000) , Unsupervised audio stream segmentation and clustering via the bayesian information criterion, *in* 'Proceedings of the ICSLP', Vol. 3, pp. 714–717.

Zue, V., Glass, J., Goodine, D., Phillips, M. and Seneff, S. (1990), The summit speech recognition system: phonological modeling and lexical access, *in* 'Proceedings of the ICASSP', Vol. 1, pp. 49–52.

Part III
Applications Using Semantic Web Technologies

Chapter 6
Personalised Multimedia Summaries

**Cathy Dolbear, Paola Hobson, David Vallet, Miriam Fernández,
Iván Cantador and Pablo Castells**

6.1 Introduction

Personalisation, in its simplest definition, is technology which enables a system to match available content, applications and user interaction modalities to a user's stated and learned preferences. Personalisation intends to make life simpler for users by anticipating their needs and interests so that, for example, they are not overwhelmed by long lists of search results when seeking images and video clips for a certain task, or that their screen is not filled with irrelevant information when they are trying to access news information.

Generally, the objective of personalisation is to enable content offerings to be closely targeted to the user's wishes, and a variety of methods have been proposed in recent years to fulfil this objective. A common method is to apply content filtering, which selects content appropriate to a user's preferences from a set of available content (see for example Chen and Kuo 2000), and the experimental aceMedia system in which personalised content is made available to an end user as part of a search operation (Evans, Fernandez, Vallet, and Castells 2006). The user's preferences may be known via the user explicitly providing information about their interests, or may be learned over time as the user interacts with the system. Another well-known technique for content personalisation is based on recommendation, which proposes content to a user based on various criteria which may include the user's previous acceptance of related content or on the consumption of related content by a peer group (see for example McNee, Riedl, and Konstan, 2006).

Since much research effort has already gone into personalised retrieval and recommendation, in this chapter we introduce a different example of the application of semantic multimedia technologies, where we apply personalisation to the creation of personalised summaries of multimedia content. In this application, we assume that our user has limited time or attention span and needs to very quickly grasp the

C. Dolbear
Ordnance Survey Research Labs, Southampton, UK
e-mail: Catherine.Dolbear@ordnancesurvey.co.uk

Y. Kompatsiaris, P. Hobson (eds.), *Semantic Multimedia and Ontologies,*
© Springer Science+Business Media, LLC 2008

essential elements contained in a video sequence. The application must generate a representative summary which meets the user's needs and expectations.

This summarisation problem has some features in common with personalised content retrieval (content filtering) and recommendation systems in that

- the user needs and interests must be available;
- there is a description of the content which enables the system to decide whether it will be offered to the user; and
- an appropriate decision system (reasoning mechanism) is available to apply appropriate processing to the content based on the user preferences.

These three elements are equally important, i.e. success or otherwise of personalisation depends partly on correctly understanding user expressed preferences and interpreting user actions to translate these latter into preferences, partly on sufficiently expressive and meaningful metadata being available in order to match the content to the user's requirements, and equally importantly, on creation of appropriate reasoning technologies to enable the match to be made.

The capture and representation of user preferences is an area known as user modelling, and is outside the scope of this book (but see Geisler and Ha 2001 for an example state of the art method). The domain of metadata expression and representation is treated in Chapters 4 and 5, and that of reasoning in Chapter 3. The use of well-defined and correctly specified annotation terms is very important, as it assists with interoperability of the reasoning tools which act on the content to achieve the desired personalisation. In other words, the personalised application examples which follow in this chapter rely on the availability of a unified and accurate set of metadata, which enable the appropriate content to be selected.

This implies that the content contains some appropriate annotation, which may have been manually added or automatically generated. A personalised search application will transform user expressed (or learned) preferences into appropriate queries which can be matched to the available content metadata. Where content is not already annotated, analysis methods (such as those described in Chapters 4 and 5) can be used to derive metadata according appropriate schema or ontologies (as explained in Chapter 2).

6.1.1 Chapter Overview

Our focus in this chapter is processing of multimedia content to create personalised summaries which meet a user's need for a shortened version of the content, to meet requirements of time, interest level and physical constraints such as storage space or available bandwidth. An example might be to produce 5 minutes' highlights from a premier league soccer match, for the busy soccer fan to view on a mobile device during their commute to work, or to share with friends when out socialising. Such a summary must not only meet time constraints (i.e. the user has specified how long the highlights can be), but must also have sufficient semantic meaning such that it can be understood as a self-contained unit.

When we intend to personalise such summaries, we also must ensure that the selected content is that which the user is most interested in, and which generates an emotional response i.e. that the user feels that the chosen content has some specific meaning for them. However, many current multimedia content summarisation methods are signal based, and do not necessarily support semantic story telling according to a user's preferences and interests. Some examples are reviewed in Section 6.2. We will also review user requirements for personalised summaries and will describe some state of the art personalisation methods, which can be applied to the personalised summarisation problem. In Section 6.2, we also introduce some high-level usage scenarios, before moving on to a specific example of soccer matches' summarisation in Section 6.3. A complementary technique for contextualising personalisation, as a means to enhance the coherence of summaries, is presented in Section 6.4.

6.2 Personalised Multimedia Summaries

Methods to automatically summarise long video sequences have been in development for some years, often with the objective of creating a short version of a long sequence to enable a user to review the material to determine if the full version would be relevant to them. Many authors have proposed the use of keyframes to represent a summary of a video sequence, for example (Chang, Sull, and Lee 1999), in which the detected keyframes are intended to provide a compact representation of the video sequence. However, representation of a continuous video sequence by a series of still images does not convey the meaning of the video, but instead can only give a quick visual summary of some of the events in the sequence.

More recent work such as Sundaram and Chang (2001) and Graves and Gong (2004) analyse the complexity and temporal action in the video content, in an attempt to generate more meaningful summaries which are composed of short temporal segments. In their experiments, Sundaram and Chang (2001) summarised well-known movies down to as little as 5% of their original length (i.e. for a 165-min movie, an 8-min segment was created). Using a combination of automatic shot generation and manual selection, this method considers both visual complexity of the content, as determined by the amount of time it would take to understand the meaning of some content following a keyframe, and the film syntax i.e. how the producer arranges film shots to create the story.

The approach taken by Graves and Gong (2004) aims at creating an entirely automatic summarisation process, based on where the system determines that there is "action" in the video sequence. Although this would lead to useful results in applications where scene activity is the most important element e.g. surveillance video, it does not necessarily translate well to summarisation of other types of material such as TV drama or operatic performances, where people and objects may be stationary for long periods of time.

In the above methods, the objective is to produce a summary of the video content which enables a user to quickly understand the content without needing to view the entire sequence. This may be useful for applications where a user must review long sequences, such as, for example, many hours of surveillance video tapes or long TV programmes or movies from a video archive. The summarisation in these cases would aim to create a universally meaningful clip so that any user could understand the essence of the full sequence. This, however, is not applicable for applications where the summarised clip is intended to be the final item to be viewed by an end user, such as would be created for sports clips services. In such applications, the user subscribes to a service which will enable them to view summaries of their favourite events (e.g. a soccer or cricket match). These summaries are intended to be accessible via mobile communications networks, and should be available soon after the match is finished. Each user subscribed to the service has their own personal preferences for what they want the summary to contain, such as favourite team, player, etc., and it is unfeasible to create multiple personalised summaries using a manual method. Therefore we seek a method of automatic generation of sports highlights from a full-length match according to the preferences of the fan, and in the next section, we will describe this method applied to soccer content.

Although the example which follows in Section 6.3 has been applied specifically to soccer sports content, the methodology is more generally applicable to summarisation problems in other sports domains. When an accurate user profile expressing the user's specific preferences relating to the content area and correctly annotated content are available (the first two key criteria discussed in Section 6.1 above), then the methodology to be introduced in Section 6.3 will enable meaningful personalised summaries to be created.

6.3 Use Case – Personalised Soccer Summaries

Personalisation of soccer highlights was selected as an example use case since the massive interest in soccer makes commercialisation of filtering techniques in this domain attractive. Manually edited soccer highlights are already being marketed as a major application for third generation mobile phones. However, since substantial expertise and time is required to edit soccer highlights by hand, an advantage of an automatic system is to allow a user to receive personalised highlights. For instance, user requirements research (Evans 2003) has shown that fans wish to see specific events involving particular players, and are very keen on viewing summaries of soccer matches when mobile, as the key activities are only a small part of the game.

Our system focused on producing coherent summaries, that is, ones that make sense as a whole, rather than being made up of individual, unrelated clips. This was based on the findings from a knowledge elicitation study with sports editors (Dolbear and Brady 2003) which showed that the important elements of a soccer highlights package are to tell the story of the match, by representing the flow of play and causal relationships between events. Young (2000) notes that coherence comes from the selection of actions whose causal and temporal relationships highlight an underlying plot. User interaction, for example in automatic narrative generation tools, allowing the user to alter the state of the world at any given point in a story, can so radically alter the world that even the most accommodating plot lines cannot survive. This raises the question of how far we can personalise a summary before losing the sense of coherence. For example, including only events involving the soccer fan's favourite player may result in a meaningless sequence of disjoint events, providing no understanding to the viewer of what actually happened in the game. We need to make sure that personalisation only takes place within a framework of coherent summarisation, in order to avoid this problem.

This section describes the implementation of an automatic soccer highlights generation system (Dolbear 2004) and addresses the issue of how to measure users' satisfaction with the content they are provided with and how this relates to the length of summary they might pay for. We also investigate the trade-off between personalisation and coherence in a summary, by developing a novel quantitative measure of summary coherence based on the causal relationships between events.

6.3.1 Previous Work

The information extraction problem has been addressed in the soccer domain using audio and video features such as colour density analysis, slow motion replay detection, penalty-box detection and speech-band energy to identify semantic events using machine-learning techniques such as Bayesian belief networks (Ekin, Tekalp, and Mehrotra 2003). With such systems, any event that can be recognised is deemed important enough to include in the summary. This leaves the generation of more meaningful summaries, containing only events relevant to a particular user, as an open area of research.

It has long been recognized in natural language processing research that an accurate summary includes all the narrative elements of the original text (Lehnert 1981), and the importance of a text unit depends directly on the number and quality of causal relations that the unit has to other text units (Trabasso and Sperry 1985). More recently, narrative coherence, modelled using tree-depth measurement in rhetorical structure theory trees, has been the basis for sentence selection algorithms for text summarisation (Mani, Bloedorn, and Gates 1998). While the authors have shown that modelling textual coherence improves summarisation results, the causal relationships in all of these previous methods have been manually annotated. As will be seen in the subsections which follow, our system is able to identify these causal relationships automatically, and we then use them to personalise the summaries.

From interviews with soccer fans asking them to rank events in priority order (Evans 2003), we have a clear idea of user preferences in the soccer domain. Goals were found to be the most important, followed by major referee decisions, sendings off, fouls, the build up to and celebrations following a goal, interviews with goal scorers or player of the match, and finally controversial incidents. This insight is used in the design of our user profile ontology in Section 6.3.2.

A frequently used method for personalising a multimedia summary, for example (Ferman, Errico, Van Beek, and Sezan 2002), is to assign a weight to each of the user's preferences, and use these weightings to vary the scores of the multimedia content entities, so that a resource allocation agent can then determine which content should be included in the personalised summary. An alternative is to use a collaborative filtering technique (Shardanand and Maes 1995). These are mainly employed in recommender systems providing personalised suggestions about items that a user may find interesting. Neighbourhoods of users with similar tastes (specified via user profiles) are formed and used to generate recommendations of items that a particular user may be interested in. Neither of these personalisation approaches allow for the coherent combination of a number of items into a summary, and so are insufficient for our purposes. This is because soccer highlights require the causal relations between the event items to be taken into account, so that the game's flow of play can be seen.

6.3.2 Method: Soccer Ontology and "Neutral" Summarisation

Since our primary focus is on information summarisation rather than extraction, we sidestep the need to extract information from the audio or video representation of soccer matches, and use the minute-by-minute "ticker-tape" reports widely available on many sports' websites. Such ticker-tapes represent a very rich source of content annotation, which, as has been explained above, is a necessary pre-cursor to any form of personalised content delivery.

While work has been done on information extraction from free-text soccer reports (Saggion, Cunningham, Maynard, Bontcheva, Hamza, Ursu, and Wilks 2002), we avoid this complexity by using a template mining technique to extract information directly from text where there is an automatically recognizable pattern. For example on websites such as the BBC's, the number of event classes that are described is limited, so we can simply search for expected words and phrases such as "Goal", "by" (followed by a player's name) and "from left half". We use a soccer ontology containing 20 classes representing common soccer events such as assist, booking, corner, foul and goal. Each event class has a start time, extra time, duration and player property associated with it, see Fig. 6.1.

Our training set consists of 126 examples of full-length soccer match descriptions, corresponding to approximately 90 min of video footage each. Their accompanying summaries were generated by manual annotation of the ticker-tapes with those events shown in the highlights broadcast on television, which we use as a "ground truth" benchmark. Events are clustered into causally related groups (which we term context groups). This is either done using the groupings chosen by the editor of the original web page (when the events are grouped into paragraphs on the web

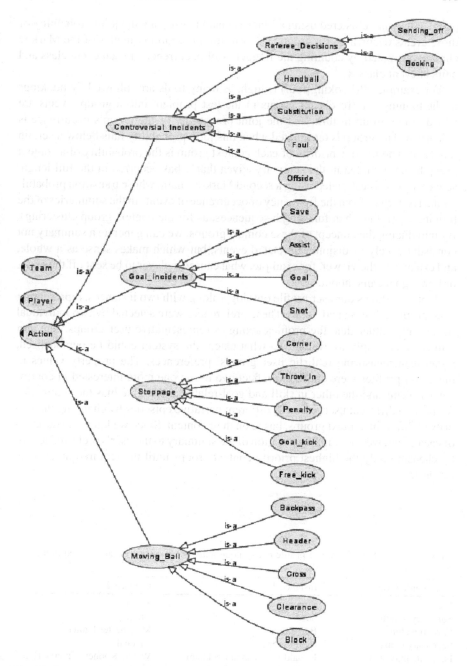

Fig. 6.1 Soccer events ontology

page) or they are clustered using a Markov chain to estimate the joint probability of those events occurring as a group. The transition probability matrix of the Markov chain is estimated by counting the frequency of occurrence of each event class and pairs of event classes.

For example, P(booking|foul) is high, as many fouls are followed by bookings in the training set. To cluster events in the test problem into a group, events are added to the group in turn, and the joint probability of the group's occurrence is calculated. The group is terminated when this joint probability falls below a certain threshold. The relative priority of each context group is the probability of a context group being included in the summary, given that it has occurred in the full-length sequence. This is estimated using a second Markov chain, whose transition probability matrix derives from the frequency of occurrence of events in the summaries of the training set (rather than full-length sequences, as for the context group clustering). By introducing the concept of these context groups, we can generate a summary not consisting solely of disjoint, unrelated events, but which makes sense as a whole, and explains to the viewer, for example, what caused a player to be sent off the pitch, or how a goal came about.

Table 6.1 shows our user profile ontology, along with two instances, representing example users Simon and Sarah. These preferences were selected by two individual soccer fans, rather than the profiles acting as representative user groups. The aim initially was simply to evaluate to what extent the system could be personalised, rather than measuring realistic user groups' preferences. The property values in these user profiles were chosen to reflect two users; one more interested in controversial events and the other in skill and goal-related events. We bias the summaries for the two different users towards different narrative episodes by changing the priority of different context groups, based on their content. Since we know the duration of each event, we can limit the duration of the summary to the user's preferred length by choosing only the highest priority context groups until the required duration is reached.

Table 6.1 Properties of the user profile class, along with values of two instances used in the personalisation experiments

User profile property	Instance 1	Instance 2
Name	Simon	Sarah
Summary length	60 s	5 min
Favourite club	Barcelona	Manchester United
Secondary clubs	Real Madrid	Arsenal
Favourite player(s)	Ronaldinho, David Beckham	Wayne Rooney, Thierry Henry
Favourite event	Goal	Goal
Second favourite event	Sending off	Penalty
Third favourite event	Foul	Shot
Fourth favourite event	Penalty	Save
Fifth favourite event	Booking	Assist

6.3.3 Characterising the Success of the Personalised Soccer Summary System

Since we were not aware of any commonly used performance measures for evaluating how closely summary content corresponded to user requirements in the literature, we chose three metrics for our evaluation. These were the accuracy of the summary duration relative to that requested by the user; how closely the content of the summary corresponded to the kind of events, players and clubs the user had indicated a preference for; and finally how coherent the summaries were.

6.3.3.1 Duration Accuracy

The first question to answer is whether our system can produce summaries of the right length for different users. We varied the requested length of the summary between 30 s and 20 min. Recall that each event has a duration property associated with it, which is derived from the times on the website ticker-tapes. These times were manually checked against the video footage and found to be accurate to the nearest second. Then the duration error between this request and the actual summary output was measured for the 126 soccer matches, in a leave-one-out fashion. The experiment was first carried out using summaries based on the priorities of individual events, and then repeated using summaries where whole context groups of events were included at a time, so that the differences in the two methods could be evaluated. Figure 6.2 shows a graph of the mean percentage error in duration accuracy for different summary lengths, and it can be seen that single-event based summarisation is more accurate than context-group based summarisation, especially for shorter summaries since an event's duration is of finer granularity than a context group's. The mean duration of a single event is 19.2 s, compared with 27.1 s for a context-group. However, beyond about 300 s, there is little advantage in using single-event based summaries, in terms of duration accuracy, and the advantage of context-group based summaries is in the additional coherence they provide to the overall summary.

Therefore, we can see that while single-event based summarisation has a smaller duration error than context-group based summarisation, since an event's duration is of finer granularity than a context group's, this advantage decreases significantly with summary length. The mean percentage error between the actual and preferred summary length also decreases as the summary length increases.

6.3.3.2 Utility

To offer the user choices like, "We know you're an Everton supporter, would you like to pay for an extra five minutes to see Everton scoring from a penalty?" we introduce a measure of how well the content presented to the user fulfils their requirements, which we term utility.

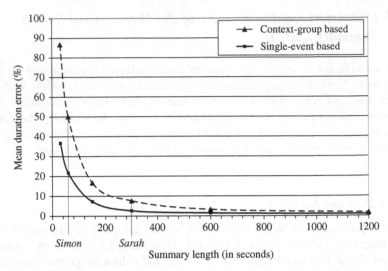

Fig. 6.2 Personalised summary duration error against summary length, with the two users Simon and Sarah's preferred summary lengths marked

Our utility function for a summary S and user profile U is defined as

$$\text{Utility}\,(S, U) = \sum_{i=0}^{N} w_i \text{frequency(events\_of\_class\_}U(i) \in S),$$

where i is the index of user profile properties, and N is the number of properties in the user profile. The weightings w_i give higher priority to the more preferred events, and those involving a favourite player or club. Figure 6.3 shows how utility increases with summary length; for Sarah the rate of increase decreases with summary length, while for Simon it increases. Simon is a tougher customer to please than Sarah, although this difference is less noticeable at shorter summary lengths. This is because Sarah's favourite events are included more often in the neutral (non-personalised) summaries than Simon's favourites. This suggests that there may be a limit on the variation away from neutral that a personalised summary can produce using our method. For future work, it would be useful to analyse representative user profiles of different types of users to evaluate how frequently real users do have profiles that require content that differs so substantially from that of a neutral summary that our coherence-based method could not generate it.

To entice a user to pay for extra content, or help them save time, the utility measure we have developed goes some way towards quantifying the additional benefit a particular user would gain from an increment in summary length. We found that utility increases with summary length, and that some users have higher utility than others, even for the neutral summaries.

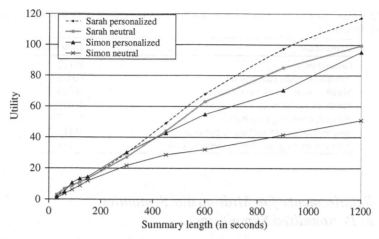

Fig. 6.3 Personalised summary utility against summary length

6.3.3.3 Coherence

We now investigate the trade-off between coherence and personalisation. To what extent is our suggestion valid that constraining personalisation to the context group level improves coherence? Our novel coherence measure for a summary S, consisting of events E_t, E_{t-1}, ... E_1 is calculated as

$$\text{Coherence}(S) = \sqrt[t]{P(E_t, E_{t-1} \dots E_2 | E_1)}.$$

That is, coherence is based on the causal relationships between the summary events, as calculated using the conditional probability of occurrence of the sequence, given the first event. Coherence is calculated here for summaries of the same length as the ground truth summaries because coherence was found to decrease with summary length. Therefore, we do not vary the summary length for Simon and Sarah's preferences in this experiment in order to make useful comparisons of their coherence. Table 6.2 shows the mean coherence of the summaries broadcast on television (the "ground truth"), compared with our neutral summaries generated using both single-event based and context-group based summarisation, and summaries personalised for Simon and Sarah.

Table 6.2 shows that coherence is much higher for context-group based summarisation than when single events are included in the summaries. The small difference in Simon and Sarah's results can be attributed to the small variations in summary lengths. As suggested in (Young 2000), personalisation reduces coherence in the summary, but the drop is much smaller for the context-group based summaries than the single-event based ones, which shows the advantages of the context group idea in retaining coherence, even in a personalised summary. Overall, it can be seen that including whole context groups in the summary, rather than just one event at a time, not only increases coherence, but mitigates the reduction in coherence due to personalisation.

Table 6.2 Mean coherence of various summaries; comparing ground truth with neutral and personalised summaries

Experiment	Coherence
Ground truth	0.112
Neutral, single-event based	0.018
Simon, event-based, personalised	0.006
Sarah, event-based, personalised	0.009
Neutral, context-group based	0.117
Simon, context-group based, personalised	0.112
Sarah, context-group based, personalised	0.113

6.3.4 Requirements for Multimedia Semantics in Personalised Summaries

Since the publication of Berners-Lee's vision of the semantic web in 2001 (Berners-Lee, Lassila, and Hendler 2001), there has been increasing interest in the use of ontologies for describing the meaning of content, both on the World Wide Web and in databases. In the sense of the term "ontology" as understood by the semantic web community, the structures we have used to describe events and user profiles are little more than metadata. That is, while they contain some limited hierarchical and possessive relationships, they do not take advantage of the expressiveness or preciseness of such semantic web languages as the web ontology language (OWL). While it is understood that metadata should be standardised, and used as a syntactical exchange mechanism, the fundamental point of an ontology is that it is not standardised, but enables individuals or groups to represent their own point of view via explicit semantics, forming part of the decentralised system of the semantic web. Extracting comprehensive semantics from multimedia, in order to populate an ontology expressed in description logics (using OWL–DL for example) is a long way off however. The semantic web community is moving towards understanding the need for provision of interfaces between standard World Wide Web Consortium (W3C), semantic web languages such as the resource description framework (RDF) and OWL, and the type of processing that needs to be carried out for extraction of semantics from multimedia, or with other concrete domains such as spatial or temporal reasoning. It is at this juncture that a way forward may lie between the standardisation requirements of multimedia metadata and the more open, decentralised technology of semantic web ontologies.

6.4 Contextual Coherence of Personalised Summaries

The previous subsections address the achievement of intra-document coherence by analysing the relations between consecutive events in a personalised summary. However in a typical session, users view more than one story, and often several documents related to each one. For example, on soccer (or rugby) match days, or during major tournaments, one would want to watch important scenes of several matches, plus a summary of results, some analysis and discussion, interviews, etc. The amount of stories, daily events and documents for each story, largely surpasses the available time of the idlest reader. Thus, it is not only important to summarise long documents to shorter versions but to select a reasonable subset of relevant documents and topics to be presented to the user out of the massive flow of available news items, and compose the pieces (summarised or not) in an effective and coherent way, according to the user's particularities and live activity. In fact, in some cases, the content is already delivered in a short format at the point of production (e.g. in news bulletins), and the summarisation need lies in the appropriate selection of items or segments. Compared with the intra-document perspective addressed in the previous section, the aggregation of summaries introduces a new dimension in the summarisation problem, where a larger variety of topics and a wider semantic heterogeneity are involved.

In this section, we argue that it is possible to further enhance the coherence of composite summaries at the aggregative level, by analysing the relations between user preferences and the current, live user focus at runtime. Indeed, an important requirement in order for a personalised summary to be perceived as relevant and meaningful by the user is to improve its coherence with the ongoing course of user activities at the time the summary is generated. The idea of contextual personalisation, proposed here, addresses the fact that human preferences are multiple, heterogeneous, changing, even contradictory and should be understood in context with the user goals and tasks at hand (Vallet, Castells, Fernández, Mylonas, and Avrithis 2007).

Even if the user is believed to have a persistent set of user interests, either learnt by the system in the profiling phase or manually provided by the user, it is assumed that such interests are not static, but vary with time and depend on the situation. In order to provide effective personalised summaries and develop intelligent personalisation algorithms, it is appropriate to not only consider a stable set of persistent user interests, but also to take into account the current user focus. Indeed, although users may have stable and recurrent overall preferences, not all of their interests are relevant all the time. Instead, usually only a subset is active at a given situation, and the rest can be considered as "noise" preferences. For instance, a user may enjoy documentaries about sea life, whereby the concept "sea" is important for his/her in the context of natural life documents, but this does not mean he/she is especially interested in sea battles when he/she is viewing a documentary about wars. Therefore, our model distinguishes a persistent component (which evolves at a slower pace) of a priori user preferences, and a temporary, ad hoc component, which is dependent on the live context within which the user engages in content retrieval tasks.

In our approach, the latter takes the form of an explicit, dynamic representation of the live semantic context as a vector of weighted domain concepts, which is built by collecting ontology elements involved in user actions, as will be described later in this chapter. This runtime representation of context is used in combination with the persistent user preferences in order to compute a focused, contextualised set of user interests. The computation of this set is achieved in two steps, consisting of a contextual expansion, followed by a contraction. In the first step, the initial preference and context sets are completed to form semantically coherent super-sets, and in the contraction, a sort of intersection of the supersets is determined. This way, the semantic runtime context is used to activate different subsets of user interests at runtime, so as to achieve a coherence with the thematic scope of user actions, in such a way that out-of-context preferences are discarded. Finally, the contextualised user interests are used to achieve a better, more accurate and reliable personalisation of the retrieval results retrieved by the system in response to user queries.

Context is an increasingly common notion in information retrieval (IR) (Finkelstein, Gabrilovich, Matias, Rivlin, Solan, Wolfman, and Ruppin 2002). This is not surprising since it has been long acknowledged that the whole notion of relevance, at the core of IR, is strongly dependent on context – in fact, it can hardly make sense out of it. However, context is a difficult notion to grasp and capture in a software system. In our approach, we focus our efforts on this major topic for content search and retrieval systems, by restricting it to the notion of semantic runtime context. The latter can be defined as the background themes under which user activities occur within a given unit of time. In this view, the problems to be addressed include how to represent the context, how to determine it at runtime and how to use it to influence the activation of user preferences, contextualise them and predict or take into account the drift of preferences over time (short and long term). In our current solution to these problems, the runtime context is represented as (is approximated by) a set of weighted concepts from a domain ontology.

The concepts that are used to represent the context are the ones that appear in user queries and annotations of clicked documents during a retrieval session. For example, if a user is querying and reading about ecologic damage in a certain region, the context may be made of domain concepts such as fire, toxic spills, air, river, fauna, etc. The initial weight of a concept in the context depends on its importance in a query, or the clicked documents where it is found. Then the weight is updated after each user request (click or query) in a way that decays with time, so that most recently involved concepts are considered most significant in reflecting the ongoing user concerns.

Our approach to the contextual activation of preferences is then based on a computation of the semantic distance between each concept in persistent user pref-erences and the set of concepts in the current context. This distance is assessed in terms of the number and length of the semantic paths linking preferences to context, across the semantic network defined by the ontology. This can be expressed as

$$CP(u, y) = P(u, y) \cdot \bigcup_{x \in \mathcal{O}, x \xrightarrow{p} y \text{ in } \mathcal{O}} C(x) \cdot w(p), \qquad (6.1)$$

where the union symbol denotes the algebraic sum (i.e. $a \cup b = a + b - a \cdot b$), $P(u, y) \in [0, 1]$ is the intensity of interest by a user u for a concept y of a domain ontology $\mathcal{O}$, $C(x) \in [0, 1]$ is the degree of importance of a concept x in the current context, $x \xrightarrow{p} y$ denotes there is a path p of semantic relations $r_i(x_i, x_{i+1})$, $i = 1, \ldots, k - 1$, connecting x to y in the ontology (i.e. $x_1 = x$, $x_k = y$), and $w(p)$ is the propagation power of each path, which depends on the semantic strength (a value in $[0,1]$) assigned to the semantic relations that make up the path, namely

$$w(p) = \prod_{i=1}^{k-1} w(r_i(x_i, x_{i+1})).$$

For instance, in the previous example, a steady user interest for sea life would be found to be in context with the retrieval session, provided that the domain ontology includes e.g. oil spill as a special case of an ecologic accident with impact on sea life, whereas a user preference for e.g. some basketball team would be out of place given the current focus of user activity. If, say, fishing industry was also in the context, the relevance of the user interest for sea life would be intensified, if the fact that the fishing industry depends on sea life is a known semantic relation in the ontology (see Fig. 6.4). Whereas the relation weights $w(r(a, b))$ are stored in the knowledge base, the weights of the paths are not stored persistently, as they are highly sensitive to changes in the KB (addition and removal of instances and relations). They are therefore computed on demand at runtime instead, and cached only for the duration of a session. For further details on this method, the reader is referred to Vallet et al. (2007).

Ultimately, the perceived effect of contextualisation is that user interests that are out of focus for a given context are disregarded, and only those that are in the semantic scope of the ongoing user activity (a sort of intersection between user preferences and runtime context) are considered for personalisation. This would mean that, for instance, information about the damage of an oil spill on the sea life would have higher priority than the economic impact, when a personalised summary about the accident is built. In practice, the inclusion or exclusion of preferences is

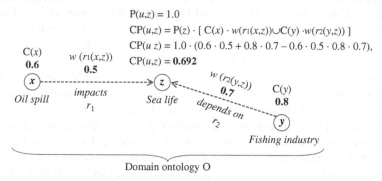

$P(u,z) = 1.0$

$CP(u,z) = P(z) \cdot [\, C(x) \cdot w(r_1(x,z)) \cup C(y) \cdot w(r_2(y,z))\,]$

$CP(u\ z) = 1.0 \cdot (0.6 \cdot 0.5 + 0.8 \cdot 0.7 - 0.6 \cdot 0.5 \cdot 0.8 \cdot 0.7)$,

$CP(u,z) = \mathbf{0.692}$

$C(x)$ **0.6** $w\ (r_1(x,z))$ **0.5**

x ------- impacts r_1 -------> z <--- $w\ (r_2(y,z))$ **0.7** depends on r_2 ---

Oil spill   Sea life $C(y)$ **0.8**

y

Fishing industry

Domain ontology O

Fig. 6.4 Contextual value of a user interest for "sea life" with respect to "oil spill" and "fishing industry" in a retrieval session

not binary, but instead ranges on a continuum scale, where the contextual weight of a preference decreases monotonically with the semantic distance between the preference and the context, as determined by Equation (6.1).

The extraction and inclusion of real-time contextual information as a means to enhance the effectiveness and reliability of long-term personalisation enables a more realistic approximation to the highly dynamic and contextual nature of user preferences. The ontology-driven representation of the domain of discourse, proposed in the previous sections, provides enriched descriptions of the semantics involved in retrieval actions and preferences, enabling the definition of effective means to relate user preferences and context. The gain in accuracy and expressiveness obtained from an ontology-based approach brings additional improvements in terms of retrieval performance.

The proposed contextualisation technique brings a clearer benefit in multi-document (or multi-topic) summarisation, involving the automatic selection of a subset of available multimedia documents (or document segments on a variety of subjects). For instance, a personalised multi-document summary may include a list of clips of several sports events, biased towards the user's favourite sports, teams, players, etc. This could include a couple of (summaries of) soccer matches, a basketball match and a golf tournament. If the user pays more attention to the golf clips, the effect of contextualisation would result in the summary automatically reorganising itself by increasing the space devoted to golf content. This would be a consequence of temporarily raising the a priori (persistent, long-term) user preference for golf, taking into account the ongoing user actions (semantic runtime context). This temporary, focused profile is what we are calling a contextualised user profile. The advantage of contextualisation is obviously higher when the initial multi-document spans across a wider subject range (e.g. including politics, sports, culture, etc.).

The contextualisation technique has been implemented in an experimental prototype, and tested on a medium-scale corpus. The latter consists of 145,316 multimedia documents (445 MB) from the CNN web site (http://dmoz.org/News/OnlineArchives/CNN.com), annotated with the KIM domain ontology and KB (Kiryakov, Popov, Terziev, Manov, and Ognyanoff 2004), publicly available as part of the KIM platform, developed by Ontotext Lab, with minor extensions. The ontology was used in OWL format (ported from its original RDF version), but our personalisation system is compatible with RDF as well.

For the experiment, we have built a testbed including ten hypothetical context situations (scenarios), each consisting of a sequence of user actions defined a priori, including queries and clicks on summary items, detailed step by step.

The results of this experiment are shown in Fig. 6.5, comparing the performance of contextual presonalisation vs. personalisation alone, and no personalisation. It can be observed that the contextualisation technique consistently results in better performance with respect to simple personalisation. The experiment shows how the contextualisation approach significantly enhances personalisation by removing out-of-context user interests, and leaving the ones that are indeed relevant in the ongoing course of action.

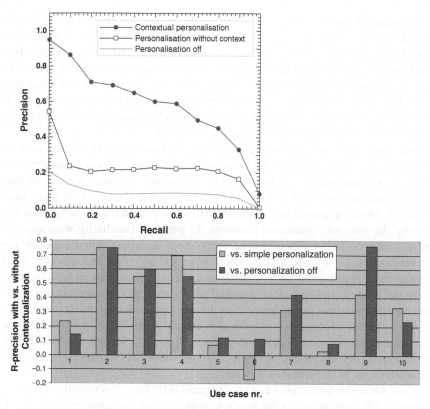

Fig. 6.5 Comparative performance of personalised search with and without contextualisation, showing the average precision vs. recall curve (*left*) and the comparative precision histogram (*right*), for ten scenarios

6.5 Conclusions

In this chapter, we have presented examples of personalisation applied to the summarisation of multimedia content. Automated content summarisation is necessary when the summary needs to be personalised to a user's specific needs or interests. For example, in a commercially viable sports clips service, each user will want action relating to their favourite team, players, league, etc. If there are thousands of subscribers to the service, it would be impossible to generate the targeted summaries for each user, but with knowledge of the user's preferences and interests, and suitable annotated content, an automated summarisation system such as that described in Section 6.3 could select exactly the right portions of the source for each user. The method we describe above takes into account the need to produce a semantic summary of the content i.e. that the resulting shortened version remains coherent and still tells the story of the whole event, rather than presenting a disjointed set of situations which can arise when purely signal-based methods are used.

Personalised summarisation was illustrated in Section 6.3 applied to one specific domain – that of soccer videos. This domain is highly representative of many sports domains where there will be opposing teams, multiple players and potentially a long match. Users will have favourite teams, players, tournaments, actions, moments (e.g. the famous "coup de boule" from the 2006 World Cup), etc. for each sport they follow, and the methodology described in Section 6.3 is generic enough to be extended beyond soccer, as long as a suitable domain ontology is defined and that user preferences appropriate to the sport are obtained.

User satisfaction in personalised systems is the main measure of success of the chosen method. Subjective testing is the most appropriate means of judging how closely a personalisation system meets the user needs. Although we can measure specific characteristics such as how closely a time target is met or how many times a favourite player appeared in a summary, only a user can tell us how satisfied they were by the summary generated for them. As people's familiarity with a subject and their interest in it varies over time, it could not be expected that a specific personalisation decision made by the system when the user first encounters it would necessarily be applicable over time as the user becomes more experienced and other issues and interests influence their personal preferences. It is also the case that a user may have different needs and interests at different times during the day e.g. leisure vs. work. Therefore, attention to context is critical in maintaining users' satisfaction in their interaction with personalisation systems, and Section 6.4 describes the use of context in improving user satisfaction in systems where multiple multimedia summaries may be presented to the user.

It was shown in Section 6.4 that user requirements for personalised content may change rapidly depending on the user's activities at any one time, but may also be subject to slow changes over a longer period, whilst retaining a static or very slowly changing set of preferences throughout stable periods in their life. The results shown in Section 6.4 show the improvements achieved when context is taken into account, and reinforce the importance for any personalisation system to use available contextual cues to better predict changes in user needs and preferences.

Acknowledgments Catherine Dolbear carried out the research presented in this chapter at Oxford University whilst the recipient of a Motorola University Partnerships in Research grant. Pablo Castells, David Vallet, Miriam Fernandez and Ivan Cantador were partly supported by the Spanish Ministry of Science and Education (TIN2005-06885).

References

Berners-Lee T., Lassila O. and Hendler J. (2001) The Semantic Web. Scientific American, May.
Chang, H.S., Sull, S. and Lee, S.U. (1999) Efficient video indexing scheme for content-based retrieval, IEEE Transactions on Circuits and Systems for Video Technology, 9(8), pp 1269–1279.
Chen, P.M. and Kuo, F.C. (2000) An information retrieval system based on a user profile. Journal of Systems and Software, 54, pp 3–8.

Dolbear C. (2004) Personalised Information Filtering using Event Causality. DPhil thesis, University of Oxford.

Dolbear C. and Brady J.M. (2003) Soccer highlights generation using a priori semantic knowledge, IEE International Conference on Visual Information Engineering, VIE 2003, University of Surrey, UK. July.

Ekin A., Tekalp A.M. and Mehrotra R. (2003) Automatic Soccer Video Analysis and Summarization, IEEE Transactions on Image Processing, 12(7), pp 796–807.

Evans A. (2003) User-centred design of a mobile football video database, Second International Conference on Mobile and Ubiquitous Multimedia, Norrkoping, Sweden, December.

Evans, A., Fernandez, M., Vallet, D. and Castells, P. (2006) Adaptive multimedia access: from user needs to semantic personalisation, IEEE International Symposium on Circuits and Systems, ISCAS 2006, Kos, Greece, 21–24 May.

Ferman A.M., Errico J.H., Van Beek P. and Sezan M.I. (2002) Content-based filtering and personalisation using structured metadata, Proceedings of the Joint Conference on Digital Libraries, ACM Portland, Oregon. July, p 393.

Finkelstein L., Gabrilovich E., Matias Y., Rivlin E., Solan Z., Wolfman G. and Ruppin E. (2002) Placing search in context: the concept revisited. ACM Transaction on Information Systems 20(1), pp 116–131.

Geisler B. and Ha V. (2001) Modeling user preferences via theory refinement, Proceedings of International Conference on Intelligent User Interfaces, Santa Fe, New Mexico, United States, pp 87–90.

Graves A. and Gong S. (2004) Wavelet-based holistic sequence descriptor for generating video summaries, British Machine Vision Conference (BMVC 2004), Kingston, UK, 7–9 September.

Kiryakov A., Popov B., Terziev I., Manov D., and Ognyanoff D. (2004) Semantic Annotation, Indexing, and Retrieval, Journal of Web Semantics 2(1), pp 49–79.

Lehnert W.G. (1981) Plot units: a narrative summarization strategy, Cognitive Science 4, pp 293–331.

Mani I., Bloedorn E. and Gates B. (1998) Using cohesion and coherence models for text summarisation, Proceedings of the AAAI Spring Symposium on Intelligence Text Summarisation, pp 69–76.

McNee S.M., Riedl J., and Konstan J.A. (2006) Making Recommendations Better: An Analytic Model for Human-Recommender Interaction. In the Extended Abstracts of the 2006 ACM Conference on Human Factors in Computing Systems (CHI 2006), Montreal, Canada, April.

Saggion H., Cunningham H., Maynard D., Bontcheva K., Hamza O., Ursu C. and Wilks Y. (2002) Extracting information for information indexing of multimedia material, Third Language Resources and Evaluation Conference.

Shardanand U. and Maes P. (1995) Social Information Filtering: Algorithms for Automating "Word of Mouth", Proceedings of Computer Human Interaction CHI'95 pp 210–217

Sundaram H. and Chang S.F. (2001) Condensing computable scenes using visual complexity and film syntax analysis. Proceedings of the International Conference on Multimedia and Expo, ICME'01. IEEE Tokyo, Japan, August.

Trabasso T. and Sperry L.L. (1985) Causal relatedness and importance of story events. Journal of Memory and Language 24(5) pp 595–611.

Vallet D., Castells P., Fernández M., Mylonas P. and Avrithis Y. (2007) Personalized content retrieval in context using ontological knowledge. IEEE Transactions on Circuits and Systems for Video Technology 17(3), Special issue on the convergence of knowledge engineering, semantics and signal processing in audiovisual information retrieval, March, pp 336–346.

Young R.M. (2000) Creating interactive narrative structures: the potential for AI approaches. AAAI Spring Symposium on Artificial Intelligence and Interactive Entertainment AAAI, Stanford, CA, March.

Chapter 7
The Role of Ontologies for 3D Media Applications

Michela Spagnuolo and Bianca Falcidieno

7.1 Introduction

From the beginning of its use, the term multimedia has been characterised by the possible multiplicity of content, by its availability in digital form and by its accessibility via electronic media. Text, audio, animations, videos, and graphics are typical forms of content combined in multimedia, and their consumption can be either linear (e.g. sound) or non-linear (e.g. hypermedia), usually allowing for some degree of interactivity.

In the last decade, we witnessed an unprecedented improvement in technologies for multimedia delivery: Internet bandwidth, compression methods, and visualisation capabilities are now allowing streaming, sharing, and rendering of multimedia content both in professional and in personal environments. The standardisation of content delivery is captured now in MPEG-4, which covers all media types. At the same time, the convergence of research in multimedia and knowledge technologies (see Chapter 1) opens up new possibilities of interaction with multimedia, as for example those addressed by multimedia content analysis, semantic annotation, and content-based retrieval. In parallel to this evolution, MPEG-7 formalises the way we will be able to *describe* the content and use these descriptions for an easier and more efficient processing (see Chapters 2 and 4).

Semantic multimedia, as the evolution of traditional multimedia, makes it possible to use and share content of multiple forms, endowed with some kind of *intelligence*, accessible in digital form and in distributed or networked environments. The success of semantic multimedia largely depends on the extent to which we will be able to compose them, and the related processing tools in systems that provide efficient and effective search capabilities, analysis mechanisms, and intuitive reuse and creation facilities, at the level of content, semantics, and context (Golshani 2006). Taking one step further, indeed, we could easily envision semantic multimedia

M. Spagnuolo
Istituto di Matematica Applicata e Tecnologie Informatiche, Consiglio Nazionale delle Ricerche, Genova, Italy
e-mail: spagnuolo@ge.imati.cnr.it

Y. Kompatsiaris, P. Hobson (eds.), *Semantic Multimedia and Ontologies,*
© Springer Science+Business Media, LLC 2008

systems of a higher level of complexity in which the generic architectural framework underpinning semantic multimedia systems could be extended to knowledge and data intensive applications, which have been historically developed in sectors that were quite far from multimedia and knowledge technologies. Throughout this chapter, we will illustrate this idea focusing on perspective applications of 3D media, a rapidly emerging new form of media in the semantic multimedia panorama.

3D media are digital representations of either physically existing objects or virtual objects that can be processed by computer applications. They may be either defined directly in the virtual world with a modelling system or acquired by scanning the surfaces of a real physical object. 3D content is relatively *recent* in the multimedia scenario: only in the last decade, indeed, computer graphics has reached a mature stage where fundamental problems related to the modelling, visualisation, and streaming of static and dynamic 3D shapes are well understood and solved. Considering now that most PCs connected to the Internet are equipped with high-performance 3D graphics hardware, it seems clear that in the near future 3D data will represent a huge amount of traffic and data stored and transmitted using Internet technologies. It has been predicted that geometry is poised to become the fourth wave of digital multimedia communication, where the first three waves were sounds in the 1970s, images in the 1980s, and videos in the 1990s.

3D media introduce also a *new* kind of content in the multimedia scenario: research on multimedia and semantic multimedia is largely devoted to pixel-based content which is at most two dimensional (e.g. images), possibly with the addition of time and audio (e.g. animations or videos), while 3D media are defined by vector-based representations. Due to its distinctive properties, the emergence of 3D content cannot be simply addressed as the problem of adding one dimension to the content: 3D media make it necessary to develop ad hoc solutions for content analysis, content- and context-based retrieval, modelling, and presentation, simply because most 2D methods do not generalise directly to 3D.

In this chapter, we will discuss issues related to the definition of semantic 3D media, taking into account the perspective of researchers in the field of computer graphics as well as the perspective of the 3D application requirements. The computer graphics community could indeed bring a significant contribution to the development of ontologies for 3D applications by taking care of defining a comprehensive schema for documenting and sharing 3D media representations, to be linked and further specialised by experts in different domains. To better understand the characteristics of the 3D scenario, Section 7.2 discusses the evolution of 3D modelling paradigms, from the traditional geometry-oriented to the emerging semantics-driven approaches. Emphasis will be given to the need of handling not only 3D shapes but also *structures* of 3D shapes as a key to link semantics to geometric data. In Section 7.3, we will analyse the levels of knowledge management required in applications, exemplifying the concepts in the scenario of product modelling, which is among the most complex and consolidated of 3D application domains. Finally, preliminary results related to the definition of ontologies for describing and processing 3D media in a semantics-aware context will be presented. These results have been obtained within the FP6-IST Network of Excellence AIM@SHAPE, whose main goal is to develop new methodologies for modelling and processing knowledge embedded in multidimensional digital objects, called shapes. Concluding remarks will end the chapter with a discussion on the main challenges that need to be addressed in order to achieve also for 3D media the same level of functionalities available in traditional media.

7.2 3D Media Representation: From Geometry to Semantics

Knowledge technologies can be effectively used in complex 3D application fields if the underlying 3D modelling approach is able to support and encapsulate the different levels of abstraction needed for describing an object form, function, and meaning in a suitable way. We will briefly overview the traditional approach to 3D modelling, as it has been adopted until now in computer graphics, and propose its evolution towards a semantics-based modelling paradigm, which is consistent with the different description levels used for traditional 2D media and reflects an organisation of the information content that ontologies dealing with 3D application domains could nicely exploit.

7.2.1 The Traditional Geometric/Visual Approach to 3D Media Representation

Modelling shapes is part of both cognitive and creative processes, and from the outset, models of physical shapes have satisfied the desire to see in advance the result of a project (Maldonado 1994). Architects, engineers, and product designers have always used physical models and graphical representations both for visualising their formal, structural, and functional hypotheses and to show other people (e.g. customers, clients, and producers) their projects. The ability of producing high-fidelity physical shape models was fundamental in the fifteenth century for originating the profession of architects, as professionals different from the master builders.

The use of computers has revolutionised this approach to shape modelling, opening new frontiers in research and application fields: computer-aided design, computer graphics, and computer vision, whose main goal is to discover basic models for representing and generating shapes. At the beginning, this effort gave rise to research in geometric modelling, which sought to define the abstract properties which completely describe the geometry of an object (*geometric model*) and the tools to handle this embedding into a symbolic structure. The visual aspect of shapes has deeply influenced the development of techniques for digital shape modelling, which have mainly focused on the definition of mathematical frameworks for approximating the outer form of objects using a variety of representation schemes.

Terminology and definitions for the foundations of geometric modelling were first introduced in the seminal article of Requicha (1980), whose basic notions have shaped the whole field to this day. The Requicha's paradigm uses four levels of

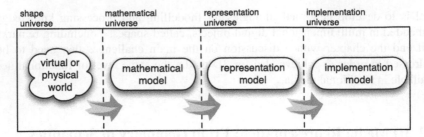

Fig. 7.1 The modelling paradigm defined by Requicha

abstraction, called universes (see Fig. 7.1) and expresses the modelling pipeline as transitions, or mappings, between these universes.

The first transition is from the *physical* to the *mathematical* universe: in this step, it is essential to capture the main properties of the objects to be modelled and to choose an appropriate mathematical abstraction (*mathematical model*). For example, if one has to model terrain data, an appropriate mathematical class of surfaces is the class of bi-dimensional scalar fields. The choice of this class will guide the following steps and will set a few basic guidelines for checking the correctness of the digital model: for example, choosing the class of bi-dimensional scalar fields will constrain the digital models to have no caves, as for each (x,y) value only one z value will be admissible.

The same mathematical model can be represented in different manners: for example, a bi-dimensional scalar field can be represented by decomposing the domain using a regular grid or a triangular mesh, and by associating the field values to the grid vertices. Considerable research activity has been developed in the two most well-known representation schemes for solids: CSG (constructive solid geometry) and B-Rep (boundary representation), which have deeply influenced current commercial geometric modelling systems. Roughly speaking, CSG represents shapes by modelling them as a composition of simpler volumes, while B-Rep represents shapes by defining their enclosing boundary surface. Figure 7.2 shows some examples of B-Rep representations of the same shape, mathematically defined by the equation of a torus. The triangle mesh is probably the most common geometric model used in computer graphics, and it is defined by a triangular network among points scattered on the shape boundary surface (a); other possibilities are regular

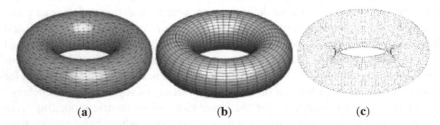

(a) (b) (c)

Fig. 7.2 Different geometric models of the same shape

quadrangular grids (b), level sets, or the point set itself (c) that is the simplest model possible, and it is defined by points on the shape whose adjacency can be determined by ad hoc algorithms or suitable spatial ordering structures.

The same geometry can be therefore represented by different discretisations (e.g. meshes, parametric surfaces, unstructured point clouds), each representation being chosen according to their advantages and drawbacks with respect to the application purposes. For example, complex triangulated meshes are badly suited to interactive animation. Simpler representations such as point set surfaces can be sufficient for special classes of applications (e.g. ray-tracing techniques only require ray-surface interrogations). The conversion between distinct representations is still a delicate issue in most systems, but there are tools to derive triangular meshes from the majority of representation schemes. The selected *representation model* will be eventually mapped into an appropriate data structure, that is computer-understandable and that will be devised according to optimisation and efficiency criteria (*implementation model*). For example, a triangular mesh can be implemented in many different ways.

It is important to point out that, for the development of semantic 3D media, the conceptualisation of the geometry in *not* an issue: geometric modelling is, by itself, the answer of the computer graphics community to the need of defining and expressing in formal terms concept and relationships concerning the geometric representation of 3D media. Shape models and related data structures encapsulate all the geometric and topological information needed to store and manipulate 3D content in digital form.

While the technological advances in terms of hardware and software have made available plenty of tools for using and interacting with the geometry of shapes, the interaction with the *semantic content* of digital shapes is still far from being satisfactory. While we have tools for viewing digital shapes even in much unspecialised web contexts – e.g. browser plugins such as scalable vector graphics (SVG) or VRML – we still miss effective and established tools to understand the meaning of an object (virtual or real), to compare it with other objects, or to decide if two parts are equivalent, similar, or different.

7.2.2 A New Paradigm for Representing 3D Media Semantics

To be able to handle semantic 3D media, we believe it is necessary to reason in terms of a new modelling paradigm which differs from Requicha's scheme in two ways: the coexistence of a real universe coupled with a semantic one and the formalisation of the mathematical universe whose models are based not only on purely geometric aspects but also on a set of multiple views, or structures, on top of the geometry.

This objective can be achieved if the 3D content is organised in a way that takes into account and supports reasoning at different levels of abstraction and that goes beyond the limits of the pure geometry. The integration and coupling of the classical shape modelling pipeline with the semantics-based one is sketched in Fig. 7.3.

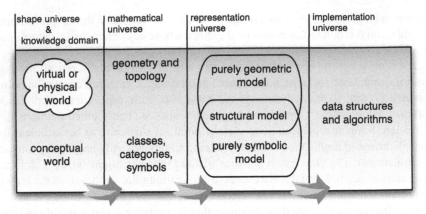

Fig. 7.3 The semantics-based modelling paradigm for 3D media

First of all, the universe of objects to be modelled has to be coupled with a *knowledge domain*, or conceptual world. In this universe, we will find abstractions of the human perception, understanding, and organisation of 3D media content and related knowledge. Entities belonging to a conceptual world and underpinning a broad conceptual domain are, for example, concepts of *similarity, features, structural decompositions*, or shape *categories*.

The conceptualisation of the knowledge domain has to adhere to a suitable organisation of the geometric data about the shapes. Generalising what has been discussed so far, we may say that shapes are characterised by a *geometry* (i.e. the spatial extent of the object), they can be described by *structures* (e.g. form features or part–whole decomposition), they have *attributes* (e.g. colours, textures, or names attached to an object, its parts, and/or its features), they have a *semantics* (e.g. meaning, purpose, functionality), and they may also have interaction with *time* (e.g. history, shape morphing, animation) (Falcidieno, Spagnuolo, Alliez, Quak, Vavalis and Houstis 2004.

We believe that the key issue to focus on is the *structural* level of representation of shape models. Structural models reflect and make explicit the decomposition of the object into its main parts/components and provide a global description of the object as a configuration of simpler parts. Examples of structural models are skeletons, obtained, for example, by volume thinning or distance transforms, or surface segmentation into patches having uniform properties. A structural representation of a shape specifies parts, attributes, and relations between them, independently and explicitly. Structural models encapsulate knowledge because they describe an object in terms of relevant parts that are context-dependent, or even user-dependent.

With respect to the traditional modelling paradigm, the simple one-level geometric model has to be replaced by a multi-layer architecture, where both the geometry and the structure contribute to the representation of the shape. At the same time, the structure is seen as the bridge towards the semantics, as it supports the annotation of the geometry with semantic information. In Fig. 7.4, we show an example of the different layers that shape representations should be able to portray, ranging from

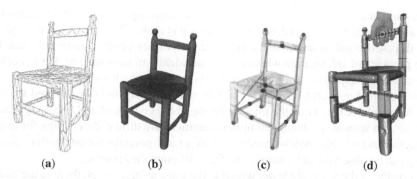

| (a) | (b) | (c) | (d) |

Fig. 7.4 The multi-layer organisation of 3D content; raw data (**a**), geometry (**b**), structural (**c**), and semantic (**d**) levels or representation

raw point measures acquired on a physical object in (a) to the semantic annotation of the digital model highlighting parts suitable for grasping the object in a virtual environment (d).

The importance of structural descriptions and representations relates also to theories of human perception, where experimental results are used for showing that people, when they interpret the meaning of a novel scene, attend to a few details only and recognise an object through basic shapes (Biederman 1987; Marr 1982). In generic domains of knowledge, they assume that each basic shape may be represented as a combination of a few generalised primitives. In more focused domains of knowledge, the basic components, or primitives, may be also linked to functional or other semantic primitive components, and the structural model generally reflects a semantics-driven segmentation of the shape.

To realise the shift towards this new modelling paradigm, it is also necessary to develop new and advanced tools for supporting semantics-based analysis, synthesis, and annotation of shape models (Mortara, Patané and Spagnuolo 2006; Attene, Katz, Mortara, Patané, Spagnuolo and Tal 2006; Abaci, Mortara, Patané, Spagnuolo, Vexo and Thalmann 2005). This step is equivalent to image analysis and segmentation for 2D media: features of a 3D model are equivalent to regions of interest in images. There is, however, a different input and a slightly different target, as image analysis is trying to understand what kind of objects are present in the scene captured by the image, while in 3D segmentation, the object is known and it has to be decomposed into meaningful components that might be used to manipulate and modify the shape at later stages. From a high-level perspective, the main differences concern the different nature of the content: descriptors used for 2D images are concerned with colour, textures, and properties that capture geometric details of the shapes segmented in the image. While one-dimensional boundaries of 2D shapes have a direct parameterisation (e.g. arc length), the boundary of arbitrary 3D objects cannot be parameterised in a natural manner, especially when the shape exhibits a complex topology, e.g. many through-holes or handles. Most notably, feature extraction for image retrieval is intrinsically affected by the so-called sensory gap: "The sensory gap is the gap between the object in the world and the information in a (computational) description derived from a recording of that scene" (Smeulders, Worring, Santini, Gupta and Jain 2000). This gap makes the description of objects an ill-posed problem and casts an intrinsic uncertainty on the descriptions due to the presence of information which is only accidental in the image or due to occlusion and/or perspective distortion. On the other hand, the boundary of 3D models is represented in vector form and therefore does not need to be segmented from a background. Hence, while the understanding of the content of a 3D vector graphic remains an arduous problem, the initial conditions are different and allow for more effective and reliable analysis results and offer more potential for interactivity since they can be observed and manipulated from different viewpoints.

Finally, at the semantic level, which is the most abstract level, there is the association of a specific semantics to structured and/or geometric models through annotation of shapes, or shape parts, according to the concepts formalised by a specific domain ontology. For example, the chair in Fig. 7.4 represented in structural form can be analysed in the domain of knowledge related to computer animation and the regions of possible grasping are annotated accordingly (see Fig. 7.4(d)). The aim of structural models is, therefore, to provide the user with a rich geometry organisation which supports the process of semantic annotation. Therefore, a semantic model is the representation of a shape embedded into a specific context, and the multi-layer architecture emphasises the separation between the various levels of representations, depending on the knowledge embedded as well as on their mutual relationships.

The multi-layer view of 3D media resembles the different levels of description used for other types of media, but there is a kind of conceptual shift when dealing with 3D media: here, we have the complete description of the object and we want to describe its main parts, or features, usually in terms of low-level characteristics (e.g. curvature, ridges, or ravines). These features define segmentations of the shape itself that is independent of a specific domain of application but that carries a geometric or morphological meaning (e.g. protrusions, depressions, and through holes).

7.3 Knowledge and Ontologies for 3D Media Applications

3D media are not only fancy-looking graphics used in entertainment applications; they are endowed with a high knowledge value carried either by the expertise needed to design them or by the information content itself. 3D graphics are key media in many sectors such as industrial design, engineering and simulation, and medicine and bioinformatics. In these applied sectors, representing a complex shape in its complete life-cycle stages is known to be highly non-trivial, due to the sheer mass of information involved and the complexity of the knowledge that a shape can reveal as the result of a modelling process. We believe that the potential of semantic multimedia technologies could be fully exploited in these application areas, where the processes deal with contents of multiple forms and types, the processing workflows are guided by knowledge and semantics, and the working environment is usually distributed. Knowledge technologies, and ontologies in particular, are quite promising in this field and offer new possibilities regarding knowledge management, retrieval effectiveness, and online collaboration compared to conventional technologies and techniques (Sevilmis, Catalano, Camossi, Cheutet and Ferrandes 2006).

An interesting example of a prospective 3D semantic multimedia system is product modelling, where a great industrial value is carried not only by the product itself – encapsulated in its corresponding 3D model – but also by the design and development history and process, the intermediate shapes that contributed to the definition of the final product, and the experts' knowledge used at the various stages of its development. Starting from a sketchy description of the various levels of knowledge management and processing occurring in the product modelling field, we will then generalise the requirements of generic ontologies and metadata for 3D application scenarios.

7.3.1 Knowledge About 3D Media: The Product Modelling Example

The interest in shape-related knowledge arises in all applications dealing with digital models of 3D shapes, either representing real objects or being created from scratch. As an example, we will discuss here *product modelling*, which is the application sector that mostly contributed to the development of techniques for modelling and processing digital 3D models. Product modelling can be informally defined as the whole work flow that goes from an idea about a new product (e.g. an appliance or a car) to the concept development and shape design, and then to a series of engineering-related steps such as testing, manufacturing, or machining the physical object. Due to the industrial push of product modelling, disciplines such as computer-aided design (CAD) and computer-aided manufacturing (CAM) strongly influenced the field of geometric modelling: they provided tools for an efficient handling of geometric data and for assisting engineers, or design professionals, in their activities. CAD systems can be regarded as the main geometry authoring tool within the product modelling work flow, while CAM systems take as input 3D models, or digital 3D media, and generate from them code to drive numerically controlled machine tools in order to manufacture the object.

Oversimplifying the whole process, we may take the CAD design and the CAM step as the beginning and end of the product modelling phase. Even in this simplified case, it is evident that the process involves a variety of data, information, and knowledge that the simple geometry cannot encapsulate by itself. Designers will be concerned more with aesthetic aspects of the model and will therefore be more used to reason in terms of qualitative properties of the geometry, such as roundness or smoothness, that may influence the shape of the product and convey some high-level feeling, such as aggressiveness or solidity in car design.

Aesthetics by itself is definitely not the single aspect to be considered since designers have also to deal with manufacturing, ergonomics, usability, or material technology. There is a variety of established methodologies that are used to integrate all these crucial aspects, and among them, concurrent engineering (CE) is a good example of a semantic 3D media environment. In a CE work flow, the various actors of the process work in parallel on a number of tasks that concur to modelling the product in order to optimise product quality while reducing development time. Therefore, CE information management is a global problem that requires a global strategy and solution, while most solutions today end up being independent.

The information management strategy should include the way design information is represented and how different processes interact with this information, across many departmental and disciplinary boundaries. Thus, to provide meaningful descriptions of a part for the different activities involved in the product development process, it is crucial to fulfil integration requirements. In the engineering community, *feature-based modelling* technology was identified as the solution for associating *functional* information to geometric data, and consequently for integrating design and downstream applications (Shah and Mäntylä 1995; Bidarra and Bronsvoort 2000).

Feature-based modelling introduced a structural level of representation in the traditional product modelling pipeline: *features*, as sets of geometric elements that are associated with some *meaning*, are a way to structure the geometry according to semantics-oriented criteria. The concept of feature is very crucial for the development of semantic 3D media also because it allows simultaneous consideration of different views of one object through the conceptualisation of different feature classes. The intuition behind this is that while the geometry of an object is unique, its description in terms of parts or functional aspects may be multiple. The same shape, indeed, may be described in different ways: considering the simple example depicted in Fig. 7.5, we might describe the same object as being formed either by a small handle attached to a box or as the result of carving out three small boxes out of a bigger one.

In the product modelling context, the different descriptions sketched in Fig. 7.5 could correspond, for example, to two different views of the same product used in

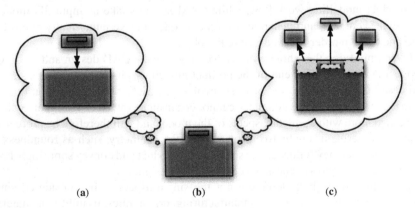

(a)   (b)   (c)

Fig. 7.5 The same object (b) may be described in different ways (a,c)

different stages of the modelling workflow. For instance, an engineer dealing with functional design would construct the object using a volume composition approach, by adding a handle to a box (see Fig. 7.5(a)). In the design scenario, indeed, the relevant features are those that carry a functional meaning as, for example, the handle for carrying the object. Conversely, in a manufacturing phase, the same object would be better described in terms of volume subtraction because the volume to be machined out identifies relevant features in the machining process (see Fig. 7.5(c)).

The central goal is to *conceptualise* shape design with classified elements, i.e. features, and add information related to design intent and other specific contexts. Most current CAD systems now support feature-based modelling, and they provide a better understanding of the relationships between the functional aspects of engineering and part shape. Feature-based modelling is the key to support CE work flows, where each design process works and updates its specific feature-based model and the modifications have to be propagated to the other concurrent design processes. So, it is necessary not only to conceptualise semantic descriptions but also to provide the mapping between different feature-based models that represent the same object under different points of view, which is still an open challenge.

It is clear that effective CE systems should be based on knowledge management and sharing mechanisms and standards that are able to provide a comprehensive formalisation and reasoning infrastructure that supports the design and production processes. Data standards, such as STEP, are very useful for exchanging low-level information but are not useful for supporting a knowledge-driven design process (Cera, Regli, Braude, Shapirstein and Foster 2002). We need to have tools for annotating 3D shapes or shape parts, ontologies able to express the functionalities of shape parts, and retrieval systems able to locate existing content according to geometric as well as semantic criteria. The functionalities provided by consolidated knowledge technologies have to be integrated with advanced tools for processing and analysis of 3D media in order to create a harmonised knowledge-driven framework for dealing with 3D media.

7.3.2 Knowledge Sources in 3D Applications

Effective and efficient information management, knowledge sharing, and integration have become an essential part of more and more professional tasks and work flows in product modelling, but it is clear that the same applies also to other contexts, from the personal environment to other applied sectors. There is a variety of information related to the shape itself, to the way it has been acquired or modelled, to the style in which it is represented, processed, and even visualised, and many more aspects to consider.

To cope with the complexity of 3D applications, we envision that application-specific ontologies should rely on a detailed formalisation of 3D media properties that does not depend on the specific application and captures the common knowledge about the shapes that can be specialised in application ontologies. Stated differently, we believe that the development of ontologies for 3D applications should resemble the abstract configuration presented in Fig. 7.3, therefore taking into account the formalisation of concepts related to *structure* as a hinge for connecting semantics.

Up to now, the few ontologies describing 3D media usually refer to partial aspects of the shape geometry, considering only the representation used for a specific application. This is, for example, the case of an interesting recent work on the use of ontologies in a computer vision system addressing the inspection of plants for horticultural applications (Koenderink, Top and van Vliet 2006). A human expert relies on a number of properties to assign quality grades to plants at the seedlings stage: for example, the leaf area and curvature, the stem length, or the regularity of the leaf shape. The expert knowledge used in the process of plant classification is then embedded in a number of tasks and sub-tasks and integrated with what the authors call a *geometrical application ontology* that supports the segmentation of the 3D model into features meaningful in that domain. The formalisation of the classification process is used to define a set of rules that are used to classify plants in an automatic manner. This expert system is coupled with an image acquisition device that measures the relevant properties on the 3D model reconstructed from the data acquired.

Apart from these few examples, we are not aware of 3D applications already working with ontologies, while there are ongoing activities related to the formalisation of background domain knowledge pertaining to application areas dealing with 3D data. This is the case of the medical domain, for example, where the foundational model of anatomy (FMA) has been conceptualised using ontologies and potentially offering a very interesting background for developing 3D semantic web applications for that domain (Rosse and Mejino Jr. 2003).

Therefore, the ingredients needed to implement a 3D semantic application should definitely include a conceptualisation of the shape itself, in terms of geometry, structure, and semantics, and of the knowledge pertaining to the application domain. In order to fulfil the requirements of complex 3D applications, we need tools and methods to formalise and manage knowledge related to the media content and to the application domain, at least at the following levels:

- *knowledge related to the geometry of 3D media*: while the descriptions of a digital 3D item can vary according to the contexts, the geometry of the object remains the same and it is captured by a set of geometric and topological data that define the digital shape;
- *knowledge related to the application domain in which 3D media are manipulated*: the application domain casts its rules on the way the 3D shape should be represented, processed, and interpreted. A big role is played by knowledge of the domain experts which is used to manipulate the digital model: for example, the correct manner to compute a finite element mesh of a 3D object represented by free-form surfaces is subject also to informal rules that should be captured in a knowledge formalisation framework;

- *knowledge related to the meaning of the object represented by 3D media*: 3D media may represent objects that belong to a category of shapes, either in broad unrestricted domains (e.g. chair, table in house furniture) or in narrow specific domains (e.g. T-slots, pockets in mechanical engineering). The shape categories can also be described or defined by domain-specific features that are the key entities to describe the media content, and these are obviously dependent on the domain.

The first level is concerned with knowledge which has geometry as its background domain. There are a variety of different representations for the geometry of 3D media that cannot be simply reduced to the classical virtual reality modelling language (VRML) descriptions and its variations, as currently supported by MPEG-4. Here, the view of 3D media is more concerned with the visualisation, streaming, and interaction aspects than with requirements imposed by applications. 3D geometry, as used in applications, has to do with a much richer variety of methods and models, and, for example, in the product modelling scenario, users might have to deal with different representation schemes for the same product within the same modelling pipeline. In this sense, describing the content of 3D media in terms of geometric data is much more complex for 3D than for 2D media. There are many attributes and properties of 3D models that scientists and professionals are using to exchange, process, and share content, and all these have to be classified and formalised thoroughly.

The second level refers to the knowledge pertaining to the specific application domain, but it has to be linked to the geometric content of the 3D media. Therefore, if we want to devise semantic 3D media systems, with some reasoning capabilities, we have to formalise also expert knowledge owned by the professionals of the field.

Finally, the third level has to do with the knowledge related to the existence of categories of shapes; as such, it is related both to generic and to specific domains. Usually in 3D applications, it is neither necessary nor feasible to formalise the rules that precisely define these categories in terms of geometric properties of the shape, besides very simple cases. However, due to the potential impact of methods for search and retrieval of 3D media, there is a growing interest in methods that can be used to derive feature vectors or more structured descriptors that could be used to automatically classify 3D media.

7.4 3D Application Ontologies: The Experience of AIM@SHAPE

The computer graphics community could bring a significant contribution to the development of ontologies for 3D applications by taking care of defining a comprehensive schema for documenting and sharing 3D media representations, to be linked and further specialised by experts in different domains. Besides knowledge related to 3D media and content, it is also important to capture knowledge embedded in the *tools* used to process shapes. Let us clarify the concept with an example: given a 3D shape, there exist a variety of different algorithms that implement the triangulation of its bounding surface; the choice of one or another depends on the properties that the resulting triangular mesh may exhibit. For example, there are methods producing equiangular triangles that are more suited for finite element analysis or methods that produce triangles that are positioned adaptively along creases of the surface. It is usually the know-how of the expert that enables the decision of one or another method. A clear classification of available tools for processing the geometry and manipulating 3D shapes might be an important building block for supporting the composition and creation of new easy-to-use tools for 3D media, whose use and selection can be made available also to professional users of 3D who are not necessarily experts in the specific domain of computer graphics.

The role of experts in 3D modelling for the development of semantic 3D media is twofold: on the one side, the identification of key properties for the description of 3D media and processing tools, and on the other side, the contribution to the development of advanced tools for the interpretation, analysis, and retrieval of 3D content. These ideas underwent a first validation phase in the course of the ongoing research activities of the project AIM@SHAPE that has produced a quite broad and comprehensive formalisation of all shape representation types, with their main attributes, and also a taxonomy of tools used for a variety of tasks in the computer graphics domain.

AIM@SHAPE expresses the expertise of computer graphics researchers, and therefore most of the effort was focused on the development of ontologies to be used as an e-Science support for scientists to discover and reuse resources in their specific area of expertise. The first step was to express relevant attributes and properties for the resources made available by the project via the repositories of the tools and shapes, respectively (Albertoni, Papaleo, Pitikakis, Robbiano, Spagnuolo and Vasilakis 2005). These attributes were initially structured in two separate taxonomies that largely extended the basic Dublin Core metadata and MPEG-4 attributes and evolved into an ontology structure called the *common ontology*.

Regarding the shapes, the structure of the ontology is simple but broad, and its general view is depicted in Fig. 7.6(a) (Vasilakis, Pitikakis, Catalano, Salem, Saboret, Papaleo, Garcia-Rojas and Sevilmis 2006). Generally, the number of properties is relatively small while the depth of the ontology is localised under the *Shape Representation* class specialisation. Note that the concept *Structural Descriptors* is a sub-class of *Shape Representation*, meaning that the concept of shape extends and includes the geometric and structural levels. Other classes that have been introduced in the shape ontology concern the concept of *shape groups*: frequently, indeed, it is necessary to have a mechanism for linking shape models under a common framework, for example, to capture a series of models that correspond to the various stages of an acquisition and reconstruction process or for capturing a series of models that correspond to different representations of the same geometry (see Fig. 7.6(b)).

Even if the focus is on 3D, the ontology for the shape models covers a large variety of representations, including images and videos. However, most of the interest in expressing detailed metadata concerns the properties of the representation models that correspond to the geometric level of representation of shapes. The hierarchy of *Shape Representation* is depicted in Fig. 7.7: the first level is completely listed, while the second and third are expanded only for the class *Geometrical*

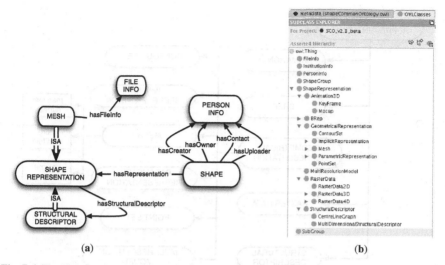

Fig. 7.6 The high-level organisation of the shape ontology (**a**) and the full list of concepts used in the ontology (**b**)

Representation. The attributes for the various classes are many and mostly related to the documentation of properties that characterise the quality of the geometric model (e.g. resolution, genus, manifoldness) or that may be relevant for retrieving models with certain metric properties (e.g. bounding box, scale of original).

In the common shape ontology, a special role is played by the class *Structural Descriptor* that abstracts the concept of structural description of shapes. Since the domain of the ontology has to do with shapes and tools in an application-neutral sense, the *Structural Descriptor* is characterised by two sub-classes only, which correspond in practice to two abstract *containers* capturing at a high level the most common structural representations used in computer graphics (see Fig. 7.7). *Centreline Skeletons* are often used to code segmentation results and are characterised as one-dimensional structures resembling the physical skeleton of the shape. *Multidimensional structures* characterise the results of structuring methods, such as the medial axis transform, that define abstract descriptions whose elements do not have uniform dimensionality. Application-specific ontologies can specialise further this class and implement in this way the link between application-specific knowledge and geometry.

The common ontology for the description of tools is less complex than the shape ontology in terms of depth, but it contains more concepts. However, the properties that define relations between concepts are localised at the first level of the hierarchy only. The tool ontology reflects a taxonomy of a variety of processing tasks that are used in the computer graphics domain, such as, modelling, parametrisation, or distance computation. Intuitively, each software tool may implement one or more basic functionalities, which in turn may be modelled by one or more algorithms. The *Functionality* hierarchy, shown in Fig. 7.8, has the main role to capture type information for the respective concepts, and this means that there are no additional

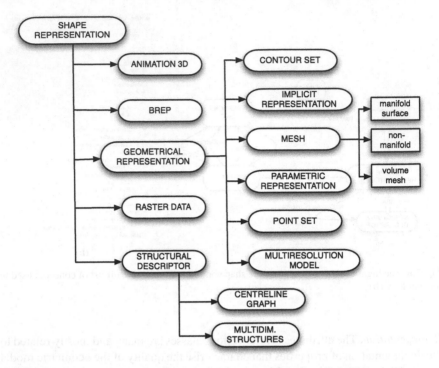

Fig. 7.7 The hierarchy originating from the *shape representation* class in the shape ontology

attributes defined and only a specific amount of instances will be created – those that represent the most specific types for each concept. More details can be found in Vasilakis et al. (2006).

In Fig. 7.9(a), the main relations formalised around the tool concept are shown, while the complete list of concepts defined in the ontology is depicted in Fig. 7.9(b). The *Shape Info* class realises the link between tools and shapes, at least at the level of shape type. The class *Shape Info* indeed is related to the class *Shape Type* which fully reflects the *Shape Representation* in the shape ontology. Again, as for the *Functionality* hierarchy, only the types are captured.

Therefore, the common ontologies define a kind of basic structure that could be exploited by task- or application-specific ontologies that could extend and specialise the common part if needed. From a technical point of view, the ontologies developed so far are expressed in OWL and are accessible via the AIM@SHAPE portal.

7.4.1 Examples of Application Ontologies

Common ontologies in AIM@SHAPE represent the knowledge about shapes and tools that is shared in a broad domain of scientists using 3D media, and this knowledge can be specialised in various areas of application. The experience reported here

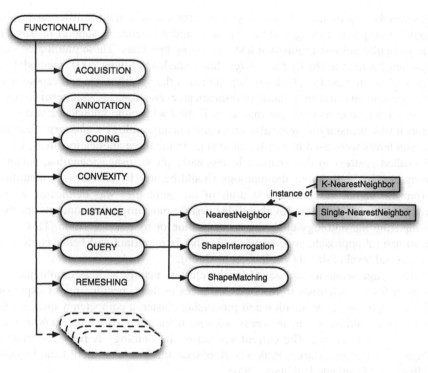

Fig. 7.8 The hierarchy originating from the *Functionality* class in the tool ontology

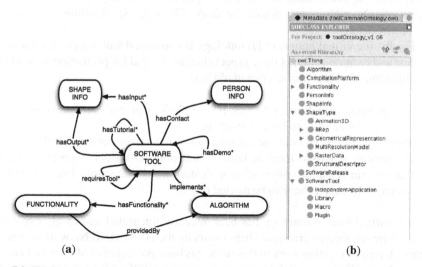

Fig. 7.9 The high-level organisation of the tool ontology (**a**) and the functionality taxonomy used in the ontology (**b**)

sketches the requirements for ontologies as expressed within three different areas of application: product design, virtual humans, and e-Science to support research in the particular field of acquisition and processing pipelines. These ontologies were developed using the *On-To-Knowledge* (Sure, Staab and Studer 2004) methodology that is characterised by a kick-off step, aimed at the specification and capturing of the requirements, and an iteration of refinement, evaluation, and maintenance steps.

It is interesting to point out that, even if the background knowledge was common, it was necessary to agree also on a common terminology – *glossary* – because several terms were used in a different manner in the three application areas, which are called *clusters* in this chapter. In this early phase, usage scenarios, potential users, and basic questions the ontology should be able to answer were identified. From this initial kick-off, a first draft of the ontologies was delineated with a middle-out approach aimed at identifying first the most important concepts and then completing the ontology either by specialisation or by generalisation. This is the most natural approach, concentrating on what is important and better controlling the desired level of detail (Vasilakis et al. 2006).

The usage scenarios envisaged by the clusters mainly address ontologies as a support for the scientists to discover resources in their specific area of expertise. For example, in the acquisition and processing cluster, a competency question the ontology should be able to answer is; *what particular acquisition tool is best suited to acquire this shape?* The current version of the ontology is fully described in Papaleo, Albertoni, Marini, Pitikakis, Robbiano and Vasilakis (2006) and Papaleo, Albertoni, Marini and Robbiano (2005).

The product design cluster has the general objective of assisting the development of shape processing tools for design. Since purposes are different in the product life cycle, the same shape can play different roles within the shape life cycle. In order to distinguish among all these concepts, it is necessary to enrich the shape representation, with its *role* within the shape life cycle. See Sevilmis et al. (2006) for further details.

Finally, the virtual human (VH) ontology is concerned with supporting the integration and harmonisation of three aspects that are crucial for professionals working in animation of virtual characters and objects:

- Human body modelling and analysis: morphological analysis, measuring similarity, model editing, and reconstruction.
- Animation of virtual humans: autonomous or pre-set animation of VH.
- Interaction of virtual humans with virtual objects: virtual – smart – objects that contain semantic information indicating how interactions between virtual humans and objects have to be carried out.

The virtual human ontology has been recently integrated and nicely expanded to the formalisation of emotional behaviours by the HUMAINE Network of Excellence. A very interesting work in this sense has been presented in Moccozet, García-Rojas, Vexo, Thalmann and Magnenat-Thalmann (2006) where a comprehensive view of the domain is given.

7.5 Conclusions

3D media content is growing both in volume and in importance in more and more applications and contexts. In this chapter, we have discussed the issues related to handling this form of content from the point of view of semantic media systems, focusing on the level at which we should be able to capture knowledge pertaining to 3D media.

3D applications are characterised by several knowledge-intensive tasks that are not limited to browsing and retrieving properly annotated material, but deal with the manipulation, analysis modification, and creation of new 3D content out of that existing. While this is true also for traditional 2D media applications, the tools and expertise needed to manipulate and analyse 3D vector-based media are still prerogative of a rather specialised community of professionals and researchers in the computer graphics field. In this sense, the computer graphics community could bring a significant contribution to the development of ontologies for 3D applications, by providing comprehensive schema for documenting and sharing 3D media and related processing tools, to be linked and further specialised by experts in different domains.

Semantics-aware classification of available tools for processing the geometry and manipulating 3D shapes might be an important building block for supporting the composition and creation of new easy-to-use tools for 3D media, whose use and selection can be made available also to professional users of 3D but not expert in the specific domain of computer graphics. The use of 3D is indeed spreading out of the traditional communities of professional users and it will soon reach an inexperienced audience. Online gaming is already proposing advanced services for the creation of personalised content to populate virtual environments like in SonyStation. To get ready for 3D, we should be able to set up a semantic 3D media environment that transforms the traditional geometric approach to a semantic-aware level of representation of 3D media, and that can help to meet the requirements of content creators and users, and start to address the grand challenges they pose:

- to make the creation and modification of 3D content (with the associated knowledge) as easy as for texts using word processors;
- to make the retrieval of 3D content as easy as with Google for texts;
- to deliver appropriate 3D content in the appropriate modality.

In this chapter, we have discussed the first steps taken in the direction of coupling knowledge technologies with traditional 3D modelling systems. The role of experts in 3D modelling for the development of semantic 3D media is twofold: on the one side, the identification of key properties for the description of 3D media and processing tools, and on the other side, the contribution to the development of advanced tools for the interpretation, analysis, and retrieval of 3D content. The results are so far encouraging and open up a number of interesting questions. First of all, it is quite evident that if we want to be able to reason about shapes at the geometric, structural, and semantic level, then we have to be also able to annotate, retrieve, and compare 3D content at each of the three layers. When these tools will be fully available, it will be also possible to use them to create new content in an easier way, searching for inspiration in existing repositories, looking for objects that resemble some prototype shape, extracting parts that have a precise functional meaning, and composing them in a new shape.

Acknowledgments This work is supported by the EU Network of Excellence AIM@SHAPE. We acknowledge the work and contribution of all project partners in the fulfillment of the results presented concerning ontologies. In particular, we thank Laura Papaleo, Neyr Sevilmis, George Vasilakis, Marios Pitikakis, Alejandra Garcia-Rojas, and all the colleagues of IMATI who have contributed to the development of ontologies with enthusiasm and energy.

References

Abaci, T., Mortara, M., Patané, G., Spagnuolo, M., Vexo, F. and Thalmann, D. (2005), Bridging geometry and semantics for object manipulation and grasping, *in* 'Proceedings of the Workshop towards Semantic Virtual Environments', SVE05, UNIGE, University of Geneva, Villars, Switzerland, pp. 110–119.

Albertoni, R., Papaleo, L., Pitikakis, M., Robbiano, F., Spagnuolo, M. and Vasilakis, G. (2005), Ontology-based searching framework for digital shapes, *in* R. M. et al., ed., 'On the Move to Meaningful Internet Systems 2005, Agia Napa, Cyprus, October 31–November 4, 2005, Proceedings', Vol. 3762 of *Lecture Notes in Computer Science*, Springer, New York, pp. 896–905.

Attene, M., Katz, S., Mortara, M., Patané, G., Spagnuolo, M. and Tal, A. (2006), Mesh segmentation: A comparative study, *in* M. Spagnuolo, A. Belyaev, S. Hiromasa, I. Fujishiro and B. Falcidieno, eds, 'Shape Modeling and Applications 2006. SMI 2006 IEEE International Conference on', IEEE Computer Society Press, Los Alamitos, CA, USA, pp. 14–25.

Bidarra, R. and Bronsvoort, W. F. (2000), 'Semantic feature modelling', *Computer-Aided Design* **32**(3), 201–225.

Biederman, I. (1987), 'Recognition-by-components: a theory of human image understanding', *Psychological Review* **94**, 115–147.

Cera, C., Regli, W., Braude, I., Shapirstein, Y. and Foster, C. (2002), 'A collaborative 3D environment for authoring of design semantics', *Computer Graphics and Applications, IEEE* **22**(3), 43–55.

Falcidieno, B., Spagnuolo, M., Alliez, P., Quak, E., Vavalis, E. and Houstis, C. (2004), Towards the semantics of digital shapes: the AIM@SHAPE approach, *in* P. Hobson, E. Izquierdo, I. Kompatsiaris and N.E.O'Connor, eds., 'European Workshop on the Integration of Knowledge, Semantics and Digital Media Technology (EWIMT2004)', IEE, London, pp. 1–4.

Golshani, F. (2006), 'Multimedia and reality', *IEEE Multimedia* **13**(1), 96–96.

Koenderink, N. J. J. P., Top, J. L. and van Vliet, L. J. (2006), 'Supporting knowledge-intensive inspection tasks with application ontologies', *International Journal of Human-Computer Studies* **64**(10), 974–983.

Maldonado, T. (1994), *Reale e Virtuale*, Feltrinelli.

Marr, D. (1982), *Vision - A computational investigation into the human representation and processing of visual information*, W. H. Freeman, San Francisco.

Moccozet, L., García-Rojas, A., Vexo, F., Thalmann, D. and Magnenat-Thalmann, N. (2006), In search for your own virtual individual, *in* Y. S. Avrithis, Y. Kompatsiaris, S. Staab and N. E. O'Connor, eds., 'Semantic Multimedia, First International Conference on Semantics and Digital Media Technologies, SAMT 2006, Athens, Greece, December 6–8, 2006, Proceedings', Vol. 4306 of *Lecture Notes in Computer Science*, Springer, New York, pp. 26–40.

Mortara, M., Patané, G. and Spagnuolo, M. (2006), 'From geometric to semantic human body models', *Computers & Graphics* **30**(2), 185–196.

Papaleo, L., Albertoni, R., Marini, S., Pitikakis, M., Robbiano, F. and Vasilakis, G. (2006), Ontology for shape acquisition and processing 2nd version, Deliverable D1.2.2.1, AIM@SHAPE IST NoE N. 506766.

Papaleo, L., Albertoni, R., Marini, S. and Robbiano, F. (2005), An ontology-based Approach to Shape Acquisition and Reconstruction, *in* 'Workshop towards Semantic Virtual Environment 2005', SVE05, UNIGE, University of Geneva, Villers, Switzerland, pp. 148–155.

Requicha, A. G. (1980), 'Representations for rigid solids: Theory, methods, and systems', *ACM Computing Surveys* **12**(4), 437–464.

Rosse, C. and Mejino Jr, J. (2003), 'A reference ontology for biomedical informatics: the foundational model of anatomy', *Journal of Biomedical Informatics* **36**(6), 478–500.

Sevilmis, N., Catalano, C., Camossi, E., Cheutet, V. and Ferrandes, R. (2006), Ontology for Product Design 2nd version, Deliverable D1.2.3.1, AIM@SHAPE IST NoE N. 506766.

Shah, J. and Mäntylä, M. (1995), *Parametric and feature-based CAD/CAM*, John Wiley & Sons, New Jersey.

Smeulders, A. W. M., Worring, M., Santini, S., Gupta, A. and Jain, R. (2000), 'Content-based image retrieval at the end of the early years', *IEEE Transaction on Pattern Analysis and Machine Intelligence* **22**(12), 1349–1380.

Sure, Y., Staab, S. and Studer, R. (2004), On-to-knowledge methodology (OTKM), *in* S. Staab and R. Studer, eds, 'Handbook on Ontologies', International Handbooks on Information Systems, Springer, New York, pp. 117–132.

Vasilakis, G., Pitikakis, M., Catalano, C., Salem, W., Saboret, L., Papaleo, L., Garcia-Rojas, A. and Sevilmis, N. (2006), Report on an integrated view of the domain ontologies – 2nd version, Deliverable D1.5.1, AIM@SHAPE IST NoE N. 506766.

Chapter 8
The Application of Semantic Web Technologies to Multimedia Data Fusion within eScience

Jane Hunter, Suzanne Little, and Ronald Schroeter

8.1 Introduction

Advances in scientific research techniques have led to an explosion of information-rich, multimedia data within the research sector. New high-throughput data capture and combinatorial experimentation techniques (involving advanced instruments capable of capturing extremely high-resolution data streams) have resulted in the generation of research data in quantities that are too great for effective assimilation. The data is not only massive in volume but is also being produced in a broad range of mediums and formats, including numerical data, spectrographic output, genomic arrays, images, 3D models, audio and video, for disciplines including nano-materials, bioinformatics, tele-medicine, geosciences, astronomy and the social sciences. Scientific discovery is increasingly dependent on reliable tools and services to support the storage, dissemination, analysis and correlation of these complex data sets by collaborating teams of globally distributed scientists.

The volume, variety and multi-dimensional nature of the content exacerbate the difficulty of describing this data adequately so it can be confidently and appropriately incorporated into existing theories or models. In order to validate and authenticate scientific results, detailed provenance metadata describing the precise methodology and derived data sets needs to be recorded. Because today's scientists are working in large geographically distributed teams or "virtual organisations", the data and metadata have to be comprehensible to people, computers and software across many different organisations, platforms and disciplines. Metadata standards and semantic interoperability are essential to enable distributed querying, analysis and integration of mixed-media and heterogeneous scientific data sets in order to maximise their reuse, extract the inherent knowledge and build new knowledge layers on top of existing data.

J. Hunter
School of Information Technology and Electrical Engineering, University of Queensland, Brisbane, Qld., Australia
e-mail: jane@itee.uq.edu.au

Y. Kompatsiaris, P. Hobson (eds.), *Semantic Multimedia and Ontologies,*
© Springer Science+Business Media, LLC 2008

The Semantic Web (Berners-Lee, Hendler and Lassila 2001) promotes inter-operability through formal languages and rich semantics. It aims to build a web where information is exchanged easily between humans and machines. Chapter 2 describes the layered standards and protocols for data definition, storage and exchange that make up the Semantic Web architecture: eXtensible Markup Language (XML) (Bray, Paoli, Sperberg-McQueen, Maler, Yergeau and Cowan 2006), Resource Description Framework (RDF) (Beckett 2004), Web Ontology Language (OWL) (McGuinness and van Harmelen 2004) and Uniform Resource Identifiers (URIs) (Berners-Lee, Fielding and Masinter 2005). Through a combination of these technologies, the Semantic Web aims to define and expose the semantics associated with data or information, in order to facilitate automatic processing, integration, sharing and reuse of the data.

Our hypothesis is that the application of Semantic Web technologies to the semantic annotation, integration and correlation of distributed mixed-media scientific data sets and scientific data processing services offers enormous potential for expediting the discovery of new knowledge. Semantic Web/grid tools enhance inter-operability through formal syntaxes, ontologies and inferencing rules. They enable innovative search, data exploration, hypothesis development and evaluation interfaces and can assist researchers in managing, assimilating and distributing data to facilitate further scientific understanding and discovery.

The remainder of this chapter is structured as follows. In the next section (Section 8.2), we describe some of the key challenges and Semantic Web technologies either currently available or emerging that could usefully be applied to eResearch or eScience problems. In Sections 8.3–8.5, we describe three case studies in which we applied, evaluated and extended Semantic Web technologies:

- fuel cell optimisation
- semantic WildNet
- Ethnographic Media Analysis.

Finally, in Section 8.6, we conclude with a brief discussion on the value-add of Semantic Web/grid technologies and where Semantic Web technologies are heading in the context of scientific multimedia data.

8.2 The Relevance of Semantic Web Technologies to eScience

eScience is the term given to large-scale scientific research that is increasingly being carried out through distributed global collaborations, enabled by the Internet and related technologies. Typically, a feature of these collaborative scientific enterprises is the need to capture and analyse very large data collections using unique scientific instrumentation and very large-scale computing resources to carry out high-performance analysis, modelling and visualisation.

The emergence over the last decade of high-throughput instruments and digital analysis techniques, such as electron microscopes, tomographic scanners, real-time sensors, microarrays, satellites and telescopes, has led to an explosion of high-resolution, information-rich, mixed-media data in quantities far greater than was previously possible. Researchers are unable to manage, analyse, interpret, assimilate and disseminate the large volumes and variety of data being produced. Hey and Trefethen (2003) describe this information explosion as the "data deluge" and note the requirements for quality metadata, storage and preservation of the increased output of scientific data from "the next generation of experiments, simulations, sensors and satellites".

The data being produced by researchers is in a broad range of mediums, formats, resolutions and dimensions and includes numerical data, spectrographic data, genomic arrays, images (2D and 3D), audio, video, spatial data and temporal data streams (from sensors). It is generated by a wide variety of instruments, software applications, software versions and operating systems. Significant pre-processing and normalisation are required before comparison or correlation is possible. Data representation standards and metadata standards are required to ease the difficulties associated with data exchange and reuse, both within and across disciplines.

Many of the great challenges in science are multi-disciplinary in nature. The data requiring correlation is often captured and described by scientists from many different disciplines. The scientific problem of "global warming" is a good example – scientists want to integrate data and information from biology, marine sciences, environmental sciences, oceanography, geosciences and astronomy in order to measure and understand the causes and effects of climate change. Different terminologies, vocabularies, models and points of view apply across these disciplines. Exchange and sharing of knowledge between researchers in different disciplines is typically hampered by conflicting terminologies, inconsistent formats, obstructive firewalls and systems with limited accessibility or interoperability. Scientific workflows and provenance capture systems vary widely in the granularity and representation of provenance data, preventing validation and verification of results. All of these issues prevent the easy retrieval, reuse and assimilation of data from multiple sources and often lead to duplication of experiments. Scientists are becoming increasingly frustrated by the barriers prohibiting seamless data sharing and integration.

Researchers need to be able to exchange data freely across domain and organisational boundaries. As De Roure and Hendler (2004) state, "... interoperability is key to all aspects of scale that characterise e-Science, such as scale of data, computation and collaboration". There are a set of key components that make up the semantic interoperability framework envisaged within the Semantic Web:

- High-quality, precise, structured metadata descriptions in standardised (XML) representations that are machine-understandable. These may be automatically generated (by instruments), manually enhanced or attached through semantic annotation tools.
- URIs – unique identifiers are essential in order to understand when two statements are referring to the same resource or object. They must also be persistent over time so links and data are not lost because they are no longer accessible.

- Resource Description Framework (RDF) – this provides a data model for objects ("resources") and relations between them that can be represented in a machine-processable XML syntax.
- RDF schema (Brickley and Guha 2004) – a vocabulary for describing properties and classes of RDF resources, with a semantics for generalisation hierarchies of such properties and classes.
- OWL (Web Ontology Language) – adds more vocabulary for describing properties and classes: including relations between classes (e.g. disjointness), cardinality (e.g. "exactly one"), equality, richer typing of properties, characteristics of properties (e.g. symmetry) and enumerated classes.
- Inferencing rules – SWRL (Semantic Web Rule language) (Horrocks, Patel-Schneider, Boley, Tabet, Grosof and Dean 2004) defines rules (in an XML syntax) which can be invoked to infer new knowledge from related RDF statements.
- RDF query language – SPARQL (Prud'hommeaux and Seaborne 2007), a protocol and query language for querying RDF statements.

In the next three sections, we describe three actual case studies in which we have applied these technologies to different disciplines to enable scientific problems to be solved more quickly through richer, machine-processable descriptions, enhanced semantic interoperability and faster data integration. In particular, our approach is to facilitate semantic interoperability across media types, vocabularies and disciplines through a common extensible ontology (Hunter 2003). This approach is flexible and easily adapted to any domain through the incorporation of domain-specific ontologies and rules.

8.3 Data-Driven Discovery of Novel Fuel Cell Materials

Fuel cells offer a clean renewable energy alternative to fossil fuels. As such, there is increasing interest in improving their efficiency and reducing their cost so they become a more attractive energy option. However, they are highly complex multi-component systems – their efficiency depends on their internal nano-structure and the complex chemical and physical processes occurring across their internal interfaces. Significant advances in the accurate modelling of fuel cell components (electrodes, membrane and catalyst layers) can be achieved through improved analysis, assimilation and modelling of existing data and more systematic, controlled design and monitoring of tests and experiments. Within the FUSION project (Hunter, Cheung, Little and Drennan 2005), we are employing Semantic Web technologies to provide a robust knowledge-mining system which will assist collaborating teams of fuel cell scientists to discover and optimise novel materials for fuel cell components.

A core component of the Solid Oxide Fuel Cell (SOFC) is an oxygen ion conducting membrane that must have mechanical and chemical stability at elevated temperatures under both reducing and oxidising conditions. Although oxygen ion conducting materials with these properties exist, they typically operate at temperatures $>750°C$. There is significant demand for new, structurally stable materials, with oxygen conductivities approaching $>10^{-1} \, S \, cm^{-1}$ at temperatures *below* $500°C$ and which are stable over a wide range of partial pressures of oxygen. A reduction in operating temperature has significant effect on the cost and engineering demands of the ancillary materials that make up the fuel cell.

Domain experts have already intuitively identified patterns that indicate fertile areas for searching for potential compounds with enhanced conductivity. The systems of immediate interest are oxide compounds that show negative thermal expansion coefficients associated with uncertainty in the oxygen position of specific bond networks and enhanced ionic conductivity. The addition of dopants to these compounds opens the structures to new conduction pathways and further improvements in conductivity. But doping further expands the number of potential ternary or quaternary compounds that satisfy our criteria into the millions. The time and effort associated with traditional trial-and-error approaches to experimental preparation, analysis and testing of these compounds is cost-prohibitive. There is obvious benefit in applying computing techniques to perform the virtual compound screening and identification process which in turn will drive the experimental programme. Hence our aims within this project are to employ Semantic Web techniques (ontology-based data integration) together with other computing technologies to

- Combine and apply innovative data integration, data mining and computational modelling techniques to the large volume of existing experimental data available, to enable domain experts to screen and identify target compounds;
- Use the outcomes of the data integration and mining phase to drive a focused programme of experimentation which will expedite the discovery of novel compounds for oxygen ion conducting membranes that can operate efficiently below $500°C$.

Figure 8.1 illustrates the key stages in our methodology.

In the past, scientists have had to manually search, retrieve and correlate data from a number of related but disparate databases in order to identify compounds with desirable structure and properties. To overcome this hurdle, we have developed an ontology (based on MatML (MatML Schema Development WG 2004), the Materials Mark-up Language) that enables the semantic integration of data from the Inorganic Crystal Database (ICSD) (FIZ Karlsruhe 2004), the thermodynamic data in the FactSage database (CRCT 2007), the ionic radii database and phase diagram data to determine materials with desirable properties and stability. For example, scientists want to retrieve answers to queries such as "Give me compounds that contain tungsten–oxygen–X (where X is a different cation), with bond lengths between Y and Z nm, with anomalies and anisotropy in the positional parameters of oxygen and with bond angles between J° and K°".

The ontology that we have developed (Fig. 8.2) relates property data to characterisation data, chemical composition and processing parameters. Further work is required to ensure community consensus and widespread adoption of such an ontology for the materials science community. The CODATA Taskforce on

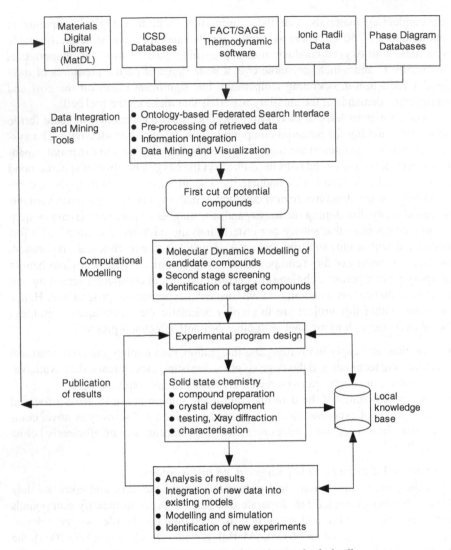

Fig. 8.1 Data-driven discovery of novel oxygen ion conductors for fuel cells

Materials Data Representation (ICSU 2006) has been given the mandate to develop a common representation for the exchange of materials science data which has widespread community agreement – the development of an ontology is one aspect of this group's focus.

Once the data has been retrieved, pre-processed (to resolve syntactic inconsistencies) and integrated, it can be presented to the domain expert for further interrogation and exploration through an interactive data mining and visualisation interface. For this we are employing a combination of two open source software tools: Weka (University of Waikato 2007) (a collection of machine learning algorithms for data mining) and OpenDX (Thompson, Braun and Ford, 2006) (the open source version of IBM's Data Explorer). Together these technologies enable data mining

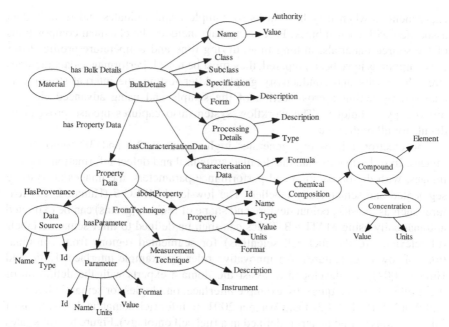

Fig. 8.2 Materials ontology for database integration

of the highly multivariate data sets in order to identify predictive trends and patterns that apply to oxide-ion conducting materials. The outcome from the interactive data mining phase is a short list of potential ternary compounds.

There is currently insufficient experimental data available to adequately describe the effects of all possible doping schemes on compound properties and structure. This is where advanced atomistic modelling becomes useful. Atomistic modelling techniques based on well-established energy minimisation methods (Islam 2002) have a proven track record in the accurate modelling of defects, local structures and ion migration mechanisms in complex oxides for potential SOFC use. Doping mechanisms will be simulated at the atomic level in relation to ion size and defect clustering to assess the possible influence on oxide-ion migration. In this way, the fuel cell scientists identify the optimum dopant and concentrations and hence can generate a very precise and targeted experimental programme.

The experimental programme consists of a detailed specification of compounds to prepare and the method of preparation. Preparation consists of a highly complex set of processing steps which are the responsibility of a team of individuals. A workflow system with a Graphical User Interface (GUI) has been developed. It enables new experiments to be defined – controllable parameters can be specified and tasks can be allocated to specific experimenters (e.g. the mixing, slip batching, tape casting and firing steps in electrolyte preparation). The system is underpinned by a MySQL database overlaid with a SPARQL query interface and Jena API (McBride 2001). Executing an experimental design invokes a workflow management process (built using Web Services and BPEL4WS (Weerawarana and Curbera 2002)) which tracks the different activities within an experiment, notifies experimenters when they have tasks to complete and validates and records data associated with each subtask. Processing data includes the chemical compositions of the source materials, milling time, drying time and temperature profile. After the compounds have been prepared, they must be tested. Performance data includes strength, density and conductivity graphs. After testing, the internal structure is analysed by taking a cross-section of the sample and using advanced electron microscopy techniques. The workflow system also captures precise provenance details for all of the data.

The electron microscopy generates high-resolution 2D and 3D tomographic images. In order to correlate the detailed structural and defect information in these images, with the preparation and performance parameters, the images need to be segmented and semantically labelled. The low-level MPEG-7 (Hunter 2001) features such as the size, colour, texture and shape of regions (grains) can be extracted automatically using MATLAB. Rules can then be defined to infer semantic labels (of relevance to the fuel cell scientists) for segmented regions from combinations of low-level features. An innovative rules-by-example interface (Little and Hunter 2004) was developed to assist the domain experts with the definition of these rules. It uses a query-by-example interface, ontologies for semantic indexing and RuleML (Boley, Tabet and Wagner 2001) to infer rich semantic descriptions of image regions (based on terms defined in a fuel cell ontology). Figure 8.3 illustrates the rules-by-example interface that enables domain experts to define rules such as

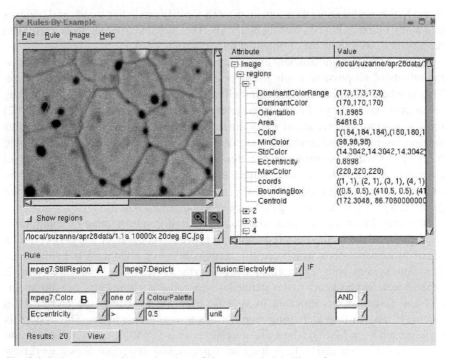

Fig. 8.3 Rules-by-example interface for defining semantic labelling rules

IF [(colour is like this) AND (texture is like this) AND (shape is like this)]
THEN (the region is a platinum substrate particle)

All of the generated and validated metadata is stored in a central knowledge repository. A query engine, visualisation engine and knowledge capture (annotation) tools sit on top of the knowledge repository. The data exploration and visualisation interface (Hunter, Falkovych and Little 2004) correlates the preparation, performance and microstructural data through the fuel cell ontology. This enables fuel cell scientists to enter queries such as

Give me the microstructural, conductivity, efficiency and voltage data for fuel cells with electrolyte porosity > 15% and average platinum substrate grain size < 200 nms.

The results of such complex queries are presented as synchronised multimedia HTML+Time (Microsoft 2007) presentations. A GUI is provided (based on the underlying fuel cell ontology) through which users can specify the search parameters, range of data and image resolutions to be displayed and the preferred format of presentations (e.g. animated slideshow or tiled thumbnails). Figure 8.4 illustrates

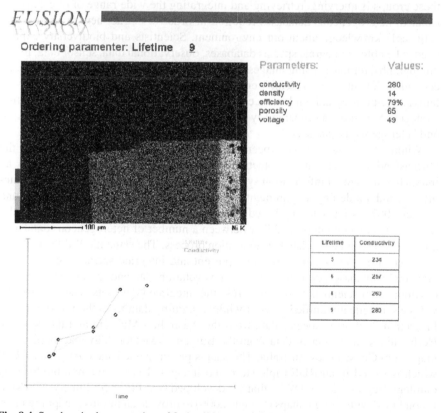

Fig. 8.4 Synchronised presentation of fuel cell images and data

the results of a presentation that synchronises a slideshow of microstructural images with a plot of corresponding data. This interface also enables new hypotheses or predictive models to be derived, saved, shared and refined as more data is acquired. Users may also specify graphically where more data is required and new experiments are initiated.

FUSION provides an integrated knowledge management system for fuel cells which ensures fast and easy integration and correlation of manufacturing, performance and microstructural data with external data sources. User feedback has been extremely positive, indicating that the system enables faster interpretation of large image collections and data sets and rapid formulation of more accurate fuel cell models. The long-term consequences are expected to be shorter development cycles, improved performance and lower costs for fuel cells.

8.4 Semantic WildNet

A large number of organisations and initiatives globally are involved in biodiversity monitoring for the purposes of conservation. One of the greatest challenges facing these groups is querying, retrieving and integrating the wide range of relevant, distributed, heterogeneous databases required in order to extract new predictive and actionable knowledge about our environment. Scientists and biodiversity experts need to be able to integrate species databases, observational data, sensor data, maps, photographs, remote sensing images, climatology data, vegetation distributions and ecological data in order to identify endangered species or fragile, threatened ecosystems and to prepare and implement environmental impact analyses and conservation strategies. Semantic interoperability is essential in order to harmonise such disparate and heterogeneous data sets.

Within Australia, we have been working with scientists and staff from the Queensland Environmental Protection Authority (EPA) in order to develop an interactive integrated information system to satisfy their data search, retrieval, integration and modelling requirements. Semantic WildNet (Henderson, Khan and Hunter 2007) is an ontology-based biogeographical system designed specifically to support semantic interoperability between a number of heterogeneous databases and also to facilitate the data harmonisation process. The semantic WildNet system uses Semantic Web technologies to represent and integrate species sighting data, taxonomic databases, climate sensor data, vegetation data and spatial data enabling environmental scientists to reason across the integrated data sets. The system provides a semantically unified view of wildlife sighting data from the Environmental Protection Authority, species data from the Australian Museum and the National Herbarium, climate sensor data from the Bureau of Meteorology and topographic maps from Geosciences Australia. The data is pre-processed and converted to RDF which is stored in an RDF triple store and integrated via a common biodiversity ontology (represented in OWL) that we developed (see Fig. 8.5). Finally, SPARQL is combined with Google maps (Google 2006) to provide an intuitive mapping interface to query the integrated data sets.

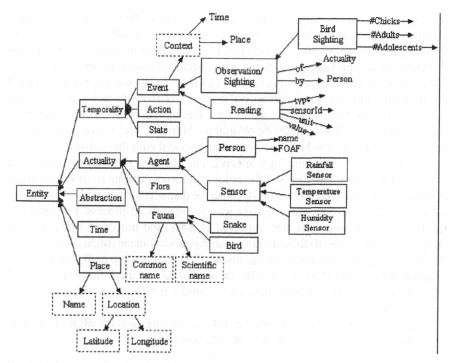

Fig. 8.5 Biodiversity ontology for semantic WildNet

The initial data sets under consideration were

- Wildlife sighting data from the EPA. This includes time of observation, scientific species name, latitude and longitude of the sightings, as well as the observer's name and field notes;
- Species data from the Australian Museum;
- Habitat data from the National Herbarium;
- Climate sensor data from the Bureau of Meteorology. This includes date/time of reading, latitude and longitude of sensor, type of reading (temperature, rainfall, humidity), unit (degree Celsius, inches, percentage);
- Topographic maps from Geosciences Australia.

The information existed in a variety of file formats, including Microsoft Excel spreadsheets, Microsoft Access tables, ESRI shape files, MIF (MapInfo) files and custom XML files. Although the data sets displayed a high degree of consistency, a certain amount of pre-processing was required to resolve syntactic and formatting inconsistencies across the data sets, e.g. conflicting date/time formats.

Protégé (Gennari, Musen, Fergerson, Grosso, Crubezy, Eriksson, Noy and Tu 2003) was used to construct the biodiversity ontology in OWL DL format. Figure 8.5 shows an overview of the core classes and properties that were defined. We developed our ontology by extending the classes within a common upper ontology (the ABC ontology (Doerr, Hunter and Lagoze 2003)) developed through previous work. For example, *flora* and *fauna* were defined as subclasses of the *Actuality* superclass. *Observation* is a subclass of *Event*. *Sighting* is an equivalent class to *Observation*. The values associated with species common names and scientific names were adopted from existing taxonomies provided by the Australian Museum and the Herbarium. As other international groups publish their ontologies associated with biodiversity and ecological data (Parr, Parafiynyk, Sachs, Ding, Dornbush, Finin, Wang and Hollander 2006; Williams, Martinez and Golbeck 2006), we expect to modify our ontology in order to harmonise it with these efforts.

Given the biodiversity ontology in OWL DL, the next step was to convert the available data sets into instances of the ontology classes. Custom scripts were developed to generate the RDF instances. Because the data sets were provided in a variety of file formats, conversion of the data was a complicated process. For example, the Excel spreadsheets were first exported as XML and processed using an XSL style sheet, to produce RDF/XML. In some cases, data inconsistencies meant that the style sheet grew too complex, so custom Perl scripts were used instead. After generating the 110,000 triples of RDF instance data, we used the Jena RDF API to store the triples in a MySQL database. Figure 8.6 provides an overview of the system architecture.

Queries were implemented using the RDF query language, SPARQL. Examples of the most common types of queries included the following:

- Retrieve all snake sightings by a particular observer;
- Retrieve all sightings of Sterna Caspia birds where a nearby climate sensor reached >26.7°C;
- Retrieve all sightings of Sterna Caspia birds within a given geographic region and above a certain elevation;
- Retrieve all sightings of Sterna Caspia birds by observers who work at the EPA.

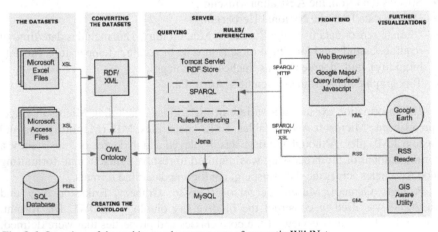

Fig. 8.6 Overview of the architectural components of semantic WildNet

One problem we encountered was the inability of SPARQL to support negative queries. For example scientists want to ask, "Give me all wet sclerophyll forest habitats in which bridled honeyeaters have *not* been observed". SPARQL does not support this kind of query.

A small amount of Jena code was required to support OWL reasoning across subsumption and equivalence relations. This enabled queries based on superclasses to retrieve data on subclasses (e.g. querying for instances of *Animal* will identify the subclasses *Bird* and *Snake*) and inherited properties (e.g. each *BirdSighting* instance inherits the *AnimalSighting* properties). Our use of OWL also helped address semantic issues associated with data equivalence and duplication. A good example is the bird whose scientific name is *Platycercus elegans*. It also has three common names: the Crimson Rosella, Yellow Rosella and Adelaide Rosella. Our translation scripts created three distinct instances of *P. elegans*. Defining these classes as equivalent classes in the OWL ontology, then searching on any of the common names will return instances of all three.

The environmental scientists we were working with requested the ability to carry out searches via standard web browsers but through a mapping interface, such as Google maps. Hence we developed a JavaScript application centred around Google maps. SPARQL queries were entered via pull-down menus, and posted to the server asynchronously, using AJAX. Results retrieved in SPARQL's XML response format were parsed and plotted onto Google maps at the relevant latitude and longitude. Figure 8.7 shows how sightings of birds are identified by a small bird icon. Clicking on one of these icons displays a speech bubble containing all of the relevant metadata. The use of Google maps allows the sightings data to be overlaid on any of three map types: map, satellite images or hybrid.

User feedback from scientists within the EPA and researchers in the Centre for Remote Sensing and Spatial Information Science has been very positive. Currently scientists have to manually retrieve data from multiple data sets and then develop and apply hard-wired mechanisms – integrating at most two data sets at a time. Our approach enables multiple data sets to be integrated and reasoned across simultaneously through an intuitive ontology-based geographical interface. Users particularly appreciated the ontology-based spatial querying tool which used a combination of a mapping interface with pull-down query menus populated from existing taxonomies. More sophisticated query mechanisms were possible than with traditional relational databases, and the results demonstrated higher precision and recall for test queries that involved the invocation of built-in subsumption and equivalence rules.

One limitation of the current system is that at the start of the project we migrated each of the legacy databases into RDF instances (that are compliant with the common OWL ontology). This enabled us to demonstrate the viability of an RDF/OWL-based architecture, but it does not take into account updates or changes to the databases that we are integrating. If we want to incorporate recent changes or updates to these databases, then we must either rerun the migration process periodically or investigate the feasibility of on-the-fly mapping. The second, more dynamic, approach would involve translating a SPARQL query based on our common

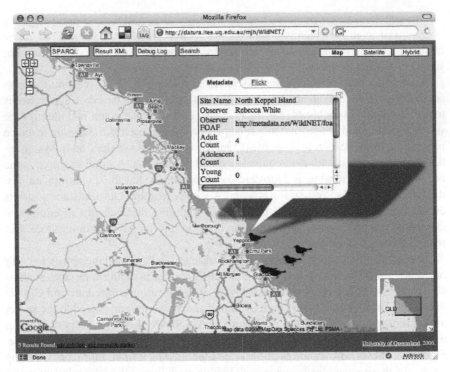

Fig. 8.7 Display of SPARQL query results on Google maps interface

ontology (Fig. 8.5) into queries applicable to each of the databases, retrieving
the relevant data sets and then mapping those on the fly to our ontology.

Despite its acknowledged limitations, semantic WildNet provides the basis for
more intelligent reactive and dynamic systems. For example, queries could be con-
figured to run periodically over the integrated data sets. Query results could then be
parsed and converted into RSS (Harvard Law 2003), allowing specific changes to
the data to be monitored and relevant persons notified. This could be very useful for
notifying scientists of environmental "hotspots" requiring timely action.

8.5 Ethnographic Media Analysis

The aim of the Ethnographic eResearch project (Schroeter and Thieberger 2006)
was to develop and evaluate tools to support collaborative research by linguists
working on endangered languages. A key focus was on tools to enable rich multi-
layered and authenticated annotation of audiovisual recordings with different transcripts, as well as other contextual information.

Because the Semantic Web is dependent on computer-understandable descriptions of web resources, annotation tools play a very important role in the Semantic Web. Annotation systems (Reeve and Han 2005) provide a means of attaching

machine-processable tags, descriptions or metadata to web resources manually. If the annotations are drawn from an ontology, then they become even more valuable. If the annotations are tags drawn from a shared conceptualisation (i.e. an agreed vocabulary or ontology), then they can be used to infer or extract new knowledge and to identify implicit relationships between resources.

Within eScience, there is a growing demand for collaborative annotation tools for multimedia content. Distributed groups of scientists want to synchronously view the same image, video or 3D object; discuss the meaning of what they are viewing; and attach notes to segments, regions or structures that can be stored, shared and retrieved at a later time. An essential requirement is the ability to authenticate the source of the annotation and to restrict access to annotations to trusted colleagues – for reasons of privacy, confidentiality or protection of intellectual property. This is particularly important within eScience, where the annotation or interpretation of the raw document or data is often more valuable than the target of the annotation.

One example of a community generating multimedia content that requires collective analysis and knowledge capture through shared annotation tools is the Paradisec project (Barwick 2005) – a web-enabled facility for collaborative digitisation, management and access to Australian researchers' ethnographic audiovisual recordings of endangered languages and music from the Asia Pacific region.

Within the "Ethnographic Media Analysis" project, we have been applying, evaluating and customising the Vannotea system (Schroeter, Hunter, Guerin, Khan and Henderson 2006) to enable discussion and annotation of recordings from the Paradisec project by geographically distributed linguists. Figure 8.8 illustrates a screen shot of Vannotea being used to annotate and compare two different recordings simultaneously.

Fig. 8.8 Vannotea being used within the Ethnographic Media Analysis project

Vannotea is a secure collaborative annotation system designed to enable teams of researchers to collaboratively annotate multimedia content (images, video, 3D objects) either synchronously or asynchronously. Its implementation involves combining and extending a number of existing open source technologies based on open standards:

- Annotea (Kahan, Koivunen, Prud'Hommeaux and Swick 2001) – a web-based annotation server developed by the W3C as part of the Semantic Web initiative which we have extended to support annotation of fine-grained contexts within multimedia objects;
- Jabber – this provides the instant messaging required for the real-time application sharing and event logging (Jabber 2005);
- Vic/Rat (McCanne and Jacobson 1995; Hardman, Sasse, Handley and Watson 1995) – these videoconferencing tools are extended to enable the recording of separate participants' H.261 streams and their conversion to tiles within a single MPEG movie;
- Shibboleth – an Internet2 middleware initiative that enables identity management and secure access to web resources shared amongst a federation of organisations (Morgan, Cantor, Carmody, Hoehn and Klingenstein 2004);
- XACML (eXtensible Access Control Markup Language) – XML-based language for defining and enforcing access control policies (Lorch, Proctor, Lepro, Kafura and Shah 2003).

Figure 8.9 illustrates the necessary components for Vannotea's deployment. On the left-hand side, content providers allow access to collections of domain-specific scientific multimedia data. They provide search, browse and retrieval interfaces to their collections through existing web portals or web applications via pre-existing

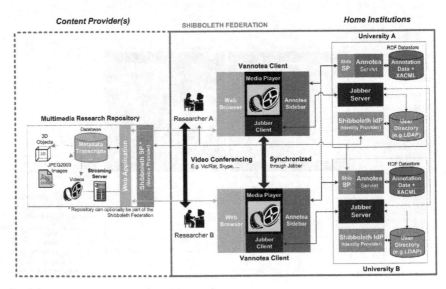

Fig. 8.9 Overview of Vannotea's architectural components

metadata, e.g. transcripts of linguistic data stored within the Paradisec collection. The content may be publicly accessible or protected through site-specific user accounts.

In the centre of Fig. 8.9 are two researchers from different institutions that are part of a Shibboleth Federation. Shibboleth is an emerging mechanism for restricting access to institutional research repositories. Institutions join a Shibboleth Federation and establish a Shibboleth Service Provider (SP). This controls sharing of data and services between institutions. Users can use SingleSignOn (SSO) from their home institution to log in and gain access to data or services within the federation. We have chosen to use Shibboleth to implement the authentication and access control over our annotation servers.

The researchers use videoconferencing tools and the Vannotea Client to collaboratively discuss, analyse and annotate the scientific multimedia content they have retrieved from a content provider. Their Vannotea clients are synchronised through Jabber messages, which ensure that all of the Vannotea clients are precisely synchronised and all researchers have exactly the same view of the multimedia content at the same time.

On the right we have the home institutions of the two researchers. Their universities provide access to services that include

- the Shibbolized Annotea server, where users can upload, search and retrieve annotations;
- a Jabber server for instant messaging;
- and a Shibboleth Identity Provider (IdP), which authenticates users when they log on. The IdP also releases attributes about each user to the Shibboleth Service Providers within the federation, e.g. to the content providers or the Annotea servers, so they can make decisions regarding access rights.

The screen shot of Vannotea in Fig. 8.8 illustrates the user interface components:

- A web browser (Internet Explorer) (left-hand side) – which provides the search and browse interface to online multimedia collections;
- An embedded media player – currently we support a range of plugins including Quicktime, Windows Media Player, Video Lan Client (upper centre) – for viewing, navigating and drawing on images, videos, and 3D objects, to highlight particular regions or segments;
- an Annotea sidebar (right-hand side) – to display, search, retrieve or respond to existing annotations – as well as create new annotations. Annotations can take the form of free text, files or URL's to related content;
- a Jabber client (bottom centre) – which enables instant message passing between current users logged into the session. It also enables contacts to be added or deleted, allows/disallows users to see presence information and enables other users to be invited into a collaborative session.

Within the Ethnographic Media Analysis project, work has focused on the mapping of incompatible transcriptions generated from different transcription tools, to be mapped to a common XML format (that includes time stamps for alignment with the corresponding recording) to enable the exchange and reuse of time-aligned transcriptions between different researchers. Assuming transcripts are stored on the annotation server in this common format, we are able to search, retrieve and display them using Vannotea and synchronise them with the replay of the recordings. In this way, Vannotea enables ethnographic researchers to share and compare their transcriptions of recordings of endangered languages – either in real-time or asynchronously.

Furthermore, the use of Vannotea within a videoconference or audioconference environment, together with the integrated Jabber chat room, provides a very rich interactive environment which both encourages and records scholarly discourse around specific multimedia content. More importantly, the addition of security through Shibboleth authentication and authorisation not only ensures authentication of the source of any annotations but can also be used to limit access to either the session or the annotations to trusted colleagues only. This is of particular importance in research projects such as the Ethnographic Media Analysis project, in which the privacy of individuals in the recordings must be protected and the intellectual property associated with the interpretations is of value.

8.6 Conclusions

This chapter began by explaining why Semantic Web technologies have enormous potential for application to the integration and analysis of the rapidly expanding pool of multimedia content being generated within scientific disciplines. It then described three case studies (from the disciplines of materials science, biodiversity and linguistics) in which Semantic Web technologies have played a central role in enabling semantic interoperability between data sets, metadata schemas, media types, instruments and software. Apart from a small number of high-profile projects (e.g. MyGrid (Stevens, Robinson and Goble 2003)), CombeChem (Coles, Frey, Hursthouse, Light, Carr, DeRoure, Gutteridge, Mills, Meacham, Surridge, Lyon, Heery, Duke and Day 2005) and within the W3C's Semantic Health Care and Life Sciences Interest Group (Baker and Cheung 2007), Semantic Web technologies are still not widely deployed or broadly adopted within eScience. We believe that this is changing. Increasingly, Semantic Web technologies are being employed to enable the scalable integration of cross-disciplinary predictive models derived from distributed heterogeneous multimedia collections. As the potential value of Semantic Web technologies is recognised and acknowledged through success stories, we can expect to see their growing adoption by eScientists.

Acknowledgments The work described in this chapter is the result of the effort and contributions by a large number of additional members of our eResearch team within the School of Information Technology and Electrical Engineering (ITEE) at the University of Queensland. In particular we would like to thank Kwok Cheung, Michael Henderson and Imran Khan. We would also like to thank John Drennan for his invaluable support, ideas, data and feedback both on the FUSION project and more generally. Financial support for this project has come from numerous sources including the Australia Research Council (ARC) Special eResearch Initiative programme.

References

Baker, C. J. O. and Cheung, K-H. (eds.) (2007). *Semantic Web: Revolutionizing Knowledge Discovery in the Life Sciences*, Springer, New York. ISBN: 978-0-387-48436-5

Barwick, L. (2005). *Networking digital data on endangered languages of the Asia Pacific region.* International Journal of Indigenous Research, 1(1), pp. 11–16.

Beckett, D. (ed.) (2004). *RDF/XML Syntax Specification (Revised)*, W3C Recommendation, W3C, February 10.

Berners-Lee, T., Hendler J. and Lassila O. (2001). *The Semantic Web*, Scientific American, May, pp 34–43.

Berners-Lee, T., Fielding, R. T. and Masinter, L. (2005). *Uniform Resource Identifier (URI): Generic Syntax*, IETF RFP 3986 (standards track), Internet Eng. Task Force, January.

Boley, H., Tabet, S. and Wagner, G. (2001). *Design Rationale of RuleML: A Markup Language for Semantic Web Rules*. Proc. SWWS'01, Stanford, July/August, pp 381–401.

Bray, T., Paoli, J., Sperberg-McQueen, C. M., Maler, E., Yergeau, F. and Cowan, J. (eds.) (2006). *XML 1.1 (Second Edition)*, W3C Recommendation, W3C, 16 August.

Brickley, D. and Guha, R. V., (eds) (2004). *RDF Vocabulary Description Language 1.0: RDF Schema*, W3C Recommendation, W3C, February 10.

Coles, S., Frey, J., Hursthouse, M., Light, M., Carr, L., DeRoure, D., Gutteridge, C., Mills, H., Meacham, K., Surridge, M., Lyon, L., Heery, R., Duke, M. and Day, M. (2005). *The 'end to end' crystallographic experiment in an e-Science environment: From conception to publication.* In, *UK e-Science All Hands Meeting 2005, Nottingham, UK, 19–23 September*. Southampton, UK.

CRCT, Thermfact Inc. and GTT-Technologies (2007). *FactSage 5.5.*

De Roure, D. and Hendler, J. A. (2004). *E-Science: The Grid and the Semantic Web.* In IEEE Intelligent Systems – Special Issue on E-Science, volume 19(1), pp. 65–71.

Doerr, M., Hunter, J. and Lagoze, C. (2003). *Towards a Core Ontology for Information Integration*, Journal of Digital Information, 4 (1). April.

FIZ Karlsruhe (2004). *ICSD (Inorganic Crystal Structure Database).*

Gennari, J., Musen, M. A., Fergerson, R. W., Grosso, W. E., Crubezy, M., Eriksson, H., Noy, N. F. and Tu. S.W. (2003). *The Evolution of Protégé: An Environment for Knowledge-Based Systems Development*. International Journal of Human-Computer Studies, 58(1), pp. 89–123.

Google (2006). Google Maps API Version 2 Documentation.

Hardman, V., Sasse, A., Handley, M., and Watson, A. (1995). *Reliable Audio for Use over the Internet*, in INET'95, Honolulu, Hawaii.

Harvard Law (2003). *RSS 2.0 Specification.*

Henderson, M., Khan, I. and Hunter, J. (2007). *Semantic WildNet: An Ontology-based Biogeographical System*, Technical Report, EcoPortal Qld Project, March.

Hey, T. and Trefethen, A. (2003). *The Data Deluge: An e-Science Perspective*. In Grid Computing – Making the Global Infrastructure a Reality, Wiley, January.

Horrocks, I., Patel-Schneider, P., Boley, H., Tabet, S., Grosof, B. and Dean M., (2004). *SWRL: A Semantic Web Rule language Combining OWL and RuleML*, W3C Member Submission, 21 May.

Hunter, J. (2001). *Adding Multimedia to the Semantic Web – Building an MPEG-7 Ontology*. International Semantic Web Working Symposium (SWWS). Stanford. July. pp 261–282.

Hunter, J. (2003). *Enhancing the Semantic Interoperability of Multimedia through a Core Ontology*. In IEEE Transactions on Circuits and Systems for Video Technology, Special Issue on Conceptual and Dynamical Aspects of Multimedia Content Description, Vol 13, No. 1, January 2003.

Hunter, J., Falkovych, K. and Little, S. (2004). *Next Generation Search Interfaces – Interactive Data Exploration and Hypothesis Testing*, 8th European Digital Libraries Conference (ECDL 2004). Bath, UK. September. pp 86–98

Hunter, J., Cheung, K., Little, S. and Drennan, J. (2005). *FUSION – A Knowledge Management System for Fuel Cell Optimization*. International Conference on Solid State Ionics. Applications: Fuel Cells. Baden–Baden. July. p 544.

International Council for Science (ICSU) (2006). *CODATA (Committee on Data for Science and Technology) Taskforce on Materials Data Interchange.*

Islam, M.S. (2002). *Computer modelling of defects and transport in perovskite oxides.* Solid State Ionics, 154, pp. 75–85.

Jabber Software Foundation (2005), *Jabber Overview.*

Kahan, J., Koivunen, M.-R., Prud'Hommeaux, E. and Swick, R. (2001). *Annotea: An Open RDF Infrastructure for Shared Web Annotations,* in Proceedings of the WWW10 International Conference, Hong Kong, pp. 623–632.

Little, S. and Hunter, J. (2004). *Rules-By-Example – a Novel Approach to Semantic Indexing and Querying of Images,* Proceedings of the Third International Semantic Web Conference, ISWC2004. Hiroshima, Japan. November. pp. 534–548.

Lorch, M., Proctor, S., Lepro, R., Kafura, D. and Shah S. (2003), *First experiences using XACML for access control in distributed systems,* in Proceedings of the 2003 ACM workshop on XML Security, 2003, Fairfax, Virginia.

MatML Schema Development Working Group (2004), *MATML – Version 3.1 Schema.* October.

McBride, B. (2001) Jena: Implementing the RDF Model and Syntax Specification. Proceedings of the Second International Workshop on the Semantic Web, SemWeb 2001, HongKong, May.

McCanne S. and Jacobson, V. (1995). *Vic: A Flexible Framework for Packet Video,* ACM Multimedia, 95, pp. 511–522, 1995.

McGuinness, D. L. and van Harmelen, F. (eds.) (2004) *OWL Web Ontology Language: Overview.* W3C Recommendation, W3C.

Microsoft MSDN Library (2007), HTML+TIME 2.0 Reference.

Morgan R.L., Cantor, S., Carmody, S., Hoehn, W. and Klingenstein, K. (2004) "Federated Security: The Shibboleth Approach", Educause Quarterly, Volume 27, Number 4.

Parr, C. S., Parafiynyk, A. Sachs, J., Ding L., Dornbush, L. S., Finin, T., Wang, D. and Hollander, A. (2006). *Integrating Ecoinformatics Resources on the Semantic Web,* Proceedings of the 15th International Conference on the World Wide Web, Edinburgh.

Prud'hommeaux, E. and Seaborne A. (eds) (2007). *SPARQL Query Language for RDF,* W3C Working Draft, W3C, 26 March.

Reeve L., Han H., (2005), *Semantic Annotation for Semantic Social Networks Using CommunityResources,* AIS SIGSEMIS Bulletin, Vol. 2, Issue (3&4), pp. 52–56.

Schroeter, R., Hunter, J., Guerin, J., Khan, I. and Henderson, M. (2006). *A Synchronous Multimedia Annotation System for Secure Collaboratories,* 2nd IEEE International Conference on E-Science and Grid Computing (eScience 2006). Amsterdam, Netherlands. December.

Schroeter, R. and Thieberger, N. (2006). *EOPAS, the EthnoER online representation of interlinear text.* Barwick, L. and Thieberger, N. (eds.) 2006. Sustainable Data from Digital Fieldwork Sydney: Sydney University Press. pp. 99–124.

Stevens, R.D., Robinson, A., and Goble, C.A. (2003), *myGrid: Personalised Bioinformatics on the Information Grid,* Proceedings 11th International Conference on Intelligent Systems in Molecular Biology June.

Thompson, D, Braun, J. and Ford R., (2006). *OpenDX: Paths to Visualization.* VIS, Inc.

University of Waikato (2007). *Weka3 : Data Mining Software in Java.*

Weerawarana, S. and Curbera, F. (2002) *Business process with BPEL4WS: Understanding BPEL4WS.* IBM, August.

Williams, R.J., Martinez, N., and Golbeck, J. (2006) *Ontologies for Ecoinformations,* Journal of Web Semantics, volume 4, Issue 4, pp. 237–242.

Part IV
Applications Using Alternative Approaches to Multimedia Ontologies

Chapter 9
Mind the Gaps – Finding the Appropriate Dimensional Representation for Semantic Retrieval of Multimedia Assets

William I. Grosky, Rajeev Agrawal, and Farshad Fotouhi

9.1 Introduction: Multimedia Retrieval

Multimedia retrieval is an enabling technology for the new semantic web, since discussing multimedia in the framework of the semantic web can be placed under the rubric of multimedia annotation. After all, the annotation modality is arbitrary; e.g. images can be annotated with text, text can be annotated with images, images can be annotated with audio, videos can be annotated with structured ontological descriptors. Techniques for carrying out appropriate annotation cover the gamut of present-day research topics in the area of multimedia semantics, including the following important areas: media object representation, genre representation and detection, event representation and detection, multimedia ontology learning, emergent semantics, and folksonomies.

Media object representation is quite important, as particular representations lend themselves better to cross-media annotations. In the past, the different media were isolated and analysed separately. For example, images had one representation, audio another, and they were rarely analysed together. More and more researchers now realise that documents of interest are multimedia, not monomedia, and thus should be represented in an integrated fashion to take advantage of various mathematical techniques for discovering latent semantics (Zhao and Grosky 2002a). A multimedia document is represented as a high-dimensional vector, where the coordinates represent particular feature values. Using various dimensional reduction techniques, researchers have distilled various concepts from multimedia document collections, where each concept represents the co-occurrence of various elementary features. If, for example, an image feature and a textual feature occur in the same concept, we may be able to say that the textual feature is an annotation for the occurrence of the particular image feature (and vice versa).

W.I. Grosky
University of Michigan-Dearborn, Dearborn, MI, USA
e-mail: wgrosky@umich.edu

Y. Kompatsiaris, P. Hobson (eds.), *Semantic Multimedia and Ontologies,*
© Springer Science+Business Media, LLC 2008

Genre representation and detection concerns itself with the ability to classify multimedia documents into various categories such as news videos, sports videos, jazz music, and classical music (Fischer, Lienhart, and Effelsberg 1995). Some work has also been done using more subjective categories, such as the various emotions evoked by particular multimedia documents (Geng, Zhuang, and Pan 2003). Events require spatial and temporal features and are manifested through video and audio multimedia documents (Westermann and Jain 2006).

Multimedia ontology learning is in its infancy, especially due to the newness of the area of multimedia ontologies in general (Chang, Sikora, and Puri 2001; Vembu, Kiesel, Sintek, and Baumann 2006). As in standard textual documents in this area, machine learning techniques should be applied to the occurrence of various multimedia features in a given corpus in the hope of finding various generalised concepts which hopefully appear in other, as yet, unexamined multimedia documents.

A folksonomy is a form of emergent semantics as it refers to a collaborative, dynamic approach to the generation of ontologies and media object semantics (Aurnhammer, Hanappe, and Steels 2006; Mika 2005). That such an approach results in a stable semantics has been shown in Cattuto, Loreto, and Pietronero (2006).

While addressing the area of multimedia retrieval, it has been widely recognized that the family of multimedia retrieval techniques should become an integration of both low-level visual features addressing the more detailed perceptual aspects and high-level semantic features underlying the more general conceptual aspects of multimedia data. Although efforts have been devoted to combining these two aspects of visual data, the gap between them is still a huge barrier in front of researchers. Intuitive and heuristic approaches do not provide us with satisfactory performance. Therefore, there is an urgent need for finding and managing the latent correlation between low-level features and high-level concepts. How to bridge this gap between visual features and semantic features has been a major challenge in this research field. It is imperative for multimedia researchers to realize that any multimedia retrieval technique has to narrow this gap down to a minimum. MPEG-7, which is discussed in detail in Chapter 2, is one such step in the right direction.

Another challenge, which multimedia researchers still are struggling with, is the *curse of dimensionality*: multimedia data is inherently of high dimensionality, making it difficult to carry out efficient querying. Thus, it is extremely interesting that various techniques for dimensional reduction have also been found to improve semantic retrieval, forming so-called *concepts* from low-level features. This chapter discusses these techniques and shows that using them in the same fashion as they have been used in traditional textual information retrieval produces quite interesting results.

The structure of this chapter is as follows: Section 9.1 provides a short introduction to semantic multimedia retrieval, while Section 9.2 discusses various dimensionality reduction techniques. In Section 9.3, we discuss our approach to dimensional reduction in the multimedia environment, and perform some illustrative clustering and retrieval experiments. Finally, in Section 9.4, we present our conclusions.

9.1.1 Why Multimedia Retrieval?

The emergence of multimedia technology and the rapid growth in the number and type of multimedia assets controlled by public and private entities, as well as the expanding range of image and video documents appearing on the web, have attracted significant research efforts in providing tools for effective retrieval and management of multimedia data. Multimedia retrieval is based on the availability of a representation scheme for multimedia content. Multimedia content descriptors may be visual features such as colour, texture, shape, and spatial relationships, audio features such as spectral properties, textual features such as keyword counts, or multimedia semantic primitives (labelled image regions, word signatures in audio).

Conventional information retrieval is based solely on text, and these approaches to textual information retrieval have been transplanted into multimedia retrieval in a variety of ways, including the representation of a multimedia document as a vector of feature values. However, "a picture is worth a thousand words". Multimedia contents are much more versatile compared with text, and the amount of visual data is already enormous and still expanding very rapidly. Hoping to cope with these special characteristics of multimedia data, content-based multimedia retrieval methods have been introduced. Many of the newer methodologies use various enabling technologies from the semantic web vision, including taxonomies (Aslandogan, Their, Yu, Zou, and Rishe 1997) and ontologies (Hyvönen, Saarela, Styrman, and Viljanen 2003).

To give an idea of the state of the art in multimedia retrieval, several tasks, which the casual user would consider quite simple, have been presented as being beyond the current technology (Rowe and Jain 2005).

- Search an archive of radio broadcasts to find an interview with a particular individual or search a picture archive to find a photo of the person visiting a particular city. This requires context to disambiguate words and identify where a particular photo was taken.
- Identifying a person across a room through the mediation of your cell phone camera. Simple face matching may return too many false positives. Using the context of the situation at hand may serve to overcome this problem.
- Make the billions of hours of home video currently stored in shoeboxes useful. Tools for organizing and retrieving this information are needed.

Just as in common-sense reasoning, it sometimes turns out that the seemingly simplest tasks are actually quite difficult. And just as in common-sense reasoning, the missing ingredient is how to take *context* into account. The earliest work in multimedia information retrieval was based on computer vision algorithms which were focused on low-level feature-based similarity search over images, video, and audio (Ballard and Brown 1982; Haralick and Shapiro 1993). In the last decade, trying to take context into account, serious efforts have been made to utilize multiple modalities available with multimedia objects in various retrieval techniques.

9.1.2 The Addition of Semantics

The different types of information that are normally associated with multimedia documents are (Grosky 1994)

- Content-independent metadata: data that is not directly concerned with content, but related to it. Examples are image format, author's name, date, and location.
- Content-based metadata: Non-information-bearing metadata: data referring to low-level or intermediate-level features, such as colour, texture, shape, spatial relationships, and their various combinations. This information can easily be computed from the raw data.
- Information-bearing metadata: data referring to content semantics, concerned with relationships of entities appearing in multimedia documents to real-world entities, as well as data referring to the relationship of a particular multimedia document or sub-document to particular users. This type of information, such as that a particular building appearing in a video is the *Sear's Tower*, or that a particular image evokes the emotion of happiness in Joe Smith, cannot usually be derived from the raw data. It must then be supplied by other means. In the first case, the building might inherit this semantic label from another video, an image, or a detailed textual description, where a similar-appearing building has already been identified. In the second case, Joe Smith may specifically inform the system of his feelings when he views this image, or, again, this information may be inherited from other images which invoke similar feelings, perhaps by their characterization as being in the same genre (Fischer, Lienhart, and Effelsberg 1995; Geng, Zhuang, and Pan 2003; Li, Ogihara, and Li 2003), or though a process of social tagging (Aurnhammer, Hanappe, and Steels 2006; Mika 2005).

Note that information-bearing metadata, commonly referred to as semantic information, however, are not extracted directly from visual contents, but represent the relatively more important meanings of multimedia objects that are perceived by human beings. These conceptual aspects are more closely related to users' preferences and subjectivity. Concepts may vary significantly in different circumstances. Subtle changes in the semantics may lead to dramatic conceptual differences. Needless to say, it is a very challenging task to extract and manage meaningful semantics and to make use of them to achieve more intelligent and user-friendly retrieval.

Low-level multimedia features are directly related to perceptual aspects of image content. Since it is usually easy to extract and represent these features and fairly convenient to design similarity measures by using the statistical properties of these features, a variety of content-based image retrieval techniques have been proposed.

High-level conceptual information is normally represented by using text descriptors. Traditional indexing for multimedia retrieval is text based. In certain content-based retrieval techniques, text descriptors are also used to model perceptual aspects. However, the inadequacy of text description is very obvious:

- It is difficult for text to capture the perceptual saliency of visual features.
- It is rather difficult to characterize certain entities, attributes, roles, or events by means of text only.
- Text is not well suited for modelling the correlation between perceptual and conceptual features.
- Text descriptions reflect the subjectivity of the annotator, and the annotation process is prone to be inconsistent, incomplete, ambiguous, and very difficult to be automated.

Rather than trying to discover a media object's hidden meaning, researchers should try to invent ways of managing media objects so as to help people make more intelligent use of them. They should initiate studies on the relationship between users and media objects. Media objects should be interpreted relative to the particular goal or point of view of a particular user at a particular time. Media objects that would satisfy a user at one time may not satisfy him at other times. Also, media objects that would satisfy one user at a particular time may not satisfy other users at any time.

Of course, content-based descriptors are necessary to this process, but they are definitely not sufficient. Thus, researchers have studied measured interactions between users and media objects, with the ultimate goal of trying to satisfy the user community by providing them with the media objects they individually require, based on their previous media interactions. Thus, the field of *emergent multimedia* semantics was born (Grosky, Patel, Li, and Fotouhi 2005; Grosky, Sreenath, and Fotouhi 2002; Santini, Gupta, and Jain 2001; Staab 2002).

The major advantage of using semantic information in multimedia retrieval is that the notion of similarity is not just based on simple low-level feature matching, but also incorporates the context of the retrieval. Figure 9.1 shows five images, the middle one of which (image 3) can have multiple semantics, two of whose values would be *forest* and *fog*. If interpreted in the context of a user browsing path (. . ., image 1, image 3, image 2, . . .), the *fog* semantics would be the primary interpretation of this image, but in the context of a user browsing path (. . ., image 4, image 3, image 5, . . .), the *forest* interpretation would predominate.

9.1.3 Multimedia Features

Until recently, managing multimedia information has been quite ad hoc. Tools that were developed by one research group could not easily be repurposed and used as components in the design of more complex systems by other research groups. This had been caused, largely, by the complexity of devising transformations between different data and metadata representation schemes used by these different groups. The growing popularity of MPEG-7 has changed this state of affairs.

Allowing for the representation of a multiplicity of multimedia features in a uniform fashion, it is becoming much easier to transform from one representation

Fig. 9.1 An image with multiple semantics disambiguated by context

scheme to another in a more automatic and transparent fashion than was previously possible. The following features have been used to represent image data:

Colour is one of the most widely used visual features in content-based image retrieval. It is relatively robust and simple to represent. Various studies of colour perception and colour spaces have been proposed, in order to find colour-based techniques that are more closely aligned with the ways that humans perceive colour (Gershon 1985).

Texture refers to the patterns in an image that present the properties of homogeneity that do not result from the presence of a single colour or intensity value (Howarth and Ruger 2004). It is a powerful discriminating feature, present almost everywhere in nature. However, it is almost impossible to describe texture in words because it is virtually a statistical and structural property.

Shape representation is normally required to be invariant to translation, rotation, and scaling (Tao and Grosky 2000).

A combination of the above features are extracted from each image and transformed into a point of a high-dimensional vector space. Using this representation, the many techniques developed by the information retrieval community can be used to advantage. As the dimensionality of the underlying space is still quite high, however, the many disadvantages caused by the curse of dimensionality also prevail. The conventional approaches that use such image attributes as colour and texture also suffer from a number of other problems, such as capturing semantics and formulating queries. To improve results, one widely popular but highly inefficient solution to this problem is to annotate images with keywords manually, after visually examining them. The image collection can then be queried on these keywords. The quality of this method, however, is dependent on the perception of the person annotating the images. Even so, this technique is used by many search engines, including Google and Yahoo. To overcome these problems associated with the above methods, we use both low-level image features, in the form of *visual keywords* (Sreenath, Grosky, and Fotouhi 2004), and text annotations for the purpose of image clustering and retrieval.

9.1.4 Mind the Gaps

In the last decade, researchers have been trying to build algorithms/techniques to bridge the different, so-called, gaps existing in multimedia retrieval. In the research literature, the focus has been on the following two gaps: semantic and sensory. We mention here another gap, the *subjective gap*, which exists due to users' needs and the descriptions of these needs. It may be difficult for a user to express what she wants from a multimedia retrieval system. Therefore, it is important that the system itself try to reconstruct them from a user's browsing and querying history. The semantic gap is the principal focus of multimedia retrieval research. A proper definition of semantic gap is given in Smeulders, Worring, Santini, Gupta, and Jain (2000):

> The semantic gap is the lack of coincidence between the information that one can extract from the visual data and the interpretation that the same data have for a user in a given situation.

In general, the semantic gap starts at the low-level features and extends to the semantics (Hare, Lewis, Enser, and Sandom 2006). Sometimes, we may identify some of the objects in an image but the context of these objects in that particular image may be missing. The semantic gap is very critical to content-based multimedia retrieval techniques.

The sensory gap exists in the multimedia world as the gap between an object and the machine's capability to capture and define that object. For example, a person in a picture with the side of his face exposed may not be recognized as a human because a human should have two eyes or a three-dimensional structure represented by a two-dimensional image (e.g. chest radiograph). The lack of resolution can also contribute to this sensory gap. It is possible that different low-level features or representations can be produced by the same object due to distance, partial occlusions, illumination, clutter, camera viewpoint, etc. Similarly, different objects can produce similar low-level features. For human eyes, it is not difficult to see this perceptual difference, but is a very difficult problem for a machine. To bridge the sensory gap, some form of contextual knowledge is required by the retrieval system. This knowledge may come while capturing the multimedia data or may be incorporated as part of domain knowledge. This contextual knowledge may be in the form of physical laws, laws about how objects behave and how people visualize the objects.

The subjective gap is similar to the semantic gap; it refers to the lack of ability of a user to describe her needs (query) to a retrieval system. The subjective gap also exists due to the non-availability of any features which can define emotions, feelings, smell, touch, and other such features. If a user needs a picture of a sweet food item, there is no method to describe what "sweet" means. At this time, if the image database has text annotations, which includes these abstract features, a query may return some results depending on the quality and level of these annotations. To bridge this gap, instead of asking the user's requirements at a very fine level, a higher level concept can be sought.

9.1.5 The Curse of Dimensionality

The curse of dimensionality was identified and defined by Bellman (1961), in connection with the difficulty of optimization by exhaustive enumeration on product spaces and refers to "the exponential growth of hyper volume as a function of dimensionality". As the dimensionality of the input data space (i.e. the number of predictors) increases, it becomes exponentially more difficult to find global optima for the parameter space, i.e. to fit models. Hence, it is simply a practical necessity to pre-screen and pre-select from among a large set of input (predictor) variables those that are of likely utility for predicting the outputs (dependent variables) of interest (StatSoft 2005).

In multimedia retrieval applications, the feature vectors are used to store information to represent high-dimensional data. Such vectors may represent anything from RGB data of individual pixels to texture and shape data for an image, and multimedia data similarity queries are based upon nearest neighbour searches of this data. In processes where the dimension of the feature vectors continues to increase, problems arise as the data tends toward the boundary of the data region and the result is that the time for a "nearest neighbour search" increases rapidly as the dimensionality increases. An interactive computer application called jCurse that can illustrate the "curse of dimensionality" by allowing the user to view a number of data distributions and perform distance measurements using a variety of metrics can be found in Eccles and Su (2004). They also argue that the expected distance increases as the dimension increases, in the case of maximum, Manhattan, and Euclidean distances, with distribution models of uniform, Gaussian, Chi-Square, exponential and a mix of these for all components of the feature vector. Tesic (2004) discusses the issue in terms of capturing and organizing large volumes of images, such as scientific and medical data, and notes that such projects require new information processing techniques in the context of pattern recognition and data mining. In multimedia databases, the volume of the data is very large, and so is the number of feature vectors. It is impractical to store all the extracted feature vectors from millions of images in main memory. The amount of time needed to access the feature vectors on storage devices overwhelmingly dominates the time needed for a search. This problem is further complicated when the search is to be performed multiple times and in an interactive environment. The high dimensionality of data can cause increased time and space complexity, degradation in the algorithm/system performance, and decreased performance in nearest neighbour search, clustering, and indexing.

There are two ways to overcome the curse of dimensionality in multimedia search and retrieval. The first is to search for approximate results of a multimedia query, and the second is to reduce the high-dimensional input data to a low-dimensional representation. In most cases, as users are interested in retrieving the results which are close to their query, exact search and retrieval can be wasteful and not required. A standard method, which has been very popular, is to map the data items into a high-dimensional feature space as points. The feature space can then be indexed using a multidimensional indexing scheme (Guttman 1984; Samet 1989). Similarity search is then equivalent to hyper-spherical range search. This search will return all multimedia objects which are similar to the query object but within a certain threshold. The problem with this method is highlighted in Beyer, Goldstein, Ramakrishnan, and Shaft (1999). If the data dimensionality is large, then the maximum and minimum distances to a given query point in high-dimensional space are almost the same under a wide range of distance metrics and data distributions. All points converge to the same distance from the query point in high dimensions, and the concept of nearest neighbours becomes meaningless.

Nearest neighbour search in high dimensions is useful when the underlying dimensionality of the data is much smaller than the actual dimensionality and when the search space is limited to only a cluster to which the query point belongs. A novel data structure called Spatial Event Cube (SEC), for conceptual representation of complex spatial arrangements of visual thesaurus entries in large multimedia datasets, is suggested by Tesic (2004). This space can be used to discover simple spatial relationships in a scientific dataset using the perceptual association rule algorithm, to distil the frequent visual patterns in image and video datasets in order to discover interesting patterns. A survey of high-dimensional search techniques for multimedia databases is presented in Bohm, Berchtold, and Keim (2001).

9.2 Dimensionality Reduction Techniques

Dimensionality reduction has been one of the most active research areas of machine learning in the recent years. Burges (2004) considers the problem of the reduction of dimensionality, a way of making the amount of data used more manageable. The author surveys various approaches to dimensionality reduction, among which are principal component analysis (PCA), kernel PCA, probabilistic PCA, projection pursuit, multidimensional scaling, isomap, locally linear embedding, Laplacian eigenmaps, and spectral clustering. Dimensionality reduction can be considered as a pre-processing step before the data is ready to be used by the system.

Dimensionality reduction reduces the number of random variables involved in an operation. There are different approaches, such as *feature selection*, which involves finding a subset of features by means of a filter, and *feature extraction*, which involves using a mapping of the multidimensional space to fewer dimensions. In some applications, it is possible to use new representations in which there has been some loss. There is a trade-off between preserving important aspects of original data and the number of dimensions desired. It is also possible to measure the degree of loss with a loss function, which provides a quantitative means for measuring errors in the representation of data; different loss functions may mean different low-dimensional representations.

In feature selection, an appropriate subset of the original features is found to represent the data. The criterion to select appropriate features is dependent on the application domain. This method is useful when a limited amount of data is present, but represented with a large number of features. In the diagnostic use of gene expression data, a classifier is used to determine the disease of a patient based on the expression of thousands of genes. For this, the classifier is trained from data of only several tens of patients (Tibshirani, Hastie, Narasimhan, and Chu 2002). It is crucial to determine a small set of relevant variables to estimate reliable parameters. The advantage of selecting a small set of features is that you then need to use few values in the calculations.

In feature extraction, new features are found using the original features without losing any important information. Feature extraction methods can be divided into linear and non-linear techniques. Linear techniques are based on getting a resultant feature set Y, which is derived using linear combinations of the original feature set X. The linear feature extraction process generally uses a weight vector w to optimise a criterion, which is also considered as a quality parameter.

Reducing or eliminating the curse of dimensionality is a goal for improving the search and retrieval capabilities of multimedia applications. In this section, we discuss various linear and non-linear dimensionality reduction techniques.

9.2.1 Linear Dimensionality Reduction Techniques

There are several linear dimensionality reduction techniques such as principal component analysis, factor analysis, projection pursuit, and independent component analysis. We will provide a brief description of some of them.

Principal Component Analysis: Principal component analysis (PCA) is a second-order method that seeks to reduce the dimension of the data by finding a few orthogonal linear combinations of the original variables with the largest variance. An excellent tutorial on PCA can be found in Smith (2002). PCA transforms the data to a new coordinate system such that the first coordinate (also called the first principal component) is the projection of the data exhibiting the greatest variance, the second coordinate (also called the second principal component) exhibits the second greatest variance, and so on. This way, the "most important" aspects of the data are retained in the lower order principal components. PCA is also called the (discrete) Karhunen-Loève transform (or KLT, named after Kari Karhunen and Michel Loève), the Hotelling transform (in honour of Harold Hotelling), singular value decomposition (SVD), or the empirical orthogonal function (EOF) method.

Projection Pursuit (PP): Projection pursuit is another linear method, which finds the most "interesting" possible projections of multidimensional data. PP can also incorporate higher than second order information, and is therefore useful for non-Gaussian datasets. A good review of PP can be found in Huber (1985). The projection index defines the "interestingness" of a direction; the task of PP is to optimize this index. A projection is considered interesting if it has a structure in the form of trends, clusters, hyper-surfaces, or anomalies. These structures can be analysed using manual or automatic methods. The scatter-plot is one such manual method, which can be used to understand data characteristics over two selected dimensions at a time. There are many methods to automate this task. A method based on the negative Shannon entropy is commonly used. The projection index can be maximised by finding an estimate of the density of the projected points and maximising the projection index operating on that estimate (Silverman 1988).

Independent Component Analysis (ICA): ICA is a generalization of the PCA and the PP concepts. ICA looks for independent variables, while PCA seeks uncorrelated variables. ICA can be divided into noiseless and noisy cases. The noiseless ICA is a special case of PP, with independence being the *interestingness* in the projection pursuit index definition. The following description is based on the survey (Hyvarinen 1999).

- The ICA of the random vector x consists of finding a linear transform $s = Wx$, so that the components s_i are as independent as possible, in the sense of maximizing some objective function $f(s_1, \ldots, s_m)$ that measures independence.
- Objective functions can be *multi-unit* contrast functions that estimate all p independent components at once, or *one-unit* contrast functions that estimate a single independent component at a time.

ICA has been used in blind source separation, feature extraction, blind convolution, and exploratory data analysis in the fields of economics, psychology, and other social sciences.

9.2.2 Non-Linear Dimensionality Reduction Techniques

Many linear dimensionality techniques, such as PCA and ICA, also have their non-linear variants. The non-linear PCA incorporates non-linearity in the objective function, though the resulting components are still linear combinations of the original data. It is possible to use such non-linear methods such as principal curves and self-organizing maps with ICA (Fodor 2002). Here, we will discuss some of the most popular non-linear dimensionality reduction techniques.

Multidimensional Scaling: Multidimensional scaling is used to analyze subjective evaluations of pairwise (dis)similarities of entities. Assume there are n items in p-dimensional space and an $n \times n$ matrix of proximity measures. Multidimensional scaling produces a k-dimensional representation ($k \leq p$) of the original data items. The distance in the new k-space reflects the proximities in the data. If two items are more similar, this distance will be smaller. The distance measures can be Euclidean, Manhattan, or maximum norm. Multidimensional scaling is typically used to visualise data in two or three dimensions, to uncover underlying hidden structure. While determining the maximum number of k, it is ensured that there are at least twice as many pairs of items than the number of estimated parameters, which results in $p \geq 4k + 1$ (Carreira-Perpinan 1997). An architecture of a distributed image retrieval system using multidimensional scaling is given in Brunelli and Mich (2000). They provide a method to quantify the effectiveness of low-level visual descriptors in a multimedia database. Multidimensional scaling has been used for scientific visualization, data mining in the areas of cognitive science, information science, psychophysics, marketing, ecology, and psychometrics.

Vector Quantization (VQ): In many applications, it is required to represent each data item by not just one single value, but using a small array, such as an image pixel. In a simple case, each image pixel is represented by three values: red, green, and blue. Using vector quantization, it is possible to quantize all the possible set of colour values by approximating them by a small subset of, say, 256 colours, therefore using only 1 byte instead of 3 bytes to represent each pixel. In VQ, the basic idea is to replace the values from a multidimensional vector space with values from a lower dimensional discrete subspace. A vector quantiser maps k-dimensional vectors in the vector space R^k into a finite set of vectors $Y = \{y_i : i = 1, 2, \ldots, N\}$. The vector y_i is called a code vector or a *codeword*, and the set of all the codewords is called a *codebook*. There is a nearest neighbour region called the *Voronoi* region associated with each codeword, y_i.

$$V_i = \{x \in R^x : ||x - y_i|| \leq ||x - y_j||, \forall j \neq i\}$$

VQ can be used for any large datasets, when adjacent data values are related in some way. VQ has been used in image, video, and audio compression. A review of vector quantisation techniques used for encoding digital images is presented in Nasrabadi and King (1988). In Subramaniam and Rao (2003), a low-complexity quantisation scheme using transform coding and bit allocation techniques, which allows for easy mapping from observation to quantised values, is developed for speech.

Laplacian Eigenmaps (LEM): In a multimedia dataset, low-dimensional data is hidden in a very high-dimensional space. For example, $n \times m$ pixels are needed to represent an image of n rows and m columns. If this image is of a certain object and has been captured using a moving camera under fixed lighting conditions, the dimensionality of the space of all images of the object is the number of degrees of freedom of the camera. The space under consideration has the structure of a low-dimensional manifold embedded in $\Re^{n^2}$ (Belkin and Niyogi 2003). This method is based on the graph–theoretic approach. A graph is built using the data items, which incorporates neighbourhood information of the dataset. A low-dimensional representation of the dataset is computed using the Laplacian of the graph that optimally preserves local neighbourhood information. The algorithm has three steps:

- Constructing the adjacency graph: Two points (nodes in graph terminology) x and y are connected by an edge if x and y are "close". To find the closeness, a Euclidean distance measure based on either a certain threshold or an n nearest neighbours approach can be used.
- Weighting the edges: One simple approach is to assign the weight of edge between points x and y as 1, if they are connected. A more complex approach can use the heat kernel.
- Compute eigenmaps: In the last step, eigenvalues and eigenvectors are computed using the graph arrived at in the previous step.

The LEM algorithm optimally preserves local information in the embeddings provided by the Laplacian eigenmaps. The LEM has been used to improve the clustering-based segmentation of multivariate images (Tziakos, Laskaris, and Fotopoulos 2004). Another non-linear dimensionality reduction technique, Locally Linear Embedding (LLE), is similar to LEM (Roweis and Saul 2000).

Diffusion Maps: Diffusion maps provide a framework based on diffusion processes that allow one to obtain a multiscale description of geometric structures of datasets as well as of spaces of functions defined on these sets. This approach uses the ideas from spectral graph theory, harmonic analysis, and potential theory (Coifman and Lafon 2006). In this framework, any arbitrary dataset can be parameterised to build embeddings called diffusion maps. It is possible to define a meaningful metric on the data using the diffusion distance. Basically, there are two steps in this approach:

- Calculating diffusion distances: In this step, the goal is to define a distance metric on a dataset that reflects the connectivity of the points within the set, similar to the weight metric in the graph. The method to determine distance is dependent on the application. Two points may be considered close if they are connected by many short paths in the graph; therefore, the diffusion distance between two points will be small. The diffusion distance is actually the sum over all paths of length less than a certain length between two points. It has been found to be more robust to noise on the data than any other distance measures.
- Deriving diffusion maps: Using the diffusion distance matrix, the eigenvalues and eigenvectors are calculated. The right eigenvectors weighted by eigenvalues generate the diffusion maps (Lafon and Lee 2006). This mapping is a parameterisation of the dataset in a low-dimensional space. Diffusion maps have been used to organize and cluster words into concepts as well as in image clustering.

9.3 The Journey of Latent Semantic Analysis from the Textual Domain to the Multimedia Landscape

Latent Semantic Analysis (LSA) presumes that there is an underlying, latent semantic structure in the usage of the words in any document collection. LSA is a popular technique in natural language processing. It is also called Latent Semantic Indexing

(LSI) in the context of information retrieval. LSA has also been used often in multimedia retrieval. In this section, we describe our multimedia clustering, search, and retrieval research, which models the multimedia retrieval problem along the lines of text information retrieval techniques.

9.3.1 Information Retrieval (IR)

Information retrieval has existed for a very long time in the form of databases. But there is a fundamental difference between databases and information retrieval. Databases store information in a highly structured fashion, and therefore querying on databases is easy. However, information retrieval is based on unstructured data and we need to apply more intelligent techniques to query this data and retrieve information which is relevant to the user (Witten, Moffat, and Bell 1999).

The information retrieval problem is posed as "matching of queries with words to documents with words". From a user's perspective, retrieval is based more on a concept than on a set of words. LSI was first proposed in Deerwester, Dumais, Landauer, Furnas, and Harshman (1990) to overcome the deficiencies of term-matching retrieval by treating the unreliability of observed term-document association data as a statistical problem. The underlying latent semantic structure in the document collection is partially obscured by the randomness of word choice with respect to retrieval. Statistical techniques were used to find this latent structure and remove the obscuring "noise". To organize and search a large text collection, clustering traditionally has been used to discover the inherent concepts embodied there (Dhillon and Modha 2001). The document collection can then be organized based on the concepts expressed through these clusters. The basic idea is to extract unique keywords from the set of documents and consider these words as features and then represent each document as a vector of weighted word frequencies in this feature space. A *term-document matrix* is created, in which rows represent the textual keywords and columns represent the documents. Then, LSA is applied on this term-document matrix to discover the latent relationships between correlated words and documents. LSA uses the truncated singular value decomposition (SVD), which projects the high-dimensional concept space to a low-dimensional concept space. This new representation can be used for various purposes:

- To apply document clustering and classification;
- To find relationships between terms or between documents;
- To query the document collection using a set of terms.

In information retrieval, synonymy (multiple words having the same meaning) and polysemy (words having multiple meanings) are two other problems. SVD also helps in recovering these relationships.

The annual Text Retrieval Conference (TREC) sponsored by the Defense Advanced Research Projects Agency and the National Institute of Standards and Technology has been organizing contests to improve IR techniques since 1992. In

Dhillon and Modha (2001), the concept decompositions are obtained by taking the least-squares approximations onto the linear subspace spanned by all the concept vectors. There are many other related schemes referred to in the literature (Bast and Majumdar 2005). They have also introduced the *curve of relatedness score* to retrieve the relevant documents using query expansion. A bipartite spectral graph partitioning algorithm that uses both left and right singular vectors is applied to cluster the documents and words simultaneously (Dhillon 2001).

9.3.2 Applications to Multimedia

After successful application of LSA in text retrieval, researchers have applied this technique in the multimedia domain. The problem is to describe a term in an image. The earliest applications used manual text annotations to describe an image, similar to the terms in a document in text retrieval. The manual text annotation may be skewed by individual users' perspectives. It is not an easy task to build a system entirely on manual text annotations. Another approach is to use the low-level features (descriptors) of an image. These features can be extracted automatically, unlike manual annotations. This approach has three steps:

- Extracting image features;
- Reduction of feature vector dimensions;
- Query image collection using some similarity metric.

The QBIC system (Faloutsos, Barber, Flickner, Hafner, Niblack, Petkovic, and Equitz 1994) stores colour, texture, shape, sketch, and object information of each image and uses techniques similar to information retrieval techniques. In this system, it is possible to integrate all of these in one single query. The user can specify the colour proportion, select regions of relevant texture, and draw a sketch of the query image. In this system, dimensional reduction was used to reduce the time taken to calculate image similarities, which was an operation of quadratic time-complexity.

In Photobook (Pentland, Picard, and Sclaroff 1996), PCA is used to create eigen-images, which are small sets of perceptually significant coefficients. This technique is referred to as *semantics-preserving image compression*. These low-level features have been used as *terms*, over which to apply standard information retrieval techniques.

In other approaches, images have been divided into blocks of pixels and then each block is described using low-level features. Various text retrieval techniques, such as inverted files, term weighting, and relevance feedback, are applied on the blocks of an image (Squire, Müller, Müller, and Pun 2000). In Westerveld (2000), image contents are combined with textual contents. The low-level image features used are HSV colour space and Gabor texture filters. The retrieval results for the text and image features are better than image-only and text-only results.

In Zhao and Grosky (2002b), an approach is presented to negotiate the gap between low-level features and high-level concepts in web documents, using LSA on vectors containing both keywords and image features of the documents. The results of this paper demonstrate the use of image features in improving text retrieval, even for text-only queries.

LSA has also been used in the video domain to improve retrieval results. To find the association between segmented frame regions, low-level video features have been combined with structural information (Hohl, Souvannavong, Merialdo, Huet, 2004).

9.3.3 Visual Keywords

The first step in any image retrieval system is to extract the image features. The feature extraction can be based on the entire image or on regions of the image resulting from a segmentation process. Such segmentation techniques have also been used to identify the objects of interest, based on their specific shapes. After segmentation, features are computed from each segmented object and used for clustering. These object segmentation techniques, however, are not very likely to succeed in broad domains. This problem may be circumvented by weak segmentation, where grouping is based on some data-driven properties. Once such features have been extracted, the images are clustered using such methods as k-means, hierarchical agglomerative clustering, or a learning-based approach.

We extract the low-level image features by subdividing an image using a template of a certain size. As template-based visual keywords are supposed to convey semantics, template sizes are crucial. This is the same problem as in classical information retrieval, where textual keywords are at the word stem level, rather than the individual word level or the paragraph level. Choose a template size too large (akin to a paragraph in classical IR), and it would contain multiple object segments and have a muddled semantics. Choose a template size too small (akin to a letter in classical IR), and its semantics would be completely undetermined. In our approach, we consider each image as a document and each template region as a word (visual keyword). Hence, each image is represented by multiple template regions. These regions are called *tiles*. Each tile is represented using the MPEG-7 *scalable colour, colour structure*, and *colour layout* colour descriptors. This results, however, in a very large number of distinct tiles. To reduce this large number of tiles, we cluster them and treat tiles in the same cluster as being the same. This is akin to the stemming operator for textual keywords. Thus, in our approach, we use a term-image matrix, where the terms consist of textual keywords and visual keywords, each visual keyword being a tile representing a particular cluster of similar tiles. We show that this image representation approach produces better image clusters than those resulting from just using image features or just using textual keywords (Agrawal, Grosky, and Fotouhi 2006a). The proposed approach has four steps:

- Extracting and clustering visual keywords;
- Creating a term-document matrix using textual keywords;

- Combining visual keywords and textual keywords information;
- Evaluating the MPEG-7 visual keyword model.

We apply LSA on the combined visual and textual space and learn co-occurrence relations among textual keywords and visual keywords. In summary, we extract the semantic relationship between text to text, image to image, and text to image in this step. The algorithm to create visual keywords is given in Fig. 9.2.

We now discuss various experiments using our keyword model. We use the image collection *LabelMe*, available through the MIT AI Lab (Russell, Torralba, Murphy, Freeman 2005). This collection allows people to annotate images online and have the annotations be updated instantly. We selected 658 images belonging to 15 categories from this collection. The categories with the number of images in each category are Boston street scenes (152), cars parked in the underground garage (39), kitchens (14), offices (24), rocks (41), pumpkins (58), apples (11), oranges (18), conference rooms (28), bedrooms (14), dining (63), indoor homes (59), home offices (19), silverware (81), and speakers (37). Figure 9.3 has images from four categories: office, bedroom, indoor home, home office.

We use a template size of 32 pixels × 32 pixels to create the non-overlapping tiles for each image. The original images in the collection have different resolutions, which vary from 2560 × 1920 to 300 × 205. The images are resized to 640 pixels × 480 pixels if they are larger to restrict the number of tiles to a fixed limit; however, the smaller images are left in their original sizes. The Multimedia digital Library for On-line Search (MILOS) software (http://milos.isti.cnr.it), which is based on the MPEG-7 XM model, is used to extract the colour descriptors SCD, CSD, and CLD. The total number of descriptors used is 140, in which we have 64 of SCD, 64 of CSD, and 12 of CLD. The maximum number of tiles an image can have is 300; the total number of tiles of 658 images is 165750. In Fig. 9.4, each row shows some example tiles from the categories shown in Fig. 9.3, but they look very

---

Input: A set of images $I = \{I_1, I_2, \ldots, I_n\}$.

Output: Visual keyword-image matrix

Algorithm:

1. Divide each image I_i into non-overlapping tiles t_i of the fixed template size.
2. Extract MPEG-7 descriptors (SCD, CLD, CSD) to form a tile vector $t_{i,j}$ for each tile t_j of image I_i.
3. Generate a tile matrix V, where each $t_{i,j}$ above is a row vector of V.
4. Normalize V and then apply SVD to reduce the dimension.
5. Apply a clustering algorithm to create C clusters out of all the tiles.
6. Compute the visual keyword–image matrix, having one column for each image and one row for each cluster, where the (i, j)th element of this matrix is the number of times tiles from the ith cluster appear in the jth image.

Fig. 9.2 Algorithm to create visual keyword matrix

Fig. 9.3 Images from the categories *offices*, *bedrooms*, *indoor homes*, *home offices*

similar to each other. Hence, they are likely to have similar low-level features. We apply a clustering algorithm *vcluster* (Karypis 2003) on these tiles to get 1500 visual keyword clusters. These clusters are then used as visual keywords to create a matrix of 658 images × 1500 clusters.

The textual keyword matrix was created from the annotation list of the image collection, and a 658 images × 506 words image-textual keyword matrix is created. The visual keyword and textual keyword matrices are then combined to create a single matrix of size 658 images × 2006 keywords, which contains both types of keywords. LSA/SVD is then applied to select only 200 principal components (coefficients), which results in a matrix of 658 images × 200 concepts.

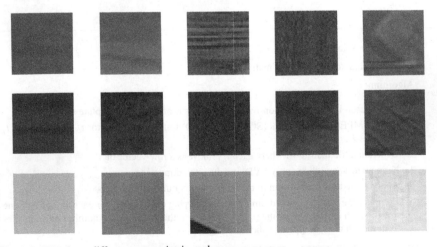

Fig. 9.4 Tiles from different categories in each row

We have conducted experiments using the following set of data:

- Full-size image (*mpfs*): Clustering is applied on the MPEG-7 colour descriptors extracted from the full-size images. Therefore, the visual keyword is actually the entire image and each vector represents the 140 MPEG-7 coefficients. We apply LSA to extract the inherent relationship among images and use only 16 coefficients to keep the error rate not more than 5%.

- Full-size image and textual keywords (*mpfstk*): In this case, we also use the textual keywords in addition to visual keywords. After combining both 140 colour descriptors and 506 textual keywords, the resultant vector has 646 coefficients for each image. We again apply SVD to extract relationships among images using both types of descriptors and also reduce the dimension of the matrix to 658 images × 38 concepts to maintain the error not more than 5% as before. Finally, we cluster the images using these image vectors.

- Tiles of each image (*mpts*): As discussed previously, images are partitioned into non-overlapping tiles, and these template-based tiles are clustered into 1500 visual-keyword clusters. After applying SVD, we select only 370 coefficients allowing 5% error. In essence, we cluster the images using visual keywords, where each visual keyword is a tile representing a particular cluster of similar tiles.

- Tiles of each image and textual keywords (*mptstk*): To see the improvement over the *mpts* dataset, we combine both visual keywords and textual keywords. We still apply SVD and surprisingly we need to select only 14 coefficients to allow 5% error with respect to the original matrix. Here we cluster the images using both visual keywords and textual keywords.

- In addition to the above datasets, we also cluster the images using only the textual keywords. There are a total of 506 text keywords for 658 images. We extract the first 142 coefficients using LSA/SVD to keep the same error as in other cases, which sufficiently captures the inherent relationship among the keywords. We find that the results are worse than the result found using any of the above datasets. The adjusted Rand Index is found to be only 0.26, lowest in all the datasets. This confirms that clustering the images merely on text keywords does not give good results.

Table 9.1 shows the result of applying the k-means algorithm for $k = 15$, which is the actual number of categories in the image collection. The adjusted Rand index is used to determine the accuracy of the clusters.

Table 9.1 Clustering results using different datasets

Dataset	Adjusted Rand Index (ARI) (Douglas 2004)
Mpfs	0.32
Mpfstk	0.39
Mpts	0.34
Mptstk	0.51
Text keywords only	0.26

The result shows that when we use low-level features extracted for full-size images (*mpfs*), ARI = 0.32, which is lower than what we get when clustering is done also using textual keywords (*mpfstk*). The more interesting results are obtained when the images are divided into tiles. We get ARI = 0.34 using only visual keywords (*mpts*), but there is a large improvement we also use textual keywords (*mptstk*).

We also conducted retrieval experiments and measured the precision at 10% and 30% recall and the average precision at 10%, 20%, ..., 100% recall (Agrawal, Grosky, and Fotouhi 2006b). The values vary between 0 and 1. We considered the entire collection of images in our database as the query dataset, to avoid favouring certain query results. The LSI dimensionless algorithm of Bast and Majumdar (2005) is used for all the retrieval experiments. The algorithm to formulate the query vector is given below:

1. Given a query image q, divide q into tiles and determine, for each tile, to which of the visual keywords clusters it belongs to. Now we have the closest cluster/concept for each tile of q.
2. Create the visual keywords vector using the information of step 1 and concatenate it with the textual keywords vector. This results in the query vector to be used for similarity matching.
3. Use this query vector and term-image matrix to find the similar images using cosine similarity.

The results of Table 9.2 show that at 10% recall, using visual keywords along with text keywords give the best results. The next best result is obtained when the full-size image and text keywords are combined. Using the text keywords alone is closely behind this. But using only low-level image features gives worse results. We can also observe that it does not really matter much in the case of using only low-level features as to whether we use the entire image or the tiles. At 30% recall, we still get the best results while using both visual keywords and text keywords. But using text keywords alone is better than the use of low-level features of the full-size image, which indicates that at a higher recall value, the utility of using the low-level features diminishes. The average precision results further indicate that visual keywords when used with textual keywords consistently provide the best representation for content-based image retrieval. Another important observation is that visual keywords alone are better than using low-level features and text for the entire image.

Table 9.2 Precision results for different datasets

Dataset	10% recall	30% recall	Average precision
Mpfs	0.68	0.51	0.41
Mpfstk	0.76	0.56	0.39
Mpts	0.69	0.54	0.43
Mptstk	0.81	0.68	0.56
Txt	0.73	0.64	0.50

9.4 Conclusion

In this chapter, we have shown the complexity of the process of semantic multimedia retrieval, and how multimedia information should be encompassed in the semantic web vision. Our work in this, so-called multimedia semantic web (Grosky, Sreenath, and Fotouhi 2002), differs from the standard semantic web paradigm in one important aspect, however. While most standard work has been concentrating on the very important problem of tool building in order to manage various sorts of high-level descriptors, the unspoken assumption seems to be that only particular users, namely document authors, should be able to describe particular multimedia documents.

We believe, on the other hand, that each user should be free to contribute to a multimedia document's overall context-based semantics. The key is to manage them in such a way as to use them to satisfy a particular user's needs and wants. Multimedia researchers can, and should, play an important role in the semantic web community, not only to extend the semantic web vision to multimedia entities through the emerging multimedia semantic web but also to show the semantic web community that their use of a unique, author-defined semantics is quite short-sighted.

References

Agrawal, R., Grosky, W.I. and Fotouhi, F. (2006a) Image Clustering Using Multimodal Keywords. SAMT 2006, Athens, Greece, pp. 113–123.

Agrawal, R., Grosky, W.I. and Fotouhi, F. (2006b) Image Retrieval Using Multimodal Keywords. ISM 2006, Athens, Greece, pp. 817–822.

Aslandogan, Y.A., Their, C., Yu, C.T., Zou, J. and Rishe, N. (1997) Using semantic Contents and WordNet in Image Retrieval. ACM SIGIR, Philadelphia, PA, USA, pp. 286–295.

Aurnhammer, M., Hanappe, P. and Steels, L. (2006) Integrating Collaborative Tagging and Emergent Semantics for Image Retrieval. Workshop on Collaborative Web Tagging, Edinburgh, Scotland.

Ballard, D.H. and Brown, C.M. (1982) Computer Vision, Prentice Hall, New Jersey, USA.

Bast, H. and Majumdar, D. (2005) Why Spectral Retrieval Works. Proceedings of ACM SIGIR, Salvador, Brazil, pp. 11–18.

Belkin, M. and Niyogi, P. (2003) Laplacian Eigenmaps for Dimensionality Reduction and Data Representation. Neural Computation, Vol. 15, No. 6, pp. 1373–1396.

Bellman, R. (1961) Adaptive Control Processes: A Guided Tour, Princeton University Press, Princeton, NJ.

Beyer, K.S., Goldstein, J., Ramakrishnan, R. and Shaft, U. (1999) When Is "Nearest Neighbor" Meaningful? International Conference on Database Theory, Springer-Verlag, New York, Vol. 1540, pp. 217–235.

Bohm, C., Berchtold, S. and Keim, D.A. (2001) Searching in High-Dimensional Spaces: Index Structures for Improving the Performance of Multimedia Databases. ACM Computing Surveys, Vol. 33, No. 3, pp. 322–373.

Brunelli, R. Mich, O. (2000) Image Retrieval by Examples. IEEE Transactions on Multimedia, Vol. 2, No. 3, pp. 164–171.

Burges, C.J.C. (2004) Geometric Methods for Feature Extraction and Dimensional Reduction: A Guided Tour. Microsoft Research Technical Report MSR-TR-2004-55, Microsoft Research, Redmond, WA.

Carreira-Perpinan, M.A. (1997) A Review of Dimension Reduction Techniques. Technical Report CS-96-09, Department of Computer Science, University of Sheffield, Sheffield, UK.

Cattuto, C., Loreto, V. and Pietronero, L. (2006) Semiotic Dynamics and Collaborative Tagging, Technical Report, Information Systems Research Lab, University of Illinois at Urbana-Champaign.

Chang, S.F., Sikora, T. and Puri, A. (2001) Overview of the MPEG-7 standard. IEEE Transactions on Circuits and Systems for Video Technology, Vol. 11, No. 6, pp. 688–695.

Coifman, R.R. and Lafon, S. (2006) Diffusion Maps. Applied and Computational Harmonic Analysis, Vol. 21, No. 1, pp. 5–30.

Deerwester, A., Dumais, S.T., Landauer, T.K., Furnas, G.W. and Harshman, R.A. (1990) Indexing by Latent Semantic Analysis. Journal of the American Society of Information Science, Vol. 41, No. 6, pp. 391–407.

Dhillon, I.S. (2001) Co-Clustering Documents and Words Using Bipartite Spectral Graph Partitioning. ACM SIGKDD, ACM Press, New York, pp. 269–274.

Dhillon, I.S. and Modha, D.S (2001) Concept Decompositions for Large Sparse Text Data Using Clustering. Machine Learning, Vol. 42, No. 1, pp. 143–175.

Douglas, S. (2004) Properties of the Hubert-Arable Adjusted Rand Index. Psychological Methods, Vol. 9, No. 3, pp. 386–396.

Eccles, I. and Su, M. (2004) Illustrating the Curse of Dimensionality Numerically Through Different Data Distribution Models. International Symposium on Information and Communication Technologies, Vol. 90, pp. 232–237.

Faloutsos, C., Barber, R., Flickner, M., Hafner, J., Niblack, W., Petkovic, D. and Equitz, W. (1994) Efficient and Effective Querying by Image Content. Journal of Intelligent Information Systems, Vol. 3, No. 3/4, pp. 231–262.

Fischer, S., Lienhart, R. and Effelsberg, W. (1995) Automatic Recognition of Film Genres. ACM International Conference on Multimedia, San Francisco, CA, pp. 295–304.

Fodor, I.K. (2002) A Survey of Dimension Reduction Techniques. Technical Report UCRL-ID-148494, Lawrence Livermore National Laboratory, Livermore, CA.

Geng, Y., Zhuang, Y. and Pan, Y. (2003) Popular Music Retrieval by Detecting Mood. ACM SIGIR, Toronto, Canada, pp. 375–376.

Gershon, R. (1985) Aspects of Perception and Computation in Colour Vision. CVGIP, Vol. 32, No. 2, pp. 244–277.

Grosky, W.I. (1994) Multimedia Information Systems. IEEE Multimedia, Vol. 1, No. 1, pp. 12–24.

Grosky, W.I., Patel, N., Li, X. and Fotouhi F. (2005) Dynamically Emerging Semantics in an MPEG-7 Image Database. Computer Journal, Vol. 48, No. 5, pp. 536–544.

Grosky, W.I., Sreenath, D.V. and Fotouhi, F. (2002) Emergent Semantics and the Multimedia Semantic Web. SIGMOD Record, Vol. 31, No. 4, pp. 54–58.

Guttman, A. (1984) R-Trees: A Dynamic Index Structure for Spatial Searching. ACM SIGMOD, Boston, MA, pp. 47–57.

Haralick, R.M. and Shapiro, L.G. (1993). Computer and Robot Vision, Addison-Wesley, New York, USA.

Hare, J.S., Lewis, P.H., Enser, P.G.B. and Sandom, C.J. (2006) Mind the Gap: Another Look at the Problem of the Semantic Gap in Image Retrieval. SPIE, Multimedia Content Analysis, Management, and Retrieval, Vol. 6073, San Jose, CA, USA.

Hohl, L., Souvannavong, F., Merialdo, B. and Huet, B., A.W.M. (2004) Using Structure for Video Object Retrieval. CIVR 2004, Vol. 3115, Dublin, Ireland, pp. 564–572.

Howarth, P and Ruger, S. (2004) Evaluation of Texture Features for Content-Based Image Retrieval. International Conference on Image and Video Retrieval, Dublin, Ireland, pp. 326–334.

Huber, P.J. (1985) Projection Pursuit. The Annals of Statistics, Vol. 13, No. 2, pp. 435–475.

Hyvarinen, A. (1999) Survey on Independent Component Analysis. Neural Computing Surveys, Vol. 2, pp. 94–128.

Hyvönen, E., Saarela, S., Styrman, A. and Viljanen, K. (2003) Ontology-Based Image Retrieval. Proceedings of WWW2003, Budapest, Hungary.

Karypis, G. (2003) CLUTO: A Clustering Toolkit Release 2.1.1, University of Minnesota, Department of Computer Science, Minneapolis, MN 55455, USA, Technical Report: #02-017.

Lafon, S. and Lee, A.B. (2006) Diffusion Maps and Coarse Graining: A Unified Framework for Dimensionality Reduction, Graph Partitioning, and Data Set Parameterization. Transaction on Pattern Analysis and Machine Intelligence, Vol. 28, No. 9, pp. 1393–1403.

Li, T., Ogihara, M. and Li, Q. (2003) A Comparative Study on Content-Based Music Genre Classification. ACM SIGIR, Toronto, Canada, pp. 282–289.

Mika, P. (2005) Ontologies are Us: A Unified Model of Social Networks and Semantics. Proceedings of the Fourth International Semantic Web Conference, Springer, pp. 522–536.

Nasrabadi, N.M. and King, R.A. (1988) Image Coding Using Vector Quantization: A Review. Transactions on Communications, Vol. 36, No. 8, pp. 957–971.

Pentland, A., Picard, R.W. and Sclaroff, S. (1996) Photobook: Content-Based Manipulation of Image Databases. Journal of Computer Vision, Vol. 18, No. 3, pp. 233–254.

Rowe, L.A. and Jain, R. (2005) ACM SIGMM Retreat Report on Future Directions in Multimedia Research. ACM Transactions on Multimedia Computing, Communications, and Applications, Vol. 1, No. 1, pp. 3–13.

Roweis, S. and Saul, L. (2000) Nonlinear Dimensionality Reduction by Locally Linear Embedding. Science, Vol. 290, No. 5500, pp. 2323–2326.

Russell, B.C., Torralba, A., Murphy, K.P. and Freeman, W.T. (2005) LabelMe: A Database and Web Based Tool for Image Annotation. MIT AI Lab Memo AIM-2005-025

Samet, H. (1989) The Design and Analysis of Spatial Data Structures. Addison-Wesley Longman Publishing Co., Inc., Boston, MA, August.

Santini, S., Gupta, A. and Jain, R. (2001) Emergent Semantics Through Interaction in Image Databases. Transactions on Knowledge and Data Engineering, Vol. 13, No. 3, pp. 337–351.

Silverman, B.W. (1988) Density Estimation for Statistics and Data Analysis. Journal of the American Statistical Association, Vol. 83, No. 401, pp. 269–270.

Smeulders, W.M.A., Worring M., Santini, S., Gupta A. and Jain, R. (2000) Content Based Image Retrieval at the End of the Early Years. Transactions on Pattern Analysis and Machine Intelligence, Vol. 22, No. 12, pp. 1349–1380.

Smith, L.I. (2002) A Tutorial on Principal Components Analysis, retrieved on Jan 21, 2007. http://csnet.otago.ac.nz/cosc453/student_tutorials/principal_components.pdf.

Squire, D.M., Müller, W., Müller, H. and Pun, T. (2000) Content-Based Query of Image Databases: Inspirations from Text Retrieval. Pattern Recognition Letters, Vol. 21, No. 13–14, pp 1193–1198.

Sreenath, D.V., Grosky, W.I. and Fotouhi, F. (2004) Using Coherent Semantic Subpaths to Derive Emergent Semantics. Knowledge-Based Intelligent Information and Engineering Systems, Eighth International Conference, LNCS, Vol. 3215, pp. 173–179.

Staab S. (Ed.) (2002) Emergent Semantics. IEEE Intelligent Systems, Vol. 17, No. 1, pp. 78–86.

StatSoft (2005) STATISTICA for Windows Version 7.1. www.statsoft.com

Subramaniam, A.D. and Rao, B.D. (2003) PDF Optimized Parametric Vector Quantization of Speech Line Spectral Frequencies. IEEE Transactions on Speech and Audio Processing, Vol. 11, No. 2, pp. 130–142.

Tao, Y. and Grosky, W.I. (2000) Image Indexing and Retrieval Using Object-Based Point Feature Maps. Journal of Visual Languages and Computing, Vol. 11, No. 3, pp. 323–343.

Tesic, J., 2004 Managing Large-Scale Multimedia Repositories. Ph.D. Thesis, Vision Research Lab, University of California, Santa Barbara.

Tibshirani, R., Hastie, T., Narasimhan, B. and Chu, G. (2002) Diagnosis of Multiple Cancer Types by Shrunken Centroids of Gene Expression. National Academy of Sciences of the USA, Vol. 99, No. 10, pp. 6567–6572.

Tziakos, I., Laskaris, N. and Fotopoulos, S. (2004) Multivariate Image Segmentation Using Laplacian Eigenmaps. EUSIPCO, Vienna, Austria.

Vembu, S., Kiesel, M., Sintek, M. and Baumann, S. (2006) Towards Bridging the Semantic Gap in Multimedia Annotation and Retrieval. First International Workshop on Semantic Web Annotations for Multimedia (SWAMM), Edinburgh, Scotland, 22 May.

Westermann U. and Jain, R. (2006) A Generic Event Model for Event-Centric Multimedia Data Management in eChronicle Applications. ICDE Workshop on eChronicles, Atlanta, Georgia, p. 106.

Westerveld, T. (2000) Image Retrieval: Content versus Context. Content-Based Multimedia Information Access, RIAO, Paris, France, pp. 276–284.

Witten, I.H., Moffat, A. and Bell, T.C. (1999) Managing Gigabytes, Second Edition, Morgan Kaufmann Publishing Company, San Francisco, California, USA.

Zhao, R. and Grosky, W.I. (2002a) Narrowing the Semantic Gap Improved Text-Based Web Document Retrieval Using Visual Features. Transactions on Multimedia, Vol. 4, No. 2, pp. 189–200.

Zhao, R. and Grosky, W.I. (2002b) Negotiating the Semantic Gap: From Feature Maps to Semantic Landscape. Pattern Recognition, Vol. 35, No. 3, pp. 593–600.

Chapter 10
Filling the Semantic Gap in Video Retrieval: An Exploration

Alexander Hauptmann, Rong Yan, Wei-Hao Lin, Michael Christel
and Howard Wactlar

10.1 Introduction: Bridging the Semantic Gap

Digital images and motion video have proliferated in the past few years, ranging from ever-growing personal photo and video collections to professional news and documentary archives. In searching through these archives, digital imagery indexing based on low-level image features like colour and texture, or manually entered text annotations, often fails to meet the user's information need, i.e. there is often a semantic gap produced by "the lack of coincidence between the information that one can extract from the visual data and the interpretation that the same data have for a user in a given situation" (Smeulders, Worring, Santini, Gupta and Jain 2000).

The image/video analysis community has long struggled to bridge this semantic gap between low-level feature analysis (colour histograms, texture, shape) and semantic content description of video. Early video retrieval systems (Lew 2002; Smith, Lin, Naphade, Natsev and Tseng 2002) usually modelled video clips with a set of (low-level) detectable features generated from different modalities. It is possible to accurately and automatically extract low-level video features, such as histograms in the HSV, RGB, and YUV colour space, Gabor texture or wavelets, and structure through edge direction histograms and edge maps. However, because the semantic meaning of the video content cannot be expressed this way, these systems had a very restricted success with this approach to video retrieval for semantic queries. Several studies have confirmed the difficulty of addressing information needs with such low-level features (Markkula and Sormunen 2000; Rodden, Basalaj, Sinclair and Wood 2001).

To overcome this "semantic gap", one approach is to utilise a set of intermediate textual descriptors that can be reliably applied to visual content concepts (e.g. outdoors, faces, animals). Many researchers have been developing automatic semantic concept classifiers such as those related to people (face, anchor, etc.), acoustic (speech, music, significant pause), objects (image blobs, buildings, graphics),

A. Hauptmann
School of Computer Science, Carnegie Mellon University, Pittsburgh PA, USA
e-mail: alex@cs.cmu.edu

Y. Kompatsiaris, P. Hobson (eds.), *Semantic Multimedia and Ontologies,*
© Springer Science+Business Media, LLC 2008

location (outdoors/indoors, cityscape, landscape, studio setting), genre (weather, financial, sports), and others (Chang, Manmatha and Chua. 2005). Automatic semantic concept detection has been investigated by numerous studies in recent years (Barnard, Duygulu, Forsyth, de Freitas, Blei and Jordan 2003; Naphade, Kristjansson, Frey and Huang 1998; Naphade and Smith 2004; Chang, Hsu, Kennedy, Xie, Yanagawa, Zavesky and Zhang 2005; Yang, Chen and Hauptmann 2004; Lin and Hauptmann 2002; Jeon, Lavrenko and Manmatha 2003; Snoek, Worring and Smeulders 2005; Yuan, Xiao, Wang, Ding, Zuo, Tong, Liu, Xu, Zheng, Li, Si, Li, Lin and Zhang 2005; Wu, Chang, Chang and Smith 2004), showing that these classifiers could, with enough training data, reach the level of maturity needed to be helpful filters for video retrieval (Hauptmann, Baron, Chen, Christel, Duygulu, Huang, Jin, Lin, Ng, Moraveji, Papernick, Snoek, Tzanetakis, Yang, Yan and Wactlar 2003; Natsev, Naphade and Tešić 2005).

In this chapter, we examine the use of high-level semantic concepts (Naphade and Smith 2004) to assist in video retrieval and its promise to bridge the semantic gap by providing more accessible visual content descriptors. The hypothesis is that a few thousand semantic concepts (Naphade, Smith, Tesic, Chang, Hsu, Kennedy, Hauptmann and Curtis 2006) that have reasonably reliable detection accuracy can be combined to yield high-accuracy video retrieval. If we can define a rich enough set of such intermediate semantic descriptors in the form of a large lexicon and taxonomic classification scheme, then robust and general-purpose content annotation and retrieval will be enabled through these semantic concept descriptors. Although a huge number of successful semantic concept detection approaches have been developed and evaluated (Smeaton and Over 2003; Snoek, Worring, Geusebroek, Seinstra and Smeulders 2006), many questions remain unanswered: What kinds of concepts are most useful? How many are needed? How accurate do they need to be? How can we use them to assist video retrieval? To gain a deeper understanding of these issues, we have conducted a set of retrieval experiments on a large-scale video collection, which constitute first steps towards answers to these questions and provide guidelines for future work.

The chapter is organised as follows. Section 10.2 begins with a case study showing that increasing the number of semantic concepts improves video retrieval. We also speculate what minimal number of concepts will be sufficient to construct a highly accurate video retrieval system. Then, in Section 10.3, we analyse the types of concepts we should add to the current lexicon. Section 10.4 explores concept combination strategies, and how users can employ these concepts for both interactive and machine-assisted video retrieval. We end with a discussion regarding the role of semantic concepts for the future of video retrieval based on the presented analyses of concept quality, quantity, combination, and use.

10.2 Are Semantic Concepts Useful to Video Retrieval?

To illustrate the usefulness of constructing a large number of high-level semantic concepts to enhance video retrieval quality, we provide a case study based on a large-scale TRECVID video collection (Smeaton and Over 2003) and two recently developed video concept lexica, namely the Large-Scale Concept Ontology for Multimedia (LSCOM) (Naphade et al. 2006) and the MediaMill challenge concept data (Snoek, Worring, van Gemert, Geusebroek and Smeulders 2006), both of which also include an "annotation corpus" for the TRECVID 2005 video collection, where for each concept in the lexicon and every shot in the collection, it was manually determined whether the concept was absent or present in the shot.

10.2.1 Description of Video Archive

In this section, we describe the video collection, the set of high-level semantic concepts, and the use cases for query topics adopted in our case study.

10.2.1.1 TRECVID 2005 Development Set

In 2001, the National Institute of Standards and Technology (NIST) started the TREC Video Track (now referred to as TRECVID; Over, Ianeva, Kraaij and Smeaton 2005) to promote progress in content-based video retrieval via an open, metrics-based evaluation, where the video corpora have ranged from documentaries, advertising films, technical/educational material to multilingual broadcast news. As the largest video collections with manual annotations available to the research community, the TRECVID collections have become the standard large-scale testbeds for the task of multimedia retrieval.

Success in the search task is measured through *precision* and *recall* as the central criteria to evaluate the performance of retrieval algorithms. Precision is the fraction of the retrieved documents that is relevant. Recall is the fraction of relevant documents that is retrieved. NIST also defines another measure of retrieval effectiveness called non-interpolated average precision over a set of retrieved documents (shots in our case). Let R be the number of true relevant documents in a set of size S; L the ranked list of documents returned. At any given index j let R_j be the number of relevant documents in the top j documents. Let $I_j = 1$ if the jth document is relevant and 0 otherwise. Assuming $R < S$, the non-interpolated average precision (AP) is then defined as

$$\frac{1}{R} \sum_{j=1}^{S} \frac{R_j}{j} I_j.$$

Mean average precision (MAP) is the mean of average precision over all queries.

In our case study, we used only the development data set from the TRECVID 2005 corpus (Over et al. 2005). This consists of broadcast news videos captured in the months of October and November 2004. The video collection includes multilingual news video captured from MSNBC (English), NBC Nightly News (English), CNN (English), LBC (Arabic), CCTV (Chinese), and NTDTV (Chinese). The development set comprises about 70 hours of video. The corpus was segmented into 61,901 shots, which were used as the units of retrieval.

10.2.1.2 Semantic Concepts

We studied three sets of high-level semantic concepts, where each set is larger than the previous ones and completely includes the smaller sets.

LSCOM-Lite The first set is generally referred to as LSCOM-Lite (Naphade et al. 2006). It is composed of 39 concepts and was released by NIST in conjunction with the TRECVID 2005 data set. The TRECVID 2005 participants jointly annotated ground truth for these concepts on the TRECVID 2005 development set.

MediaMill The second set of concepts was created by the MediaMill group in the Netherlands (Snoek et al. 2006). They annotated 101 concepts on the same data set, with a challenge to other researchers to use these concepts, annotations, and low-level features to develop better concept detection systems. Since only 75 of these concepts were present in our largest LSCOM concept lexicon, we limited our evaluation to those 75 concepts to achieve direct comparability.

LSCOM The largest set of concepts contained 320 concepts, developed as part of the LSCOM effort (Naphade et al. 2006). While the full LSCOM set contains over 2600 concepts, many of them are unannotated or contain no positive instances in the TRECVID 2005 collection. For this study, we used 320 LSCOM concepts that were annotated with at least several positive instances. LSCOM is a collaborative effort of multimedia researchers, library scientists, and end users to develop a large, standardised taxonomy for describing broadcast news video. These concepts have been selected to be relevant for describing broadcast video, feasible for automatic detection with some level of accuracy and useful for video retrieval. LSCOM additionally connects all its concepts into a full ontology. However, we only used the LSCOM concepts as a flat lexicon in our experiments. All shots relevant to all concepts had been annotated for the TRECVID 2005 development set.

10.2.1.3 Use Cases

Our video retrieval experiments were conducted on 83 "use case" queries to uncover the relationship between the number of concepts, detection accuracy, and retrieval performance. These 83 queries were used because truth annotations for relevant shots were available for each query on the same TRECVID 2005 video development collection, which had also been annotated with truth for the concept lists.

To measure the usefulness of large numbers of concepts for video retrieval, "use cases" had been defined by the LSCOM activity (Naphade et al. 2006). Here, in consultation with user communities of broadcast news professionals and intelligence analysts, a number of scenarios were identified, which were well covered in the TRECVID 2005 data set. The scenarios covered unexpected breaking news events such as natural disasters, as well as long-standing news stories, such as "US

Elections". Each of these events had aspects with associated video clips that the users would have liked to access and review in detail.

The scenarios were designed to be (a) independent of the concept lexicon used in the annotation corpus and (b) a realistic setting for an information seeker in the sampled user communities. For example, the use cases included the following broad scenarios:

- *Afghanistan:* battles, disarmament, demobilisation, and reintegration
- *Iraq:* Fallujah, car bombs, improvised explosive devices, and assassinations
- *Eritrea:* War by proxy
- *Global:* Oil crisis.

For each scenario, a set of topics was derived, which would be answerable by video documents in the collection. The topics were intended to emphasise the visual aspect of the video, not the accompanying audio narrative. Thus for the "Afghanistan" use case scenario, some example topics were

- battles/violence in the mountains
- armoured vehicles driving through barren landscapes
- mountainous scenes with openings of caves visible
- people wearing turbans and carrying missile launchers.

These topics, in turn, were mapped into very specific, visual queries, e.g. looking for shots of

- a person with head-scarf greeting people
- military formations engaged in tactical warfare, or part of a parade
- military hospital with vehicles in foreground
- masked men with guns and/or any other weapons.

To carry out some quality assessments of concept utility, LSCOM derived relevance judgments for 83 use-case queries. LSCOM adopted a labelling strategy similar to the "pooling" used in TRECVID (Over et al. 2005). In this strategy, the top results from various systems are labelled, while the bottom results are simply assumed to be negative. LSCOM approximated this approach by feeding the query topics to interactive retrieval systems and having multiple annotators perform "interactive searches" over the collection by essentially issuing text and image queries and finding as many relevant shots as possible during a 30-minute period. This provided an approximate, but high-quality set of labels, useful for evaluating the quality of various concept-based search methods for the queries.

10.2.2 Retrieval Experiments

To evaluate the retrieval utility of the LSCOM-Lite, the MediaMill, and the full LSCOM concept sets, we designed experiments based on the automatic search task in TRECVID, where an automatic video retrieval system searches for relevant documents without any human feedback or intervention. As a baseline, we generated the standard text retrieval output by searching the speech transcript for automatically extracted text keywords from each search query. As one of the most important retrieval components for video retrieval, text retrieval finds a number of top-ranked documents based on the similarity between query keywords and documents' textual features. Textual features can be extracted from a number of information sources such as speech transcript, closed captions, and video optical character recognition (VOCR). Unless textual features are not available in the video data (such as in surveillance video), text search is usually the most effective single modality to handle semantic queries in video retrieval systems (Hauptmann and Christel 2004). Given the annotations of high-level concepts and relevance judgments of search queries at our disposal, we can linearly combine the semantic concept predictions with the text retrieval outputs to determine how much these search queries would be affected. Specifically, we compared the baseline text retrieval results to the results after incorporating (a) the LSCOM-Lite set of 39 concepts, (b) 75 concepts from the 101 concept MediaMill challenge which overlapped with the LSCOM concepts, and (c) 320 of the LSCOM concepts that had at least a few positive instances in the annotations.

Let us begin with the most ideal case, where we assume that the semantic concept detection is perfect (equivalent to directly using the concept truth annotation) and that the combination method of concepts is optimal. Although impractical, these results serve as an upper bound to indicate how useful the concepts can be. In previous work (Yan and Hauptmann 2003), we developed a theoretical framework for studying the performance limits over both monotonic and linear combination functions. In brief, the approach computes the optimal linear combination performance with the semantic concepts f_i fixed. Let D represent the documents, Q is the query, i is the index of the corresponding ranking features, and N is the total number of ranking features. We denote the linear combination $F(D, Q) = \sum_{i=1}^{N} \lambda_i f_i(D, Q)$ and $AP(F(D, Q))$ as the average precision of order list σ, where σ is determined by retrieval score $F(D, Q)$ with respect to D. Therefore, our task can be rewritten as a bounded constrained global optimisation problem,

$$\text{LLB} = \max_{\lambda_i} \text{AP}\left(\sum_{i=1}^{k} \lambda_i f_i(D, Q)\right),$$

where LLB is the locally fixed linear bound. Note that this bound allows different concept combination weights for different queries.

To get a more realistic estimate (as opposed to the perfect "oracle" detection) of the concept utility with state of the art concept detection approaches, we repeated the experiment after introducing noise into the perfect concept prediction (but still with an oracle combination). The results from TRECVID 2006 semantic concept classification evaluation (Smeaton and Over 2003; Smeaton, Over and Kraaij 2006) show that the current best semantic concept classification systems can average slightly less than 0.2 MAP over the LSCOM-Lite concepts. Because mean average precision is a rank-based measure and difficult to simulate, we approximated this MAP with a breakeven precision-recall point at 0.2. Breakeven precision-recall is usually a good approximation for mean average precision. They are equivalent to each other if the precision-recall curve is mirror symmetric to the line of precision = recall. This was easily achieved by randomly switching the labels of positively annotated shots to be (incorrectly) labelled as negative and conversely switching some negatively labelled shots to incorrect positive examples, until we achieve the desired breakeven point where precision is equal to recall. This made the concept labels appear roughly equivalent to a detector with MAP of 20%. Clearly this is a relatively simple approximation of true performance. More realistic would be to allow the simulated accuracy of individual concept detectors to vary around the global mean of 0.2, as opposed to giving all the same accuracy.

Figure 10.1 shows the retrieval results of combining semantic concepts for the three sets under different noise levels on the queries for text-only retrieval and retrieval with the LSCOM-Lite, the MediaMill, and the larger LSCOM concept sets. Oracle detection and oracle combination results are labelled OD + OC. The results using simulated "noisily detected" concepts (labelled OC + ND) are also shown at 50%, 20%, and 10% breakeven precision-recall (shown as "50% PR", "20% PR", and "10% PR", respectively). Realistic combination estimates (RC) assume the combination algorithm is only half as effective as perfect combination, and these bars are shown with 10% breakeven precision-recall as "RC + ND, 10% PR". We can observe a substantial improvement from the additional semantic concepts. For example, video retrieval performance can reach 37% MAP after the full

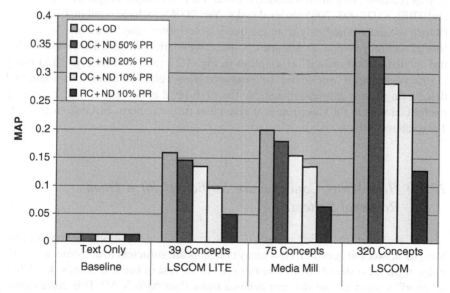

Fig. 10.1 Mean Average Precision (MAP) for different levels of concept detection accuracy and combination effectiveness. ©IEEE 2007 (Hauptmann et al. 2007)

LSCOM set of concepts are incorporated, which is impressive given that the base-line text-only retrieval MAP is only 1%. The surprisingly low baseline of text-only retrieval, achieved using configuration parameters typical for video retrieval from text sources, can be attributed to the strong visual specificity of the queries, which cannot be answered by merely searching the audio transcript. The quality of the Chinese and Arabic speech recognition and machine translation for the non-English portions of the corpus also contributed to the low text-only retrieval score. These experiments confirm the huge potential of high-level concepts for effective video retrieval. As we introduce detection noise into the semantic concepts, the retrieval performance keeps decreasing when more and more positive shots are switched to negative ones. This shows that detection accuracy of semantic concepts has a noticeable effect on the quality of video retrieval accuracy. However, even if the breakeven precision-recall of these sets of concepts is only 10%, the retrieval MAP can still be boosted to an absolute 26% MAP with the full set of LSCOM concepts. This suggests that although the prediction provided by the state of the art automatic concept detection algorithms is far from perfect, they can still substantially improve the standard text-only retrieval output.

It is worth mentioning that the above discussions assume the true relevant docu-ments for each query are available and therefore we can use learning approaches to estimate the optimal combination model. In practice, we would not be able to col-lect ground truth for every possible query that users may submit. Hence, it is more reasonable for us to derive concept combination models based on some obtainable query properties, such as query description, query context, user profile, or inter-active relevance feedback (see Section 10.4 for further discussions on the selec-tion of realistic combination models). Based on recent results reported on the offi-cial TRECVID 2003–2005 retrieval tasks (Yan 2006), realistic combination models (which are determined only from the query description) may result in a 30%–50% loss of accuracy compared with the optimal combination models. Thus we modeled the "realistic combination" assumption in Fig. 10.1 (and later in Fig. 10.2) using a 50% degradation over oracle combination. However, even taking this additional discounting factor into consideration, the high-level concepts can still be a very useful component for video retrieval given that they can boost MAP from absolute 1% to above 10%.

10.2.3 How Many Concepts are Sufficient for a Good Retrieval System?

One of the most interesting aspects of this work is that these results now provide hints to answer the question: How many concepts are sufficient to construct a "good" video retrieval system? To be more rigorous in the rest of the discussions, we define a "good" system as one that can achieve more than 65% MAP. This corresponds to the current MAP accuracy that has been reported for the best web (text) search engines (Beitzel, Jensen, Frieder, Chowdhury and Pass 2005). In order to investigate this problem more thoroughly, we need to extrapolate our MAP numbers on three extant concept sets to some "imaginary" concept sets with larger sizes under the assumption that the additional concepts have a similar quality to the existing concepts. The first step for extrapolation is to determine a reasonable extrapolation function for the given points in order to determine the relationship between MAP and the size of the concept set. Theoretically, there are an infinite number of functions that can fit the given three numbers. However, we can impose a reasonable assumption on the function space to determine a unique extrapolation function, i.e. the maximum MAP increment brought by a new concept is proportional to the difference between the current MAP and the upper limit 1. In other words, the higher the current MAP is, the less benefit a new concept can offer. Guided by this assumption, we derive the following partial differential equation,

$$\frac{dm}{dx} \propto (1 - m),$$

where m is the value of MAP, x is the number of concepts, and the boundary condition is $m(\infty) = 1$. Solving this equation yields

$$m(x) = 1 - \exp(ax + b),$$

where a, b are two parameters which can be determined with curve fitting approaches.

Figure 10.2 plots the true MAPs on three concepts sets as well as the fitted curves using the proposed exponential function over both perfect concepts and noisy

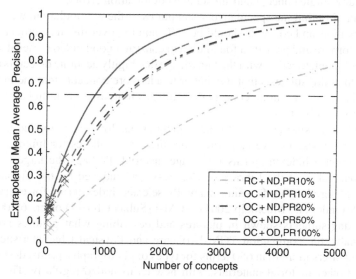

Fig. 10.2 Extrapolated mean average precision vs. the number of high-level concepts. ©IEEE 2007 (Hauptmann et al. 2007)

concepts under oracle combination, as well as the noisy detection at 10% breakeven precision-recall and realistic combination, which assumes a 50% degradation in the combination step. The figure shows the true MAPs on the three original concept sets indicated by "x". The corresponding fitted curves are plotted with the *solid line* representing the oracle detectors (OD) with oracle combination (OC), and the *dashed line* signifying extrapolation using the noisy detectors (ND) with 50%, 20%, and 10% breakeven precision-recall (PR). Realistic combination estimates (RC) assume the combination algorithm is only half as effective as perfect combination and are shown with 10% breakeven precision-recall as "RC+ND,PR10%". The *horizontal dashed line* represents a comparison MAP of 0.65, which is what has been achieved by some of the best web search engines on text document collections. The fitted curves in Fig. 10.2 provide a fairly accurate estimation on the target points. The curves allow us to study the behaviour of video retrieval systems in depth as if there were many more concepts available than the current status quo.

To reach the level of a "good" retrieval system, we will only need around 800 concepts if we can obtain perfect detection accuracy for each concept. There is a trade-off between the minimal number of concepts and the concept detection accuracy. The lower the detection accuracy, the more concepts we are likely to need to accurately retrieve the video content. If overall accuracy of concept detection is only 10%, we will need more concepts to achieve the same level, i.e. around 1,200–1,300 concepts.

The biggest surprise comes in the realistic combination scenario, which tries to approximate the combination behaviour of real systems when compared to oracle combination (Yan 2006). Here, Fig. 10.2 shows that using 3,000 or more concepts will be sufficient for accurate retrieval, despite a fairly low detection accuracy of 10% for any single concept and substantial combination errors.

Keeping in mind the speculative assumptions of the extrapolation, we conclude that a few thousand concepts should be sufficient to cover the most crucial content in video corpora and provide a foundation to construct good video retrieval systems. This experiment, together with the knowledge that highly accurate detectors are very difficult to build, suggests that it is better to add more concepts into the mix rather than building very accurate concept detectors, as long as we can find a reasonable method to combine them.

The idea of using concepts to index pictures has long been applied by librarians and archivists, and we can draw from their vocabularies for finding concepts and meaningful indexing terms for image material. Perhaps the largest index of image material is at the Library of Congress, and indexed by the Thesaurus for Graphic Materials (TGM), using manually selected index terms for every library item (Alexander and Meehleib 2001). TGM-I (Subject Terms) offers 69,000 terms for indexing subjects shown in pictures and describing what pictures are about. Additionally, the companion TGM-II (Genre and Physical Characteristic Terms) document offers more than 650 terms for types of photographs, prints, design drawings, and other pictorial materials, with new terms added regularly. The Art and Architecture Thesaurus by the Getty Research Institute (Petersen 1994) is another standard source for image and video description with a "structured vocabulary of more than 133,000 terms, descriptions, bibliographic citations, and other information relating to fine art, architecture, decorative arts, archival materials, and material culture." Additionally, there are numerous smaller controlled vocabularies for stock photography collections, museums, and news organisations. None of these are designed for video collections, nor do they take into account whether the descriptors are automatically detectable.

One might simply propose to automatically index as many concepts as possible, for example, taking all index terms from the Thesaurus for Graphic Materials. However, in practice, obtaining annotations and building automatic detectors is by no means trivial, and developing concept detectors of very low retrieval utility would waste effort, or even worse, degrade the performance of large-scale concept-based retrieval systems. Note also that our extrapolations are based on the assumption that additional "imaginary" semantic concepts should have a similar quality (such as detection accuracy, proportion of the positive data and so on) to the existing 320 LSCOM concepts.

To address this, Section 10.3 investigates which concepts should be chosen, while Section 10.4 looks at concept combination issues, including what happens if concept combination is left under a user's interactive control.

10.3 What Kinds of Concepts Should be Chosen?

The above experiments suggest that several thousand high-level concepts should be able to support highly accurate video retrieval systems, however, these concepts should not be randomly selected. The effort to annotate and construct a good concept classifier is significant. The most well-known concept is a "face". Face detectors have been studied in computer vision for almost three decades, and only recently have reliable commercial products became available (Zhao, Chellappa, Phillips and Rosenfeld 2003). Another reason concepts should not be selected randomly is that in order for our assumptions to hold, the chosen concepts must be similar in retrieval utility to the existing ones. We thus argue that our efforts should only be put towards adding those concepts that are likely to be beneficial to as many queries as possible. The effort of developing a new concept, providing large amounts of training data and implementing automatic detection algorithms can then be amortised over many queries. The research question is how to define these "helpful" concepts.

To find out which concepts should be chosen for indexing video collections, we analysed the TRECVID'05 video archive annotated with the 320 LSCOM concepts, and calculated how each concept contributes to retrieving shots relevant to the search queries. We classified the LSCOM concepts into seven categories, proposed by the Large-Scale Concept Ontology for Multimedia (LSCOM) workshop (Hauptmann 2004). The total number and examples of each category are shown in Fig. 10.3 and Table 10.1, respectively. The largest category is Scene (39% of the 320 concepts), closely followed by Objects (32%).

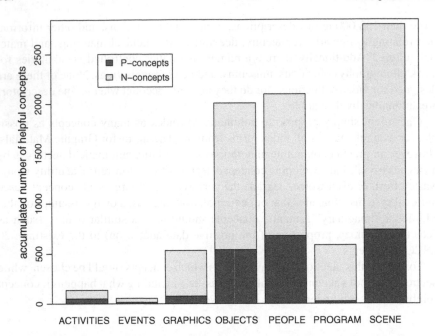

Fig. 10.3 The number of LSCOM concepts in each category as listed in Table 10.1. Scene, Objects, People are the three largest categories. ©IEEE 2007 (Hauptmann et al. 2007)

Table 10.1 LSCOM concepts are manually classified into seven categories. Each row list examples in each category. ©IEEE 2007 (Hauptmann et al. 2007)

Category	Examples
Program	Entertainment, sports, commercials
Scene	Snow, urban, road
People	Reporter, single person female, Tony Blair
Objects	Animal, boat, computers
Activities	People marching, vending, walking and running
Events	Explosion and fire
Graphics	Charts, logo, map

10.3.1 Determining Concept Utility

We employ an information-theoretic measure, mutual information (MI) (Cover and Thomas 1991), to determine if a concept is "helpful" in retrieving the shots relevant to a query. MI has been effective in tasks like feature selection for text categorisation (Yang and Pedersen 1997). Let us denote the relevance of a shot as a random variable R, and the presence or absence of a concept in a shot as C, where R and C are binary random variables. The mutual information between R and C, $I(R; C)$ is defined as follows,

$$I(R;C) = \sum_{r,c} P(r,c) \log \frac{P(r,c)}{P(r)P(c)},$$

where $r \in \{\texttt{relevance, irrelevance}\}$, $c \in \{\texttt{absence, present}\}$. MI can be interpreted as the degree to which the randomness of R is reduced with knowledge of C. If one becomes more certain about the relevance of a shot after knowing the presence or absence of a concept (i.e. MI is greater than zero), the concept is defined as a *helpful* concept for the topic. In practice, it is difficult to obtain zero mutual information when the data set is not extremely large. We thus define a concept C as helpful only when the entropy of R using Maximum Likelihood Estimates is reduced more than 1%, which is an empirically determined, minimal threshold that can filter out most spurious effects.

We further divide the helpful concepts into two types: *positively* helpful concepts (P-concept) and *negatively* helpful concepts (N-concept). The presence of P-concepts in a shot increases the degree of relevance. Conversely, the presence of N-concepts decreases the degree of relevance. N-concepts can be used as filters to the narrow retrieval search space. P-concepts and N-concepts are determined by *pointwise mutual information*, defined as follows:

$$I_P(r;c) = \log \frac{P(r,c)}{P(r)P(c)}.$$

If $I_P(\texttt{relevance;presence})$ of a concept is greater than $I_P(\texttt{relevance; absence})$, it is a P-concept for a given topic, and an N-concept otherwise. For example, for the topic "find shots of an airplane taking off", "sky" is a P-concept and "animal" is an N-concept.

10.3.2 Concept Frequency and Retrieval Utility

Given an unannotated, large video archive, how many concepts are there? As a practical question, how much video do annotators have to watch before a reasonable set of concepts are identified? To answer these questions, we first plot concept frequency (i.e. the number of shots where a concept appears) against the rank of a concept by concept frequency.

The linear relationship between concept frequency and rank in the log–log scale approximately follows Zipf's Law (Zipf 1972), as first observed by Kender and Naphade (2005). The good news is that top-ranked concepts are extremely frequent and a set of common concepts may be quickly collected without browsing through much of an archive. To give a quantitative answer, we simulate the following scenario: An annotator browses a video archive from the first shot of the first video, and writes down new concepts right after they appear. The results are plotted in Fig. 10.4, where the x-axis is the number of shots that an annotator has watched, and the y-axis is the accumulated concept frequency, i.e. the number of unique concepts identified so far times the frequency of each concept.

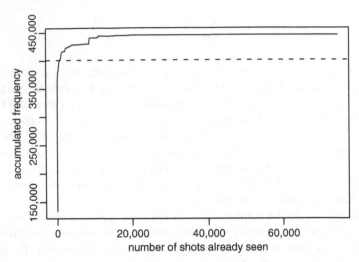

Fig. 10.4 A simulation to show that video concepts in an archive can be quickly identified. ©IEEE 2007 (Hauptmann et al. 2007)

Imagine an annotator browsing the TRECVID archive from the first shot (in Fig. 10.4 the x-axis increases from 0 to all shots in the TRECVID) and identifying video concepts that have not been seen before. For each new video concept, we accumulate its concept frequency and plot the accumulated frequency on the y-axis. The *dashed line* in Fig. 10.4 marks 90% of total concept occurrences. By merely watching 0.9% of the archive, the annotator can accumulate a set of concepts that will account for 90% of the total concept occurrences.

The result is very encouraging: By watching merely 0.9% (3053 seconds) of the archive, an annotator can gather a set of concepts that account for 90% of all concept occurrences in the TRECVID 2005 video development collection. Thus, new concepts for the global concept lexicon can be identified very efficiently, in order to accumulate the target 3,000–4,000 concept lexicon.

The bad news, however, is that most concepts occur very infrequently. Ninety per cent of the concepts occur fewer than 100 times in the 74,523 shots, which makes it very difficult to develop automatic detectors because statistical learning algorithms require large numbers of training examples (Naphade and Smith 2004). Are these rare concepts really important for answering video retrieval queries? We investigate how concept frequency is related to video retrieval utility, and plot the number of search queries that are improved by a concept (both positively or negatively) against concept frequency in Fig. 10.5. To summarise the results succinctly, we fit cubic splines on the three sets of data points. Cubic splines do not assume linear structure. Note that the choice of regression methods is less important here than illustrating the relationship between the number of improved topic searches and the concept frequency.

In Fig. 10.5, the presence of P-concepts increases the degree of relevance of a shot to a query, while the presence of N-concepts decreases the degree of relevance.

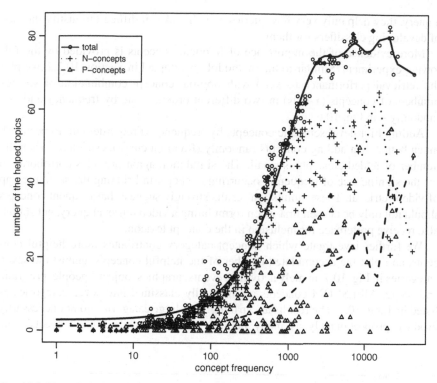

Fig. 10.5 The relationship between the frequency of a concept and the number of queries it improves. Note that the x-axis is in log scale. ©IEEE 2007 (Hauptmann et al. 2007)

As can be seen from these plots, the number of queries that a concept improves is strongly related to its frequency. The results clearly show that rare concepts are unlikely to benefit more than one query (as shown by the "total" curve in Fig. 10.5). For example, a rare concept, "castles", occurs only 25 times and helps only one query, "find shots of tourist sites". The number of topics where concepts can improve the search results (the curve labelled total in 10.5) stays low for concepts with frequency less than 100. Only after concept frequency exceeds 100 can concepts help retrieval for multiple queries. As an example of a frequent concept, "person", occurs 21,060 times and benefits 76–82 queries.

We further break down the total number of improved queries by the type of help they receive. As concept frequency increases, N-concepts are more likely to benefit more queries (the N-concept curve in Fig. 10.5), which is not completely surprising as frequent concepts remove large numbers of irrelevant shots more effectively than rare concepts. P-concepts demonstrate a similar trend but to a lesser degree (the P-concept curve). In summary, frequent concepts are more important because they benefit retrieval of more search topics, either positively or negatively, than rare concepts. Even though rare concepts are very discriminative if they positively affect a query, they help only very few queries, which makes it difficult to justify the cost of developing classifiers for them.

More evidence of the importance of frequent concepts is provided by the following experiment. Similar to the methodology adopted in Section 10.2.2, we plot the retrieval performance (y-axis) with optimal concept combination of various numbers of concepts (x-axis) in two different orders – one by frequency and one randomly – in Fig. 10.6.

Adding high-level semantic concepts by frequency (FreqOrder curve) performs much better than adding concepts randomly (Random curve), especially when the number of added concepts is small. The simulation again provides corroboration for the significance of frequently occurring concepts in bridging the semantic gap of video retrieval. These simulation results strongly suggest that frequent concepts should not only be chosen first when formulating a video retrieval query, but should also receive preference for inclusion in the concept lexicon.

We further investigate which concept category contributes more helpful concepts, and plot the accumulated number of the helpful concepts against the seven categories in Fig. 10.7, namely activities, events, graphics, objects, people, program, and scene. All LSCOM concepts are manually classified into seven categories as listed in Table 10.1. The results are striking: The large categories do not necessarily produce proportionately as many helpful concepts. While both "Objects" and

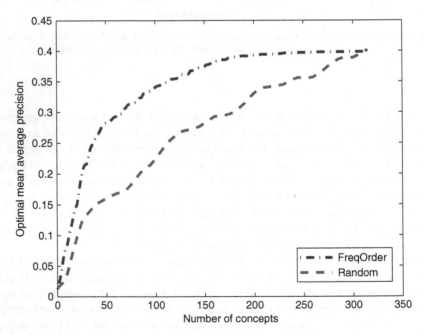

Fig. 10.6 Adding high-level concepts by frequency (FreqOrder curve) performs better than adding concepts randomly (Random curve), especially when the number of added concepts is small. ©IEEE 2007 (Hauptmann et al. 2007)

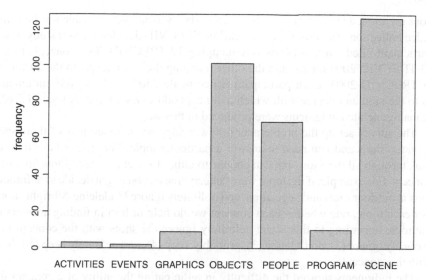

Fig. 10.7 The accumulated number of concepts that benefit video retrieval in each category is disproportional to the number of concepts in a category (cf. Fig. 10.3). ©IEEE 2007 (Hauptmann et al. 2007)

"Scene" are large categories, "Scene" contributes disproportionally the largest number of helpful concepts.

10.4 How can we Use the Concepts to Help Video Search?

Our theoretical analysis has uncovered the potential of using high-level concepts to augment video retrieval results. However, we do not know if this means users can actually derive this benefit in their searches. Since most users would start with a text query expressing their information need, the open question is whether this information need can be related to the correct, helpful concepts in a realistic retrieval setting. In this section, we discuss some possible approaches to incorporate high-level concepts into the retrieval output and analyse their applicability, including interactive manual selection methods and automatic selection methods.

10.4.1 User Study: Evaluating Manual Selection of Concepts

How easy is it for people to select helpful concepts for queries? The goal of our user study was to determine whether people associate semantic concepts to information needs accurately, and if they are consistent. Twelve university employees and students participated in the study, with eight participants being very familiar with TRECVID concepts, topics, and video information retrieval and the remaining four relative novices. Since this study was conducted at the same time as the annotations mentioned in the earlier sections, truth data was not yet available for the same video collection. Therefore, we used earlier TRECVID data for the user study. Each participant filled out two tables, one mapping 10 TRECVID 2004 concepts to the 23 TRECVID 2004 topics, and the other mapping the 17 concepts to the 24 topics in TRECVID 2003. Each participant hence made $230 + 408 = 638$ judgments as to the sign and degree with which a concept addresses a topic. A total of 7,656 human-generated judgments were produced in this way.

The survey set up the problem as follows: Suppose there are tens of thousands of video shots and you need to answer a particular topic. You do not have time to look through all the shots, but can choose to either look at or ignore shots having a concept. For example, if the topic were "cherry trees", you might decide to definitely look at outdoor shots and vegetation, and definitely ignore Madeleine Albright shots. For each topic, rate whether each concept would help or hurt in finding answers to the topic according to this scale: definitely ignore the shots with the concept (1), probably ignore (2), don't know (3), probably keep (4), and definitely keep (5) shots with this concept.

The judgments showed the difficulty in anticipating the utility of a concept for a given topic, even with such a small-sized corpus of concepts (17 and 10 for TRECVID 2003 and 2004). The overall correlation of ratings between pairs of subjects was weak for both TRECVID 2003 and TRECVID 2004. From the 66 pairings of raters, on TRECVID 2003 the Pearson product moment correlation coefficient values ranged from 0.37 to 0.77, mean 0.58, STD 0.07. For TRECVID 2004, the coefficient values ranged from 0.27 to 0.70, mean 0.56, STD 0.09. The Pearson correlation coefficient shows that with both concept-topic sets there was very weak positive correlation, indicating that users do not agree on which concepts are likely to help a given query.

The collective evidence shows much disagreement between the raters across the concept-topic associations: Over 20% of the TRECVID 2003 associations and 17% of the TRECVID 2004 associations have at least one rater scoring the association as definitely ignore, while another rated it as definitely keep. By contrast, only 12% of TRECVID 2003 associations and 13% of TRECVID 2004 associations had strong uniformity of all 12 raters within one ratings point of each other on the 5-point scale. We were interested in looking at the concept-topic associations where raters did have greater agreement, i.e. those associations with ratings having a relatively low standard deviation. Figures 10.8 and 10.9 present the top quartile of associations having the best ratings' agreement (which correlated to a standard deviation of < 0.7 for both sets). Empty cells in the tables indicate concept topic associations having higher levels of disagreement amongst the 12 subjects.

One other piece of information is shown in Fig. 10.8 and 10.9: The cells corresponding to the 54 instances of topics improved by a concept are shaded grey. Of 33 such TRECVID 2003 topic-concept associations, 14 were found with high agreement by raters, 2 others were found by raters with high agreement but rated as don't know rather than keep, and 17 were rated with a variety of opinions. Of the 21 TRECVID 2004 topic-concept associations, 6 were found with high agreement by raters but 15 were rated with a variety of opinions. When participants expressed a

Concept Key:	14 building	18 female speech	22 non-studio setting	
11 outdoors	15 road	19 car truck bus	23 sporting event	26 violence
12 face in news	16 vegetation	20 aircraft	24 weather news	27 Albright
13 3+ people	17 animal	21 speech in news	25 zoom in	

	11	12	13	14	15	16	17	18	19	20	21	22	23	24	25	26	27
100 aerial views	4.9			4.8	4.8			2.9				4.6			3.0		1.2
101 basketball		2.8						1.4					5.0	1.3			1.1
102 pitcher throw	4.7						1.3						5.0				1.1
103 Yasser Arafat		4.9	3.9	3.2										1.1	3.2		
104 airplane	4.9									4.9					2.9		
105 helicopter	5.0				3.6					4.8		4.7					
106 Tomb...Soldier	5.0		3.6									4.8		1.4			
107 rocket	4.8				3.1							4.6		1.3	3.2		
108 Mercedes logo					4.5						2.6			1.4			1.4
109 tanks	4.8					3.5						4.8					
110 diver								3.3				4.7			3.2		1.0
111 locomotive	4.9							2.9					1.3				1.3
112 flames	4.7							3.2	3.1			4.7					
113 snow peaks	5.0						2.4	3.1				4.8			3.1		1.3
114 bin Laden		4.9						3.3				4.7		1.3	3.3		
115 roads/cars	5.0				4.9			3.3				4.8					1.2
116 Sphinx	4.9							3.0				4.8	1.2	1.4	2.9		1.4
117 city crowd	4.9		5.0		4.7			3.3				4.8			2.9		
118 Mark Souder		5.0						3.3									
119 M. Freeman				3.0				3.1							3.3		
121 coffee cup																	
122 cats							4.9	3.3							3.6		
123 Pope		4.9					1.4	2.8						1.4			
124 White House	4.9		3.5	4.9				3.3			3.5	4.7	1.2		3.2		

Fig. 10.8 Average association on 5-point scale (1 = ignore, 5 = keep) from 12 raters assessing TRECVID 2003 concept relevance to TRECVID 2003 topics; blank cells indicate higher levels of rater disagreement, grey cells denote objective retrieval improvement according to truth data for topics and concepts. ©IEEE 2007 (Hauptmann et al. 2007)

rating, the rating agreed with the pooled truth data. There was clear consistent opinion on over half the shaded cells. Also, raters expressed consensus intuitions that were not supported by the pooled truth. Of the 43 topic-concept pairs in TRECVID 2003 and 8 in TRECVID 2004 marked with high agreement as positively associated in Fig. 10.8 and 10.9, 29 of the 43 and 2 of the 8 were not substantiated by empirical truth.

Additional interactive search experiments in Christel and Hauptmann (2005) further present strong evidence that semantic concept sets, if capable of being produced to reasonable levels of accuracy, could indeed benefit the user in addressing "generic" topics beyond what they could find using existing video retrieval systems, but that "specific" topics are already addressed adequately through other means (such as text search against the narrative text in news). However, we also must conclude that users are unable to reliably find the right concepts to exploit from very small concept sets. As the concept corpus grows, users will need automated recommendation or selection systems to combine concepts effectively in order to achieve the benefit levels projected in Section 10.2.

TRECVID 2004	28 boat	29 Albright	30 Clinton	31 train	32 beach	33 basket	34 plane	35 people	36 violence	37 road
125 street	1.3					1.2		4.9		4.8
126 flood		1.1	1.3			1.0	1.3			
127 dog		1.1				1.0	1.1	4.8		
128 Hyde										
129 Dome	1.2				1.0	1.0				
130 hockey	1.0	1.2	1.2	1.2	1.0		1.0			1.3
131 keys	1.2	1.3	1.3			1.1	1.0			
132 stretcher		1.4	1.4				1.3			
133 Saddam						1.0				
134 Yeltsin						1.0			3.3	
135 Donaldson										
136 golf		1.3				1.2	1.0			
137 Netanyahu						1.0				
138 steps						1.1	1.3			
139 weapon						1.0			4.7	2.8
140 bike						1.0	1.3			4.6
141 umbrella						1.2				
142 tennis	1.4				1.3		1.2			
143 wheelchair										
144 Clinton			5.0			1.2				
145 horse						1.0	1.1			
147 fire		1.1	1.1			1.0				
148 sign						1.3	1.3	4.8		4.3

Fig. 10.9 Average association on 5-point scale (1 = ignore, 5 = keep) from 12 raters assessing TRECVID 2004 concept relevance to TRECVID 2004 topics; blank and grey cells same meaning as Figure 10.8. ©IEEE 2007 (Hauptmann et al. 2007)

10.4.2 Automated Assistance

Given the difficulty for users to manually identify which concepts are beneficial, automatic concept selection might turn out to be a better alternative, if it could find relevant concepts for each query without explicit human intervention. In this section, we describe several types of automatic concept selection methods and discuss their advantages and disadvantages.

(1) The simplest approach to handle high-level semantic concepts is to match the name of each concept with the query terms. If a concept name is found to be relevant, then its detection outputs can be used to refine the initial retrieval results. For example, the semantic concept of "building" detection will be helpful for retrieving the query of "finding the scenes containing buildings in New York City". This method is very intuitive to understand and simple to implement. However, in practice it is unrealistic to expect a general query topic to explicitly indicate all related concepts in the description. For example, the concept of "outdoor" could be useful for the query of "finding people on the beach" but it does not show up in the query directly.

(2) To extend the power of simple query matching, we can follow the idea of global query expansion strategies in text retrieval, which attempts to enrich the query description from external knowledge sources such as a co-occurrence thesaurus

(Qiu and Frei 1993), created based on global term-to-concept similarities, or a semantic network (ontology) organised to provide semantic relations between keywords, e.g. WordNet (Fellbaum 1998). These approaches have been successfully applied in the multimedia retrieval task (Volkmer and Natsev 2006; Neo, Zhao, Kan and Chua 2006) and show promising retrieval results by introducing extra concepts from external knowledge sources. However, apart from some useful semantic concepts, these approaches are also likely to introduce additional noisy concepts to the query and thus might yield unexpected deterioration of the search result quality. They are also not able to build up connections between queries and concepts that may not have any a priori obvious semantic connection, but are present in the corpus e.g. Madeleine Albright is strongly associated with "walking down stairs". This is only clear after examining the corpus, which shows her frequently descending from the plane as she arrives for state visits. Moreover, even when the subset of relevant concepts are perfectly detected, it remains a challenge for these query matching approaches to derive a good strategy to combine all the high-level semantic concepts with other text/image retrieval results.

(3) As another alternative, we can leverage the semantic concepts by learning their combination strategies from a pre-collected training collection, e.g. learning query independent combination models (Amir, Hsu, Iyengar, C.-Y.Lin, Naphade, Natsev, Neti, Nock, Smith, Tseng, Wu and Zhang 2003) and query-class based combination models (Yan, Yang and Hauptmann 2004; Chua, Neo, Li, Wang, Shi, Zhao, Xu, Gao and Nwe 2004). These approaches can automatically determine the weighting between different concepts and handle the hidden semantic concepts without any difficulties. However, since these learning approaches can only capture the general patterns that distinguish relevant and irrelevant training documents, their power is usually limited by the number of available training data.

(4) We can also consider local analysis approaches that can adaptively leverage semantic concepts on a per query basis without the support of training data. For these approaches, initial retrieved documents are examined in real time to determine the concepts to expand. The essence of local strategies is to utilise retrieved documents as pseudo-positive/negative examples to select expanded discriminative query concepts to improve the retrieval performance. For example, a retrieval approach called probabilistic local context analysis (pLCA) (Yan 2006) has been proposed, which can automatically leverage useful high-level semantic concepts to improve the initial retrieval output without any training data. However, the success of this type of approach usually relies on a set of initial retrieval outputs that exhibit a reasonable accuracy. If the initial retrieval performance is unsatisfactory, it is possible for local analysis approaches to degrade the retrieval results.

All four types of approaches, that is "term matching" of concepts to queries, global query expansion, query class analysis, and local context analysis, have proved to be successful in handling high-level semantic concepts in various studies, although they all come with their own limitations. Moreover, the applicability of these methods is not mutually exclusive. Instead, a composite strategy can usually produce a better result than any single approach. How to automatically determine the best strategy or strategies to incorporate high-level concepts into the retrieval is an interesting direction for future exploration.

10.5 Conclusions and Future Work

Using the TRECVID video collection and truth annotations from 320 concepts, we simulated and extrapolated performance of video retrieval under different assumptions of concept detection accuracy. The experimental results confirmed that a few thousand semantic concepts could be sufficient to support high-accuracy video retrieval systems. Surprisingly, when sufficiently many concepts are used, even low detection accuracy can potentially provide good retrieval results as long as we find a reasonable way to combine them.

We also derived suggestions regarding the type of concepts that will be most helpful and the frequency of desirable concepts to include in the set. We first showed that frequent concepts play a more vital role in video retrieval than rare concepts. Unlike rare concepts that benefit none or only one specific topic, recurrent concepts of frequency greater than 100 helped multiple search topics, either by filtering out irrelevant results or by promoting relevant shots. Second, frequent concepts can be easily identified with a small, randomly sampled collection, since it was shown that even 1% of the video collection can cover around 90% of the concepts occurring in the entire collection. Finally, "Scene" concepts (and to a lesser degree "People" related concepts) were shown to be very helpful and should be developed first. Although there are many concepts in the "Objects" category appearing in the archive, they usually benefit very few queries, making them virtually irrelevant for general search queries. Ultimately, despite many hints, we leave unanswered the question whether this many appropriate semantic concepts can actually be found, and, specifically, which ones they should be.

In order to utilise the semantic concepts in the realistic retrieval setting, we discussed a number of approaches for concept combination based on either manual selection or automatic determination. Since a user study shows that it is difficult for users to predict which concept will help for a specific query, we suggest several (semi-) automatic ways to find the best combination of concepts that will be relevant to a specific query, including semantic matching, learned combination, and relevance feedback.

There are currently efforts underway to connect large concept lists into ontologies or graphs. One such effort is the LSCOM concept ontology, which assembles over 2000 semantic concepts into an ontology derived from the CYC (Reed and Lenat 2002) ontology. This ontology is limited to visible and detectable concepts. In the Shatford-Panofsky hierarchy (Shatford 1986), which distinguishes pre-iconographic, iconographic, and iconological aspects of an image, the ontology tends to describe the pre-iconographic aspects, related to the "factual", elementary, and easily understandable aspects of an image. The ontology excludes more abstract notions such as "pleasant", "happy", "social", or "scary". These are descriptions which Panofsky would characterise as iconographic (related to an artistic motif) or "iconological" (related to underlying cultural principles that determine the symbolism of an image). While limited-domain efforts at connecting concepts to specialised ontologies for retrieval have been shown to be effective (Wang, Liu and Chia 2006; Srikanth, Varner, Bowden and Moldovan 2005), the effectiveness of a large-scale ontology for general news retrieval has not been demonstrated. An alternative to manually constructed ontologies that encapsulate human knowledge and preconceptions is to allow the data to connect related concepts automatically, and suggest their joint use for retrieval. This could be done with something as simple as the chi-square measure (Yang and Pedersen 1997), or through more refined graphic models that explore independence and overlap of concepts in a larger lexicon. Potentially, both interactive retrieval and automatic retrieval could benefit from suggestions of structurally related concepts for specific queries, but the evidence for this is still outstanding.

Above all, we hope that this divide-and-conquer approach using large numbers of semantic concepts as an intermediate layer will allow us to develop thousands of concepts that can be somewhat reliably identified in many contexts, and with sufficient numbers of these concepts available, covering a broad spectrum of visible things, users will finally be able to bridge the semantic gap. Ultimately, this chapter arrives at the conclusion that "concept-based" video retrieval with fewer than 5,000 concepts, detected with minimal accuracy of 10% mean average precision is likely to provide high-accuracy results, comparable to text retrieval on the web, in a typical broadcast news collection. These observations serve as a foundation for continuing investigations instantiating such a large collection of concepts for retrieval.

Acknowledgments This research was supported in part by the National Science Foundation (NSF) of the United States under Grant No. IIS-0205219.

References

Alexander, A. and Meehleib, T. (2001) , 'The thesaurus for graphic materials: Its history, use and future', *Cataloging and Classification Quarterly* **31**(3/4), 189–212.

Amir, A., Hsu, W., Iyengar, G., Lin. C. -Y., Naphade, M., Natsev, A., Neti, C., Nock, H. J., Smith, J. R., Tseng, B. L., Wu, Y. and Zhang, D. (2003) , IBM research TRECVID-2003 video retrieval system, *in* 'NIST TRECVID-2003'.

Barnard, K., Duygulu, P., Forsyth, D., de Freitas, N., Blei, D. and Jordan, M. (2002), 'Matching words and pictures', *Journal of Machine Learning Research* **3**, 1107–1135.

Beitzel, S., Jensen, E. C., Frieder, O., Chowdhury, A. and Pass, G. (2005) , Surrogate scoring for improved metasearch precision, *in* 'SIGIR '05: Proceedings of the 28th annual international ACM SIGIR conference on Research and development in information retrieval', ACM Press, New York, NY, USA, pp. 583–584.

Chang, S.-F., Hsu, W., Kennedy, L., Xie, L., Yanagawa, A., Zavesky, E. and Zhang, D.-Q. (2005) , Columbia university TRECVID-2005 video search and high-level feature extraction, *in* 'NIST TRECVID'.

Chang, S. F., Manmatha, R. and Chua., T. S. (2005), Combining text and audio-visual features in video indexing, *in* 'IEEE ICASSP 2005', Vol. 5, pp. 1005–1008.

Christel, M. and Hauptmann, A. G. (2005) , The use and utility of high-level semantic features, *in* 'International Conference on Image and Video Retrieval (CIVR'05)', Vol. 3568 of *Lecture Notes in Computer Science*, Singapore, pp. 134–144.

Chua, T. S., Neo, S. Y., Li, K., Wang, G. H., Shi, R., Zhao, M., Xu, H., Gao, S. and Nwe, T. L. (2004) , Trecvid 2004 search and feature extraction task by NUS PRIS, *in* 'NIST TRECVID'.

Cover, T. and Thomas, J. (1991) , *Elements of Information Theory*, Wiley-Interscience, New York, NY, USA.

Fellbaum, C. (1998) , *WordNet: An Electronic Lexical Database*, MIT Press, Cambridge, MA, USA.

Hauptmann, A. (2004) , Towards a large scale concept ontology for broadcast video, *in* 'Third International Conference on Image and Video Retrieval (CIVR)', pp. 674–675.

Hauptmann, A. G., Baron, R., Chen, M.-Y., Christel, M., Duygulu, P., Huang, C., Jin, R., Lin, W.-H., Ng, T., Moraveji, N., Papernick, N., Snoek, C., Tzanetakis, G., Yang, J., Yan, R., and Wactlar, H. (2003) , Informedia at TRECVID 2003: Analyzing and searching broadcast news video, *in* 'Proceedings of TRECVID'.

Hauptmann, A. G. and Christel, M. G. (2004) , Successful approaches in the TREC video retrieval evaluations, *in* 'Proceedings of the 12th annual ACM international conference on Multimedia', ACM Press, New York, NY, USA, pp. 668–675.

Hauptmann, A., Yan, R., Lin, W.-H., Christel, M. and Wactlar, H. (2007) , 'Can high-level concepts fill the semantic gap in video retrieval? a case study with broadcast news', *IEEE Transactions on Multimedia* **9**(5), 958–966.

Jeon, J., Lavrenko, V. and Manmatha, R. (2003) , Automatic image annotation and retrieval using cross-media relevance models, *in* 'Proceedings of the 26th annual international ACM SIGIR conference on Research and development in informaion retrieval', ACM Press, New York, NY, USA, pp. 119–126.

Kender, J. and Naphade, M. (2005) , Visual concepts for news story tracking: Analyzing and exploiting the NIST TRECVID video annotation experiment, *in* 'Conference on Computer Vision and Pattern Recognition', pp. 1174–1181.

Lew, M., ed. (2002) , *Intl. Conf. on Image and Video Retrieval*, Vol. 2383 of *Lecture Notes in Computer Science*, Springer, The Brunei Gallery, SOAS, Russell Square, London, UK.

Lin, W.-H. and Hauptmann, A. G. (2002) , News video classification using SVM-based multi-modal classifiers and combination strategies, *in* 'MULTIMEDIA '02: Tenth ACM international conference on Multimedia', ACM Press, New York, NY, USA, pp. 323–326.

Markkula, M. and Sormunen, E. (2000) , 'End-user searching challenges indexing practices in the digital newspaper photo archive', *Information Retrieval* **1**(4), 259–285.

Naphade, M. R., Kristjansson, T., Frey, B. and Huang, T. (1998) , Probabilistic multimedia objects (multijects): A novel approach to video indexing and retrieval in multimedia systems, *in* 'Proceedings of ICIP', Vol. 3, pp. 536–540.

Naphade, M. R. and Smith, J. R. (2004) , On the detection of semantic concepts at TRECVID, *in* '12th annual ACM international conference on Multimedia', ACM Press, New York, NY, USA, pp. 660–667.

Naphade, M., Smith, J., Tesic, J., Chang, S.-F., Hsu, W., Kennedy, L., Hauptmann, A. and Curtis, J. (2006) , 'Large-scale concept ontology for multimedia', *IEEE MultiMedia* **13**(3), 86–91.

Natsev, A., Naphade, M. and Tešić, J. (2005) , Learning the semantics of multimedia queries and concepts from a small number of examples, *in* '13th ACM International Conference on Multimedia', pp. 598–607.

Neo, S.-Y., Zhao, J., Kan, M.-Y. and Chua, T.-S. (2006) , Video retrieval using high level features: Exploiting query matching and confidence-based weighting, *in* 'Proceedings of the Conference on Image and Video Retrieval (CIVR)', Vol. 4071 of *Lecture Notes in Computer Science*, pp. 143–152.

Over, P., Ianeva, T., Kraaij, W. and Smeaton, A. (2005) , Trecvid 2005 - an overview, *in* 'Proceedings of TRECVID 2005', NIST, USA.

Petersen, T. (1994) , *Art & Architecture Thesaurus*, second edn, Oxford University Press, UK.

Qiu, Y. and Frei, H.-P. (1993) , Concept based query expansion, *in* 'Proceedings of the 16th annual international ACM SIGIR conference', ACM Press, New York, NY, USA, pp. 160–169.

Reed, S. and Lenat, D. (2002) , Mapping ontologies into CYC, *in* 'AAAI Conference, Workshop on Ontologies For The Semantic Web'.

Rodden, K., Basalaj, W., Sinclair, D. and Wood, K. (2001) , Does organisation by similarity assist image browsing?, *in* 'CHI '01: Proceedings of the SIGCHI conference on Human factors in computing systems', ACM Press, New York, NY, USA, pp. 190–197.

Shatford, S. (1986) , 'Analyzing the subject of a picture: A theoretical aproach.', *Cataloging and Classification Quarterly* **6**, 39–62.

Smeaton, A. F., Over, P. and Kraaij, W. (2006) , Evaluation campaigns and TRECVid, *in* 'MIR '06: Proceedings of the 8th ACM International Workshop on Multimedia Information Retrieval', ACM Press, New York, NY, USA, pp. 321–330.

Smeaton, A. and Over, P. (2003) , TRECVID: Benchmarking the effectiveness of information retrieval tasks on digital video., *in* 'Proceedings of the International Conference, on Image and Video Retrieval'.

Smeulders, A., Worring, M., Santini, S., Gupta, A. and Jain, R. (2000) , 'Content-based image retrieval: the end of the early years', *IEEE Transactions Pattern Analysis and Machine Intelligence* **22**(12), 1349–1380.

Smith, J. R., Lin, C. Y., Naphade, M. R., Natsev, P. and Tseng, B. (2002) , Learning concepts from video using multi-modal features, *in* 'International Thyrrhenian Workshop for Digital Communications IWDC', Capri, Italy.

Snoek, C., Worring, M., Geusebroek, J.-M., Seinstra, F. and Smeulders, A. (2006) , 'The semantic pathfinder: Using an authoring metaphor for generic multimedia indexing', *IEEE Transactions Pattern Analysis Machine Intelligence* **28**(10), 1678–1689.

Snoek, C., Worring, M. and Smeulders, A. (2005) , Early versus late fusion in semantic video analysis, *in* 'Proceedings of ACM Multimedia', pp. 399–402.

Snoek, C., Worring, M., van Gemert, J. C., Geusebroek, J.-M. and Smeulders, A. (2006) , The challenge problem for automated detection of 101 semantic concepts in multimedia, *in* 'ACM Multimedia', pp. 421–430.

Srikanth, M., Varner, J., Bowden, M. and Moldovan, D. (2005) , Exploiting ontologies for automatic image annotation, *in* 'Proceedings of the 28th Annual International ACM SIGIR (SIGIR 2005)', pp. 552–558.

Volkmer, T. and Natsev, A. (2006) , Exploring automatic query refinement for text-based video retrieval, *in* 'IEEE International Conference on Multimedia and Expo (ICME)', pp. 765 – 768.

Wang, H., Liu, S. and Chia, L.-T. (2006) , Does ontology help in image retrieval?: a comparison between keyword, text ontology and multi-modality ontology approaches, *in* 'MULTIMEDIA '06: Proceedings of the 14th annual ACM international conference on Multimedia', ACM Press, New York, NY, USA, pp. 109–112.

Wu, Y., Chang, E. Y., Chang, K. C.-C. and Smith, J. (2004) , Optimal multimodal fusion for multimedia data analysis, *in* 'Proceedings of the 12th annual ACM international conference on Multimedia', pp. 572–579.

Yan, R. (2006) , Probabilistic Models for Combining Diverse Knowledge Sources in Multimedia Retrieval, PhD thesis, Carnegie Mellon University.

Yan, R. and Hauptmann, A. G. (2003) , The combination limit in multimedia retrieval, *in* 'Proceedings of the eleventh ACM international conference on Multimedia', pp. 339–342.

Yan, R., Yang, J. and Hauptmann, A. G. (2004) , Learning query-class dependent weights in automatic video retrieval, *in* 'Proceedings of the 12th annual ACM international conference on Multimedia', pp. 548–555.

Yang, J., Chen, M. Y. and Hauptmann, A. G. (2004) , Finding person x: Correlating names with visual appearances, *in* 'International Conference on Image and Video Retrieval (CIVR'04)', Ireland.

Yang, Y. and Pedersen, J. (1997) , A comparative study on feature selection in text categorization, *in* 'Proceedings of the 14th International Conference on Machine Learning (ICML)', pp. 412–420.

Yuan, J., Xiao, L., Wang, D., Ding, D., Zuo, Y., Tong, Z., Liu, X., Xu, S., Zheng, W., Li, X., Si, Z., Li, J., Lin, F. and Zhang, B. (2005) , Tsinghua university at TRECVID 2005, *in* 'NIST TRECVID 2005'.

Zhao, W., Chellappa, R., Phillips, P. J. and Rosenfeld, A. (2003) , 'Face recognition: A literature survey', *ACM Computing Surveys* **35**(4), 399–458.

Zipf, G. (1972) , *Human Behavior and the Principle of Least Effort: An Introduction to Human Ecology*, Hafner Publishing Company, New York.

Part V
Conclusion

Chapter 11
Conclusions Relating to Semantic Multimedia and Ontologies

Yiannis Kompatsiaris and Paola Hobson

11.1 Reflections on Semantic Multimedia and Ontologies

Semantic multimedia analysis, as shown in the previous chapters, has already started producing useful results in many domains and applications. As mentioned in Chapter 10, for example, after detailed analysis and experimentation, it was found that "...although the prediction provided by the state-of-the-art automatic concept detection algorithms is far from perfect, they can still substantially improve the standard text-only retrieval output." At this stage of research and development, it is important to understand the advantages and limitations of automated semantic analysis in terms of several factors, and this understanding can help to make the correct decisions for adopting the use of such approaches into practical systems and provide to personal, professional, enterprise and scientific users the benefits of these approaches. For example, the performance of each approach in generic versus specific applications and more importantly the opportunities to combine semantic analysis with existing systems in order to provide added value to the offered service rather than trying to build services purely based on semantic analysis functionalities has benefits in multiple application domains, as shown in Part III of this book.

The applications described in Chapters 6–8 demonstrate the breadth of opportunity for exploitation of semantic multimedia concepts in consumer, professional and scientific domains. Despite their disparate features and domains of use, these applications have in common that the developed systems must be reliable and easily usable by their intended end user. This poses requirements of accuracy and tractability at the back-end system level, and requirements of simplicity and comprehension at the user presentation level.

Systems which automate decision making on behalf of a user will be successful only if the user has confidence that the decisions are accurate and that the actions taken reliably replicate those which the user would have done if the system were

Y. Kompatsiaris
Centre for Research and Technology – Hellas, Informatics and Telematics Institute, Thermi-Thessaloniki, Greece
e-mail: ikom@iti.gr

Y. Kompatsiaris, P. Hobson (eds.), *Semantic Multimedia and Ontologies,*
© Springer Science+Business Media, LLC 2008

manually driven. In the case of media analysis, this implies that the resulting meta-data consistently describes the content as users might label it themselves. In fact, one of the benefits of multimedia analysis based on accepted standards, as was presented in Chapters 4 and 5, is that standardised annotations are produced which are not subject to noise and subjectivity which can arise in systems requiring manual annotation. The appropriateness of the annotation is best measured by the success of the applications which use it, and as we saw in Chapter 10, a granularity of annotation using appropriately chosen labels can be defined to solve specific retrieval problems, as illustrated by TRECVID. Also, as illustrated in Chapters 7 and 8, specific domain ontologies can be defined by the users themselves for specialist applications, ensuring a tight coupling between the system requirements and system implementation. However, this implies a high investment for the application owner in time and specialist knowledge resources in setting up the initial system. Such investment will, of course, be recovered many times over by the time-savings and efficiency benefits that the system brings. Taking a standardised approach ensures longevity and extensibility of the system as new knowledge and processes become available.

Personalisation systems, such as the personalised summarisation method described in Chapter 6, are somewhat harder to evaluate as the acceptability of the outcome is dependent on the user's subjective perception. However accurately the content may be labelled, if a user asks the system to assemble, for example, a humorous summary of some video content, they will only feel satisfied if the selection meets their particular perspective on what is funny. Over a period of time, the system can learn the user's preferences and more accurately match their needs, but if the system makes early mistakes, the user's first impressions of the application may be negative and they may be reluctant to trust the system for further recommendations. Involving representative end users in the design loop is essential in such applications, to ensure that the most appropriate system is implemented.

11.2 Harmonisation of Multimedia Ontologies

Consistency and interoperability of annotations and metadata appear as recurring themes throughout this book. Commercial exploitation of semantic technologies relies on the creation of a broad ecosystem, encompassing multiple devices, plat-forms, communication bearers and applications, where a consumer can feel confi-dent that what they are buying can be integrated with other equipment and appli-cations that they use, and that such devices and software will not become obsolete within a short time. Interoperability of metadata was the subject of a W3C Incubator Group on Multimedia Semantics, and the reports from this group (available online) hint at routes towards solutions.

Concerning multimedia ontologies and ontology or more general logic-based approaches for semantic multimedia analysis, there are already very interesting results as can be seen by Chapters 2–4 and in the applications described in Part III of this book. As it can be seen, especially in Chapters 3 and 4, the combination of multimedia and knowledge- or logic-based approaches is not so straightforward, and it requires significant research effort and advances until multimedia analysis can really benefit from logic-based advances. Multimedia content and analysis have specific requirements which must be taken into account. One of the most typical is the existence of uncertainty in multimedia content analysis, which has to be taken into account by the formal knowledge-based approaches or requires further research and development into new ways to handle it. There are several initiatives working towards this direction, among them the W3C Multimedia Semantics Incubator Group and a number of EC part-funded research projects under the 6th framework IST programme, such as aceMedia, K-Space, BOEMIE, X-Media and MESH (see Web Resources section for further information on these projects).

11.3 For Further Reading and Research

The area of semantic multimedia and ontologies is emerging as one of the fastest moving research domains, partly due to its intrinsic difficulty, which stimulates the interest of researchers, and partly due to its anticipated commercial prospects, which attract commercial attention. The interested reader is encouraged to browse the list of references below, in addition to those appended to each chapter, and in particular, the works of Stamou and Kollias (2005) and the Special Issue on Semantic Image and Video Indexing in Broad domains from the IEEE Transactions on Multimedia (2007) are highly recommended.

Further Reading

Cardoso, J. and Sheth, A. (Eds) (2006) *Semantic Web Services, Processes and Applications*, Springer, New York.

Nack, F., van Ossenbruggen, J. and Hardman, L. (2005) That obscure object of desire: multimedia metadata on the Web, Part 2. *IEEE Multimedia* 12(1): 54–63.

Snoek, C. and Worring, M. (2005) Multimodal video indexing: a review of the state-of-the-art, *Multimedia Tools and Applications*, Springer Science and Business Media, New York.

Staab, S. and Studer, R. (2004) Handbook on ontologies, *International Handbooks on Information Systems*, Springer-Verlag, Heidelberg.

Stamou, G. and Kollias, S. (Eds) (2005) *Multimedia Content and the Semantic Web*, Wiley, New York.

Stamou, G., van Ossenbruggen, J., Pan, J. and Schreiber, G. (2006) Multimedia annotations on the semantic Web. *IEEE Multimedia* 13(1): 86–90.

Troncy, R., Bailer, W., Hausenblas, M., Hofmair, P. and Schlatte, R. (2006) Enabling multimedia metadata interoperability by defining formal semantics of MPEG-7 profiles. *SAMT 2006*: Vol. 4306, pp. 41–55, December 6–8 2006, Athens.

Uren V., Cimiano P., Iria J., Handschuh S., Vargas-Vera M., Motta E. and Ciravegna F. (2006) Semantic annotation for knowledge management: Requirements and a survey of the state of the art. *Web Semantics: Science, Services and Agents on the World Wide Web*, 4(1): pp. 14–28. January.

van Ossenbruggen, J., Nack, F. and Hardman, L., (2004) That obscure object of desire: Multimedia
    metadata on the Web, Part 1. *IEEE Multimedia* 11(4): 38–48.
IEEE Transactions On Multimedia, special issue on Semantic Image and Video Indexing in Broad
    Domains, Volume: 9 Issue: 5, August 2007.
International Journal of Semantic Computing, (2007) Vol 1 No 1, March.

Web Resources

aceMedia project	http://www.acemedia.org
aceMedia ontology harmonisation	http://www.acemedia.org/aceMedia/reference/ multimedia_ontology/index.html
AIM@SHAPE Network of Excellence	http://shapes.aimatshape.net
Boemie project	http://www.boemie.org/
CODATA committee	http://www.codataweb.org/06conf/meetings/22oct06-1.html
Ethnographic eResearch project	http://ethnoer.unimelb.edu.au/
FactSage 5.5	http://www.factsage.com
freedb	http://www.freedb.org
Garcia, Roberto, PhD thesis	http://rhizomik.net/~roberto/thesis
Google Maps documentation	http://www.google.com/apis/maps/documentation/upgrade.html
Grace note	http://www.gracenote.com
HTML+TIME 2.0	http://msdn2.microsoft.com/en-us/library/ms533102.aspx
HUMAINE Network of Excellence	http://emotion-research.net/
Inorganic Crystal Structure Database	http://www.fiz-karlsruhe.de/ecid/Internet/en/DB/icsd/
Jabber Software Foundation	http://www.jabber.org/
K-Space Network of Excellence	http://www.k-space.eu/
Last.fm	http://www.last.fm/
MatML	http://www.matml.org/downloads/matml31.xsd
MESH project	http://www.mesh-ip.eu/
MPEG-7 Ontologies	http://rhizomik.net/ontologies/mpeg7ontos

Multimedia digital library for on-line search	http://milos.isti.cnr.it/
OWL	http://www.w3.org/TR/owl-features
Pandora	http://www.pandora.com/
Paradisec project	http://paradisec.org.au/home.html
RDF Schema	http://www.w3.org/TR/rdf-schema/
RDF Syntax	http://www.w3.org/TR/rdf-syntax-grammar/
ReDeFer	http://rhizomik.net/redefer
RSS 2.0 specification	http://cyber.law.harvard.edu/rss/rss.html
Semantic WildNet	http://www.itee.uq.edu.au/~eresearch/projects/ecoportalqld/papers/SemWildNET.pdf
SonyStation	http://stationexchange.station.sony.com/
SPARQL description	http://www.w3.org/TR/rdf-sparql-query/
StatSoft, Electronic Textbook	http://www.statsoft.com/textbook/glosc.html, 2005
TRECVID	http://www-nlpir.nist.gov/projects/trecvid/
TRECVID on line proceedings	http://www-nlpir.nist.gov/projects/tvpubs/tv.pubs.org.html
TVAnytime	http://www.tv-anytime.org
W3C multimedia semantics incubator (MMSEM XG)	http://www.w3.org/2005/Incubator/mmsem/
W3C MMSEM XG report on MPEG-7	http://www.w3.org/2005/Incubator/mmsem/XGR-mpeg7/
W3C MMSEM XG report on semantic interoperability	http://www.w3.org/2005/Incubator/mmsem/wiki/Semantic_Interoperability
Weka	http://www.cs.waikato.ac.nz/ml/weka/
XQuery description	http://www.w3.org/TR/xquery/
X-Media project	http://www.x-media-project.org/

Index